Federalism and Internal Conflicts

Series Editors
Soeren Keil
Institute of Federalism
University of Fribourg
Fribourg, Switzerland

Eva Maria Belser
University of Freiburg
Freiburg, Switzerland

This series engages in the discussions on federalism as a tool of internal conflict resolution. Building on a growing body of literature on the use of federalism and territorial autonomy to solve ethnic, cultural, linguistic and identity conflicts, both in the West and in non-Western countries, this global series assesses to what extent different forms of federalism and territorial autonomy are being used as tools of conflict resolution and how successful these approaches are.

We welcome proposals on theoretical debates, single case studies and short comparative pieces covering topics such as:

- Federalism and peace-making in contemporary intra-state conflicts
- The link between federalism and democratization in countries facing intra-state conflict
- Secessionism, separatism, self-determination and power-sharing
- Inter-group violence and the potential of federalism to transform conflicts
- Successes and failures of federalism and other forms of territorial autonomy in post-conflict countries
- Federalism, decentralisation and resource conflicts
- Peace treaties, interim constitutions and permanent power sharing arrangements
- The role of international actors in the promotion of federalism (and other forms of territorial autonomy) as tools of internal conflict resolution
- Federalism and state-building
- Federalism, democracy and minority protection

For further information on the series and to submit a proposal for consideration, please get in touch with Ambra Finotello ambra.finotello@palgrave.com, or series editors Soeren Keil soeren.keil@unifr.ch and Eva Maria Belser evamaria.belser@unifr.ch.

More information about this series at
https://link.springer.com/bookseries/15730

Soeren Keil • Sabine Kropp
Editors

Emerging Federal Structures in the Post-Cold War Era

palgrave
macmillan

Editors
Soeren Keil
Institute of Federalism
University of Fribourg
Fribourg, Switzerland

Sabine Kropp
Otto-Suhr-Institut für Politikwissenschaft
Freie Universität Berlin
Berlin, Germany

Federalism and Internal Conflicts
ISBN 978-3-030-93668-6   ISBN 978-3-030-93669-3 (eBook)
https://doi.org/10.1007/978-3-030-93669-3

© The Editor(s) (if applicable) and The Author(s), under exclusive licence to Springer Nature Switzerland AG 2022

This work is subject to copyright. All rights are solely and exclusively licensed by the Publisher, whether the whole or part of the material is concerned, specifically the rights of translation, reprinting, reuse of illustrations, recitation, broadcasting, reproduction on microfilms or in any other physical way, and transmission or information storage and retrieval, electronic adaptation, computer software, or by similar or dissimilar methodology now known or hereafter developed.

The use of general descriptive names, registered names, trademarks, service marks, etc. in this publication does not imply, even in the absence of a specific statement, that such names are exempt from the relevant protective laws and regulations and therefore free for general use.

The publisher, the authors and the editors are safe to assume that the advice and information in this book are believed to be true and accurate at the date of publication. Neither the publisher nor the authors or the editors give a warranty, expressed or implied, with respect to the material contained herein or for any errors or omissions that may have been made. The publisher remains neutral with regard to jurisdictional claims in published maps and institutional affiliations.

This Palgrave Macmillan imprint is published by the registered company Springer Nature Switzerland AG.
The registered company address is: Gewerbestrasse 11, 6330 Cham, Switzerland

Acknowledgements

Finalizing any edited book is always the result of a lot of work, dedication and support by numerous people. First and foremost, we would like to thank all the contributors to this volume. Their hard work and their willingness to include our feedback to discuss their cases with us and help us form the theoretical insights developed in the Introduction and Conclusion have been exceptionally rewarding for us as editors. While we acknowledge that much theory-building remains to be done in order to conceptualize emerging federal structures, what we have tried to start here would not have been possible without the clear, coherent and deep insights provided by the authors of the different chapters.

We would like to thank Palgrave Macmillan, and here specifically Ambra Finotello and Karthika Devi for their support to this project and their faith in us and the authors. Chloe Doherty provided exceptional support in copy-editing and developing the index for this book, and it would not be as well-written without her input. We are very grateful for her commitment to making this book better and ensuring coherence and clarity throughout.

Soeren Keil would like to thank his colleagues at the Institute of Federalism, especially Eva Maria Belser, Thea Bächler and Bernhard Altermatt. The work has benefitted from several discussions with friends and colleagues, in particular Paul Anderson, Michael Breen, Jelena Dzankic, Achim Munz, Johanna Schnabel and Michael Siegner. Sabine Kropp would also like to thank Johanna Schnabel and the members of the Standing Group "Federalism" of the German Political Science Association for their suggestions and comments on how to fix the phenomenon of "emergence", to which the book refers.

Finally, we would like to dedicate this book to the people who make it all worthwhile and possible. Our families have always supported our work and we are deeply indebted to them for this.

Contents

Part I Introduction: Theoretical and Empirical Dimensions   1

1 The Emergence and Regression of Federal Structures:
   Theoretical Lenses and Analytical Dimensions   3
   Sabine Kropp and Soeren Keil

Part II Case Studies   31

2 Belgium: Federalism as a Stopover?   33
   Petra Meier

3 Spain and the United Kingdom: Between Unitary State
   Tradition and Federalization   49
   Paul Anderson

4 Federal Regression and the Authoritarian Turn in Russia   73
   Stanislav Klimovich and Sabine Kropp

5 Why No Federalism? The Challenges of Institutionalizing
   a Multilevel Order in Ukraine   95
   Sabine Kropp and Jørn Holm-Hansen

6   The Emergence of Complex Federal Political Systems in
    the Western Balkans   115
    Soeren Keil

7   Federalism and Conflict Resolution in Nepal and
    Myanmar   141
    Michael G. Breen

8   India: An Emerging or Fragile Federation?   165
    Wilfried Swenden

9   Learning from Iraq? Debates on Federalism and
    Decentralization for Post-War Syria   189
    Eva Maria Belser and Soeren Keil

10 Federalism in Ethiopia: Emergence, Progress and
    Challenges   215
    Yonatan Tesfaye Fessha and Beza Dessalegn

11 The 'Federal Solution' to Diversity Conflicts in South
    Africa and Kenya: Partial at Most   233
    Nico Steytler

12 Institutional Instability and (De)federalizing Processes
    in Colombia   259
    Kent Eaton

13 Federalism in the European Union   277
    Eva G. Heidbreder

Part III   Concluding Remarks   301

14 Conclusion: Emergence, Operation and Categorization
    of Federal Structures in the Post-Cold War Era   303
    Soeren Keil and Sabine Kropp

Index   327

Notes on Contributors

Paul Anderson is Senior Lecturer in Politics and International Relations at Liverpool John Moores University, UK. His research interests include territorial autonomy, constitutional politics and conflict resolution. He has written on aspects of British and Spanish politics, with particular focus on the Scottish and Catalan independence movements. Anderson is the co-lead of the University Association for Contemporary European Studies-James Madison Charitable Trust (UACES-JMCT) funded research network "(Re)Imagining Territorial Politics in Times of Crisis".

Eva Maria Belser holds a Chair for Constitutional and Administrative Law at the University of Fribourg (since 2008), Switzerland, and a UNESCO Chair in Human Rights and Democracy (since 2014). Since 2008, she is Co-director of the Institute of Federalism and heads its international centre. She is a member of the board of the Swiss Centre of Expertise in Human Rights and co-directs the thematic cluster "Institutional Aspects of Human Rights Implementation". Her publications include several books on fundamental rights, constitutional law and federalism in Switzerland and in comparative perspective. Her latest English-speaking publication is *The Principle of Equality in Diverse States - Reconciling Autonomy with Equal Rights and Opportunities*, 2021 (co-edited with Thea Bächler, Sandra Egli and Larence Zünd).

Michael G. Breen is Lecturer in Public Policy Melbourne Early Career Academic Fellowship (MECAF) at the University of Melbourne, Australia. He completed his PhD from Nanyang Technological University, Singapore, in 2017 and was awarded the prestigious McKenzie Postdoctoral

Fellowship from the University of Melbourne in 2018. Breen's research focuses on federalism in Asia and the management of ethnic diversity. Recent publications include *The Road to Federalism in Nepal, Myanmar and Sri Lanka: Finding the Middle Ground* (2018, Routledge) and *Deliberative Democracy in Asia* (Routledge 2021, co-edited with Baogang He and James S. Fishkin).

Beza Dessalegn is Assistant Professor of Law at Hawassa University, School of Law, Ethiopia. He was a postdoctoral fellow in the Department of Public Law and Jurisprudence at the University of the Western Cape. His research interests focus on minority rights, federalism, human rights and constitutional law. He has written a number of articles in peer-reviewed journals on matters relating to electoral laws, political participation of regional minorities, subnational autonomy and local governments in Ethiopia.

Kent Eaton is Professor of Politics at the University of California, Santa Cruz, USA. His research focuses on territorially defined interests, identities and institutions in Latin America, with a special interest in movements for territorial autonomy, the design and performance of federal institutions and the causes and consequences of decentralization. His most recent book is *Territory and Ideology in Latin America: Policy Conflicts Between National and Subnational Governments* (2017). In addition, he is the co-author/editor of three monographs on decentralization, including *The Democratic Decentralization Programming Handbook* (2009), *The Political Economy of Decentralization Reforms* (2010) and *Making Decentralization Work* (2010).

Yonatan Tesfaye Fessha is Professor of Law at the University of the Western Cape, South Africa. His teaching and research focuses on examining the relevance of constitutional design in dealing with the challenges of divided societies. He has written widely on matters pertaining to, but not limited to, federalism, constitutional design, autonomy and politicized ethnicity. His publications include books on *Ethnic Diversity and Federalism: Constitution Making in South Africa and Ethiopia* (2016) and *Federalism and the Courts in Africa: Design and Impact in Comparative Perspective* (co-edited, 2020). He has contributed to constitution-building projects, including in Sudan, South Sudan and Yemen. He was a Marie-Curie Fellow at the Institute for Comparative Federalism at Eurac Research, Italy, and a Michigan Grotius Research Scholar at the University of Michigan.

Eva G. Heidbreder is Professor of Political Science and has a Chair in Multilevel Governance in Europe at the Otto von Guericke University Magdeburg, Germany. Former positions include the Heinrich Heine University Düsseldorf, the Hertie School of Governance Berlin and guest professorships at the Humboldt University of Berlin as well as the Freie Universität Berlin, and the University of Konstanz. She has written widely on the EU, including work on enlargement, administrative cooperation and democratic participation.

Jørn Holm-Hansen is a political scientist and senior researcher at the Norwegian Institute for Urban and Regional Research, Oslo Metropolitan University, Norway. His research is mainly focused on political development in Europe's eastern countries. Holm-Hansen's latest research projects have been about the accommodation of regional diversity in Ukraine, state-society network governance in Russia and welfare reform in Russia. Ongoing projects are about Russian-Norwegian cooperation in the High North and the populist versus pragmatic Russia-Europe nexus.

Soeren Keil is the Academic Head of the International Research and Consulting Center at the Institute of Federalism, University of Fribourg, Switzerland. Before that, he was Reader in Politics and International Relations at Canterbury Christ Church University, UK. He is also a visiting professor at the Centre International de Formation Européenne (CIFE), Nice, France. His research focuses on the use of territorial autonomy as a tool of conflict resolution, the political systems of the Western Balkan states and the process of EU enlargement. His recent publications include *Power-Sharing in Europe—Past Practice, Present Cases, and Future Directions* (Palgrave Macmillan 2021, co-edited with Allison McCulloch).

Stanislav Klimovich is a PhD student at Freie Universität Berlin, Germany, and research associate in the Project "Variations of Governance in Hybrid Regimes: Business, State and Civil Society in Russia". He is also Reader in Russian Politics at University of Potsdam. In 2016 he achieved his Master's Degree in Political Science from the Higher School of Economics, HSE Moscow. His academic interests are in the field of governance in Russia, as well as federalism and decentralization in non-democratic contexts.

Sabine Kropp is Professor at the Freie Universität Berlin, Germany, where she holds the chair of German politics. She has widely written on comparative federalism, parliamentarism, German politics and East

European politics, with a special emphasis on Russian politics. She is head of the research projects "Variations of Governance in Hybrid Regimes: Business, State and Civil Society in Russia" and "Political Cohesion Under Conditions of Fiscal Scarcity—German Federalism in the Time of COVID-19".

Petra Meier is Professor of Politics in the Faculty of Social Sciences at University of Antwerp, Belgium. Her research focuses on the representation of gender and other social markers in politics and policies, targeting the (re)production of social inequalities through formal and informal institutions. Recent research on the Belgian federal system addresses the interplay of territorial reform and democracy, the trade-off between demos and demoi, the mobilization of social groups in ethnofederations and the organization of its dual and competitive nature in times of crises and the COVID-19 pandemic. For a list of recent publications, see https://www.uantwerpen.be/en/staff/petra-meier/publications/.

Nico Steytler is the South African Research Chair in Multilevel Government, Law and Development at the Dullah Omar Institute of Constitutional Law, Governance and Human Rights, University of the Western Cape, South Africa. He was a technical advisor to the Constitutional Assembly during the drafting of the 1996 South Africa. His research focuses on multilevel government principally in South Africa and Africa, but also further afield. His recently publications include Steytler, Arora and Saxena (eds) *The Value of Comparative Federalism: The Legacy of Ronal L. Watts* (2021); Fombad and Steytler (eds) *Democracy, Elections and Constitutionalism in Africa* (2021); Fombad and Steytler (eds) *Corruption and Constitutionalism: Revisiting Control Measures and Strategies* (2020); and Fombad and Steytler (eds) *Decentralisation and Constitutionalism in Africa* (2019).

Wilfried Swenden is Professor of South Asian and Comparative Politics at The University of Edinburgh, UK, and Head of Politics and International Relations. He has written extensively on comparative federalism, territorial party politics and centre-state relations, especially in India. He recently edited special issues on Indian federalism for *India Review* (2017) and *Territory, Politics and Governance* (2021), and his earlier work on Indian federalism has appeared in *Government and Opposition* (2018), the *International Political Science Review* (2020), *Regional and Federal Studies* (2020), *Swiss Political Science Review* (2016, 2021) and *Seminar* (2019). He is completing a manuscript on Indian politics and government (with Chanchal Kumar Sharma) contracted with Palgrave Macmillan.

Abbreviations

ANC   African National Congress
BBI   Building Bridges Initiative
BJP   Bharatiya Janata Party (the Indian People's Party)
BiH   Bosnia and Herzegovina
CC   Constitutional Court (*Corte Constitucional*)
CFR   European Charter of Fundamental Rights and Freedoms
CIC   Commission for the Implementation of the Constitution
CKRC   Constitution of Kenya Review Commission
CPN   Communist Party of Nepal
DPA   Dayton Peace Agreement
EAOs   Ethnic Armed Organisations
ECB   European Central Bank
ELN   Ejercitó de Liberación Nacional
EP   European Parliament
EPRDF   Ethiopian People's Revolutionary Democratic Front
ESM   Ethiopian Student Movement
EU   European Union
FARC   Fuerzas Armadas Revolucionarias de Colombia
FBiH   Federation of Bosnia and Herzegovina
FDRE   Federal Democratic Republic of Ethiopia
HoF   House of the Federation
IFP   Inkatha Freedom Party
IGR   Intergovernmental relations
ISIS   Islamic State of Iraq and Syria
KADU   Kenyan African Democratic Union
KANU   Kenya African National Union
KNC   Kurdish National Council

KPRF	Communist Party of the Russian Federation
LDPR	Liberal Democratic Party of Russia
M-19	*Movimiento 19 de Abril*
NATO	North Atlantic Trade Organization
NCA	National Ceasefire Agreement
NLD	National League for Democracy
NPC	National Planning Council
NSCN-IM	National Socialist Council of Nagaland
OCADs	*Organos Colegiados de Administración y Decisión* (administrative and decision-making collective organs)
OFA	Ohrid Framework Agreement
OHR	Office of the High Representative
OTG	Oficinade Treballde la Generalitat
PDETs	*Programas de Desarrollo Territorial* (Territorially Focused Development Programs)
PSOE	Unidas Podemos coalition
PYD	Kurdish Democratic Union Party
RS	Republika Srpska
RSFSR	Russian Soviet Federative Socialist Republic
SGR	*Sistema General de Regalías* (General Royalty System)
SNNP	Southern Nations, Nationalities and Peoples' Region
SNP	Scottish National Party
TFEU	Treaty on the Functioning of the European Union
TPG	Turkey and the Kurdish People's Protection Units
UN	United Nations
UNMIK	UN Mission in Kosovo
USDP	United Solidarity and Development Party
WWII	World War II
ZOMAC	16 Zones Most Affected by the Conflict

LIST OF FIGURES

Fig. 1.1   Emergence and regression of federal structures   8
Fig. 1.2   Analytical dimensions to explore federalization   10
Fig. 14.1 Categorization of emerging federal structures   320

List of Maps

Map 2.1	Communities and regions in Belgium. *Source*: Belgium.be	38
Map 3.1	Spain. *Source*: https://d-maps.com/carte.php?num_car=2211&lang=en	50
Map 3.2	The UK. *Source*: https://d-maps.com/carte.php?num_car=5544&lang=en	51
Map 4.1	Russia's Federal Subjects. *Source*: Own compilation	75
Map 5.1	Ukraine. *Source*: https://d-maps.com/carte.php?num_car=5010&lang=en	97
Map 6.1	Balkans region. *Source*: https://d-maps.com/carte.php?num_car=69052&lang=en	116
Map 6.2	Bosnia and Herzegovina, territorial and ethnic organization. *Source*: https://reliefweb.int/map/bosnia-and-herzegovina/federation-bosnia-and-herzegovina	126
Map 7.1	Nepal. *Source*: https://d-maps.com/carte.php?num_car=5522&lang=en	142
Map 7.2	Myanmar. *Source*: https://d-maps.com/carte.php?num_car=4164&lang=en	143
Map 8.1	India. *Source*: https://d-maps.com/carte.php?num_car=4184&lang=en	166
Map 9.1	Syria. *Source*: https://commons.wikimedia.org/w/index.php?search=syria+ethnic+groups&title=Special:MediaSearch&go=Go&type=image	190
Map 9.2	Iraq Ethnic groups. *Source*: https://commons.wikimedia.org/w/index.php?search=iraq+ethnic+groups&title=Special:MediaSearch&go=Go&type=image	191

Map 10.1	Ethiopia. *Source*: https://d-maps.com/carte.php?num_car=4259&lang=en	216
Map 11.1	South Africa. *Source*: https://d-maps.com/carte.php?num_car=4415&lang=en	234
Map 11.2	Kenya. *Source*: https://d-maps.com/carte.php?num_car=239&lang=en	235
Map 12.1	Columbia. *Source*: https://d-maps.com/carte.php?num_car=4095&lang=en	260
Map 13.1	The EU. *Source*: https://d-maps.com/carte.php?num_car=260684&lang=en	278

List of Tables

Table 1.1	Analytical Dimensions and Case Selection	23
Table 7.1	Categories of Ethnic Groups in Nepal and Myanmar, and Proportion of Population	144

PART I

Introduction: Theoretical and Empirical Dimensions

CHAPTER 1

The Emergence and Regression of Federal Structures: Theoretical Lenses and Analytical Dimensions

Sabine Kropp and Soeren Keil

Federal Arrangements as Institutional Orders in Flux

The end of the Cold War has witnessed an increasing interest in the study of federal systems. Their number has grown substantially, and in all parts of the world, new federal states have emerged. Today, about 40% of the world's population live in political systems that are designated 'federal' (Burgess, 2017). The rationale for establishing federal arrangements are manifold. Institutional designers respond to demands of ethno-cultural

---

S. Kropp (✉)
Otto-Suhr-Institut für Politikwissenschaft, Freie Universität Berlin, Berlin, Germany
e-mail: sabine.kropp@fu-berlin.de

S. Keil
Institute of Federalism, University of Fribourg, Fribourg, Switzerland
e-mail: Soeren.keil@unifr.ch

© The Author(s), under exclusive license to Springer Nature Switzerland AG 2022
S. Keil, S. Kropp (eds.), *Emerging Federal Structures in the Post-Cold War Era*, Federalism and Internal Conflicts,
https://doi.org/10.1007/978-3-030-93669-3_1

groups by creating multilevel architectures. International organizations diffuse federal models in order to resolve violent conflicts. Democratization or state-building agendas of transitional states also suggest federalization. Sporadically, federal structures are inherited from the past after state dissolution and subsequently undergo more or less comprehensive transformations.

This book focuses on federal arrangements which are in the making. Its main objective is to explore why and how federal structures emerge, how nascent federal arrangements function in practice and why they regress. We posit that a static conception of federalism (Braun, 2004, 132–134) would fail to be attentive to gradual change or even ruptures, which may occur in the course of federalization. Federal systems are highly dynamic institutional settings (Friedrich, 1968; Benz & Broschek, 2013). They are objects of frequent adaptations, never achieving a perfect balance, but revolving around an equilibrium at best (Benz & Kropp, 2014).

The core argument of this book extends Carl Friedrich's observations from 1968, namely that federalism should be understood as a process, not as a fixed institutional design. What Friedrich (1968) demonstrated in the case of the US, and what Benz and Broschek (2013) also highlighted for other Western (or 'classic') federations, applies to new federal settings that emerged in the post-Cold War era (Popelier, 2018). What distinguishes these new federal arrangements from their more established classic counterparts is on the one side the process of federalization (the why and how), and on the other side the actors that drive this process (the who).

We claim that teleological views on federalization would be misleading. Federalization often remains an 'unfinished', rudimentary, principally reversible process, which does not necessarily end in full-fledged, consolidated federations. The 'imperfection' of federal arrangements may result from reforms and agreements that have introduced a few federal institutions, which do not account for a coherent federal setting. Processes of federalization sometimes peter out due to power shifts or changing agendas of incumbents. If 'truncated' institutions consolidate, they do not form a system which is truly 'federal', but reside in a grey zone blending unitary and federal models. These systems cannot easily be classified as unitary states (for an attempt to classify West European states, see Dardanelli, 2019, 282), because they have clear areas of self-rule. But they are also not considered 'federations' because they often lack main elements of federalism, such as the absence of effective shared rule (as is the case in the UK or Spain), or they lack proper democratic accountability and the rule of law (in Russia and Ethiopia, for example). To avoid terminological confusion, we therefore refer to 'federal arrangements' or 'federal structures' in the following.

A key argument of this book is that assessing the dynamics of federalization by selecting only full-fledged federations would be incomplete. Because the process can ebb and flow, federalization rarely happens as a one-directional development. Federal structures often undergo traits of de-federalization and regression (see, e.g., for Nigeria, Babalola, 2019, as well as Shakir, 2017 for Iraq; Franck, 1968; Kavalski & Zolkos, 2008; see Russia in this volume). This focus not only changes our analytical vantage point but also directs the case selection in this book (see Table 1.1): It attracts notice to federal arrangements that are not bolstered by corresponding federal practices; it spotlights countries featuring federal practices or 'federalization debates', but lack elaborated federal institutions; it explores unfinished, 'truncated' and rudimentary federal settings; it investigates why some formative periods have led to regression while federal institutions are maintained, but also examines why they ended in mature federal systems.

Conceptual Clarifications in Research on Federal Arrangements

Before we explore the reasons why and how federal structures emerge, some conceptual clarifications are essential. Viewing federal systems through a wider lens, researchers have argued that the difference between a genuine federal order and a unitary, albeit decentralized setting is rather malleable than strict (Livingston, 1952, 88). In their seminal work on regional governance, Hooghe et al. (2016) also leave the question unanswered when a state featuring a high level of regional authority becomes 'federal'. Economic theories generally employ a fuzzy understanding of federalism which widely overlaps with the term 'decentralization'. In fact, it is not easy to define discriminatory factors indicating what exactly constitutes a federal system and what is a 'decentralized' system. For example, Kenneth Wheare excluded Canada from his discussion on federations some 60 years ago, because for him it was too close to the union state found in the UK (Wheare, 1964). The Forum of Federations, the world's largest think tank on federalism, includes countries with 'devolved governance' as a matter of interest, considering that devolution and federalization are ongoing, principally reversible processes (Forum of Federations, 2021). Why, then, is this volume not simply dedicated to 'multilevel' systems, which are more or less decentralized?

We argue that decentralization and federalization are different explananda. Decentralization describes the autonomy of subcentral governments vis-à-vis the central authorities (Dardanelli, 2019, 275). There is common sense that all federations consist of at least two levels of government, each vested with autonomous responsibilities and financial resources. All feature a mix of self-rule and shared rule (Watts, 1998, 120; 1999; Elazar, 1987, 33–79). Shared rule captures an involvement of subcentral tiers and entities into central law-making and their participation in checks and balances (Dardanelli, 2019, 275), thus adding a second dimension to the idea of regional autonomy, which is constitutive for decentralized systems. More concretely, each multilevel system must answer the question: Who has the right to change the assignment of responsibilities (Hueglin & Fenna, 2015, 16)? In contrast to merely decentralized systems, where the central government can adopt competencies unilaterally (notwithstanding political pressures), federations establish procedural and constitutional safeguards (see Bednar, 2009, 95–131) protecting against unilateral centralization. But even this argument was recently questioned as local (decentralized) governments may also enjoy constitutional protection (Dardanelli, 2019, 273). Hence, it was suggested that while the degree of decentralization (as autonomy vis-à-vis the central government) should be measured on a continuum ('differences of degree'), unitary and federal systems can be distinguished by 'differences of kind' (Dardanelli, 2019, 278–280), which, from our point of view, mainly build on the elements of shared rule.

Considering this debate, we decided to look onto emerging federal structures in the post-Cold War era through the lens of federalism research for a couple of reasons. Decentralization is not necessarily a pre-stage of federalization. 'Federalization' is a process that can be initiated in centralized as well as in decentralized political systems. It often starts long before the characteristics of a 'federation' are institutionalized. Consequently, studying the explanandum of federalization presupposes looking at preceding debates or federal practices. This corresponds to the basic notions of discursive institutional theory (Schmidt, 2008), whose proponents suggest that discourses and ideas, which become part of federal debates, can gain enough strength to trigger institutional change. This is why we argue that research on emerging and regressing federal structures should start with observing 'federal debates', which, again, may come up in decentralized as well as centralized political systems.

Federal arrangements come in many shapes and forms. Elazar included unions, constitutionally decentralized states, federations, confederations, federacies, which provide areas that are not incorporated into the constitutional state (Elazar, 1987, 54–57), associated states, condominiums, leagues and joint functional authorities in his wider discussion on federal political systems. Some are quasi-federal arrangements, but not fully sovereign federal states, such as the European Union (EU). Others focus extensively on self-rule while limiting provisions for shared rule, such as the UK, Spain and Italy. In countries such as Myanmar and India, we can find the opposite effect—a strong focus on shared rule between the states and the center, but a lack of genuine self-rule for the states. Other countries have undergone periods of international administration and lack full constitutional sovereignty, such as Bosnia and Herzegovina. In some countries, federalization has stopped or slowed down, and the center remains dominant in daily decision-making (Russia), while in other countries decentralization and federalization have gone so far that the nature of the state is put into question (Belgium).

Emerging federal structures may remain 'incomplete' and not consolidated, as the process of federalization is often not linear. Institutional change often proceeds gradually, for example, when new elements are added to the existing institutional framework (layering), converted (as 'redeployment' of old institutions to new purposes), or displaced by alternative rules (Streeck & Thelen, 2005, 30; Mahoney & Thelen, 2010). In countries like Russia or Bosnia, which do possess a written federal commitment, federal institutions are a constituent part of conflicting constitutional principles (see Streeck & Thelen, 2005, 21), not bolstered by corresponding federal practices and cut back by centralizing reforms (Russia). In other words, some formally federal states have found practical approaches to problems that make the system 'federal' mainly in the name. A federal system may then have 'the shell of a formal federation but it lacks the substance in its operation' (Burgess, 2017).

Burgess' differentiation between federal institutions and federal practices also allows for investigating the opposite scenario: Unitary institutions can be employed by federalizing actors (often parties) *as if* they were federal—then the process starts before federal institutions are visible. But one should also be aware that federal practices do not automatically transform into a federal arrangement. In this understanding, federalism is not only a constitutional, but also an operative principle (Livingston, 1952, 929).

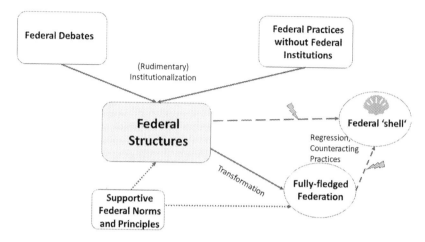

Fig. 1.1 Emergence and regression of federal structures

Figure 1.1 outlines how the above-mentioned concepts and terms relate to each other. Processes are principally reversible; federal structures can regress or wither away (Streeck & Thelen, 2005, 29–30). It also reveals that vital federations cannot survive without supportive habits, principles and norms—a matter also elaborated by institutional theory (Scott, 2014, 60). According to most theories on federalism, these principles are neatly interwoven with liberal democracies: elites and citizens are expected to acknowledge diversity and to respect pluralism, autonomy and comity, just to mention some crucial aspects. Correspondingly, the classic distinction between federalism and federation (King, 1982; Burgess, 2006) indicates that federalism—as a set of principles—does not necessarily end in federal structures (or a full-fledged federation) that live up to these principles.

The focus of this book includes the study of rudimentary, sometimes asynchronous, non-linear processes, which do not necessarily end in consolidated federal settings. This leads to the major research questions to which this volume is dedicated: Why have federal structures emerged in the past decades? And, as there are strong theoretical grounds for assuming that *when and how* federal structures emerge also affects *how* they will work later on: How do these arrangements function in practice?

Why Do Federal Structures Emerge, and How Do They Function in Practice?

Research largely lacks a clear outline of why and how federal structures emerge. One prominent starting point for unpacking this issue has been provided by the seminal work of Stepan (Stepan, 1999), who distinguished three ideal-type trajectories. One is named 'coming-together federalism', suggesting that formerly autonomous entities pool their sovereignty to form a nation state, to overcome the aftermath of civil war and/or to provide public goods (security, welfare), which the single territories cannot produce (Germany, Switzerland, the US). The second one describes the opposite path: formerly unitary states (like Belgium) (gradually) transform into a federal state to prevent the country from breaking apart. This model was labelled 'holding-together-federalism' (see also Breen, 2018b). The third type is contested because it is questionable whether violence and coercion are compatible with federal values like comity or mutual respect. It is named 'putting-together-federalism' and materializes if a hegemon usurps formerly independent territories. A prominent example is the former Soviet Union, which featured a striking mismatch between formally federal structures (including the right to secede), but was non-federal, markedly centralistic in operation (see also Kavalski & Zolkos, 2008).

This typology serves as a useful vantage point. Nonetheless, we argue that it is not fine-grained enough to understand why most federal systems emerged after the end of the Cold War. The following framework differentiates between seven analytical dimensions, which are not mutually exclusive, but intersect and occur in different combinations. These dimensions are rooted in different analytical traditions: in structuralist explanations, as provided by the concept of a 'federal society', in approaches derived from the research agenda of new institutionalism, and in international politics, which considers the influence of regional powers or the role of international actors imposing federal models in post-war countries (see Fig. 1.2). The authors of the chapters were asked to take these dimensions up as far as instructive for their respective case study. All seven analytical lenses elaborate specific perspectives on why federal structures emerge. They supplement or replace the rationalist logics of the initial 'federal bargain', which was deemed to be driven by territorial expansion, military threat and benefits through a common market (Riker, 1964, 12–15). They also consider that the context in which federalization starts affects how the federal system is subsequently operated (the 'how'), and therefore allow for drawing tentative assumptions on the functionality and democratic quality of federal structures after their establishment (the 'why').

Processes of Adaptation: Federal Society as a Source of Federalization

The first concept to which we refer is the 'federal society' (Livingston, 1952, 85, 88; Stein, 1968; see Fig. 1.2). It suggests that societies featuring multiple ethnic, political and historical schisms between populations are deemed to be predestined for transforming into a federal system. A 'federal society' is considered one in which the most politically salient aspects of identification and conflict are related to specific territories (Erk, 2007, 4). Federal institutions are conceptualized as the dependent variable in this framework, as they are expected to achieve congruence with the underlying social structure. This basically structuralist approach predicts a gradual match of the institutional architecture with diverse ethno-linguistic structures.

The concept was further specified because the predicted 'fit' with diverse social structures is anything but an automatic institutional response.

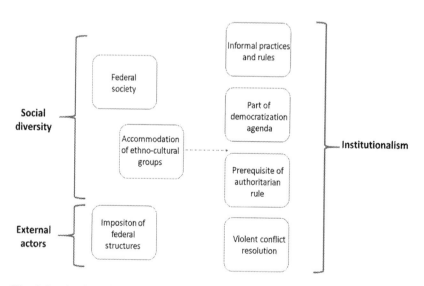

Fig. 1.2 Analytical dimensions to explore federalization

Correspondingly, Erk and Koning (2010) understand gradual shifts in the direction of federal systems as a 'dialectical relationship between the underlying social structure and the overarching institutional configuration', considering organizations of collective interest, such as parties and intermediaries, as key drivers because they translate underlying social factors into the processes of federalization. We argue that the concept needs to be further adapted for the purpose of this volume because the bulk of studies on federal societies is focused on the lessons learnt from classic federations in the West (see, e.g., Burgess, 2012). Much recent research explored adaptive processes in established democracies and is bound to a number of implicit assumptions. Perspectives change, however, when the concept is applied to fragile post-war societies or hybrid regimes, as was done by numerous chapters collected in this book.

Particularly in 'hybrid' regimes featuring limited democratic quality and flawed rule of law (Hale, 2011), and more so in authoritarian regimes, institutional choices do not 'emanate from the social structure' (Erk, 2007, 9)—for a couple of reasons. *Firstly*, political elites are less responsive to the citizens' demands if pluralism is limited and the rule of law is defective. Then, citizens face difficulty in holding incumbents accountable. Moreover, in non-democratic or hybrid regimes, political parties often do not transform social conflicts into political institutions, as elites tend to neglect the accommodation of societal diversity, act in favor of their own clientele and privilege their own reference group (see the cases of Myanmar, Ukraine or the Balkans in this volume). *Secondly*, in post-war countries, where ethnic and religious conflicts need to be settled, international organizations sometimes intervene into constitutional developments by diffusing and manufacturing federal models (or decentralization), which do not provide an accurate 'fit' to the underlying social structure (see Iraq in this volume). *Thirdly*, some countries have not adopted federal institutions, although they accommodate territorially diverse societies (Ukraine) because they fear that federal institutions would enhance processes that break the state apart. The situation becomes even more complicated when central governments in reconfiguring and nationalizing states must cope with transborder nationalism of external 'kin-states' that take responsibility for their co-nationals abroad and interfere in the relations with minority groups (see Ukraine, Myanmar in this volume; Brubaker, 1996, 55–69; 2011). This may become a strong argument to reject a federal system. One should also be aware that diversity alone does not constitute a 'federal society'—a point which we further pursue when discussing the difficult task of accommodating ethno-cultural groups.

Federalization and the Accommodation of Ethno-cultural Groups

In fact, all long-standing democracies that score highest on indexes of linguistic and ethnic diversity are federal (Stepan, 1999, 20). Federalism is expected to help countries 'manage the problems that come with ethnic and linguistic diversity' (ibid.), particularly if heterogeneity can be grouped alongside territorial borders. Not seldom, however, claims for more regional autonomy remain a permanent source of tension. Accommodating diversity becomes particularly complicated if ethnic, linguistic and economic conflicts are mutually reinforcing.

Different analytical concepts reflect the requirements that come with diverse societies. While the notion of a 'federal society' refers to long-term adaptive processes, some scholars and institutional designers deliberately craft concepts deemed useful to accommodate social diversity by creating appropriate institutions (see Fig. 1.2). One of them, which has gained relevance in some of the case studies in this book, is *ethnic federalism*. The concept implies that all federal subunits are constructed as far as possible around ethnic groups (concentrated within definable territories), each of them equipped with considerable autonomy (see Ethiopia and Nepal in this volume). If one ethnic or linguistic group dominates, the largest community can be split up into a number of subunits. This has been attempted in Nigeria over the years, where rightsizing the state and its federal units remains an ongoing struggle. The concept is also implemented in Spain and India, which have equally struggled with demarking internal borders and dealing with secessionist demands.

The concept of ethnic federalism is ridden with prerequisites. Ethnic, religious and linguistic groups neither are often concentrated social entities nor do they settle on well-defined territories (Erk, 2017). If ethnic groups are 'nested' (like in the Russian doll), ethnic federalism requires jurisdictions that secure the autonomy rights of majority groups that, at the same time, may have minority status in the respective upper-level territory. Ideally, such models combine federalism with far-reaching decentralization. The claim for decentralized responsibilities, however, may stir conflict between ethnic communities and the regional government, particularly if sub-federal territorial autonomy was recently wrested from the central state and now becomes contested 'from below'.

Time and again, regional elites employ ethnic divisions to mobilize against other communities (see the experiences of India in this volume). Then, federalization may even fuel ethno-national conflicts, or abet partition and secession (Jenne, 2009). Organizing politics around ethnic issues tends to transform any other conflict into an ethnic one (Anderson, 2013, 34). Once implanted into a federal structure, territorial conflicts become institutionalized. This is what has been outlined in the 'paradox of federalism' (Erk & Anderson, 2009): Fluid identities become fixed through the recognition of diversity, which may eventually pave the way for disintegration. Particularly groups which possess political autonomy, dispose of natural resources, or command military forces are inclined to claim more autonomy at the cost of the federal entirety. Current debates in Iraq and the quest for independence of the Iraqi Kurdish region serve as a perfect example for this (see also Myanmar, Russia in this volume).

A number of preconditions must be given to make ethnic federalism work: Federal arrangements must not challenge the security of the entire state; ethnic groups must be basically loyal; and the group claiming autonomy must not make irredentist claims (Kymlicka, 2007, 39–41). Evidently, these requirements do not materialize in conflict-ridden societies, or indeed any diverse society in which multiple ethnic groups share the same territory (Norman, 2006). This is why some ethnic federal systems provide institutional flexibility to redraw the boundaries of sub-federal units and communities, as has happened along linguistic lines in India (Swenden in this volume), and also been practiced in Ethiopia (Fessha and Dessaleghn in this volume).

One should be aware that ethnicity and religion are contested principles of political organization. From the angle of liberal democracies, ethnic federalism appears as a flawed institutional arrangement. As a tendency, the model is operated in a way that runs contrary to an equal treatment of populations and individuals. Consciousness of ethnic identity as a territorial principle tends to exclude other societal groups, particularly if identities are clear-cut and do not overlap. Kymlicka has noted that federalism may appear as a regressive compromise with pre-modern ethnic allegiances (Kymlicka, 2007). In liberal democracies, however, political and citizen rights are deemed universal; this implies that individual rights cannot be limited to group affiliation.

Moreover, the model tends to hamper effective governance. It typically creates multiple administrative tiers, either run by the federal or by the subcentral governments, which parallel each other (see Bosnia in this volume). Such an organization not only is costly, but also abets clientelism and patronal networks if offices are distributed alongside the principle of ethnicity.

In short, ethnic federalism faces two important dilemmas—on the one side there is a conflict between inclusion and autonomy (who should be included and how to prevent new forms of discrimination and exclusion), and on the other side, there is a trade-off between the need to install institutional mechanisms to ensure peace and group cooperation, which may limit the democratic qualities of the government system. This might raise the question why at all institutional designers seek to implement such models. Here one should consider that elites usually do not fabricate ethnic divisions; they are rather pre-existing (Anderson, 2013, 261).

Informal Practices: Heralding or Etiolating Federal Systems?

The awareness that practices might be federal, while formal institutions are not, turns our attention to the meaning of informal rules and channels: Which role do informal rules play in the emergence and operation of federal systems?

By 'informality', Helmke and Levitsky (2004, 727) understand socially shared rules, which are not fixed by law but communicated and enforced outside officially sanctioned channels. Informality can take different shapes, and each of its manifestations relates differently to the formal political institutions. In federal systems, informal channels are a necessary condition to make formal institutions work. They are deemed predominantly 'supportive' because they enable federal entities to coordinate their policies to cope with externalities and overcome vetoes or blockades. Such basically supportive channels are often employed in established federations, and sometimes they become strongly institutionalized as intergovernmental councils (Behnke & Mueller, 2017).

Analyzing emerging federal arrangements after the end of the Cold War, it becomes evident that institutions are often underpinned by informal channels whose effects are diametrical to the spirit of federalism. These phenomena are denoted *'etiolation'* or *'depletion'* in the following (see also Streeck & Thelen, 2005, 30), as informal structures can wither federal institutions over time. For example, when administrative tasks and fiscal resources are allocated to local and regional entities in the course of federalization, patronal politics and corruption can solidify (Hale, 2015; Freille et al., 2007; see Ukraine, Russia, India, Bosnia, Ethiopia and Kenya in this volume). Such processes are particularly conspicuous in fragile states where elites representing different ethno-linguistic groups use contestation to hijack the state, promote their own ethnic groups and foster clientelism and consistent state weakness (Dzankic, 2018). Recent research on Bosnia and Herzegovina, for example, has spelled out that not only state capture happens at a central level, but that highly decentralized countries are prone to state capture also at a regional and local level—thereby increasing the dominance of patronalism and clientelism (Kapidzic, 2019; for Argentina and Mexico, see Gibson, 2012).

Taking a more optimistic view, one might argue that clientelism can add routes to power for minority groups outside the formal institutional setup (see Steytler on Kenya and South Africa in this volume) and secure some *de facto* power-sharing between social groups. The question is whether this already heralds the emergence of 'federal structures'. It is a legitimate concern that patronalism and clientelism, as deep-seated social rules, finally run counter to the values and norms of a 'federation' (such as comity and mutual respect, see Burgess, 2006). But there might also be other 'federalizing' practices that are less problematic: parties can peripheralize a basically unitary system, and the formation of party groups within parliaments can revolve around territorial issues.

Vice versa, can federal institutions lay the ground for transforming clientelism and patronalism into informality which is supportive to democratic governance? This issue is raised in several chapters across this volume. While there is evidence that a federal system can make a difference in pushing for the promotion of diversity accommodation and peaceful conflict transformation (see, e.g., Keil & Kudlenko, 2015; Keil & Anderson, 2018), there is also consistent reluctance among scholars and policymakers alike in promoting federalism as the driver for transformative change toward practices which support democratic governance and the rule of law (for a more critical evaluation, see McGarry & O'Leary, 2007; Freille et al., 2007; on this in the context of Sri Lanka and Myanmar, see Breen, 2018a; on Iraq, see Danilovich, 2019). Even worse, federal institutions, once established, seem to strengthen already existing practices, which either undermine the spirit of federalism or subvert democracy (or affect both), as some of the contributions to this book will reveal (see, e.g., the case of Russia).

Federalization as Part of the Democratization Agenda

Nevertheless, federalization has usually been perceived as an integral part of democratization agendas and deemed a contradiction to authoritarian rule. Although the dominant view in academia remains focused on a connection and mutual enforcement between federalism and democracy (see for empirical evidence, Burgess & Gagnon, 2010), the nexus between the two has not remained uncontested (Grgic, 2017; Benz & Kropp, 2014; Benz & Sonnicksen, 2017).

Most work has focused on how federalism affects democracy—on the operation of federalism (the 'how'), but not on how federalization materializes as part of the democratization agenda (the 'why'). Introducing federal structures as a constituent element of democratization may become a Herculean task particularly in transitional regimes, to which some of the book chapters are dedicated. Once established, federal institutions can even generate the reverse effect (Obydenkova & Swenden, 2013; Filippov & Shvetsova, 2013). For example, if parties develop around territorial and/or ethnic or linguistic issues during transition, sub-federal incumbents often act as representatives of their own territory, but not of the entire state. Then, the central government is tempted to recentralize responsibilities, to limit party competition and to constrain pluralism in order to hold the state together (as was the case in Russia).

Even in established democracies, federal structures may work at the cost of democratic quality (Benz & Kropp, 2014; Kropp, 2015; Benz & Sonnicksen, 2017; Stepan, 1999; Lane & Ersson, 2005). Due to their institutional complexity, they are by nature opaque and often create blurred and overlapping responsibilities. They often strengthen the power of executives, which are negotiating in intergovernmental bodies, and concomitantly diminish parliamentary scrutiny. Federal systems also abet opportunistic and populistic strategies because they enable governments to shirk and shift the blame onto the governments of the other territorial units (Bednar, 2009, 16). Some of them have tolerated subnational authoritarianism for a considerable time period (Gibson, 2012, for the US, Argentina and Mexico; see India in this volume). Federal structures can make regimes oscillating between democracy and authoritarian rule for a considerable time period. All this suggests that federalism is not a magic wand which always fosters freedom and protects individuals from despotism (Hamilton et al., 1989), and that its alleged benefits must be critically reassessed (Benz & Sonnicksen, 2015, 2017, 2021; Benz & Kropp, 2014). Democratization agendas building on federalization as their constituent element are ridden with prerequisites. It seems plausible that if malfunctions even occur in mature federations, side effects will materialize more than ever in unstable post-war systems and nascent democracies where constitutional principles are frequently contested (for examples, see Keil, 2013 for Bosnia, as well as Shakir, 2017 for Iraq).

Federal Institutions as a Prerequisite of Authoritarian Rule

Even though the relationship between federalism and democracy is ambivalent, there is still common ground that 'authoritarian federalism' is a contradiction in terms. Authoritarian regimes by definition employ strict chains of subordination, undermine checks and balances, restrict pluralism, suppress opposition and thwart the rule of law. Hence, it is legitimate to ask whether research on federal structures should be extended to non-democratic regimes.

This book does not basically challenge this skepticism. But we find fully authoritarian regimes (like Russia), where federal structures continue to exist. This combination creates ambivalent situations for political elites. It is not impossible that even invalidated power-sharing institutions generate uncertainty because sub-national elites might subvert the claim to power of the central government. Why then do non-democratic leaders maintain and nurture federal arrangements?

Here we argue that federal institutions provide considerable benefits to authoritarian leaders (Kropp, 2019, 226). Elites can more easily be co-opted into the regime, if the access to offices and mandates is multiplied. Under the terms of defective rule of law, federal structures allow central governments to punish subnational incumbents as scapegoats for policy failures and shift the blame to subordinate entities. If this strategy is successful, it might help foster the legitimacy of the central government (see Breen, this volume). Moreover, technocratic authoritarian regimes can employ multilevel architectures as a testing ground for promoting loyal and competent satellites, and for probing new policy solutions. In authoritarian regimes, where electoral competition and government turnover are widely abandoned, good performance can help stabilize the regime's legitimacy on the output side. In other words, federal structures in non-democratic regimes may lead to 'increasing returns', which make investments into new institutions unlikely (Pierson, 2004: 35), but the 'returns' are contrary to what normative theories on federalism expect to achieve. There are rather good reasons for authoritarian leaders to employ a multilevel structure. Note, however, that this variant of 'federal arrangement' is anything else but a true 'federation'—it is merely a federal 'shell' (see

Fig. 1.1). One cannot completely rule out, however, that even such a shell will be reanimated at a later point of time.

In post-conflict states, Bosnia, Myanmar, South Africa or Ethiopia among others, authoritarian rule is the standard practice *before* any federalization takes place. The challenges of synchronizing democratization and federalization become even more urging not only when elites have been able to capture state institutions in a conflict-ridden society, but when what would become the new (or reestablished) territorial units are also ruled by authoritarian leaders, who take their legitimacy from ideology (as the left-wing FARC in Columbia or the Maoist insurgents in Nepal), or from claimed leadership over ethnic groups. This has been the case with the ethnic armed organizations in Myanmar, the different armies during the conflict in Bosnia, and throughout most of the civil war in Ethiopia. Here, authoritarianism might flourish not just as a result of dominance by either the center in a more centralized setting (Russia) or by the regions, as a result of extensive decentralization (as is the case in Bosnia). It might even become a key ingredient in center-periphery relations.

Federal Structures and Peacebuilding

The last decades have also been witnessing the increased use of federal institutions as an instrument of peacebuilding. In countries such as Bosnia, Iraq and Nepal, federal arrangements have not only been part of the wider agenda of post-war, post-authoritarian transition to democracy, but also been intrinsically linked to ensuring peace and transforming violence into non-violent behavior through political means.

While theoretical debates on this topic remain limited (see, e.g., Brancati, 2008), there is growing evidence of the usefulness of federalism as a tool of conflict resolution in numerous case studies (Keil, 2019). Dawn Walsh (2018, 1) rightly points out: 'Territorial self-government [...] is at the heart of many current and proposed conflict resolution settlements.' The logic behind the use of federal structures as key elements of peace settlements is simple. Since the end of the Cold War, a substantial transformation of violent conflicts has taken place. While wars between states have de facto become a phenomenon of the nineteenth and twentieth centuries, the last 30 years have seen an increased number of civil wars within (often post-colonial) states, but also hybrid wars, in which external actors directly or indirectly support different parties (Kaldor, 2012).

Conflicts are much more focused on access to resources, rights to self-determination, and participation and inclusion in the state, or if this is seen as not desirable or possible, the creation of new states through secession. Because of this, proponents of federalism and consociational power-sharing point out that territorial autonomy for certain groups, mixed with elite power-sharing at the center, can help solve and transform violent conflict (O'Leary, 2013).

It comes therefore as no surprise that literally every recent or ongoing conflict in the world, at one point or another, has seen suggestions for federalization as part of the conflict resolution instruments. Cox et al. (2017) or Aasland and Kropp (2021) refer to 'social cohesion' as the key to success in deeply divided (post-conflict) societies, while Burgess (2012) highlights the commitment and behavior of elites—what he calls 'the federal spirit'. In addition to strengthening democratic decision-making, local accountability and protecting minority rights, the toolbox of instruments includes mechanisms such as bottom-up approaches in the rebuilding of destroyed infrastructure and economies. Moreover, trust-building mechanisms through compromise and consensus policies are required in shared rule institutions such as second chambers, and the possibility of policy experimentation and divergence needs to be given, as this can lead to learning effects and better policies across a federation.

What sounds straightforward in theory has turned out to be much more complex in practice. Getting actors to agree on power-sharing and federal arrangements has been no mean feat. Previous research indicates, however, that the success of power-sharing arrangements, and with it of federalism as a tool of conflict resolution, remains mixed (Norris, 2008; Keil & Anderson, 2018; Keil, 2019). War-torn societies suffer not only from mistrust, a danger of recurrent violence and a frequent lack of basic forms of governance, but also from the aftermath of the violent conflict: refugees, physical destruction, mental trauma, displacement and war crimes, sometimes ongoing even after the direct end of hostilities. To build any kind of functional state, let alone a federal democracy, in such an environment is challenging at best and near-impossible at worst (Ghani & Lockhart, 2008).

There is a growing list of countries that have adopted federal structures in order to overcome war, internal conflict, state fragility and counter violence as a result of secessionist claims of certain groups. The list includes as diverse countries as Bosnia and Herzegovina (1995), Ethiopia (1995), Iraq (2005) and Nepal (2015), with ongoing debates about the use of federalism as a tool of conflict resolution in South Sudan, Syria, Cyprus and Myanmar, among others. None of these regimes can be classified as stable and fully functional. While some have been working reasonably well (such as South Africa), others have witnessed increased violence (Iraq), state weakness (Bosnia) and democratic stagnation. Even countries that have been listed as success stories, because they have protected peace and ensured democratic governance, such as Belgium and South Africa, have recently seen increased tensions on their federal systems, be it through elite contestation and the undermining of democracy (South Africa under President Zuma), or because federalism and the strict power-sharing elements have raised questions about their functionality, as is the case of Bosnia (Keil, 2018) and Belgium (Meier in this volume; Caluwaerts & Reuchamps, 2014). The mixed experience with federalization in post-war countries becomes even more evident when evaluating the imposition of federal arrangements.

Imposed Federal Structures vs. 'Putting Together Federalism'

Stepan's (1999) categorization of federal origins includes 'putting together federations', federal states created by a hegemon, who enforces state cohesion and territorial integrity through a mixture of force and some local autonomy. While the Soviet Union serves as an example for this category, substantial questions about the application of the federal idea within the Soviet Union remain (see, e.g., Burgess, 2012). Nancy Bermeo (2002, 2004) uses the category of 'internationally imposed federations', referring to a growing number of federal and decentralized states, in which models of territorial power-sharing have been introduced without the consent of the local elites (and the people). Bosnia has become a classic model for imposed federalism, as its constitution was mainly written in the US State Department, and negotiations about its future setup excluded major Bosnian stakeholders (Keil, 2013). More recently, Iraq has also been identified as an imposed federal arrangement, a country in which American constitution-makers pushed federal structures as a tool of rewarding the Kurds for their loyalty and ensuring some kind of participation of the major groups in the state (Belser, 2020, see Belser and Keil in this volume).

While Bosnia and Iraq might be the most obvious cases, there are other ones, which are more complex to assess. In Nepal, for example, peace-building and democratization were linked with an agenda of federalization, and it was heavily supported by experts working for the United

Nations (Breen, 2018a; Breen in this volume). In South Africa, international experts, as well as numerous international organizations, supported the transition from Apartheid and provided important input into the constitutional debate, although final decisions were taken by local elites (Fessha, 2010; Steytler, in this volume). Likewise, ongoing discussions about decentralization and federalism are supported by international organizations (such as the United Nations in Syria—see Keil and Belser in this volume; or the Organization for Security and Co-operation in Europe (OSCE) and the Council of Europe in Ukraine—see Kropp and Holm-Hansen in this volume). Hence, there is a fine line between 'external imposition' on the one side and 'external support and advice' on the other.

The increased role of international involvement in the settlement of internal conflicts raises a number of issues, when looked at from the perspective of new federal systems. *First*, while international involvement in one shape or form is becoming the standard in the settlement of ongoing protracted conflicts, its consequences, impacts and negative side effects are yet to be fully visible. Full international intervention surely is not the solution to building sustainable federal states and instead can manifest consistent state weakness and legitimize state capture.

Second, Roger Mac Ginty's (2011) critique of international peacebuilding remains valid—without local input and support, it is likely to lead to resistance, which might result in a return to violence. Hence, the key is finding the right balance—avoiding complete imposition but providing an international framework which can support the transition from war to peace and from authoritarianism to federal democracy. This balance is not easy to find, but evidence from South Africa (Steytler in this volume) and Nepal (Breen in this volume) indicates that it can be found—and that international actors can play a supportive role. Germany is often listed as an example, where external state-building after the Second World War and territorial decentralization have succeeded in protecting democracy, rebuilding the country and ensuring stability—again after the unification of East and West Germany in 1990 (Gunlicks, 2003). While Germany suffered similar problems compared to other post-conflict societies, its population was nevertheless much more homogenous. Additionally, the clear military and moral defeat of the Nazi regime also helped to rebuild Germany differently, and federal structures, as a historical legacy, were still anchored in the collective memory: context remains of key importance when evaluating the emergence of new federal systems and their operationalization (Burgess, 2006, 76–101, 2012; Mahoney & Thelen, 2010, 31).

Finally, when looking at the priorities of international actors and domestic elites in a specific conflict, a complex mix of expectations, hopes, wishes and long- and short-term interests emerges, while clear guidelines and definitions on what 'success' means are absent. The priorities of international actors enforcing federalization are often shifting and difficult to evaluate. It remains a challenging task to assess for how long international actors need to remain committed to a post-war country, before such a mission deserves the label of 'success'. The short-term aim of ending violence is often connected with the longer-term aim of establishing functioning statehood, often aimed at a functioning federal democracy (for the Dayton Peace Agreement, see Keil & Kudlenko, 2015), but federal structures alone do not enhance functionality and democracy, as was discussed above.

ANALYTICAL DIMENSIONS AND CASE SELECTION

Focusing on processes of federalization, the book aims at mapping a widely unstudied field. 'Emergence' and 'regression' of federal arrangements come in different shapes: as an introduction of single federal institutions, as a redeployment of already existing federal structures, sometimes combined with new institutions, as federal practices, or as a federal shell, which is not bolstered by federal norms and practices (see Fig. 1.1). Consequently, the cases selected for this book focus on different degrees of federalization. The book also includes imposed federal structures (see Table 1.1) and considers countries in which federal structures are not introduced at a single point of time but come as gradual and devolutionary institutional change (see the UK and Spain). There are cases where the territorial levels and policy domains were not simultaneously objects of federal change, and where federalization proceeds as an asynchronous and incomplete development (for the EU, see Fabbrini, 2017; Heidbreder in this volume). To explore the conditions under which a country has adopted some kind of federal structures, the book includes federal states which are regarded as being full-fledged and consolidated. Particularly, the process in Belgium has not been without its challenges, many of which can also be seen in other federalizing countries (see Meier in this volume).

Even though the approach is explorative, it is possible to derive some tentative assumptions from the seven analytical dimensions about why federal arrangements emerge, and how they function in practice. *First*, we

Table 1.1 Analytical Dimensions and Case Selection

Country	Federal Society	Accommodation of Ethnic Minorities	Informality	Democratization	Authoritarian Tendencies	Violent Conflict Resolution	Imposition by External Actors
Belgium	✓	✓			X	X	X
Spain	✓	✓	✓	X	X	X	X
UK	✓	✓	✓		X	X	X
Russia	X	✓	✓	X	✓	X	X
Ukraine	X	✓	✓	X	X	✓	✓
Bosnia and Herzegovina	✓	✓	✓	✓	✓		
North Macedonia	✓	✓	✓			✓	X
Kosovo	X	✓	✓	✓	✓	✓	✓
Myanmar	✓	✓	✓	✓	✓	✓	X
Nepal	✓	✓	✓	✓	✓	✓	X
India	✓	✓	✓	X	✓	X	X
Iraq	X	✓		X	✓	✓	✓
Syria	X	✓	X	✓	n/a	✓	X
Ethiopia	✓	✓	✓	X	X	✓	X
South Africa	✓	✓	✓	✓	X	X	X
Kenya	✓	✓	✓	X	X	✓	X
Colombia	X	X	✓	✓	X		X
European Union	✓	✓	✓	X	✓	X	X

Source: Own compilation

European Union: Due to incomplete federalization and democratization, autocratic tendencies are tolerated. *India*: In terms of accommodation of minority rights and violent repression (particularly in relation to Kashmir), the situation has been deteriorating since 2014. *Kenya*: Since the last rigged elections in 2017, some country experts argue it shows some autocratic tendencies consider the adaptive mechanism described by the concept of a 'federal society' to be found mainly in democracies, and to be less effective in hybrid or authoritarian regimes for a number of reasons, among them the lack of elite responsiveness and the diminished role of parties as intermediaries. *Second*, the accommodation of ethnic, linguistic or religious minorities is expected to be a main driver of federalization. Models like 'ethnic federalism', however, seem to generate basic dilemmas as soon as they are operated in practice. *Third*, if federal structures are imposed by external actors without the participation of domestic elites and the people, they are predestined to become dysfunctional—in terms of both efficiency and democracy, while its meaning for peacekeeping is probably ambiguous at best.

Fourth, processes of federalization and decentralization have more often than not been part of a broader agenda aimed at regime change. For the outlined reasons, it is plausible that such agendas do often not end in sustainable federal structures. *Fifth*, emerging federal arrangements are often home to informal institutions, such as clientelism or patronalism. Federal structures seem to foster these variants of informality because they embed them into an institutionalized frame. *Sixth*, there is reason to assume that non-democratic regimes employ federal structures because they provide specific benefits to authoritarian incumbents. This, again, suggests that under these circumstances the federal arrangement withers and becomes a mere 'shell' that is neither bolstered by federal practices nor supported by internalized federal norms. *Finally*, the promises of federalization as a tool for peacebuilding and power-sharing do often not materialize; the real effects depend on complex, context-dependent configurations of conditions, some of which are outlined by the other analytical dimensions.

These configurative logics (see Blatter & Haverland, 2012) suggest a case study design. In that, the research strategy of this book is still more explanatory than confirmatory (see Gerring, 2004, 2008). While most chapters study a single unit—a federal system—and its emergence or regression over time, others offer a pairwise comparison to work out different (or similar) trajectories.

Table 1.1 summarizes the characteristics of the selected cases. Each case either has started with some kind of federal debate or has emerged as a federal structure in the post-Cold War era. Some have been substantially reformed and moved toward decentralization and federalism in recent years (for the UK and Spain, Anderson). Some contributions examine countries in which federalism and decentralization is discussed as a prospect in wider debates about state reform, conflict resolution and democratization. This included the chapters on Syria and Iraq (Belser and Keil), Nepal and Myanmar (Breen), South Africa and Kenya (Steytler), and Ukraine in this volume (Kropp and Holm-Hansen). Nearly all cases included in this book must cope with the challenge to accommodate linguistic, ethnic, religious groups or castes (India, Swenden). Colombia is an exception in this respect because the conflict mainly reflects an ideological cleavage (Eaton). Some studies shed light on regressing federal systems, because either authoritarian tendencies (see Russia by Klimovich and Kropp, Ethiopia by Fessha and Dessaleghn and Myanmar by Breen) or undemocratic practices (India by Swenden) have been established, while in other cases federal structures have enabled state capture and ethno-nationalist elite domination, as pointed out in the chapter on the Balkans (Keil) or on Syria and Iraq (Belser and Keil). The EU can be considered an incomplete federal model, as it operates very much along federal lines, but remains stuck between a supranational body and an intergovernmental organization (as further explained by Heidbreder).

Note that the cases are categorized in the table by using binary choices, which are not able to capture all nuances. As 'emergence' and 'regression' are by definition phenomena in flux, the attributions are shifting over time. Therefore, the table mainly serves as a tool to achieve a rough overview and identify suitable cases. The categorization was discussed with the authors of the book chapters, who will explain and differentiate the classification in the corresponding case studies. With the case selection, the book includes similar and different trajectories and outcomes, and allows for identifying typical characteristics and deviant cases. In the concluding chapter, we will revisit the theoretical and empirical evidence and assign the cases to a typology of emerging federal structures.

References

Aasland, A., & Kropp, S. (Eds.). (2021). *The accommodation of regional and ethno-cultural diversity in Ukraine*. Palgrave Macmillan.

Anderson, L. D. (2013). *Federal solutions to ethnic problems: Accommodating diversity*. Routledge.

Babalola, D. (2019). *The political economy of federalism in Nigeria*. Palgrave Macmillan.

Bednar, J. (2009). *The robust federation. Principles of design*. Cambridge University Press.
Behnke, N., & Mueller, S. (2017). Better together? The purpose of intergovernmental councils in federal states. *Regional & Federal Studies, 5*.
Belser, E. (2020). A failure of state transformation rather than a failure of federalism? The case of Iraq. *Ethnopolitics, 19*(4), 383–401.
Benz, A., & Broschek, J. (2013). Conclusion. Theorizing federal dynamics. In A. Benz & J. Broschek (Eds.), *Federal dynamics: Continuity, change, and the varieties of federalism* (pp. 366–388). Oxford University Press.
Benz, A., & Kropp, S. (2014). Föderalismus in Demokratien und Autokratien – Vereinbarkeiten, Spannungsfelder und Dynamiken. *Zeitschrift für Vergleichende Politikwissenschaft/Comparative Governance and Politics, 8*, 1–27.
Benz, A., & Sonnicksen, J. (2015). Federalism and democracy—Compatible or at odds with one another? Re-examining a tense relationship. In C. Fraenkel-Haeberle, K. Kropp, F. Palermo, & K.-P. Sommermann (Eds.), *Citizen participation in multi-level democracies* (pp. 15–30). Leiden, Boston.
Benz, A., & Sonnicksen, J. (2017). Patterns of federal democracy. Tensions, friction or balance between two government dimensions. *European Political Science Review, 9*(1), 2–25.
Benz, A., & Sonnicksen, J. (2021). *Federal democracies at work. Varieties of complex government*. Toronto University Press.
Bermeo, N. (2002). The import of institutions. *Journal of Democracy, 13*(2), 96–110.
Bermeo, N. (2004). Conclusion: The merits of federalism. In N. Bermeo & U. Amoretti (Eds.), *Federalism and territorial cleavage* (pp. 457–483). John Hopkins University Press.
Blatter, J., & Haverland, M. (2012). *Designing case studies. Explanatory approaches in small n-research*. Palgrave Macmillan.
Brancati, D. (2008). *Peace by design: Managing intrastate conflict through decentralization*. Oxford University Press.
Braun, D. (2004). Föderalismus. In L. Helms & U. Jun (Eds.), *Politische Theorie und Regierungslehre. Eine Einführung in die politikwissenschaftliche Institutionenforschung* (pp. 130–162). Campus.
Breen, M. (2018a). *The road to federalism in Nepal, Myanmar and Sri Lanka—Finding the middle ground*. Routledge.
Breen, M. (2018b). The origins of holding-together federalism: Nepal, Myanmar, and Sri Lanka. *Publius—The Journal of Federalism, 48*(1), 26–50.
Brubaker, R. (1996). *Nationalism reframed: Nationhood and the national question in the New Europe*. Cambridge University Press.
Brubaker, R. (2011). Nationalizing states revisited: Projects and processes of nationalization in post-Soviet states. *Ethnic and Racial Studies, 34*(11), 1785–1814.

Burgess, M. (2006). *Comparative federalism. Theory and practice.* Routledge.
Burgess, M. (2012). *In search of the federal spirit—New theoretical and empirical perspectives in comparative federalism.* Oxford University Press.
Burgess, M. (2017). Federalism and federation: Putting the record straight. *50 Shades of Federalism.* Retrieved April 4, 2020, from http://50shadesoffederalism.com/theory/federalism-federation-putting-record-straight/
Burgess, M., & Gagnon, A. (Eds.). (2010). *Federal democracies.* Routledge.
Caluwaerts, D., & Reuchamps, M. (2014). Combining federalism with consociationalism: Is Belgian consociational federalism digging its own grave? *Ethnopolitics, 14*(3), 277–295.
Cox, D., Sisk, T., & Hester, E. (2017). Introduction. In F. Cox & T. Sisk (Eds.), *Peacebuilding in deeply divided societies—Toward social cohesion?* (pp. 1–12). Palgrave Macmillan.
Danilovich, A. (Ed.). (2019). *Federalism, secession, and international recognition regime—Iraqi Kurdistan.* Routledge.
Dardanelli, P. (2019). Conceptualizing, measuring, and mapping state structures—With an application to Western Europe, 1950–2015. *Publius: The Journal of Federalism, 49*(2), 271–298.
Dzankic, J. (2018). Capturing contested states: Structural mechanisms of power reproduction in Bosnia and Herzegovina, Macedonia and Montenegro. *Southeastern Europe, 42*(1), 83–106.
Elazar, D. (1987). *Exploring federalism.* University of Alabama Press.
Erk, J. (2007). *Explaining federalism. State, society and congruence in Austria, Belgium, Canada, Germany and Switzerland.* Routledge.
Erk, J. (2017). Nations, nationalities, and peoples: The ethnopolitics of ethnofederalism in Ethiopia. *Ethnopolitics, 16*(3), 219–231.
Erk, J., & Anderson, L. (2009). The paradox of federalism: Does self-rule accommodate or exacerbate ethnic divisions? *Regional & Federal Studies, 19*(2), 191–202.
Erk, J., & Koning, E. (2010). New structuralism and institutional change: Federalism between centralization and decentralization. *Comparative Political Studies, 43*(3), 353–378.
Fabbrini, S. (2017). Intergovernmentalism in the European Union. A comparative federalism perspective. *Journal of European Public Policy, 24*(4), 580–597.
Fessha, Y. (2010). *Ethnic diversity and federalism—Constitution making in South Africa and Ethiopia.* Routledge.
Filippov, M., & Shvetsova, O. (2013). Federalism, democracy, and democratization. In A. Benz & J. Broschek (Eds.), *Federal dynamics* (pp. 167–184). Oxford University Press.
Forum of Federations. (2021). Website https/forumfed.org, retrieved March 1, 2022.

Franck, T. (Ed.). (1968). *Why federations fail: An inquiry into the requisites for successful federalism*. New York University Press.

Freille, S., Haque, M. E., & Kneller, R. (2007). Federalism, decentralisation and corruption. Retrieved November 1, 2021, from https://ssrn.com/abstract=951110 or https://doi.org/10.2139/ssrn.951110

Friedrich, C. (1968). *Trends of federalism in theory and practice*. Frederick A. Praeger Publishers.

Gerring, J. (2004). What is a case study and what is it good for? *American Political Science Review, 98*(2), 341–354.

Gerring, J. (2008). Case selection for case study analysis: Qualitative and quantitative techniques. In J. Box-Steffensmeier, H. E. Brady, & D. Collier (Eds.), *Oxford handbook of political methodology* (pp. 645–684). Oxford University Press.

Ghani, A., & Lockhart, C. (2008). *Fixing failed states—A framework for rebuilding a fractured world*. Oxford University Press.

Gibson, E. (2012). *Boundary control: Subnational authoritarianism in federal democracies* (1st ed.). Cambridge University Press.

Grgic, G. (2017). *Ethnic conflict in asymmetric federations—Comparative experience of the former Soviet and Yugoslav regions*. Routledge.

Gunlicks, A. (2003). *The Länder and German federalism*. Manchester University Press.

Hale, H. E. (2011). Hybrid regimes—When autocracy and democracy mix. In N. J. Brown (Ed.), *Dynamics of democratization: Dictatorship, development, and diffusion* (pp. 23–45). Johns Hopkins University.

Hale, H. E. (2015). *Patronal politics: Eurasian regime dynamics in comparative perspective*. Cambridge University Press.

Hamilton, A., Madison, J., & Jay, J. (1989). *The federalist papers*. Bantam.

Helmke, G., & Levitsky, S. (2004). Informal institutions and comparative politics: A research agenda. *Perspectives on Politics, 2*(4), 725–740.

Hooghe, L., Marks, G., Schakel, A. H., Chapman Osterkatz, S., Niedzwiecki, S., & Shair-Rosenfield, S. (2016). *Measuring regional authority—A postfunctionalist theory of governance* (Vol. 1). Oxford University Press.

Hueglin, T. O., & Fenna, A. (2015). *Comparing federalism: A systematic inquiry*. University of Toronto Press.

Jenne, E. K. (2009). The paradox of ethnic partition: Lessons from *de facto* partition in Bosnia and Kosovo. *Regional & Federal Studies, 19*(2), 273–289.

Kaldor, M. (2012). *New and old wars—Organized violence in a global era*. Polity.

Kapidzic, D. (2019). Subnational competitive authoritarianism and power-sharing in Bosnia and Herzegovina. *Southeast European and Black Sea Studies*, online first. Retrieved April 20, 2020, from https://doi.org/10.1080/14683857.2020.1700880

Kavalski, E., & Zolkos, M. (Eds.). (2008). *Defunct federalisms—Critical perspectives on federal failures*. Routledge.

Keil, S. (2013). *Multinational federalism in Bosnia and Herzegovina*. Ashgate.
Keil, S. (2018). Föderalismus in Bosnien und Herzegowina. In T. Flessenkemper & N. Moll (Eds.), *Das politische System Bosnien und Herzegowinas—Herausforderungen zwischen Dayton-Friedensabkommen und EU-Annäherung* (pp. 77–90). Springer.
Keil, S. (2019). Federalism as a tool of conflict resolution. In J. Kincaid (Ed.), *A research agenda for federalism studies* (pp. 151–161). Cheltenham and Northampton.
Keil, S., & Anderson, P. (2018). Decentralization as a tool of conflict resolution. In K. Detterbeck & E. Hepburn (Eds.), *Handbook of territorial politics* (pp. 89–106). Edward Elgar.
Keil, S., & Kudlenko, A. (2015). Bosnia and Herzegovina 20 years after Dayton: Complexity born of paradoxes. *International Peacekeeping*, 22(5), 471–489.
King, P. (1982). *Federalism and federation*. The Johns Hopkins University Press.
Kropp, S. (2015). Federalism, people's legislation, and associative democracy. In C. Fraenkel-Haeberle, S. Kropp, F. Palermo, & P. Sommermann (Eds.), *Citizen partizipation and multilevel governance* (pp. 48–66). Brill.
Kropp, S. (2019). The ambivalence of federalism and democracy: The challenging case of authoritarianism—With evidence from the Russian case. In N. Behnke, J. Broschek, & J. Sonnicksen (Eds.), *Multilevel governance: Configurations, dynamics, consequences* (pp. 213–229). Palgrave Macmillan.
Kymlicka, W. (2007). Multi-nation federalism. In B. He, B. Galligan, & T. Inoguchi (Eds.), *Federalism in Asia* (pp. 33–56). Edward Elgar.
Lane, J.-E., & Ersson, S. (2005). The riddle of federalism: Does federalism impact on democracy? *Democratization*, 12, 163–182.
Livingston, W. S. (1952). A note on the nature of federalism. *Political Science Quarterly*, 67, 81–95.
Mac Ginty, R. (2011). *International peacebuilding and local resistance—Hybrid forms of peace*. Palgrave Macmillan.
Mahoney, J., & Thelen, K. A. (2010). A theory of gradual institutional change. In J. Mahoney & K. A. Thelen (Eds.), *Explaining institutional change. Ambiguity, agency, and power* (pp. 1–37). Cambridge University Press.
McGarry, J., & O'Leary, B. (2007). Federation and managing nations. In M. Burgess & J. Pinder (Eds.), *Multinational federations* (pp. 180–211). Routledge.
Norman, W. (2006). *Negotiating nationalism—Nation-building, federalism, and secession in the multinational state*. Oxford University Press.
Norris, P. (2008). *Driving democracy—Do power-sharing institutions work?* Cambridge University Press.
O'Leary, B. (2013). Power sharing in deeply divided places: An advocate's introduction. In J. McEvoy & B. O'Leary (Eds.), *Power sharing in deeply divided places* (pp. 1–66). Pennsylvania University Press.

Obydenkova, A., & Swenden, W. (2013). Autocracy-sustaining versus democratic federalism: Explaining the divergent trajectories of territorial politics in Russia and Western Europe. *Territory, Politics, Governance*. https://doi.org/10.1080/21622671.2013.763733

Pierson, P. (2004). *Politics in time. History, institutions, and social analysis*. Princeton University Press.

Popelier, P. (2018). Dynamic federalism. *50 Shades of Federalism*. Retrieved April 20, 2020, from http://50shadesoffederalism.com/tag/dynamic-federalism/

Riker, W. H. (1964). *Federalism: Origin, operation, significance*. Little, Brown & Company.

Schmidt, V. (2008). Discursive institutionalism: The explanatory power of ideas and discourse. *Annual Review of Political Science, 11*, 303–326.

Scott, R. W. (2014). *Institutions and organizations. Ideas, interests, and identities* (4. Aufl). Sage.

Shakir, F. (2017). *The Iraqi federation—Origin, operation, significance*. Routledge.

Stein, M. (1968). Federal political systems and federal societies. *World Politics, 20*(4), 721–727.

Stepan, A. (1999). Federalism and democracy: Beyond the U.S. model. *Journal of Democracy, 10*(4), 19–34.

Streeck, W., & Thelen, K. (2005). Introduction: Institutional change in advanced political economies. In W. Streeck & K. Thelen (Eds.), *Beyond continuity. Institutional change in advanced political economies*. Oxford University Press.

Walsh, D. (2018). *Territorial self-government as a conflict management tool*. Palgrave Macmillan.

Watts, R. (1998). Federalism, Federal Political System, and Federation. *Annual Review of Political Science, 1*(1), 117–137.

Watts, R. (1999). *Comparing Federal Systems*. 3rd ed. McGill-Queen's University Press.

Wheare, K. (1964). *Federal government* (4th ed.). Oxford University Press.

PART II

Case Studies

CHAPTER 2

Belgium: Federalism as a Stopover?

Petra Meier

Historically speaking, Belgium only recently transformed from a unitary to a federal state. This was in 1993, whereas the Belgian state was founded back in 1830. The Saint Michael Agreement signatures in 1993 concluded a fourth state reform, which finalized the federal system. One could assume that citizens would pay attention to this relatively recent state architecture, but they do not tend to do so. Even more, they worry less about it than—part of—the political elite, as they are eager to move beyond a federal system, so they treat this ambition like it were the most salient issue on the agenda (Deschouwer, 2013; Reuchamps et al., 2017; Sinardet et al., 2017; Swenden, 2013). While Belgium is known for being an important breeding ground for surrealist art, this could be extended to politics. There are probably few Western democracies where the cleavage in politics is so large between citizens and politicians. Therefore, this, in combination with the fact that the transformation of the Belgian state architecture from a unitary to a full-fledged federal system took but 25 years; the absence of a concrete blueprint of where to go or how to get there; the unique

P. Meier (✉)
University of Antwerp, Antwerp, Belgium
e-mail: petra.meier@uantwerpen.be

© The Author(s), under exclusive license to Springer Nature Switzerland AG 2022
S. Keil, S. Kropp (eds.), *Emerging Federal Structures in the Post-Cold War Era*, Federalism and Internal Conflicts,
https://doi.org/10.1007/978-3-030-93669-3_2

structure of the Belgian federal state architecture; and the ongoing political turmoil, make an interesting case to explore.

Following the logic underlying this volume, the current chapter first explains why Belgium shifted from a unitary to a federal state architecture. It then addresses the process of federalization and how Belgium currently tends to shift beyond the stage of a federation. The subsequent section investigates how the federation functions, discussing deficits with respect to democracy and efficiency criteria. Finally, the conclusion wraps up the main findings.

From Consensus Democracy to Consensus Federation: The Triggers of Federalization

Belgium is an example of what Stepan (1999) would call holding-together federalism. It is a unitary state which transformed into a federal one to avoid the country falling apart, in this case due to linguistic tensions. This definition does not hold completely, as the initial impetus was to solve conflict. Therefore, there was neither a strong tendency to plead or strive for the dissolution of the Belgian state nor a concrete danger for it to fall apart. There was, however, a political deadlock requiring creative compromises to deblock the political situation. The central state had been dominated by a French-speaking elite ever since its foundation in 1830, although the population in Flanders, including the capital city of Brussels, spoke Dutch. This elite, who also dominated the financial and economic sectors, ran the Belgian political system. The Flemish movement was initially culturally oriented, striving for both the recognition of Dutch as an official language equal to French and the use of Dutch in cultural, civic and public matters. This led to a series of language laws regulating the use of Dutch in sectors such as courts (1873), public administration (1878), public schools (1883) or the army (1887) (De Winter & Baudewyns, 2009; see also Mabille, 2011; Witte et al., 2016). Flemish requests for a liberation from French-speaking domination were first strengthened by the high price Flemish soldiers paid during World War I (WWI), but then hampered by collaboration between the German occupier and part of the Flemish movement during World War II (WWII). In the 1960s three factors strengthened Flemish claims (De Winter & Baudewyns, 2009). First, the increasing economic dominance of Flanders took advantage of the Golden Sixties, developing a tertiary economy and new industrial branches around the port of Antwerp, among others. Meanwhile, Wallonia started suffering a backlash from the old industry. This economic dominance underscored the imbalance in political, economic and financial powers, fueling Flemish self-confidence. Second, there was a liberation of the political agenda with the signing of the School Pact in 1958. The founding of the Belgian state had been—amongst others—characterized by a struggle between Catholic and Liberal forces on the separation of church and state. Belgium, and especially Flanders, had, and continues to have, a strong Catholic tradition, historically granting the Catholic Church an important stake in public and private matters. This cleavage dominated much of political life until it was pacified in the School Pact of 1958, thereby removing it from the political agenda and leaving room to deal with other issues. Third, there was a direct political trigger, related to the ongoing francization of Brussels and especially its Flemish surroundings, which quickly occupied the political agenda. At the time, the official language of a municipality depended on the number of inhabitants speaking that language as recorded during a population census. While French was still the language facilitating social mobility, there was also an increased move of French-speaking inhabitants from Brussels to the Flemish suburbs. These factors led to an increasing number of Dutch-speaking municipalities having to provide French or even bilingual facilities, when at least 30% of the residents declared to speak that language. At the beginning of the 1960s, six more municipalities in the periphery of Brussels were concerned, an evolution the Flemish movement wanted to stop (Witte, 1993). Striving for the improved recognition and guaranteed use of Dutch, it wanted a fixed language border to avoid further francization of Dutch-speaking territories. While the Flemish movement wanted part of the territory to be governed in Dutch, French-speaking politicians held an opposite view and defended the free use of language everywhere in Belgium (Van Dyck, 1996). In 1962 increased political mobilization on the issue led to an abolition of all language censuses, the definition of a language border and the division of Belgium into fixed language zones. In 1970 the Gilson Act was enshrined in the first state reform, laying the foundation for the federal state architecture still characterizing Belgium. It is difficult to estimate whether Belgium would not have evolved into a federation had other measures been decided upon to solve the crisis regarding the expanding Brussels 'oil stain', a term that refers to the francization of the Flemish areas surrounding Brussels. Two points are clear, though. First, there was no concrete plan to do so at the outset. While it is often underscored that those forming the initial compromise intended to avoid federalization, the ambitions of some of the main political protagonists of that time, such as the young Wilfried Martens, the eventual prime minister of several governments during the 1980s, were federal (Martens, 2006). It is clear, however, that the architects of the first state reform and its run-up did not have a blueprint of the final product in mind (Deschouwer, 2012). The rationale was to find constitutional and operational ways to govern the increasingly divided Belgian society.

Belgium is a typical example of a consociational or consensus democracy à la Lijphart (1977, 2012). Political problems were pacified through political elites' negotiations of pacts. The higher the stakes, the more comprehensive—but not necessarily coherent—the pacts. It is this way of functioning that, in the end, transformed Belgium from a unitary to a federal state. Consensual democracy was designed to overcome the socioeconomic and religious cleavages, and federalism was developed to appease the ethnolinguistic division (Meier & Bursens, 2020). The underlying logic was and is to organize separately what was difficult to run as a joint venture (Deschouwer, 2012). This explains the centrifugal competitive character of the Belgian federation with minimal mechanisms of cooperation. In this respect it appears that the route to a federal state architecture was one of path dependency, with 1962 as the initial critical juncture redirecting the given path, a juncture that was itself the continuation of older sociopolitical constellations. In any case, this path dependency is still clearly visible in the structure and working of the federation, but especially in all its current problems. Second, the division along linguistic lines to stop the formal francization of the Flemish municipalities around Brussels was not an isolated act. Indeed, it went hand in hand with the reform of other institutions (De Winter & Baudewyns, 2009). In 1960 the public radio and television company split into separate Dutch- and French-speaking ones, with the Ministry of National Education following suit in 1965. In 1968 the Catholic University of Leuven became a Dutch-speaking institution, leading to the foundation of the French-speaking Catholic University of Louvain-La-Neuve, literally the new Leuven. Two years later, the Dutch-speaking moved out of the French-speaking Université Libre de Bruxelles and founded the Vrije Universiteit Brussel, again literally its equal in name. Similar tendencies were found in political parties. While the three traditional parties, the Christian Democrats, the Liberals and the Social Democrats, formally split in 1968, 1971 and 1978 respectively, the Christian Democrats already functioned with both a

Dutch-speaking and a French-speaking wing since the end of WWII, while the Social Democrats organized their internal structure along regional lines in 1963 (Delwit et al., 2011). Hence, not only did institutions split along linguistic lines, but the political elite increasingly did so, too.

From Consensus Federation to Centrifugal Federation: The Problems of Gradual Institutional Reform

The Belgium state has had a full-fledged federal architecture since the fourth state reform of 1993. The main reason for this does not so much reside in the fact that the changed Article 1 of the Constitution designated Belgium a federal state constituted of communities and regions. Rather, it is the fact that from then onward, the legislatives of all these federal entities were directly elected (with the exception of that of the French Community; see infra), had their own executives and transformed the Senate into a chamber representing the communities. The three former state reforms had produced the building blocks to compile this gradually evolving federal state architecture. Looking back at this process, it seems that the first state reform of 1970 mainly set out the basic logic of the future federal state and established the rules according to which the game should be played, both when it came to the later federation and its negotiation (Deschouwer, 2012). The second state reform of 1980 laid the foundations for the federal entities, excluding the Brussels Capital Region, the outlines of which were drawn during the third state reform in 1988–1989. The fourth state reform of 1993 is considered the concluding piece of that process, whereas the fifth and sixth state reforms of 2000–2001 and 2011 further fine-tuned the system without fundamentally altering its basic structure. The first state reform laid the foundation of what later became a complex federal structure with a double layer of federal entities, communities and regions. While both communities and regions deal with different policy matters for which they have full competencies, and while only the regions have fiscal power, they do not cover different geographic areas. Both the communities as well as the regions neatly cover the complete Belgian territory, partly overlapping—which is what makes the system so complex and everything so interdependent. Regions are competent for territorial matters. For that purpose, the country is divided into three geographically bounded entities: Flanders, Wallonia and the Capital

Region of Brussels. Communities, on the contrary, are in charge of person-related policies, such as culture, language policies, education and preventive health. For that purpose, the population is divided into three groups: the Flemish Community, the French Community and the—relatively small—German-speaking Community. Notwithstanding their person-related character, the Communities are confined to specific territories because of the language border: the Flemish Community and the French Community respectively to Flanders and Wallonia; the Capital Region of Brussels has a bilingual status; and the German-speaking Community covers the German-speaking municipalities of the Walloon Region along the border with Germany. This implies that the Flemish Community executes its competencies in FlandersFlanders, the French Community in Wallonia, minus the German-speaking municipalities, both of them in Brussels, and the German-speaking Community in the Walloon Region (Map 2.1). To further complicate matters, the Flemish Community and Region merged their institutions, while they do not cover concurring territories. These federal entities were not that neatly established back in 1970. The first state reform introduced the principle of a double layer of federal entities, communities and regions. It also launched the communities, but until 1995, their legislatures and executives operated within the boundaries of the national legislature and executive, being composed by part of its members. Only the institutions of the German-speaking Community were established in the early 1970s, as the then still national legislatures and executives did not comprise enough members from that community. The first state reform, however, did establish language groups in the national

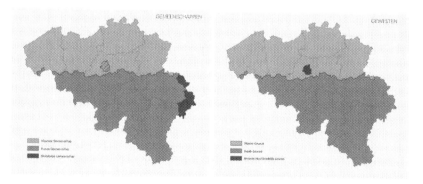

Map 2.1 Communities and regions in Belgium. *Source*: Belgium.be

House of Representatives and the Senate. All Members of Parliament (MPs) and Senators belonged to but one language group. This affiliation to a language group was important, as the first state reform also contained a number of minority protecting rules. The French-speakers, roughly 40% of the Belgian population, were afraid of becoming a structural minority. Therefore, (i) the government would have to be composed of an equal number of Dutch- and French-speaking ministers, with the exclusion of the prime minister, who is to be linguistically neutral; (ii) measures regarding relations between the language groups would need to be agreed upon by special majorities, implying not only a two-thirds majority overall, but also a simple majority within each language group; and (iii) whenever three-quarters of a language group's members considered the relations between the language groups to be in danger, they could launch the so-called alarm bell procedure, putting the issue into the government's hands. These rules were the bargaining chip for the language border, which was strongly demanded by the Flemish movement and was the definition of the bilingual geographic zone of Brussels. These rules would, by their very meaning, also apply to the negotiations of all future state reforms. The second state reform of 1980 established the contours of the Flemish and Walloon Region, even though their legislatures and executives, similar to those of the communities, operated as part of the national legislative and executive until 1995. However, the executives of communities and regions were no longer accountable to the national government, and the communities and regions obtained full legislative power. Also, the competencies of the communities were extended from specific cultural matters to the more generic person-related competencies. This extension of policy-making competencies of the federal entities was a constant factor of each subsequent state reform, to an extent that this downloading has left little in the hands of the federal level by now. It was also in the wake of the second state reform that the Flemish Community and Flemish Region decided to merge their administrations, legislative and executive. Finally, the second state reform established a Court of Arbitration, which would become the Constitutional Court during the fifth state reform. What was not set up in 1980 was the Brussels Capital Region, as no agreement could be found on its precise boundaries, its statute and how to protect the—by then—Dutch-speaking minority. From a Dutch-speaking city with a French-speaking elite, Brussels had evolved into a largely French-speaking city, only to be further fueled by its increasing internationalization. Because the Flemish movement had requested the abolition of the language census, no exact data were—or are—available, but the Dutch-speaking population was estimated to constitute less than one-fifth of the population of Brussels. It took nearly a decade of political turmoil, and a series of collapsing governments, to define the Brussels Capital Region during the third state reform of 1988–1989. It was to be limited to the bilingual area of Brussels, defined in the 1960s, and disposed of the same policy competencies as the other regions, but could not touch upon its institutions (Popelier, 2019), governing by ordinances. The latter implied that decisions by the Brussels Capital Region could be nullified by the federal government. The third state reform also notably saw the Dutch-speaking minority protecting rules applied to the Brussels Capital Region, mirroring those established for the French-speaking minority at the federal level. Similar to the German-speaking Community, the Brussels Capital Region functioned autonomously from the start. Next to the setting up of the Brussels Capital Region, the third state reform was also important for the new intergovernmental structures. These were the Federal Consultation Committee and the cooperation agreements. The latter are in many cases optional but sometimes a necessary condition for the downloading of policy competencies (such as in the case of public transport, downloaded to the regions during the third state reform). The fourth state reform of 1993 set the capstone on what had been constructed during the three previous ones. From then onward the legislatures of all federal entities were to be elected directly (with the exception of the French Community, who opted for an indirect composition of the MPs of the Walloon parliament and a number of French-speaking MPs elected to the parliament of the Brussels Capital Region). These elections were to be held simultaneously with those for the European Parliament, which means that the legislatures of the federal entities could not be dissolved prematurely. The federal entities formed their own governments and had their own administration, which had partly been transferred from the federal level. The increasing relevance of the federal entities also became apparent in a considerable reduction in size of the federal executive and legislative. The executive was set to a maximum of 15 members, while the federal House of Representatives shrank from 212 to 150 members and the Senate from 184 to 71. The latter was also to be composed differently to better represent the communities. Also telling is the fact that the federal entities were granted *in foro interno in foro externo*, meaning that these entities are responsible for foreign policy to the extent that they have domestic political competencies. With that, the federalization of Belgium was achieved, and the structures, institutions, processes and tools that had been developed did indeed consolidate. However, it became quickly apparent that the appetite for more on behalf of—part of—the Dutch-speaking elite was not satisfied and that the federal system did not work smoothly. Both the French-speaking and other Dutch-speaking parties feared that the strong Dutch-speaking Radical Right Populists Vlaams Blok (now Vlaams Belang) might in the future block Brussels' institutions. The Dutch-speaking parties held 10 out of 75 seats after the 1995 elections, 11 after those of 1999. Any Dutch-speaking party managing to obtain a handful of seats could block the entire decision-making procedure by relying on the rules protecting the Dutch-speaking minority. Also, the French Community did not have the resources to finance education. Communities, different from regions, do not have fiscal power and rely exclusively on federal money, whereas their policy competencies, especially education, require important financial means. The Flemish Community does not face this problem as its institutions merged with those of the Flemish Region, allowing for a transfer of financial means from regional to community competencies. The French Community does not have this possibility. The fifth state reform of 2000–2001 provided the Dutch-speaking minority with a supplementary protection by guaranteeing the Dutch-speaking parties just below a fifth of the seats in the parliament of the Brussels Capital Region (17 out of 89). It also improved the financial means of the communities. More important from the point of view of what makes a system a full-fledged federal one, is the fact that the Court of Arbitration was upgraded to become a Constitutional Court. It acts as a supreme court, interprets the Constitution and guards over the correct application of the division of competences between government levels. The sixth state reform of 2011 further adjusted the system, especially in shifting the power balance from the federal level to that of the federal entities. This is apparent in several factors. First, the fiscal power of the regions extended considerably (Decoster & Sas, 2012). Second, social security, which, up until then, was seen as a federal competence and an important cornerstone of state-wide interpersonal solidarity (Popelier & Cantillon, 2013), was touched upon as the competence of child benefit was downloaded. Third, the elections of the House of Representatives, not those of the federal entities' legislatives, were tied to those of the European Parliament. This allowed for the federal entities to further develop their own political dynamic and rhythm. Finally, the Senate was stripped of nearly all its competencies and functions and instructed to be indirectly composed of MPs from the legislatives of the federal entities representing their community (Dandoy et al., 2015).

From Solution to Problem: How Federalism Affects Coordination and Democracy

All of this makes for a centrifugal federal system with an overlapping double layer of federal entities. Only one layer, that of the regions, has fiscal power, but both have extensive policy competencies, at the expense of the federal level, which was gradually stripped of most of its competencies. Because the underlying logic is one of organizing separately, it is difficult to run as a joint venture, so policy competencies tend to be exclusive. There is a strong tendency toward self-rule and little shared rule, notwithstanding the fact that the different policy-making levels are highly interdependent as policy fields often touch both person- and territory-related matters, and that the communities depend on federal money. More than mechanisms of cooperation, the Belgian federation disposes of mechanisms to solve (potential) conflicts of competences or of interests (Reuchamps, 2013; Swenden, 2010, 2013; Swenden & Jans, 2006). Regarding conflicts of competences on a proactive level, it is worth mentioning the ex-ante check of new legal initiatives emanating from the federal or unit level by the Council of State. Ex-post reviews of competences are in the hands of the Constitutional Court. Political conflicts of interest are dealt with by the Federal Consultation Committee. Coordination is most developed whenever the different governments have to act with a single voice at the EU level, which provides the federal level with an important coordinating function in matters in which it has little or no say (Beyers & Bursens, 2013; Happaerts et al., 2012). Notwithstanding the German-speaking minority and the bilingual status of the Brussels Capital Region, the federation is rather bipolar as there are no state-wide parties and as the two major language groups are always positioned opposite each other. On top of this, in Flanders center (and radical) right parties tend to dominate, while the Social Democrats still have a strong position in Wallonia, and Brussels generates its own political dynamics. Both the political elite and public opinion operate in separate bubbles, even in the bilingual area of the Brussels Capital Region. All of this hampers consociational power-sharing. As underscored before, this federal system gradually evolved as an answer to tensions among language groups, becoming itself a self-fulfilling prophecy for at least two reasons. First, the structures, rules and procedures established made the language groups drift further apart as no bridging structures, processes or mechanisms were developed. For instance, it took a long time for the Federal Consultation Committee to become functional and meet on a regular basis. Secondly, and probably more importantly, the structures, rules and procedures established turned Belgium into an ethnofederation, in which every institution is permeated by the language groups (Celis & Meier, 2017). This involves every decision to be dragged into the ethno-linguistic cleavage. For instance, the executive of the Brussels Capital Region is to be negotiated in two steps. The parties of each language group sit together separately to decide which of them will govern together. Once they have decided upon the coalition within each language group, the parties meet to form the executive for the Brussels Capital Region. While the system was developed to appease tensions in a highly divided society, frictions became apparent over time. This can be seen clearly in the deadlock after the federal elections of 2007, when the Dutch- and French-speaking parties took a seemingly long—as viewed during that time—period of 194 days to negotiate a government (De Winter & Baudewyns, 2009). At some point during those negotiations, former Prime Minister Dehaene (1991–1999) entered and discovered to his great shock that negotiators no longer knew each other, let alone had conducted preliminary informal talks. While (in)formal networks that comprised Dutch- and French-speaking politicians and made the federal system function were still in place after the federalization, the younger generation did not develop similar networks, resulting in a diminished use of formal channels to meet and cooperate. The government negotiations in the wake of the federal elections of 2007 bluntly uncovered this. While the consensual character of the Belgian political system allowed the latter to turn into a federation, the design of this federal system gradually undermined its consensual character. It is true that formally speaking, Belgium still meets many of the criteria to qualify as a consensus democracy (Lijphart, 2012), but one important feature of the former system is to negotiate pacts consisting of elites cooperating to bridge the cleavages. Furthermore, this cross-linguistic bridging disappeared with the older generations of politicians. Both the political elite and public opinion were largely split. And once habits and practices caught up with the institutional split, problems rather than benefits emerged. Next to this important but rather informal feature, there are characteristics of the federal system, which have been described above and which hamper a smooth and efficient functioning of the federal system. Case specific deadlocks became apparent, as seen in the difficulties to adopt common positions in supranational and international negotiations on climate or trade related policies. The issue became even more topical in the heat of the COVID-19 pandemic, as the latter mercilessly uncovered the logistic costs of the Belgian federal system. The pandemic contributed to the general sentiment of a political deadlock. In addition to the issues mentioned previously, the Belgian federation's design and functioning uncovers some worrisome democratic deficits (Meier & Bursens, 2020). A first deficit relates to Belgium's clear case of executive federalism in which the executive holds an intense dominance over the legislative. A second deficit concerns Belgium's ethnofederal character that sees the multiple constituting demoi exerting extreme control over the encompassing demos. As such, neither executive federalism nor ethnofederalism are problematic from a democratic point of view. The problem resides in the fact that both are pushed to an extreme so that they undermine the Belgian federal system to function as a truly democratic system. Indeed, the more broadly observable tendency of executive dominance is strengthened by the way the Belgian federation with its rules and procedures were designed (Fiers, 2006; Randour, 2018). First, the legislatures are left out of the picture in both cooperation mechanisms and conflict-solving procedures. They rely on executives, not on legislatives: cooperation agreements are negotiated amongst executives; the Federal Consultation Committee is exclusively composed of members of the different executives; and the alarm bell procedure puts the issue under concern into executive hands. All of this leads to a domination of the executive both within and across government levels. Second, from the moment Belgium turned into a full-fledged federation at the beginning of the 1990s, the Senate's reform to make it represent the communities went hand in hand with a dismantling of its competencies. This process was pushed to an extreme during the sixth state reform (Dandoy et al., 2015). Already apparent in the 1990s, but even more so today, the Senate is clearly the inferior of the two chambers of the federal legislature. There is no balanced bicameral system. The legislature is supposed to act as a meeting place for the communities to meet only nine times a year and is left with no competencies so to speak. This powerlessness of the Senate shows how intergovernmental relations in Belgium are not meant to pass through legislative hands. Both features of executive dominance resulting from the federal system's design are further strengthened by the absence of state-wide parties. In Belgian politics this absence turns party leaders into central brokers when it comes to directing important negotiations and controlling party members in the executive and in the legislative (De Winter et al., 2006; De Winter & Dumont, 2006; Pilet & Meier, 2018). The excessive dominance of the executives over the legislatures puts constraints on the government's representative character both within and across each of the administration levels (unit and federal level). It hampers essential features of the legislative's democratic control over the executive. The second deficit mentioned above is related to the fact that Belgium is an ethnofederation with an extreme dominance of the multiple constituting demoi over the encompassing demos. The system is characterized not only by this domination, but especially by the almost complete lack of any formal recognition of the latter. Strong constitutional protection of the minorities, including language parity in governments, guaranteed representation of the language groups in the legislative of the Brussels Capital Region, the division of MPs into language groups in the House of Representatives and double-majority requirements (Pilet & Pauwels, 2010) are built upon a logic of representing and protecting the demoi, not the demos. Furthermore, at the federal level, citizens can only vote for and sanction half of the executive during elections as there are no state-wide electoral parties, circumscription or college (De Grauwe & Van Parijs, 2009, 2014; Deschouwer & Van Parijs, 2007). Similarly, in the bilingual Brussels Capital Region, citizens must choose between voting for and sanctioning the Dutch-speaking or the French-speaking branch of the executive as there are no regional parties. While voters cannot vote for all executive actors, these executives take decisions that affect them. The excessive ethnofederalization of Belgium dilutes the representative character of the federation, impeding the accountability of governments to citizens (Deschouwer, 2006).

Conclusion: The Paradox of Federalism

Over time Belgium evolved from a consensus democracy to a consensus federation to a centrifugal federation, but the solution became the problem. Caluwaerts and Reuchamps (2014) nicely document this paradox of federalism by arguing that federalism and consensus democracy can go hand in hand as both reject the principle of a majoritarian democracy. The problem, therefore, resides in the fact that the downloading of competencies was meant to appease tensions, even though such a centrifugal tendency of self-rule only has an appeasing effect in the short term. In the long run it feeds the request for more self-rule. The federalization thus installed a dynamic it was actually meant to extinguish (Swenden, 2013). This has two implications. At some point there is little left to download, and the unit level is so strong that it is no longer bothered by a paralyzed federal level. Both are the case in Belgium. In sum, centrifugal federalism is a limited pacification strategy (Caluwaerts & Reuchamps, 2014). While path dependency may explain the route the transformation of the Belgian state architecture took, it looks like Belgium ended up in a blind alley. The question, therefore, is how to move forward. While the dominant tendency of the Flemish Regionalists N-VA and the Vlaams Belang is to claim a confederation, if complete independence cannot be reached, alternative voices suggest stronger cooperation and other mechanisms tempering centrifugal tendencies to make the Belgian federation work more effectively (De Grauwe & Van Parijs, 2011; Popelier & Cantillon, 2013; Swenden, 2013).

REFERENCES

Beyers, J., & Bursens, P. (2013). How Europe shapes the nature of the Belgian federation: differentiated EU impact triggers both cooperation and decentralization. *Regional and Federal Studies, 23*(3), 271–291.

Caluwaerts, D., & Reuchamps, M. (2014). Combining federalism with consociationalism: Is Belgian consociational federalism digging its own grave? *Ethnopolitics, 14*(3), 277–295.

Celis, K., & Meier, P. (2017). Other identities in ethnofederations: Women's and sexual minorities' advocacy in Belgium. *National Identities, 19*(4), 415–432.

Dandoy, R., Dodeigne, J., Reuchamps, M., & Vandeleene, A. (2015). The new Belgian Senate. A (dis)continued evolution of federalism in Belgium? *Representation, 51*(3), 327–339.

De Grauwe, P., & Van Parijs, P., eds. (2009). *Electoral engineering for a stalled federation. A country-wide electoral district for Belgium's federal Parliament.* Re-Bel E-book 4. Retrieved September 20, 2019, from www.rethinkingbelgium.eu/rebel-initiative-files/ebooks/ebook-4/Re-Bel-e-book-4.pdf.

De Grauwe, P., & Van Parijs, P., eds. (2011). *Social Federalism: How is a multilevel welfare state best organized?*. Re-Bel E-book 9. Retrieved April 7, 2020, from www.rethinkingbelgium.eu/rebel-initiative-files/ebooks/ebook-9/Re-Bel-e-book-9.pdf.

De Grauwe, P., & Van Parijs, P., eds. (2014). *The malaise of electoral democracy and what to do about it.* Re-Bel E-book 14. Retrieved September 20, 2019, from www.rethinkingbelgium.eu/rebel-initiative-files/ebooks/ebook-14/Re-Bel-e-book-14.pdf.

De Winter, L., & Baudewyns, P. (2009). Belgium: Towards the breakdown of a nation-state in the heart of Europe? *Nationalism and Ethnic Politics,* 15(3-4), 280–304.

De Winter, L., & Dumont, P. (2006). Do Belgian parties undermine the democratic chain of delegation? *West European Politics,* 29(5), 957–976.

De Winter, L., Swyngedouw, M., & Dumont, P. (2006). Party system(s) and electoral behaviour in Belgium: From stability to Balkanisation. *West European Politics,* 29(5), 933–956.

Decoster, A., & Sas, W. (2012). Feiten en cijfers over de nieuwe financieringswet. In P. Popelier, D. Sinardet, J. Velaers, & B. Cantillon (Eds.), *België, quo vadis? Waarheen na de zesde staatshervorming?* (pp. 311–342). Intersentia.

Delwit, P., van Haute, E., & Pilet, J.-B. (2011). *Les partis politiques en Belgique.* Les éditions de l'Université de Bruxelles.

Deschouwer, K. (2006). And the peace goes on? Consociational democracy and Belgian politics in the twenty-first century. *West European Politics,* 29(5), 895–911.

Deschouwer, K. (2012). *The politics of Belgium. Governing a divided society.* Palgrave.

Deschouwer, K. (2013). Party strategies, voter demands and territorial reform in Belgium. *West European Politics,* 36(2), 338–358.

Deschouwer, K., & Van Parijs, P. (2007). Une circonscription électorale pour tous les Belges. *Revue Nouvelle,* 62(4), 12–23.

Fiers, S. (2006). Evoluties in het parlementair bestel. In E. Witte & A. Meynen (Eds.), *De geschiedenis van België na 1945* (pp. 263–288). Standaard Uitgeverij.

Happaerts, S., Schunz, S., & Bruyninckx, H. (2012). Federalism and intergovernmental relations: The multi-level politics of climate change policy in Belgium. *Journal of Contemporary European Studies,* 20(4), 441–458.

Lijphart, A. (1977). *Democracy in Plural Societies: A Comparative Exploration.* Yale University Press.

Lijphart, A. (2012). *Patterns of democracy: government forms & performance in thirty-six countries.* Yale University Press.

Mabille, X. (2011). *Nouvelle histoire politique de la Belgique.* CRISP.

Martens, W. (2006). *De memoires. Luctor et emergo.* LannooCampus.

Meier, P., & Bursens, P. (2020). The democratic state of the federation. In A. Benz & J. Sonnicksen (Eds.), *Federal democracies at work. Varieties of complex government.* University of Toronto Press. XX-XX.

Pilet, J.-B., & Meier, P. (2018). Ze halen hun slag wel thuis. Over particratie en het aanpassingsvermogen van Belgische partijen. *Res Publica,* 60(4), 321–345.

Pilet, J.-B., & Pauwels, T. (2010). De vertegenwoordiging van taalgroepen in België : de weg naar een hyperinstitutionalisering. In K. Celis, P. Meier, &

B. Wauters (Eds.), *Gezien, gehoord, vertegenwoordigd? Diversiteit in de Belgische politiek* (pp. 47–68). Academia Press.

Popelier, P. (2019). Asymmetry and complexity as a device for multinational conflict management. A country study of constitutional asymmetry in Belgium. In P. Popelier & M. Sahadzic (Eds.), *Constitutional asymmetry in multinational federalism. Managing multinationalism in multi-tiered systems* (pp. 17–46). Palgrave Macmillan.

Popelier, P., & Cantillon, B. (2013). Bipolar federalism and the social welfare state: A case for shared competences. *Publius: The Journal of Federalism, 43*(4), 626–647.

Randour, F. (2018). *Defining and explaining the negotiation autonomy of Austrian, Belgian and German federal executives in the Council of the European Union vis-à-vis their domestic parliaments: An outcome oriented, case specific and qualitative comparative analysis.* ESPO.

Reuchamps, M. (2013). Structures institutionnelles du fédéralisme belge. In R. Dandoy, G. Matagne, & C. Van Wynsberghe (Eds.), *Le fédéralisme belge. Enjeux institutionnels, acteurs socio-politiques et opinions publiques* (pp. 29–61). Academia-L'Harmattan.

Reuchamps, M., Sinardet, D., Dodeigne, J., & Caluwaerts, D. (2017). *Reforming Belgium's federalism: comparing the views of MPs and voters Government & Opposition,* 52(3), pp. 460-482.

Sinardet, D., De Winter, L., Dodeigne, J., & Reuchamps, M. (2017). Language identity and voting. In K. Deschouwer (Ed.), *Mind the gap: Political participation and representation in Belgium* (pp. 113–131). Rowman & Littlefield.

Stepan, A. C. (1999). Federalism and democracy: Beyond the U.S. model. *Journal of Democracy, 10*(4), 19–34.

Swenden, W. (2010). Why is Belgian federalism not more asymmetrical? In F. Requejo & K.-J. Nagel (Eds.), *Federalism beyond federations. Asymmetry and processes of resymmetrisation in Europe* (pp. 13–36). Ashgate.

Swenden, W. (2013). Conclusion: 'the Future of Belgian Federalism—Between Reform and Swansong?'. *Regional & Federal Studies, 23*(3), 369–382.

Swenden, W., & Jans, T. M. (2006). 'Will it stay or will it go? Federalism and the sustainability of Belgium. *West European Politics, 29*(5), 877–894.

Van Dyck, R. (1996). 'Divided we stand'. Regionalism, federalism and minority Rights in Belgium. *Res Publica, 38*(2), 429–446.

Witte, E. (Ed.). (1993). *De Brusselse rand. Brusselse thema's 1.* VUBPRESS.

Witte, E., Meynen, A., & Luyten, D. (2016). *Politieke geschiedenis van België van 1830 tot heden.* Manteau.

CHAPTER 3

Spain and the United Kingdom: Between Unitary State Tradition and Federalization

Paul Anderson

Introduction

Spain and the United Kingdom (UK) are not federations. They have been variably viewed as unitary states, but in line with Rokkan and Urwin's (1982) typology of constitutional configurations, they are best described as union states, that is, states in which pre-union constitutional arrangements are preserved notwithstanding the incorporation of parts of the territory through treaty and agreement. This was certainly the case in the aftermath of the Treaty of Union between the Kingdoms of Scotland and England in 1707 and can also be traced in the Spanish case as relates to the fifteenth-century dynastic union of the Crowns of Aragon and Castile. Union states do not entail a formal division of powers as is standard in a federation, but over recent decades, political standardization in Spain and the UK has given way to processes of political decentralization. In both cases the territorial question has mutated over time, marked by different

P. Anderson (✉)
Liverpool John Moores University, Liverpool, UK
e-mail: P.D.Anderson@ljmu.ac.uk

© The Author(s), under exclusive license to Springer Nature Switzerland AG 2022
S. Keil, S. Kropp (eds.), *Emerging Federal Structures in the Post-Cold War Era*, Federalism and Internal Conflicts,
https://doi.org/10.1007/978-3-030-93669-3_3

degrees of salience in support for self-government on the one hand and independent statehood on the other. This territorial and constitutional contestation is manifested in the distinct conceptions of state, nation and national identity found in sub-state territories as well as competing constitutional visions and nationalist projects (Anderson & Keil, 2016). These conflicting constitutional doctrines and the autonomy models rolled out in both states are shaped by the historical trajectories of the constituent units and the conception of both Spain and the UK as plurinational states. As Keating (2015, 189) attests, '[I]n plurinational states, unlike in mono-national ones, whether federal or unitary, there is no single constitutional story, or principle to which all others can be reduced.' (Maps 3.1 and 3.2)

Spain and the UK have much in common. Both are economically developed European liberal democracies with constitutional monarchies. Both states are plurinational and have developed complex systems of asymmetric territorial autonomy to manage the self-determination demands of

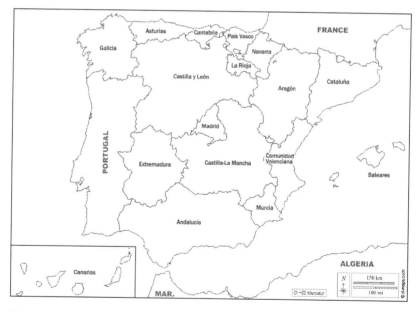

Map 3.1 Spain. *Source*: https://d-maps.com/carte.php?num_car=2211&lang=en

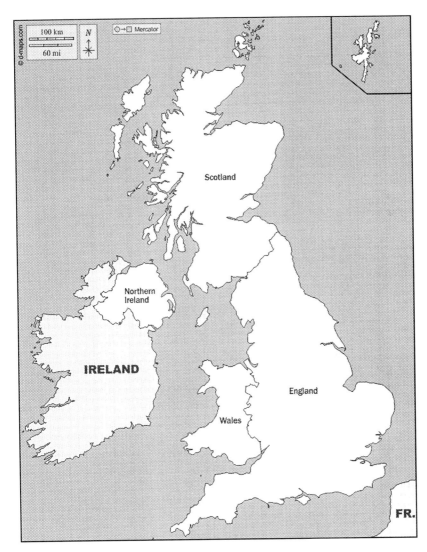

Map 3.2 The UK. *Source*: https://d-maps.com/carte.php?num_car=5544&lang=en

their territorially concentrated national minorities, namely in the Basque Country and Catalonia in Spain and Northern Ireland and Scotland in the UK. Further, both states have active secessionist movements, albeit neither state has a constitutional provision permitting independence. Tellingly, both states have responded to secessionist challenges in different ways. In the UK a referendum on Scottish independence took place in 2014, and while votes have taken place in Catalonia in 2014 and 2017 respectively, the Spanish government and Constitutional Court have gone to great lengths to emphasize the illegality of voting on Catalan independence. This, as will be discussed in the first section of this chapter, is rooted in the overarching conceptions of the Spanish and British states; the latter's configuration as a plurinational union is an accepted reality, while the definition of the Spanish state varies between a majority position of an indissoluble mononational nation-state and a minority vision of a nation of nations in which the sub-state units have a right to internal (and for some, external) self-determination (Brown Swan & Cetra, 2020).

Taking the cases of Spain and the UK, this chapter examines the territorial evolution of these federal political systems, paying particular attention to the existence (or lack thereof) of elements of federalism and federation. As will be discussed, neither Spain nor the UK functions as a proper federation, but there is an identifiable trend of federalization in both cases. They are, in Watts' (2008, 8) parlance, 'federal political systems', states which have developed their own institutional arrangements and political processes vis-á-vis political decentralization to manage their state-specific circumstances. The evolutionary nature of decentralization in Spain and the UK resonates with Friedrich's (1968) conception of federalism as a dynamic process, an institutional approach which develops over time, able to evolve and adapt to shifting circumstances within the state.

This chapter is divided into four sections. The first section charts the historical evolution of the territorial question in Spain and the UK, including the overarching philosophies guiding the constitutional interpretations of the state and the rationale developed to move power away from the center in the late 1970s in Spain and 1990s in the UK. The second section examines the main characteristics of these federal political systems, with specific focus on notions of recognition, self-rule and shared rule. The third section tackles some of the ongoing limitations and challenges to the complex autonomy systems. This section not only examines challenges from sub-state governments in the shape of secession, but also examines the pernicious implications of the unitary thrust and centralizing tendencies of state elites in both cases. The final section concludes.

The Territorial Question in Historical Context

Spain and the UK may share numerous similarities, but their historical trajectories as relates to questions of territorial accommodation and contestation have varied. The evolution of unionism in the UK has witnessed the development of an approach comfortable with the idea of a plurinational union, notwithstanding traditional inimicality toward self-government (Kidd, 2008). The variegated historical processes which led to the different unions between the four countries (England, Northern Ireland, Scotland and Wales) have proven relatively hospitable to the plurinational makeup of the state, albeit tensions remain and have occasionally flared up over time, particularly regarding (Northern) Ireland and more recently Scotland. In contradistinction, Spain's historical trajectory has been punctuated by prolonged periods of dictatorship marked by significant opposition to the plurinational idea. Tensions over the territorial organization of the Spanish state have existed since its creation and subsequent state and nation-building processes have proved weak in the face of pre-existing and vociferous nationalisms in places such as Catalonia and the Basque Country (Balfour & Quiroga, 2007). Centuries later, in Spain as much as in the UK, territorial politics remains a moving target, suspended in a state of flux (Anderson, 2018).

Spain

The Spanish state emerged from the dynastic union between the Kingdoms of Aragon and Castile in the late fifteenth century and subsequent merging of the crowns in 1516. The Crown of Aragon included three separate kingdoms—Aragon, Catalonia and Valencia—that were united in a confederation in which a sense of national distinctiveness in each territory was preserved (Balcells, 1996). In the aftermath of the dynastic union, the territories retained their own institutions, culture and language, but a creeping process of political centralization and cultural homogenization engineered by Castile between the seventeenth and eighteenth centuries precipitated violent rebellion and ultimately the dominance of Castile over the existing territories after the surrender of Barcelona in 1714. From here on a centralized model of governance that sought to replicate the French Jacobin model was imposed upon the territories. This process of Castilianization continued through the eighteenth, nineteenth and twentieth centuries, but failed in its aim to build a unitary nation with a culturally homogenous population. Instead, such centralist processes emboldened rather than weakened minority nationalist movements.

The processes of Spanish state and nation-building saw pre-existing autonomy regimes abolished and a centralized model of governance imposed on the regions of the newly formed Spain. This process of identity construction was enshrined in Spain's first constitution in 1812, which sought to create 'a centralized bureaucracy, an internal market, common taxation and judicial and cultural homogenization' (Moreno, 2001, 45). Centralization processes continued until the establishment of the Second Spanish Republic in 1931, albeit the preceding period was punctuated by short-lived endeavors such as the federalized structures of the First Spanish Republic (1873-74). The Second Spanish Republic was inaugurated in 1931 and resulted in a policy of territorial accommodation, including autonomy statutes for the Basque Country, Catalonia and Galicia. The Second Republic was neither a unitary nor federal state but an 'integral state', one which was unitary in nature, but willing to recognize and accommodate its ethnoterritorial diversity (Balfour & Quiroga, 2007, 35). The victory of the Francoist forces in 1939, however, precipitated a 40-year period of dictatorial rule, and the Second Republic's policy of accommodation and recognition was replaced by political repression and cultural genocide. Minority nationalism was a *bête noir* of the Franco regime, but the persecution of nationalist projects in the Basque Country and Catalonia served to galvanize a sense of distinctiveness among the Basques and Catalans; a re-emergence of nationalism and support for self-government ensued (Guibernau, 2004).

General Franco sought to completely eradicate any form of minority nationalism, including political parties, regional institutions, languages and cultures that did not conform to his mononational vision of Spain. In these regional territories, however, clandestine movements opposed to the Franco regime emerged, committed to engineering a democratic alternative to the dictatorial regime and restoration of the right to self-government for Spain's historical regions (McRoberts, 2001). In the subsequent transition to democracy after Franco's death in 1975, a right to autonomy for the Basque Country, Catalonia and Galicia was considered a crucial element of a successful transition. The transition, unsurprisingly, was fraught with complications, including the challenge of satisfying pro-democratic forces, namely in the historic territories, without offending the autonomy-cautious Spanish nationalists who (had) supported the Franco regime. Numerous proposals were mooted as to what sort of territorial organization the Spanish state should take, from a centralized state to a symmetrical federation, as well as some confederal ideas advocated by nationalists in Catalonia and the Basque Country (Moreno et al., 2019, p. 246). The vehement opposition of the historic territories to a centralized and unitary structure meant that democracy and decentralization became mutually reinforcing bedfellows. As Roller (2002, pp. 71-72) notes, 'it was widely accepted that a refusal or reluctance to address the issue of regional autonomy and cultural, linguistic and historical differentiations would endanger the consolidation and establishment of the post-Franco democratic regime'. The newly drafted Constitution detailed an open model of autonomy with differentiated processes for the historic territories and aspiring regions. In the event, what emerged was the State of Autonomies, an asymmetrical arrangement with 17 autonomous communities.

The 1978 Constitution was a creature of its time, reflected in the ambiguity of some of its articles, including the tacit recognition of Spain's internal diversity, the fuzzy boundaries to delineate competences and the lack of self-definition as to what sort of state Spain is. Consequently, there remains ongoing debate as to whether the state is unitary or federal. Arzoz (2012, p. 179) succinctly encapsulates this lack of clarity in his description of Spain as a 'multinational quasi federal unitary state'. The initial territorial model that evolved took an asymmetric turn, including in the division of competences as well as constitutional recognition of fiscal autonomy for the Basque Country and Navarre based on historic privileges (Bossacoma Busquets & Sanjaume-Calvet, 2019). Article Two of the Constitution recognized the right to autonomy of nationalities and regions, although these are not enumerated in the Constitution. The same article, however, underlined the 'indissoluble unity of the Spanish Nation', thus enshrining a mononational conception of the state and prohibition of a right to secede.

The Spanish experience of autonomy from the state's inception to the present day has oscillated between periods of centralization and decentralization. Decentralization was an integral component in the Spanish transition to democracy and indisputably attributed to the peaceful nature of the transition, but the anticipated evolution of the system to a full-fledged federation has yet to come to fruition. The incumbent territorial model has evolved since its initial inception in the late 1970s, but the model falls short of the requisites of federation and has become increasingly contested by the state's national minorities.

UK

The United Kingdom of Great Britain and Northern Ireland—to give the state its formal title—is a relatively young state composed of four distinct nations: England, Northern Ireland, Scotland and Wales. Each of the peripheral Celtic nations has a distinct relationship with the English center: Wales was annexed by England in the early sixteenth century, Scotland voluntarily joined union with England in 1707, and Ireland was brought into the British parliamentary state in 1801. Assimilationist policies were pursued in Scotland vis-à-vis the Highlands, but the union between England and Scotland is oft-described as an 'incorporating union', a political partnership that allowed Scotland to maintain its cultural distinctiveness (Mitchell, 2014). In a similar vein some form of institutional independence was afforded to Ireland in the aftermath of union, but this was limited and largely overshadowed by the explicit discriminatory policies of the British government toward the dominant Irish Catholic population. Strategies of assimilation were also rather forceful in the case of Wales whereby Wales' administrative, economic, legal and political systems were assimilated into the English entity and the Welsh language was largely extirpated from public life. Over centuries, a distinct sense of national identity and national distinctiveness has developed in Scotland, Northern Ireland and Wales in tandem with the development of an overarching British state identity (Colley, 1992).

The British Unionist project is not rooted in a single culture or identity and instead is construed as a political arrangement in which the constituent nations of the UK, despite being culturally distinct, are politically and legally linked with the center (Kidd, 2008). Keating (2015, 179) has described Unionism as 'genius' and predicated on 'an intellectual sleight of hand that can present the state as unitary at the center, but differentiated at the periphery'. In this sense the UK has never strictly conformed to the textbook definition of a unitary state. This is evidenced in the retention of pre-union institutions, but also in the administrative devolution arrangements developed throughout the twentieth century which saw the creation of territorial offices of state for Scotland, Wales and Northern Ireland with varying responsibilities over limited policy areas. The existence of such arrangements, however, did not alter the predominantly unitary vision of the union espoused by British politicians, which also entailed vehement opposition to the notion of self-government.

The idea of self-government in the UK has a long pedigree within the British state, including an identifiable tradition of British federal thought (Burgess, 1995). Federalism, or as it was framed in the UK 'home rule all round', was mooted and ultimately failed as a territorial solution to eschew Irish secession at the end of the nineteenth century, but support for home rule grew in Scotland and Wales. The rationale behind the Liberal Party's home rule plans was rooted in the 'holding together' notion of federalism, a tool which could satisfy regional demands for autonomy while simultaneously maintaining and even strengthening the union. In line with the unionist position outlined above, however, support for home rule among the political elite was tempered by claims that devolving powers would erode parliamentary sovereignty and undermine the legislative supremacy of the Westminster Parliament, encourage further autonomy claims and lead to state disintegration. The outbreak of World War I, armed rebellion in Ireland and the consequent establishment of the Irish Free State, overtook debate in the UK on the merits of decentralizing power, but discussions on the creation of regional legislatures in Scotland and Wales continued for much of the twentieth century (Mitchell, 1996). Electoral gains made by the Scottish and Welsh nationalist parties—Scottish National Party (SNP) and Plaid Cymru—forced the issue onto the agenda throughout the 1960s-70s and culminated in referenda in 1979 on the establishment of devolved legislatures. The proposal was overwhelmingly rejected in Wales, while in Scotland a narrow majority voted in favor, but this fell short of procedural requirements that 40% of the eligible electorate vote yes.

The experience of almost two decades of Conservative rule, however, accompanied by the anti-devolutionist and unitary approaches of Prime Ministers Margaret Thatcher and John Major precipitated growing concern in the Celtic nations that Westminster had become insensitive to Scottish and Welsh distinctiveness and thus increased attention to the merits of self-government. Under Thatcher a less accommodating strategy of inflexible unionism and a 'hyper-unionist verging on unitarist' conception of the union opposed to self-government emerged (Kidd & Petrie, 2016, 39). During this period, constitutional restlessness in Scotland translated into fervent civil society movement in favor of a Scottish Parliament and a gradual shift in the thinking of the Labour Party. In the aftermath of Tony Blair's New Labour victory in 1997, referenda were held in Scotland, Wales and Northern Ireland, and devolution rolled out to all three nations. In a similar vein to Spain, devolution was linked with discussion on democracy, couched in the language of 'modernization' and 'democratic renewal'. The rolling out of power to Scotland, Wales and Northern Ireland took the form of a highly asymmetrical model, with focus on building out rather than building in; little thought was given to processes of shared rule (Anderson, 2022). Further, the supremacy of the Westminster Parliament remained unaffected by devolution and it retained its right to legislate for the whole of the UK, even in devolved matters.[1] As former Prime Minister Gordon Brown (2014, 259) avows, '[t]he 1998 settlement held to the orthodoxy that Westminster is sovereign and that power devolved is power retained'.

Decentralization processes in both Spain and the UK put the states on a federalizing trajectory, but neither state has become, or indeed is likely to become in the near future, a full-fledged federation. In the case of Spain, decentralization became intimately linked with the country's democratization process, promoted as a tool to accommodate sub-state diversity within the parameters of the existing Spanish state as well as 'a tool of reconciliation, state-building [and] economic efficiency' (Anderson, 2020, 44). Similarly, devolution in the UK had several rationales including democratic renewal, administrative and economic efficiency, and accommodating the self-determination demands of the constituent nations (Morgan & Mungham, 2000, 24). In the event, what emerged in both Spain and the UK, are two distinct models of autonomy with federalizing tendencies; there is an identifiable trend of federalism notwithstanding the absence of federation.

Examining the Accommodation Framework: Recognition, Self-rule and Shared Rule

The development of 'diversity-cognizant institutional frameworks' (Gagnon & Tremblay, 2019, 137) has grown in recent decades as states seek to accommodate their minority national communities within the confines of the existing state. To do so, states, particularly plurinational ones, have put in place various strategies of diversity management (including both territorial and non-territorial autonomy) to enable national minorities to manage their own affairs and preserve their national identities while

---

[1] This was, however, limited by the Sewel Convention—a political convention that dictated Westminster 'would not normally legislate' on devolved matters without the respective legislatures' consent.

the extant borders of the larger state remain unaltered (Keil & Anderson, 2018). Drawing upon three crucial elements used in federal frameworks for minority accommodation—symbolic recognition, self-rule and shared rule (Swenden, 2013)—this section examines how these have been used in the British and Spanish cases as strategies of accommodation within the framework of the states' territorial models.

Symbolic Recognition

Symbolic recognition is a key aspect of 'crafting successful territorial strategies for a plurinational state' that demonstrates 'that national political elites are willing to identify the state as plurinational and recognize that it encompasses multiple, but possibly complementary identities' (Swenden, 2013, 71). Such recognition may take the shape of official recognition of statehood for minority nations, the acknowledgement of the plurinational character of the state in its constitution as well as in other state symbols such as flags and anthems.

Symbolic recognition has been the principal component in the UK's accommodation strategy. The relative ease with which the UK has recognized its plurinational character facilitated the maintenance of autarchic institutions in the pre-existing states, namely Scotland, and has been further embodied in the name and symbols of the state. As Keating (2001, 104) attests, the UK's name reflects 'its plurinational composition, while the union flag is no more than the superimposition of the flags of the component nations'. The articulation of the UK's plurinational makeup has allowed for the development of multi-layered conceptions of identity as well as differentiation between the concepts 'nation' and 'state'. Further, provisions were inserted in the Scotland and Wales Acts in 2016 and 2017 respectively to recognize the permanency of the Scottish and Welsh Parliaments. Qualifications as to what permanency means render the legal enforceability of the provisions rather meaningless, but their inclusion are nonetheless constitutionally significant, not least given their symbolic importance in recognizing the guaranteed existence of the sub-state legislatures.

Contrary to the UK, Spain has been historically uncomfortable with recognition of its plurinationality. The Constitution, promulgated in the aftermath of the transition to democracy, recognized the existence of 'Spaniards and peoples of Spain'. Yet, while there is a commitment to internal self-determination and the protection of multiculturalism, including other languages spoken in the state, the Constitution falls short of recognizing its plurinationality. Instead, it propagates a mononational view of the state in which Spain is conceived as a traditional nation-state with one official language and one *demos*, the Spanish *demos*, to whom 'national sovereignty belongs'. The term 'nationalities' was not defined in the Constitution and thus entailed only implicit recognition of the historical territories of the Basque Country, Catalonia and Galicia. Subsequent attempts by both Basque and Catalan governments to have the national status of their communities recognized have been successively rebuffed by the Spanish government, including the Declaration of Barcelona in 1998,[2] the Basque government's 'Plan Ibarretxe' in 2005 and statute reform in Catalonia in 2006. The latter, for example, advocated recognition of Catalonia as a nation, while the former was a more radical strategy of sovereignty-association (Elias & Mees, 2017). The predominant mononational narrative of Spain enshrined in the Constitution and endorsed by successive governments over the last four decades has inhibited any extension of symbolic recognition to Spain's national minorities and, as will be discussed below, has even engendered a harmonization strategy to dilute claims of national distinctiveness.

Self-rule

Self-rule is broadly defined as the decision-making powers within the jurisdiction of sub-state national or regional parliaments. In Spain self-rule was very much framed as a necessary concession to secure the support of minority nationalists during the transition. This has also been the case as the autonomy system has evolved whereby further powers have been granted to the historic nationalities in return for the support of Basque and Catalan parties in the Spanish Parliament during periods of minority government (Field, 2016). The Constitution recognized the right of self-government of the nationalities and regions, and the open-ended model on the division of powers 'provided a menu for decentralization a la carte', enabling the historic territories to become powerful autonomous communities (Moreno et al., 2019, 248). Few powers, however, are under the exclusive purview of the autonomous communities and are instead 'shared'

---

[2] The 1998 Declaration of Barcelona was an initiative between Basque, Catalan and Galician nationalist parties demanding formal recognition of Spain's internal plurality, including nationhood for the aforementioned territories.

or 'concurrent', thus limiting the autonomous capacity of the communities. What is more, the Constitution imbues the central government with authority to intervene in community jurisdiction through Basic Laws. The use of Basic Laws has been a repeated feature since the transition to democracy and has been largely interpreted by the historic nationalities as unfair encroachment by the central government in community jurisdiction and part of a wider competence-harmonization agenda to dilute their initial asymmetric guarantees (Máiz et al., 2010). As Requejo (2017) notes, the fact that the central government can freely encroach upon the competences of the autonomous communities undermines any claim that Spain is a federation.

The various legislative acts devolving power in the UK entailed different approaches to devolution, including a reserved powers model in Scotland and Northern Ireland and a corporate body model in Wales. In the latter no law-making powers were initially devolved, while The Scotland Act devolved to the Scottish Parliament all powers except those specifically reserved to the UK Parliament. The resulting model of autonomy in the UK has thus been described as 'one of the most complex examples of asymmetric autonomy' (McGarry, 2012, 129). In a similar vein to the autonomous communities in Spain, the powers and responsibilities of the Scottish, Welsh and Northern Irish governments and legislatures have increased over the years. In Scotland the devolution of further powers has been in reaction to the electoral success of the SNP and thus an attempt on the part of the British government to stifle support for independence. This was most clearly seen during the independence referendum campaign in 2014 in which all three main parties in Westminster agreed to devolve further powers to Scotland in the event of a vote against independence (Keating & McEwen, 2017). In Wales and Northern Ireland, devolution has also been enhanced, particularly in the former which now has law-making powers. The fiscal responsibilities of all three nations have also increased, yet this also takes an asymmetric route. Northern Ireland, for instance, controls corporation tax given its unique location in sharing a land border with an independent state (Ireland), while the fiscal powers of the Scottish and Welsh legislatures have been enhanced since 2012 and 2014 respectively. In contrast with the Spanish model, central government encroachment on devolved policy jurisdictions is limited by the Sewel Convention, which dictates that the UK government would not normally legislate on devolved matters without the permission of the devolved legislatures. The convention has largely operated without much controversy since the inception of devolution in the late 1990s, but as confirmed by the Supreme Court in January 2017, and the subsequent passing of legislation pertaining to Brexit notwithstanding the refused consent of some and at times all the devolved legislatures, the convention is a political not legal convention; whether the devolved legislatures grant consent or not, legislation can proceed through Parliament regardless (McHarg, 2018). There is little doubt that the devolved nations possess significant self-rule, but the continued legislative supremacy of the Westminster Parliament—which remains the only source of legal sovereignty—undermines self-government provisions and inhibits the development of the UK in a conscious federal direction.

Shared Rule

Shared rule, which refers to the participation of sub-state entities in the decision-making processes of the central government, has been a neglected dimension of power in both the UK and Spain. In both cases few mechanisms for collaboration and cooperation between the central governments and their devolved counterparts have developed, not least the absence of territorially representative second chambers and effective intergovernmental infrastructure. Devolution in the UK was solely concerned with self-rule. There were discussions prior to the establishment of the devolved legislatures regarding shared rule mechanisms, but emphasis was on self-governing structures rather than increasing the voices of the devolved nations at the center. As a result, opportunities for influence at the center on the parts of the devolved administrations have been significantly limited. An infrastructure of intergovernmental relations has developed in the UK, but it is under-institutionalized and in recent years has become a source of significant tension (Anderson, 2022). The principal mechanism is the Joint Ministerial Committee (JMC), which brings together all four governments, but the JMC has been subject to much complaint since its inception, particularly its hierarchical structures and lack of co-decision-making process. The lack of intergovernmental influence is further impeded by the absence of a territorially representative second chamber. Debate on reforming the House of Lords is almost as old as the institution itself, but only recently has discussion shifted in the direction of creating a federal-like upper chamber. The Labour Party, for instance, advocated the creation of a 'Senate of the Nations and Regions' in its 2015 election manifesto, but evidence of serious proposals to create a territorial chamber are scarce. Akin to the UK, shared rule in Spain is a limited affair. The Senate is described in the Constitution as 'the House of territorial representation', but its capacity to act as such is circumscribed by its functions (or lack thereof) and composition, which is largely based on provinces rather than autonomous communities. What is more, the politicized nature of the chamber—a result of its unofficial organization along party lines—further inhibits opportunity to facilitate intergovernmental interaction. As in the UK, intergovernmental infrastructure has developed in Spain, particularly the Conference of the Presidents and Sectoral Conferences, albeit these vertical forums have had varying levels of success. Sectoral conferences have engendered fruitful collaboration between the Spanish and autonomous governments, though they remain forums of debate and information-sharing as opposed to institutions of joint decision-making (García Morales, 2009). In a similar vein to the UK, the absence of solid shared rule in Spain negates its federal development. The discussion above details the experience of the Spanish and UK systems with the most important repertoires used to classify federal systems in plurinational contexts. Symbolic recognition, self-rule and shared rule all form part of the accommodative strategies employed in the UK and Spain to manage sub-national movements, although the arrangements differ in each case and have varying degrees of success. As one would expect, self-rule, through its vertical distribution of power, has been most successful in alleviating the grievances of national minorities in both cases, albeit the thirst for further powers and independent statehood has not been completely quenched. Self-rule arrangements, however, have enabled the autonomous regions to develop their own legislative agendas and promote and protect their distinct national identities and cultural heritage. Self-rule, however, is a fragile arrangement; asymmetry can be diluted, powers taken away and central government dominance imposed. The absence of shared rule in both Spain and the UK is a likely causal effect for the ongoing push in Scotland and Catalonia for independence. It is a truism that in both cases increasing attention has been paid to shared rule mechanisms, but the territorial models in their current configurations remain weak in facilitating sub-national influence and intergovernmental interaction at the center. The general understanding of the UK as a plurinational state has engendered a high degree of symbolic recognition, including acceptance that the four component parts of the UK constitute separate nations. This, as discussed supra, is not the case in Spain, whereby interpretations of the Spanish state are divided between mononational and plurinational understandings. Aspirations for further symbolic recognition on the part of Catalonia, for instance, have successively fallen on deaf ears. It is no coincidence, therefore, that the rejection of demands for further self-rule, enhanced shared rule and explicit recognition has developed alongside increasing support for independence.

Ongoing Challenges: Between Centralization and Disintegration

Having evaluated the principal institutional arrangements used in Spain and the UK to reconcile territorial integrity and cultural heterogeneity, this section discerns three of the main challenges facing Spain and the UK, particularly as relates to any future federalization process: Secessionism, the unitary approach of state governments and the absence of a federal and plurinational spirit.

Secessionism

Analysis of the impact of federal structures on secessionism has identified 'a paradox': 'the very same institutions that appear to be able to calm secession, reduce or eliminate the possibility of conflict and manage diversity, might actually work in the opposite intended direction' (Anderson, 2010, 131). Scholars on both sides of the debate are able to draw upon empirical evidence to substantiate the various secession-inducing and secession-preventing hypotheses. As McGarry and O'Leary (2015, 15) note, 'for every Switzerland, Canada, Belgium and India, there is at least one Austro-Hungary, Soviet Union, Yugoslavia and Pakistan'. The existence of secessionist movements in Spain and the UK, specifically in Catalonia and Scotland, have illuminated the challenges faced by states when seeking to use federal tools as mechanisms for diversity management. Indeed, a quick glance at the success of pro-secession parties in both Scotland and Catalonia in recent years lends credence to the secessionist-inducing argument; autonomy in both cases appears to have fueled rather than diluted demands for external self-determination. The decentralized models utilized in Spain and the UK are designed to contain rather than empower the state's national minorities. This lack of empowerment, evident, for example, in the absence of a guaranteed role for sub-state administrations in central government decision-making, reinforces the hierarchical and subordinated notion of decentralization in both states. In the UK the British government conceded the holding of a referendum on Scottish independence in the aftermath of the majority SNP government elected in 2011, but despite the rhetoric employed during this campaign regarding an equal partnership between Scotland and the rest of the UK, the recent Brexit debate has reinforced the hierarchical design of devolution, affirming that devolution 'at root [is] little more than the delegation of powers which can be revoked unilaterally at any time' (Keating, 2018, 48). In Spain increasing dissatisfaction with the Spanish territorial model and little prospect of serious reform has precipitated unprecedented civil society activity and growing support in favor of holding a referendum on independence as well as independence itself (Anderson, 2019). On the part of Spain's main political elites, outright hostility to asymmetry, opposition to constitutional recognition and, akin to Scotland, the absence of mechanisms to guarantee voice at the center, betray what Kymlicka (2001, 105) describes as the 'latent ethnocentrism' of the majority community. This, in turn, has intensified mounting tensions between Spain and Catalonia and increased support for secession to the extent that the pursuit of independent statehood is considered an easier feat than reform of extant Spanish structures. Federalism would ultimately address some if not many of the grievances of the Catalan and Scottish independence movements, but the success of secessionist parties and their territorial preferences for independence evidently present a challenge to evolving federal processes.

The Unitary Mindset

Notwithstanding several decades of decentralization in Spain and the UK, a unitary conception of the state prevails, manifested in limited conceptions of political authority and sovereignty. Unlike a federal understanding of sovereignty as divided between the federal government and federalized units, no such notion of shared sovereignty exists in either the UK or Spain. In plurinational contexts sovereignty is very much a contested term (Keating, 2001). This unitary understanding of political authority is thus translated into the normative thinking and institutional structures of the states, which perpetuate a hierarchical, majoritarian and monist vision of the states in spite of their plurinational reality. In the UK this is most clearly reinforced by the doctrine of parliamentary sovereignty based on the notion that the Westminster Parliament is supreme and thus the devolved institutions set up in the late 1990s are legally subordinate to the center. The Spanish Constitution enshrines a similarly monist interpretation of sovereignty and declares that national sovereignty belongs to the Spanish people as a whole, an argument oft-cited by pro-union politicians to defend their opposition to a referendum in Catalonia on independence. The unitary conception of the state in Spain and the UK is also evidenced in the identifiable centralization approaches of the central governments. This is clearest in the Spanish case vis-à-vis encroachment in competence jurisdiction through Basic Laws, Organic Laws, central government spending power and the pursuit of competence symmetrization. The latter has not only seen an attempt to forge a symmetric federation in line with the American federal model, but involved standardization processes, such as the Partido Popular (PP) government's Organic Law for the Improvement of Educational Quality (2013), which sought to standardize educational curricula and limit the teaching of school subjects in languages other than Spanish. The UK government's approach to EU withdrawal between 2016 and 2020, specifically the repatriation of powers from Brussels and protection of the UK's internal market, also betrayed a centralizing agenda. Notwithstanding extant devolved arrangements, including the reserved model of devolution, the British government sought to take control of all repatriated powers, invoking the national interest of protecting its internal market as the main rationale. This aggressively unitary approach illuminated a rather conservative and antedated interpretation of the UK Constitution that denied the decentralizing trajectory of the UK since the late 1990s. The default position of centralization spotlights the unitary conception of power in the upper echelons of British politics. A push for the centralization of authority is not unique to Spain and the UK, but it illuminates the hierarchical and statist thinking of the states' political elites. As discussed above, this unitary conception has given way to the imposition of hierarchical structures and thus the institutional domination of national minorities and jars with the proper functioning of federalism in a plurinational state. Left unchecked, this majoritarian and unitary thrust poses a significant threat to any strategy of federalization in both cases.

The Precarious Plurinational and Federal Spirit

Modelled on the German constitutional principle of *Bundestreue*, Burgess (2012, vi) defines the federal spirit 'as a shorthand expression of a set of values and principles that guide action and behavior among political elites'. Undergirding this spirit are a range of federal values and principles, *inter alia*, autonomy, equality, loyalty, partnership, recognition and respect. In plurinational states the entrenchment of these values and principles is considered crucial, not least if the objective of the state is to remain together composed of both the majority and minority groups. In this vein Taylor's (1994) 'politics of recognition' and Gagnon's (2014) 'politics of dignity and hospitality' illustrate the approach to constitutional and institutional accommodation. In Spain and the UK, there is a somewhat identifiable plurinational and federal spirit, but this remains precarious and undermined by the actions and thinking of the central governments and, in some cases, sub-state nationalist movements. On the parts of the central governments and majority political elites in Spain and the UK, the absence of a strong plurinational and federal spirit is reinforced by the dominance of unitary and majoritarian thinking. In Spain this is much more prominent given processes of competence symmetrization, but also in the absence of symbolic recognition and the contestation of the plurinational nature of the state, which sees opposition and outright hostility from some political elites—particularly those on the right of the ideological axis—to any plurinational recognition of the state. Further, the intransigent approach of the central government in managing the Catalan secessionist challenge, in which the default position of the Rajoy government was to forego dialogue in favor of recourse to the Courts, further illuminates the lack of plurinational and federal thinking (Anderson, 2021). The recent debates in the UK vis-à-vis EU withdrawal illuminated a lack of federal thinking too, reinforced by the unilateral actions of the central government and the litigation of the Supreme Court. On the latter, the Supreme Court's ruling on the status of the Sewel Convention in January 2017 betrayed a conservative understanding of the UK Constitution inasmuch as 'after twenty years of a federalizing tendency…it was insisting on the fundamentally unitary nature of the UK constitution' (Keating, 2018, 46). As discussed in the previous section, the UK government's repatriation plans also illustrated the limp plurinational and federal spirit in the UK, further exacerbating the already tenuous bonds of trust between the UK and devolved governments. Majority nations have an integral role to play in the development of a more plurinationally sensitive and federal political spirit in both the UK and Spain, but so too do the minority nations. The existence of secessionist governments in Catalonia and Scotland present an evident challenge, and while these movements often berate the central governments for the absence of inclusive and collaborative mechanisms to facilitate their participation in the organs of the central state, the ratcheting up of competing and contesting nationalist claims have significantly colored relations between the central and sub-state governments and further eroded trust between the administrations. This breakdown in trust, evident in both cases, requires a certain degree of self-discipline, self-restraint and sensitivity on all sides, but has been lacking in recent years. Notions of loyalty, partnership, recognition and respect remain abstract terms not translated into practical operation.

Conclusion—Toward a Federal Moment?

This chapter has explored the emergence of the federal trajectories of Spain and the UK and detailed the principal components of the territorial models and ongoing challenges the states face. Neither Spain nor the UK functions as a full-fledged federation, but their models of territorial accommodation have an identifiable federal tinge, notwithstanding the absence of important components such as shared rule. In the UK symbolic recognition and institutional apparatus have been used to accommodate the state's internal pluralism, while the evolution of the Spanish territorial model underlines the success of democratization projects in plurinational contexts. The frameworks of accommodation institutionalized in both states illuminate the attractiveness of decentralization as a tool of minority accommodation, but at the same time demonstrate the limits of such piecemeal reform, particularly the focus on self-rule at the expense of shared rule. In both Spain and the UK, federalism continues to be mooted as an appropriate institutional response to the self-determination demands of the states' national minorities. In the UK concern for the constitutional implications of EU withdrawal has seen increased interest in the conflict-ameliorating, democracy-enhancing and holding-together characteristics of federalism, including senior figures in the Labour Party, not least its leader Keir Starmer. Yet, while federalism offers Labour a territorial strategy that sets it apart from its main political rivals, it remains peripheral to the territorial strategies of other political elites; pro-union Conservatives remain hesitant to see the devolved nations become further detached from the center, while Scottish nationalists have little interest in UK-wide constitutional reform. In Spain the formation of the Partido Socialista Obrero Español-Unidas Podemos coalition after the November 2019 election increased the opportunity for further federalization of the Spanish state, including commitments to clarify competence jurisdiction and enhance shared rule. Akin to the UK, however, the prospects of full-fledged federalism remain weak; those on the right of the ideological spectrum consider federalism a recipe for state disintegration, while Catalan nationalists—despite traditional support for federalism—are likely to view such plans with deep suspicion. It is perfectly possible, as argued by King (1982, 76), to have federalism without federation. Spain and the UK are cases in point. Yet, while federalism has influenced and continues to permeate the territorial frameworks in both cases, its evolution remains limited by the absence of shared rule and a genuine commitment to a federal way of thinking. At times of prolonged constitutional turbulence in both cases, federalism has much to offer as an enhanced model of territorial accommodation, but it remains a marginalized option. The experience of territorial politics in Spain and the UK illuminates the predilection of political elites for muddling through various territorial challenges and crises. Recent events in both cases, however, underline that muddling through is no longer good enough; reform is required, not least if the states wish to maintain their current territorial configurations. The origins, evolution and challenges of the territorial models in Spain and the UK mark a distinct juncture in the study of new federal models, particularly in plurinational settings, and further illuminate that models of accommodation have yet to reach a stable equilibrium between the competing territorial demands of majority and minority communities. As the third decade of the twenty-first century unfolds, so too will the territorial configurations of the British and Spanish states. In true Friedrichian fashion, and notwithstanding the absence of a conscious federal teleology, federalization will remain an evolving process.

REFERENCES

Anderson, L. M. (2010). Towards a resolution of the paradox of federalism. In J. Erk & W. Swenden (Eds.), *New directions in federalism studies* (pp. 126–140). Routledge.

Anderson, P. (2021). A consociational compromise? Constitutional evolution in Spain and Catalonia. In S. Keil & A. McCulloch (Eds.), *Power-Sharing in Europe: Past practice, present cases, future directions* (pp. 201–225). Palgrave Macmillan.

Anderson, P. (2022). Plurinationalism, Devolution and Intergovernmental Relations in the United Kingdom. In Y. Fessha, K. Kossler, & F. Palermo (Eds.), *Intergovernmental relations in divided societies: A comparative perspective (pp. 91–122).* Routledge.

Anderson, P. (2020). Decentralisation at a crossroads: Spain, Catalonia and the territorial crisis. *Ethnopolitics, 19*(4), 342–355.

Anderson, P. (2019). Independence 2.0: Digital activism, social media and the Catalan independence movement. *Catalan Journal of Communication & Cultural Studies, 11*(2), 191–207.

Anderson, P. (2018). *Territorial Politics in a State of Flux: Autonomy and Secession in the UK and Spain.* PhD Thesis.

Anderson, P., & Keil, S. (2016). Minority nationalism and the European Union: The Cases of Scotland and Catalonia. *L'Europe en Formation, 379*, 40–58.

Arzoz, X. (2012). New developments in Spanish federalism. *L'Europe en formation, 363*, 179–188.

Balcells, A. (1996). *Catalan nationalism: Past and present.* Palgrave.

Balfour, S., & Quiroga, A. (2007). *The Reinvention of Spain: Nation and identity since democracy.* Oxford University Press.

Bogdanor, V. (2001). *Devolution in the United Kingdom* (2nd ed.). Oxford University Press.

Bossacoma Busquets, P., & Sanjaume-Calvet, M. (2019). Asymmetry as a device for equal recognition and reasonable accommodation of majority and minority nations. A country study on constitutional asymmetry in Spain. In P. Popelier & M. Sahadžić (Eds.), *Constitutional asymmetry in multinational federalism: Managing multinationalism in multi-tiered systems* (pp. 429–460). Palgrave Macmillan.

Brown, G. (2014). *My Scotland, our Britain: A future worth sharing.* Simon & Schuster.

Brown Swan, C., & Cetra, D. (2020). Why stay together? State nationalism and justifications for state unity in Spain and the UK. *Nationalism and Ethnic Politics, 26*(1), 46–65.

Burgess, M. (2012). *In search of the federal spirit: New theoretical and empirical perspectives in comparative federalism.* Oxford University Press.

Burgess, M. (1995). *The British tradition of federalism.* Leicester University Press.

Colley, L. (1992). *Britons: Forging the nations 1707-1837.* Yale University Press.

Elias, A., & Mees, L. (2017). Between accommodation and secession: Explaining the shifting territorial goals of nationalist parties in the Basque Country and Catalonia. *Revista d'Estudis Autonòmics I Federals, 25*, 129–165.

Field, B. (2016). *Why minority governments work: Multilevel territorial politics in Spain.* Palgrave Macmillan.

Friedrich, C. (1968). *Trends of federalism in theory and practice.* Frederick A. Praeger Publishers.

Gagnon, A. G. (2014). *Minority nations in an age of uncertainty: New paths to national emancipation and empowerment*. University of Toronto Press.

Gagnon, A.-G., & Tremblay, A. (2019). Federalism and diversity: A new research agenda. In J. Kincaid (Ed.), *A research agenda for federalism studies* (pp. 129–139). Edward Elgar.

García Morales, M. (2009). Instrumentos y vías de institucionalización de las relaciones intergubernamentales. In X. Arbós, C. Colino, M. García Morales, & S. Parrado (Eds.), *Relaciones Intergubernamentales en el Estado autonómico: la posición de los actores* (pp. 41–134). Institute d'Estudis Autonòmics.

Guibernau, M. (2004). *Catalan nationalism: Francoism, Ttansition and democracy*. Routledge.

Keating, M. (2018). Brexit and Scotland. In P. Diamond, P. Nederhaard, & B. Rosamond (Eds.), *The Routledge handbook of the politics of Brexit* (pp. 40–49). Routledge.

Keating, M. (2015). Why no federalism in the United Kingdom? In A. G. Gagnon, S. Keil, & S. Mueller (Eds.), *Understanding federalism and federation* (pp. 177–193). Ashgate.

Keating, M. (2001). *Plurinational democracy: Stateless nations in a post-sovereignty era*. Oxford University Press.

Keating, M., & McEwen, N. (2017). The Scottish independence debate. In M. Keating (Ed.), *Debating Scotland: Issues of independence and union in the 2014 referendum* (pp. 1–27). Oxford University Press.

Keil, S., & Anderson, P. (2018). Decentralization as a tool for conflict resolution. In K. Detterbeck & E. Hepburn (Eds.), *Handbook of territorial politics* (pp. 89–106). Edward Elgar.

Kidd, C. (2008). *Union and Unionisms: Political thought in Scotland 1500-2000*. Cambridge University Press.

Kidd, C., & Petrie, M. (2016). The independence referendum in historical and political context. In A. McHarg, T. Mullen, A. Page, & N. Walker (Eds.), *The Scottish independence referendum: Constitutional and legal implications* (pp. 29–52). Oxford University Press.

King, P. (1982). *Federalism and federation*. Johns Hopkins University Press.

Kymlicka, W. (2001). *Politics in the vernacular: Nationalism, multiculturalism and citizenship*. Oxford University Press.

Máiz, R., Caamaño, F., & Azpitarte, M. (2010). The hidden counterpoint of Spanish federalism: Recentralization and resymmetrisation in Spain (1978-2008). *Regional and Federal Studies, 20*(1), 63–82.

McGarry, J. and O'Leary, B. (2015) "Territorial pluralism: Taxonomizing its forms, virtues, flaws", In Basta, K., McGarry, J. and Simeon, R. (e ds.) *Territorial pluralism: Managing difference in multinational states*. UBC Press, pp. 13-54.

McHarg, A. (2018). Constitutional change and territorial consent: The Miller Case and the Sewel Convention. In M. Elliot, J. Williams, & A. L. Young (Eds.), *The UK constitution after Miller: Brexit and beyond* (pp. 159–167). Hart.
McGarry, J. (2012). Asymmetric autonomy in the United Kingdom. In M. Seymour & A. G. Gagnon (Eds.), *Multinational federalism: Problems and prospects* (pp. 129–148). Palgrave Macmillan.
McRoberts, K. (2001). *Catalonia: Nation building without a state*. Oxford University Press.
Mitchell, J. (2014). *The Scottish question*. Oxford University Press.
Mitchell, J. (1996). *Strategies for self-government: The campaigns for a Scottish Parliament*. Polygon.
Moreno, L. (2001). *The federalization of Spain*. Frank Cass Publishers.
Moreno, L., Colino, C., & Hombrado, A. (2019). Spain: Constitutional transition through the gradual accommodation of territories. In G. Anderson & S. Choudhry (Eds.), *Territory and power in constitutional transitions* (pp. 237–254). Oxford University Press.
Morgan, K., & Mungham, G. (2000). *Redesigning democracy: The making of the Welsh assembly*. Poetry Wales Press.
Requejo, F. (2017). "Is Spain a federal country?", 50 *Shades of Federalism*. http://50shadesoffederalism.com/case-studies/spain-federal-country/
Rokkan, S., & Urwin, D. (1982). *The politics of territorial identity*. Sage.
Roller, E. (2002). Reforming the Spanish Senate: Mission impossible? *West European Politics, 25*(4), 69–92.
Swenden, W. (2013). Territorial strategies for managing plurinational states. In J. Loughlin, J. Kincaid, & W. Swenden (Eds.), *Routledge handbook of regionalism and federalism* (pp. 61–75). Routledge.
Taylor, C. (1994). The politics of recognition. In C. Taylor & A. Gutmann (Eds.), *Multiculturalism* (pp. 25–75). Princeton University Press.
Watts, R. (2008). *Comparing federal systems*. McGill-Queen's University Press.

CHAPTER 4

Federal Regression and the Authoritarian Turn in Russia

Stanislav Klimovich and Sabine Kropp

Introduction[1]

Russia provides a particularly instructive case for studying the emergence and regression of federal institutions. The past 30 years of multilevel development have been a changeful back and forth. After the breakup of the Soviet Union, which was illustratively labeled as "putting-together federalism" due to the subjugation of bordering nations (Stepan, 1999),

---

[1] We are grateful to the German Research Foundation for funding the project 'Variations of Governance in Hybrid Regimes. Business, State and Civil Society in Russia' (GOVRUS, GZ: KR 3458/1-1, AOBJ:642363). This chapter is partly based on the project's conceptual framework.

S. Klimovich • S. Kropp (✉)
Otto-Suhr-Institut für Politikwissenschaft, Freie Universität Berlin, Berlin, Germany
e-mail: stanislav.klimovich@fu-berlin.de; sabine.kropp@fu-berlin.de

© The Author(s), under exclusive license to Springer Nature Switzerland AG 2022
S. Keil, S. Kropp (eds.), *Emerging Federal Structures in the Post-Cold War Era*, Federalism and Internal Conflicts, https://doi.org/10.1007/978-3-030-93669-3_4

Russia inherited formally federal, albeit excessively centralized, administrative structures. Since the early 1990s, Russian federalism has taken a highly dynamic path. With the Constitution adopted by nationwide voting on December 12, 1993, Russia became a federal system based on the principles of self-rule and shared rule. Breathing life into "sleeping" institutions taken from the Soviet past, the existing multilevel order was transformed into a remarkably decentralized system. After Putin had been elected president in 2000, he deliberately converted the federal order into a strongly recentralized, widely de-federalized institutional architecture. This process went hand in hand with the authoritarian closure of the regime (Map 4.1).

The following sections take a diachronic perspective, elucidating how the country has undergone processes of federalization and subsequent recentralization. The chapter addresses a key issue of institutional theory, as it indicates how strategic action of central actors and concomitant subversive informal practices may undermine a formally federal constitution. Moreover, the Russian case corroborates recent doubts on whether federalization is naturally conducive to democratization (Filippov & Shvetsova, 2013; Obydenkova & Swenden, 2013). Reconsidering this nexus, it will be shown that an increasingly authoritarian regime may profit from maintaining a multilevel architecture, while the "deactivated" federal institutions cause latent uncertainty that elites at both territorial levels must cope with.

The "Spontaneous Decentralization": Russia in the 1990s

Soviet Federalism as a Preexisting "Shell"

Prior to its dissolution, the Soviet Union consisted of 15 Soviet republics, out of which the Russian Soviet Federative Socialist Republic (RSFSR) was the only one which provided an additional federal structure. The Soviet Constitution granted each republic the right to exit the union. The right to secede pretended some kind of territorial autonomy, but in fact each government (executive committee) was strictly subordinated to the government residing at the upper territorial level. Significantly, the party monopoly (Art. 6, Soviet Constitution of 1977) granted each party committee of the Communist Party the right to instruct the government of the respective region or communality, but at the same time, each party

4 FEDERAL REGRESSION AND THE AUTHORITARIAN TURN IN RUSSIA 75

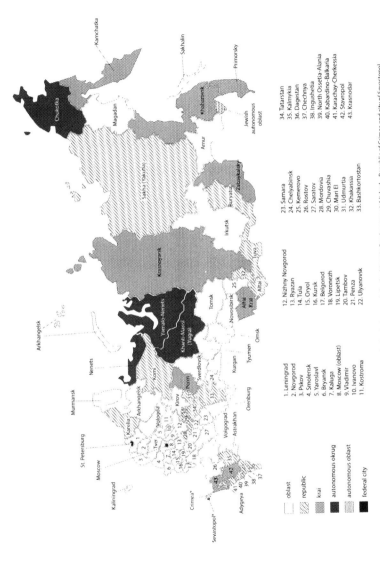

Map 4.1 Russia's Federal Subjects. *Source:* Own compilation

unit remained subordinate to the party committee at the upper territorial level. This so-called principle of *dual subordination* de facto invalidated federal self-rule. According to the Constitution, the lower territories were not autonomous but formed a part of the upper ones. The former Soviet state theory described this organization with the metaphor of the Russian doll (*matryoshka*). This principle also informed socioeconomic and budgetary planning and undermined any fiscal decentralization. Moreover, the sub-federal governments faced insurmountable obstacles to coordinate the deconcentrated agencies and branch enterprises located in their territories, as each of these bodies was part of a strict hierarchy running to the ministries in Moscow, which, again, were dominated by the central party committee. Altogether, the multilevel order "Soviet style" was characterized by tight chains of subordination and excessive centralization, turning federal institutions into a mere shell (Burgess, 2017).

Another striking feature, which became most relevant during the reconstruction of the Russian state in the 1990s, was the ethnic and significantly asymmetric character of the RSFSR's territorial organization. This characteristic significantly fostered elites' and citizens' consciousness of ethnic differences; it is still a formative element of the Russian federal structure. Before the dissolution of the Soviet Union, the regional level consisted of 49 predominantly ethnic Russian regions (*oblasts*) and six *krais*, ten autonomous *okrugs* (districts) and a Jewish autonomous oblast', two federal cities (Moscow and Leningrad) and, importantly, the 21 (ethnic homeland) republics, where a titular nation accounted for a more or less significant share but not necessarily for the majority of the population. Up until today, this organization is widely retained, even though some mergers reduced the number of federal units, as will be shown below.

Piecemeal Federalization in the 1990s and Its Effects

After the collapse of the Soviet Union, Russia inherited an asymmetric federal structure, within which economic and political disparities were mutually reinforcing. The collapse of the planning economy and the subsequent, widely contingent transformation further increased the already existing regional differences. As in the Soviet planning economy, industries were settled in the federal subjects under "strategic" aspects, and key enterprises were allocated unevenly among the regions. Particularly those in ethnic republics, which disposed of gas and oil extractive industries and natural resources, and feature majorities (or strong minorities) of titular nations (such as Tatarstan, Bashkortostan, Sakha), found themselves in a strong position vis-à-vis the center. In the center-periphery conflicts of the 1990s (described below), the leaders of the ethnic homelands, resource-poor as well as resource-rich ones, managed to form an alliance and defend their privileges against the "Russian" regions by playing the ethnic card. Interestingly, these claims served as a coordinative mechanism which was not based on a specific ethnic affiliation, but on ethnicity as such. During the constitutional debate in 1993, a proposal was launched by some federal officials aimed at eliminating the asymmetries by creating so-called *zemli* (like the German *Länder*). Not surprisingly, the ethnic republics fiercely combatted this draft and even threatened to exit the federation should they lose their privileged status. Nonetheless, the envisioned redrawing of federal units was also objected to by the Russian *oblasts* because their elites feared losing their seats in the regional legislatures alike (Solnick, 1995, 57).

The constitutional referendum held in 1993 uncovered the fragile state of Russia's federation. At that time the federal subjects became an apple of discord in the fierce conflict between the president and the Supreme Soviet (parliament), which was still dominated by a reform-averse majority of deputies. Significantly, the constitutional draft, which introduced strong presidential powers, gained 58.4% of all votes, but was rejected in 17 federal subjects. As a reaction, President Yeltsin suspended the mostly conservative regional legislatures, which were not convened between 1993 and 1994–1995. Lacking horizontal checks and balances at regional level, the federal system featured a strong executive bias at that time. The Constitution of 1993 reinforced multiethnic federalism[2] as the initial point for any further negotiation on the distribution of power and resources between Moscow and the regions. It enabled the republics (but not the *oblasts*) to adopt their own constitutions and sign international treaties, but at the same time it assigned most responsibilities to the federal government.

The first war in Chechnya, an ethnic republic in the North Caucasus which aimed at separating from Russia and thus became a massive threat

---

[2] More than 190 ethnic groups are registered in Russia today. Most ethnic republics accommodate majorities of ethnic Russians. Among those providing a strong share of the titular nations are Chechnya, Dagestan, Ingushetia, Tuva, Chuvashia, or Tatarstan. The titular nations are privileged with respect to elite selection and quotas and are often granted special linguistic and cultural rights. Legal acts must also be published in the language of the titular nations.

to the integrity of the Russian Federation, ended in a retreat of the Russian army and finally led to the agreement of Khasavyurt in August 1996. It shed light on the federal government's limited control of the regions at that time.

Despite its fragility, the federal system helped to prevent the disintegration of the country and to avoid violent interethnic conflicts (with the prominent exception of Chechnya). To integrate the insubordinate regions, Yeltsin adopted a "contractarian approach to Russian state-building" (Solnick, 1995, 55). As of 1994, Yeltsin signed 46 bilateral power-sharing contracts and more than 100 agreements with the ethnic republics and the regions (*oblasts*), offering considerable privileges particularly to the ethnic republics. During this period of "spontaneous decentralization," the federal government condoned that the federal subjects had "swallowed up" formerly centralized responsibilities. Yeltsin's approach caused side effects, however, because the contracts compromised the democratic quality of sub-federal governance: legal violations were the order of the day, while the democratic quality in some federal subjects fell below that of the national regime (see Gel'man, 2010; Obydenkova & Swenden, 2013).

The contracts regulated the control over natural resources, questions of state sovereignty, taxation, fiscal transfers, the right to establish foreign trade relations and so on (Gobuglo, 1997). Establishing disparities between the federal subjects became a major objective of the bargaining (Solnick, 1996, 17). Strikingly, more autonomy was demanded particularly by those regions, which were economically underdeveloped (albeit possessing natural resources) and whose elites were non-Russian and privileged already under the Soviet regime. Finally, the bilateral contracts deepened the already existing asymmetries between the ethnic republics and the Russian regions (*oblasts*). While the former preferred the model of a loose confederation over a vertically integrated federation, the latter supported the idea of a more unitary state (Dowley, 1998, 364–377). To regain sovereignty, Yeltsin claimed the right to appoint and dismiss the governors until 1996—a rule which ultimately undermines the federal principle—but he left the presidents of ethnic republics untouched.

The federal bargaining further increased the budgetary disparities between the federal subjects. While the Russian regions retained 64% of the taxes in 1994, the ethnic republics were able to keep 82% on average (Solnick, 1995, 54). As an effect of Yeltsin's contractarian approach, Russia represented a "bifurcated" federal system at that time. While the center-periphery relations with the ethnic republics became essentially federal, those with the Russian regions remained rather unitary. Thwarting collective action of the federal subjects throughout the outlined first-come first-served procedure; however, Yeltsin was at least able to avert the disintegration of the Russian state.

Yet, bargaining came with a high price for the federal order: as the distribution of competences was incrementally negotiated, the federal system lacked a coherent structure. The president sought to co-opt opponents by rewarding the most defiant federal subjects, even at the cost of the loyal ones (Solnick, 1995, 56). In the end numerous discrepancies between regional and federal laws emerged (Stepan, 2000, 144). These contradictions undermined the unity of law and subverted the rule of law principle. Moreover, by sustaining clientelistic relations and patronage between the center and the periphery, the federal contracts paved the way for informal practices that worked at the cost of the democratic quality. It should be mentioned, however, that as of 1998, in order to cut back federal asymmetries, Yeltsin already refrained from renewing the bilateral treaties with the regions.

Vertically integrated parties are particularly conducive to hold a federation together. In multinational federations, however, parties remain often "truncated" and regional parties represent diverse ethnic or linguistic groups. They tend to peripheralize the multilevel system. In Russia such a structure materialized soon after the Communist Party had lost its monopoly in November 1991, because there was no political party able to integrate the diverging territorial units. Newly founded parties did not gain sufficient strength to establish party branches throughout the Russian territory. The political space was shaped by organizations weakly rooted in society. Most of them revolved around charismatic leaders, their regional networks and patronage connections. This personalization strongly worked in favor of regional incumbents and businesspeople, who managed to extend their local power base. Consequently, subnational party pluralism remained rudimentary, enabling sub-federal elites to create regional fiefdoms and concomitantly abet the consolidation of subnational authoritarian regimes (Gel'man, 2010; see also Gibson, 2012, 25). At the same time regional party structures, which may stabilize federalism as an operative practice, remained too weak to peripheralize the multilevel system in a sustainable way. In the 2000s Putin was able to fill this void by creating a hegemonic party linking the territorial levels to each other, as the sections below will reveal.

At the end of the 1990s, Russian federalism was everything but a perfect federation. However, within less than one decade, Russia had turned into a multilevel system in which regional and federal elites had begun to reconstruct their roles, while the—albeit fragile—federal setup was reconfigured step by step. "Emergence" meant an uncoordinated, stepwise transformation of the Soviet "shell" into a fragile federal system. Its structure reflected the volatile distribution of power between the center and the diverse units. In comparative research the Russian case serves as an example to study how political entrepreneurs can reshape federal institutions within a brief time period, if federal institutions are neither bolstered by corresponding attitudes nor anchored in societal organizations. Both aspects provided an open flank in the 1990s, as will be shown in the subsequent sections.

DE-FEDERALIZING PROCESSES IN THE PUTIN ERA

When Putin came to power in 2000, he inherited an asymmetric, decentralized and centrifugal federal order. Due to the relative weakness of the federal government, the governors were able to regulate a considerable share of the regions' socioeconomic development. They had established subnational regimes remarkably differing in their democractic quality (Gel'man, 2010; Hale, 2011). The governors had gained considerable strength in the bargaining between the center and the regions (Treisman, 2001). The Constitution, albeit with a tendency to strong presidential rule, entitled the federal subjects to influence federal legislation in the upper chamber, the Federation Council.

Establishing a new administrative regime, Putin's predominant goal was to recentralize the multilevel order. Under his rule, key federal institutions have consistently been weakened through both *para-politics*, that is, informal practices that undermined formal institutions, and *para-constitutionalism*, that is, new custom-made institutions aimed at "substituting" the Constitution (Petrov, 2011a; Sakwa, 2010). As a result of his piecemeal reforms (2000-2008), both shared rule and self-rule—as the constituent principles of federalism—have been subverted, as the federal government was able to replace the previously imperfect bargaining model by the so-called power vertical—a term that indicates the overall dominance of the center over the constituent federal units (Sharafutdinova, 2010). In general, the autonomy of the regions is severely constrained by the fact that joint jurisdictions (Art. 72, Constitution of the RF) are de facto exercised by the federal government. The federal level administers the bulk of responsibilities, including tax collection. Expensive social tasks are implemented by the regions, most of which suffer from budgetary deficits.

A series of synchronized strategic measures to centralize political, administrative and fiscal responsibilities were undertaken. They affected all relevant federal institutions: the composition of the upper chamber was changed, federal agencies were created to monitor sub-federal politics and the selection process of the regional governors was once more altered. Importantly, Putin succeeded in establishing a hegemonic party, *United Russia*, integrating the different territorial levels within the party organization. Moreover, he propelled several mergers of federal subjects and enforced the redistribution of resources and responsibilities across the single levels of government. These multidimensional measures enforced the de-federalization of the country and at the same time stabilized authoritarian rule, as the subsequent sections will reveal.

The Federation Council and Its Substitutes

The reform of the upper chamber ranked high on Putin's centralization agenda. The regional governors and the heads of regional legislatures represented their respective territory in the Federation Council *ex officio*, and thus created a significant counterweight to the president at the end of the 1990s. As the Federation Council was able to veto the laws that passed the State Duma as well as overcome presidential vetoes (presupposing a two-thirds majority in both chambers), the heads of regions obtained considerable bargaining power in the law-making process (Art. 105-107, Russian Constitution of 1993). They could also block presidential personnel initiatives for main federal offices (Art. 102). In addition, the parliamentary immunity granted to all Federation Council members made them invulnerable against legal prosecution (Remington, 2003; Sharafutdinova, 2010). The upper chamber served as an arena for direct communication and networking between the governors without involving the federal government. Principally, this could have enforced the formation of horizontal, inter-regional alliances able to oppose Moscow.[3] Yet, the governors failed to create sustainable coalitions, as they pursued the interests of their own

---

[3] In the 1990s, some nascent structures of horizontal, inter-regional cooperation, such as *Bol'shaya Volga* or *Chernozeml'ye*, had emerged.

region and preferred exclusive bilateral bargaining with the federal government to collective action (Hyde, 2001; Sakwa, 2000). Intergovernmental relations finally resembled a spider web of command, consisting of "hyper-developed" radials running to Moscow and weak concentric threads (Petrov, 2011b, 97).

In order to cut back the governors' power, a new selection mode of Federation Council membership was adopted in 2002. The governors and heads of legislatures were replaced by two delegates, one of them representing the executive and the other one the legislative powers of each region. The Kremlin soon obtained control over the selection process. As a side effect, most delegates lacked the ties with the regions they were supposed to represent (Remington, 2003; Ross & Turovsky, 2013; Turovsky, 2007). Morphing into a platform of honorable retired governors and formerly high-ranked government officials, the Federation Council finally lost political weight (Ross, 2010). Since then, cases of law rejections have become rare, and personnel appointments proposed by the president hardly fail in the second chamber (Petrov, 2011a; Ross & Turovsky, 2013). While the Federation Council alone[4] vetoed 13% of all laws (141 out of 1045) in 1996–1999 and 8% (61 out of 781) in 1999–2003, in the current seventh convocation of the State Duma (October 2016 to July 2020), only five bills (out of 1998) failed to pass the upper chamber (Statistics of the State Duma, n.d.). Moreover, obtaining the right to appoint up to 10% of the members as representatives of the entire federation (and not of a constituent unit, i.e. 17 seats) in 2014, the president expanded his formal influence. The recent constitutional amendments passed in July 2020 entitled former presidents to become lifelong members of the Federation Council, while the total number of federal representatives in the upper chamber increased up to 30 seats (out of 170) (Art. 95).

Concurrently, a para-constitutional substitute—the "State Council"—was created to compensate the governors for being ousted from the Federation Council. The "Council of Legislators" functions as an equivalent body for the heads of regional legislatures, who had also been members of the Federation Council. It was not equipped with substantial powers, however (Ross, 2010). The State Council, again, was legitimated by a presidential decree. It serves as an advisory and consultative body for

---

[4] Together with the president, the Federation Council vetoed an additional 11% of bills (113) in 1996-1999, but just 1% (10) in 1999-2003. In the last two convocations of the State Duma, there were no cases of collective bill rejections.

the president. The regional governors employ it as a direct communication channel with the president. Due to its current composition, it lacks the influence on legislation the former Federation Council had exerted, however. From July 2020, the State Council is mentioned in Article 85 as a constitutional body designed to coordinate other public organs and to define the priorities of foreign and domestic policy. As such, it supports the genuine responsibilities of the president.

Para-constitutionalism at Work: Federal Districts and Presidential Envoys

Concomitantly, the federal government enlarged its capacity to monitor the sub-federal levels. An additional administrative layer, consisting of seven (now eight) federal districts (*okruga*), was introduced. These super-regions are headed by a representative of the president, the so-called presidential envoy (*polpred*). It is worth noting that even this massive intervention did not require any constitutional amendment because the presidential envoys are designated officials of the presidential administration. The basic task of this new institution was described in vague legal terms: it shall provide for administrative reform, ensure a clear separation of responsibilities between the center and regions, and guarantee that regional laws conform to the federal ones (Nelson & Kuzes, 2003).[5] In some cases the presidential envoys combined the function of being an official of the presidential administration with that of a high-ranked member of the federal government (vice-premiers). The accumulation of offices fosters their own position and tightens the Kremlin's grip onto the respective super-region.[6] Backed by the president, the envoys became powerful actors, while the federal districts functioned as a crucial pivot within the Russian power vertical. The *polpredy* appoint officials to regional key positions, monitor the governors, bring deviating regional legal acts in line with the federal ones and coordinate the policies of the regional units within their realm (Petrov, 2002).

[5] A considerable share of regional constitutions and statutes, legislative and executive orders violated federal laws or even invalidated the federal constitution (Sakwa, 2000, 16-17; Hyde, 2001, 731; Ross, 2003, 41). The evaluations range from about a quarter to 70% of regional legislative acts, which deviated from federal laws.
[6] For example, in the Northern Caucasus, Aleksandr Khloponin ensured that both the president's and the federal government's policies were implemented (2010-2014). His colleague Yuri Trutnev has occupied the corresponding positions in Russia's Far East since 2013.

Regional Governors: From Direct Election to Appointment and Back to Election?

In 2004 Putin abolished the direct election of the regional governors. Until 2012, they were appointed by the president and approved by the regional legislatures. This shift was regarded as a major attack on the regions' autonomy because it ultimately counteracts the principle of vertical checks and balances. Thereafter, the governors lost legitimacy and autonomy in the bargaining with Moscow and became, first and foremost, the "agents" of the president. Nevertheless, it was the regional leaders who initially helped establish legislative majorities for "United Russia." The loss of autonomy of the federal units took place without substantial protests, even in the ethnic republics, because the governors were unable to act collectively and were at the same time offered a third or even fourth time in office (see below).

The renewed federal-regional political contract implies that regional incumbents secure socioeconomic stability and deliver the desired electoral results to the center (Sharafutdinova, 2010). Particularly units in the Northern Caucasus and Southern Siberia feature abnormal electoral results. There, an overwhelming (over 80% or even 90%) support for Putin and "United Russia" was generated in all federal presidential and parliamentary elections. Due to their incorporation into the power vertical and frequent rotation, most of the governors have become the federal government's agents. They are responsible for managing socioeconomic stability and for delivering political support to the Kremlin, rather than acting as apologists of regional autonomy.

Although the direct gubernatorial elections had been reintroduced as a response to the mass protests in 2011-2012, a system of "filters" guarantees that the federal government is able to control the nomination procedure. A pool of candidates approved by the president and his hegemonic party was created (Blakkisrud, 2015; Goode, 2013), effectively restricting the choice of the regional citizens. Their function as "principal" is naturally marginalized under the terms of authoritarian rule (Kropp, 2019, 224), although Russian citizens continue to address demands to the regional authorities. The renewed federal-regional contract is mainly aimed at securing the governors' loyalty and averting potential risks. Strikingly, the federal government does not promote the governors for good economic or social performance in the region (Rochlitz et al., 2015; Libman & Rochlitz, 2019, 39–69). Neither can incumbents maintain their position, even if they are able to deliver the expected vote packages (Golosov & Tkacheva, 2018). This has become a self-evident task for any head of region.

Currently, two variants of the governors' selection are employed. In the first scenario the federal government secures the reelection of loyal incumbents if they are regarded as popular enough to win. In the second one highly unpopular governors are replaced by more promising candidates during the ongoing legislative period. The Kremlin supplies these candidates with resources necessary to win the electoral campaign.

Recent research points out that the reintroduction of direct elections did not link the governors more neatly to the regions (Kynev, 2019). Instead, the number of governors coming from outside, lacking a regional network (the so-called *varyagi* or "outsiders"), continues to increase. Behind the democratic façade, the reform fostered the federal government's grip onto the regions: governors can only survive with the president's support. From the Kremlin's point of view, the new selection mode proves to be effective: since 2012, in only four cases candidates supported by the federal center failed to win the election—2015 in Irkutsk oblast', 2018 in Khabarovsk krai, Vladimir oblast', and in the Khakassia republic.

The Role of Political Parties

The development of the Russian party system demonstrates how recentralization can be achieved by creating a hegemonic party able to co-opt even unruly regional elites and to reintegrate the various territorial units. By "verticalizing" the party system and limiting party pluralism, Putin expanded his patronage system (Filippov & Shvetsova, 2013). Still in the late 1990s, the regional governors had managed to form an electoral coalition represented in the first chamber, the Russian State Duma. In the 1999 elections the bloc *Fatherland–All Russia* obtained 13.3%, but finally lost the elections against *Unity*, a party supporting the finally victorious Putin. Thereafter, *Fatherland–All Russia* was no longer able to organize collective action. In 2001 Putin managed to co-opt the union of the regions by merging it with *Unity;* the merger transformed into the hegemonic party of power *United Russia*. Significantly, most governors joined the party, the more so as they were offered a third term of office (69 governors) or even a fourth term (17 governors) (Chebankova, 2007, 294). This deal demonstrates that governors were more interested in keeping their offices than in adhering to abstract federal principles, like self-rule or vertical checks and balances. *United Russia* soon became dominant in all federal and regional legislatures while regional and ethnic parties were officially forbidden (Kynev, 2018, 88). The hegemonic party ensured constitutional majorities and legal support for the president's initiatives (Remington, 2008). Today, *United Russia* is surrounded by three major satellites: the communist *KPRF*, the nationalist *LDPR* and the left-wing *A Just Russia* (Golosov, 2011).

Limited electoral competition allows the regime to channel potential protest. Since "non-systemic" oppositional forces are represented in the regional parliaments, the still existing federal structures provide the loyal "opposition" with some access to the political system. Yet it is questionable whether candidates can represent regional interests effectively. The satellite parties are corrupted because they are endowed with "reserved" seats in the Federation Council and the State Duma. In order to co-opt the "opposition," the federal government and *United Russia* refrain from nominating candidates in particular districts, thereby ensuring the victory of "loyal" oppositional candidates. Moreover, one of the strategies securing the reelection of regional incumbents in the gubernatorial elections is to offer the most promising challenger a seat in the Federation Council, or provide a direct mandate to the State Duma as compensation for his or her withdrawal or non-participation in the electoral campaign.

Furthermore, the federal government grants a gubernatorial position to each of the satellites—in August 2020, Oryol oblast' to the *KPRF*, Smolensk oblast' to the *LDPR* and Omsk oblast' and Chuvashia to *A Just Russia*. If challengers from *KPRF* or *LDPR* defeat Putin's candidates unexpectedly though, they will experience hard pressure. Significantly, up to now only two governors, elected against the will of the federal center, have remained in power.

Imposed Mergers of Regional Units and the Limits of Institutional Engineering

A striking example demonstrating how the federal government aims to transform the federal order is the mergers of federal units that have been undertaken since the mid-2000s. The mergers at the same time reveal the limits of institutional engineering from above. In full-fledged democratic federations, such endeavors usually depend on the cooperation of respective regional elites and an agreement of the electorate. In Russia the federal subjects were merged in a top-down method (Chebankova, 2009,

173). The procedure is regulated by a federal constitutional law (N6-FKZ, N7-FKZ). Formally initiated by the respective governors and heads of parliaments, the proposal requires presidential support to be confirmed by regional referenda. In case of successful popular vote, the president initiates a federal constitutional law that creates a new federation subject. The federal constitution must be amended (art. 65) and approved by a two-thirds majority in the State Duma and a three-quarters majority in the Federation Council. Note that all five fusions were informally initiated by the federal center and involved the so-called *matryoshka* ("Russian doll") regions, where independent constituent units of the Russian Federation were simultaneously parts of other (neighboring) sub-federal entities.[7]

A basic argument supporting these plans was that the involved ethnic units suffered from severe budgetary deficits while the share of the ethnic (non-Russian) titular population decreased due to overall demographic trends. The federal government intended to solve the problems by fusing these territories with economically stronger neighboring regions. Regional elites, particularly from the ethnic units that were doomed to disappear during the reform, were granted fiscal and economic benefits for their loyalty (Busygina, 2017). Moscow succeeded with all initiated mergers; the number of federal subjects was finally reduced from 89 to 83 by the end of 2008. Yet the Kremlin refrains from pursuing its plans, if they might impair interethnic consent, as the following example reveals.

The federal government tried to fuse the resource-rich Nenets, Yamalo-Nenets and Khanty-Mansi autonomous okrugs, which are the largest oil and gas extracting regions in Russia, with the surrounding federal units. Reviving the idea to merge the Nenets autonomous okrug (NAO) with its neighboring region, Arkhangelsk oblast' and their governors signed a corresponding memorandum in May 2020. Shortly after, regional and local politicians in NAO launched a protest against this plan. The citizens' resentments culminated in a rejection of Putin's recent constitutional amendments. Only one day after the

---

[7] Perm oblast' and Komi-Permyak autonomous okrug merged into Perm krai in 2005; Krasnoyarsk krai, Evenki autonomous okrug and Taimyr (Dolgan-Nenets) autonomous okrug merged into already existing Krasnoyarsk krai in 2007; Kamchatka oblast' and Koryak autonomous okrug merged into Kamchatka krai in 2007; Irkutsk oblast' and Ust-Orda Buryat autonomous okrug merged into already existing Irkutsk oblast' in 2008; Chita oblast' and Agin-Buryat autonomous okrug merged into Zabaykalsky krai in 2008.

constitutional referendum, the NAO's governor announced the termination of the plan (*RBK, July 2, 2020*).

The Reallocation of Resources and Responsibilities

In order to tighten the "power vertical" and to overcome the competential disorder caused by Yeltsin's bilateral contracts, Putin enforced significant competential shifts among the federal levels. Since the early 2000s, fiscal revenues have incrementally been centralized (Stoner-Weiss, 2006; Starodubtsev, 2018, pp. 78-101) while expensive administrative responsibilities, particularly social welfare tasks, have remained at the sub-federal level (Remington et al., 2013). Hence, the governors act on shaky ground because they are held responsible for the region's welfare, but lack the fiscal resources necessary to perform.

Fiscal recentralization is an efficient tool to subvert regional autonomy and change the system of intergovernmental relations. Accordingly, the federal government concentrated fiscal revenues at the federal level, particularly the VAT and natural resource extraction tax. Equalization grants were transformed into conditional transfers, which significantly reduces the autonomy of sub-national authorities (Golovanova, 2018). As a result, the regions are no longer able to compete for investments by offering tax incentives to businesses, not even in a *"race to the bottom"* manner (Treisman, 2001, 2007). In contrast to the more balanced allocation of budgetary revenues between federal and regional levels in the 1990s (Starodubtsev, 2018, 134), the federal revenue share now is about 60% (Ministry of Finance, n.d.). Significantly, Russia's fiscal centralization is even stronger than that of unitary China (Rochlitz et al., 2015; Libman & Rochlitz, 2019, 8–38). With the reallocation of tax revenue, the federal government was able to tighten its "golden"—not to say "iron"—rein. The regional governments are now forced to renegotiate transfers by exchanging loyalty for money, a situation which abets non-transparent, informal bargaining (Zubarevich, 2018).

Unfinanced mandates exacerbated the disbalance between responsibilities and scarce fiscal resources. Such mandates transfer responsibilities to the sub-federal levels while the necessary additional expenditures are neither included in the regional budgets nor covered by federal transfers. Striking examples are Putin's May Decrees 2012, which provide an ambitious masterplan for developing Russia's economy and require considerable regional (co-)financing, or his populist commitments during the electoral campaign, especially in the social sphere. In light of the overall economic stagnation and Western sanctions, Putin's promises aggravated the desperate situation for most regions: up to 90% of them indicated budget deficits in 2013-2015 (Zubarevich, 2017), while at the same time social expenditures, such as increasing salaries for teachers and doctors, must be financed through new debts. For the first time in modern Russian history, the federal Ministry of Finance employed its right to impose external administration on highly indebted regions in 2018 (in Kostroma oblast' and Khakassia republic, *TASS*, January 19, 2019).

Concluding Discussion

The past three decades of post-Soviet history have witnessed two distinctive phases in the development of the Russian federal system. The former shell of hyper-centralized, albeit formally federalized institutions inherited from the Soviet past, was brought to life in the Yeltsin era, but it remained fragile, based on ad-hoc negotiations, and prone to secessionist claims. It lacked the safeguards necessary to stabilize federal checks and balances (Bednar, 2009), first and foremost, federal attitudes of political elites, courts defending the contested multilevel institutions and a party system able to strengthen federal practices. Notwithstanding its ethno-federal composition, the federal order was not rooted in a federal culture and thus, highly susceptible for strategic moves. The containment of centrifugal dynamics, the taming of the unruly governors and recentralization, including tax collection, were at the top of Putin's political agenda. The federal pendulum swung back. Russia is, therefore, a textbook example for what was denoted "depletion" of weak federal institutions and federal regression in the introductory chapter to this book, after a period of emerging federalism (see Kropp and Keil in the Introduction).

De-federalizing dynamics continue. Significant measures were taken by the constitutional amendments of July 2020 (N1-FKZ). In addition to the changes discussed above, the president now obtains the right to appoint attorney generals of regions without approval by regional legislatures; the constitutional court can review regional laws before they are signed by governors. Moreover, a "unified system of public authority" is designed to integrate federal, regional and local levels of government (Arts. 131 and 132); this concept fundamentally contradicts the principle of self-rule. Not coincidentally, it reminds of the Soviet "unified system of state power" (Art. 89, Soviet Constitution of 1977), which was based on the indivisibility of state sovereignty as a basic rule (Uibopuu, 1979, 178) and is an explicit anti-federal idea. The veto powers of the Federation Council and the State Duma were further reduced. With these amendments, Putin managed to "constitutionalize" his personalist rule. Nevertheless, while the federal government has aimed at subordinating the sub-federal entities by recentralizing responsibilities and resources since the 2000s, the vague rules of the game still offer some room for maneuver for ad-hoc renegotiation and exclusive bargaining.

Despite Putin's all-encompassing recentralization agenda, the federal structure provides an—albeit limited—reserve of executive powers for regional elites, whose loyalty is not a matter of course. This sparks uncertainty and may lead to unintended dynamics. As some ethnic republics, especially in the Northern Caucasus, fully depend on federal financial support, their loyalty vis-à-vis the federal center depends on its ability to pay. Moreover, regional elites may accept the governors-outsiders. As long as the *varyagi* manage to avoid serious conflicts with local communities and maintain the cohabitation with the sub-federal elites, their position is not questioned. If they fail or alter the intra-elite status quo in the region, however, both the governor *and* the president risk losing support. Recent electoral campaigns revealed that even the president's candidates can, indeed, lose subnational elections; also, the president has to make some concessions to regional protesters.

Centralization is a concomitant feature of authoritarian rule. Power sharing and vertical checks and balances, on which true federalism builds, conflict with the authoritarian ruler's abundant claim to power. By definition, federalism "perforates" strict hierarchies and undermines the monolithic bloc of authoritarian rule. Why then, do authoritarian leaders nurture and sustain a multilevel state organization?

The first answer is simple. In Russia the federal structure was inherited from the Soviet past; some of its basic characteristics, most of all the ethno-federal composition, reflect a path-dependent development. It was impossible to remove these federal characteristics without shaking the fragile post-Soviet Russian state to its very foundations and stirring the already latent centrifugal tendencies. Secondly, the federal order allows the federal government to shift the blame for ineffective policy outcomes and potential popular discontent to the subnational levels of government (Bednar, 2009, 1–16). The federal government can punish regional governors as "scapegoats," if popular discontent increases (Kropp, 2019, 226). Thirdly, despite abundant centralization, the federal structure multiplies offices and mandates, allowing for the co-optation of elites. In this respect the federal system serves as an institutionalized structure for patronage and clientelism. On the one hand, these informal institutions may help contain centrifugal tendencies and stabilize the loyalty of regional elites, particularly of the governors, who still possess some leeway to establish their own personal rule in the regions. On the other hand, patronage and clientelism undermine the democratic quality. Hence, it was concluded that federalism Russian style is "autocracy-sustaining" (Obydenkova & Swenden, 2013).

The back and forth of Russian (de-)federalization offers particularly illustrative material to study processes of federal emergence and subsequent regression. Currently, nothing indicates that Russia's "sleeping" federal system, or at least single of its haggard federal institutions, can be awakened, and that this might fan attempts to achieve some re-democratization.

References

Bednar, J. (2009). *The robust federation. Principles of design.* Cambridge University Press.

Blakkisrud, H. (2015). Governing the governors: Legitimacy vs. control in the reform of the Russian regional executive. *East European Politics, 31*(1), 104–121.

Burgess, M. (2017). "Federalism and federation: Putting the record straight", in *50 Shades of Federalism.* Retrieved April 4, 2020, from http://50shadesoffederalism.com/theory/federalism-federation-putting-record-straight/.

Busygina, I. (2017). How does Russian federalism work? Looking at internal borders in the Russian federation. *Journal of Borderlands Studies, 32*(1), 105–119.

Chebankova, E. (2007). Putin's struggle for federalism: Structures, operations, and the commitment problem. *Europe-Asia Studies, 59,* 279–302.

Chebankova, E. (2009). *Russia's Federal relations: Putin's reforms and management of the regions.* Routledge.

Dowley, K. M. (1998). Striking the federal bargaining in Russia: Comparative regional government strategies. *Communist and Post-Communist Studies, 31,* 359–380.

Filippov, M., & Shvetsova, O. (2013). Federalism, democracy, and Democratization. In A. Benz & J. Broschek (Eds.), *Federal Dynamics* (pp. 167–184). Oxford University Press.

Gel'man, V. (2010). The dynamics of sub-national authoritarianism: Russia in comparative perspective. In V. Gel'man & C. Ross (Eds.), *The Politics of Sub-National Authoritarianism in Russia* (pp. 1–18). Ashgate.

Gibson, E. (2012). *Boundary control: Subnational authoritarianism in federal democracies (1. publ. ed.)*. Cambridge University Press.
Gobuglo, M. N. (1997). *Federalizm vlasti i vlast' federalizma*. Moskva.
Golosov, G. (2011). The regional roots of electoral authoritarianism in Russia. *Europe-Asia Studies*, 63(4), 623–639.
Golosov, G. V., & Tkacheva, T. (2018). Let my people run: Pre-election resignations of Russia's governors, 2013–2015. *Problems of Post-Communism*, 65(4), 243–252.
Golovanova, N. (2018). Intergovernmental transfers. Diversity of terms and Russian practice. *Financial Journal*, 2, 24–35.
Goode, J. P. (2013). The revival of Russia's gubernatorial elections: Liberalization or Potemkin reform? *Russian Analytical Digest*, 139, 9–11.
Hale, H. E. (2011). The myth of mass Russian support for autocracy: The public opinion foundations of a hybrid regime. *Europe-Asia Studies*, 63(8), 1357–1375.
Hyde, M. (2001). Putin's federal reforms and their implications for presidential power in Russia. *Europe-Asia Studies*, 53(5), 719–743.
Kropp, S. (2019). The ambivalence of federalism and democracy: The challenging case of authoritarianism—with Evidence from the Russian case. In N. Nathalie Behnke, J. Broschek, & J. Sonnicksen (Eds.), *Multilevel governance: Configurations, dynamics, consequences* (pp. 213–229). Palgrave Macmillan.
Kynev, A. (2019). Phenomenon of governors – 'outsiders' as indicator of recentralization. Experience of 1991-2018 Years. *Politeia*, 2(93), 125–150.
Kynev, A. (2018). Political parties and parliament. In I. Studin (Ed.), *Russia: Strategy, policy and administration* (pp. 87–96). Palgrave Macmillan.
Libman, A., & Rochlitz, M. (2019). *Federalism in China and Russia*. Edward Elgar Publishing.
Ministry of Finance. (n.d.). Retrieved July 3, 2020, from https://www.minfin.ru/ru/statistics/conbud/.
N1-FKZ. Zakon Rossiyskoy Federatsii o Popravke k Konstitutsii Rossiyskoy Federatsii ot 14.03.2020.
N6-FKZ. Federal'nyi Konstucionnyi Zakon ot 17.12.2001 N6-FKZ "O Poryadke Prinyatiya v Rossiyskuyu Federaciyu i Obrazovaniya v Ee Sostave Novogo Subyekta Rossiyskoy Federacii".
N7-FKZ. Federal'nyi Konstucionnyi Zakon ot 31.10.2005 N7-FKZ " O Vnesenii Izmeneniy v Statyi 10 i 11 Federal'nogo Konstucionnogo Zakona "O Poryadke Prinyatiya v Rossiyskuyu Federaciyu i Obrazovaniya v Ee Sostave Novogo Subyekta Rossiyskoy Federacii".
Nelson, L. D., & Kuzes, I. Y. (2003). Political and economic coordination in Russia's federal district reform: A Study of four regions. *Europe-Asia Studies*, 55(4), 507–520.

Obydenkova, A., & Swenden, W. (2013). Autocracy-sustaining versus democratic federalism: Explaining the divergent trajectories of territorial politics in Russia and Western Europe. *Territory, Politics, Governance, 1*(19), 86–112.

Petrov, N. (2002). Seven faces of Putin's Russia: Federal districts as the new level of state—territorial composition. *Security Dialogue, 33*(1), 73–91.

Petrov, N. (2011a). The political mechanics of the Russian rgime. *Russian Politics & Law, 49*(2), 34–69.

Petrov, N. (2011b). Russia's political elites in 2010. Twenty years on. In N. Bubnova (Ed.), *20 years without the Berlin Wall: A breakthrough to freedom* (pp. 91–135). Carnegie Moscow Center.

Remington, T. F. (2003). Majorities without mandates: The Russian Federation Council since 2000. *Europe-Asia Studies, 55*(5), 667–691.

Remington, T. F., Soboleva, I., Sobolev, A., & Urnov, M. (2013). Economic and social policy trade-offs in the Russian regions: Evidence from four case studies. *Europe-Asia Studies, 65*(10), 1855–1876.

Remington, T. F. (2008). Patronage and the party of power: President–Parliament relations under Vladimir Putin. *Europe-Asia Studies, 60*(6), 959–987.

Rochlitz, M., Kulpina, V., Remington, T., & Yakovlev, A. (2015). Performance incentives and economic growth: Regional officials in Russia and China. *Eurasian Geography and Economics, 56*(4), 421–445.

Ross, C. (2010). Federalism and inter-governmental relations in Russia. *Journal of Communist Studies and Transition Politics, 26*(2), 165–187.

Ross, C. (2003). Putin's federal reforms and the consolidation of federalism in Russia: One step forward, two steps back! *Communist and Post-Communist Studies, 36*(1), 29–47.

Ross, C., & Turovsky, R. (2013). The representation of political and economic elites in the Russian federation council. *Demokratizatsiya, 21*(1), 59–88.

Sakwa, R. (2000). Russian regionalism, policy-making and state development. In S. Harter & G. Easter (Eds.), *Shaping the economic space in Russia: Decision making processes, institutions and adjustment to change in the El'tsin Era* (pp. 11–34). Ashgate.

Sakwa, R. (2010). The dual state in Russia. *Post-Soviet Affairs, 26*(3), 185–206.

Sharafutdinova, G. (2010). Subnational governance in Russia: How Putin changed the contract with his agents and the problems it created for Medvedev. *Publius: The Journal of Federalism, 40*(4), 672–696.

Solnick, S. L. (1995). Federal bargaining in Russia. *East European Constitutional Review, 4*, 52–58.

Solnick, S. L. (1996). The political economy of Russian federalism. A framework for analysis. *Problems of Post-Communism*, November/December, pp., 13–25.

Starodubtsev, A. (2018). *Federalism and regional policy in contemporary Russia*. Routledge.

Statistics of the State Duma. (n.d.). Retrieved July 3, 2020, from http://www.gosduma.net/legislative/statistics/.

Stepan, A. (2000). Russian federalism in comparative perspective. *Post-Soviet Affairs, 16*(2), 133–176.

Stepan, A. (1999). Federalism and democracy: Beyond the U.S. model. *Journal of Democracy, 10*(4), 19–34.

Stoner-Weiss, K. (2006). Russia: Authoritarianism without authority. *Journal of Democracy, 17*(1), 104–118.

TASS. (19 January 2019). Retrieved July 3, 2020, from https://tass.ru/ekonomika/4887785.

Treisman, D. (2001). *After the deluge: Regional crises and political consolidation in Russia*. University of Michigan Press.

Treisman, D. (2007). *The Architecture of government: Rethinking political decentralization*. Cambridge University Press.

Turovsky, R. (2007). The mechanism of representation of regional interests at the federal level in Russia: Problems and solutions. *Perspectives on European Politics and Society, 8*(1), 73–97.

Uibopuu, H.-J. (1979). Soviet federalism under the new Soviet Constitution. *Review of Socialist Law, 5,* 171–185.

Zubarevich, N. (2017). The Burden of the regions: What has changed in ten years? *Russian Politics & Law, 55*(2), 61–76.

Zubarevich, N. (2018). Regional and local government. In I. Studin (Ed.), *Russia: Strategy, policy and administration* (pp. 367–380). Palgrave Macmillan.

CHAPTER 5

Why No Federalism? The Challenges of Institutionalizing a Multilevel Order in Ukraine

Sabine Kropp and Jørn Holm-Hansen

Why Study Devolutionary Processes in Ukraine Through the Lens of Federalism?

All long-standing democracies that score highest on indexes of linguistic and ethnic diversity are federal states (Stepan, 1999, 20). From this point of view, Ukraine with its multiple 'ethnic, political, and historical schisms between populations, and significant economic regional disparities' (Marlin, 2016, 278) would be predestined for transforming into a federal

---

This chapter forms part of the ARDU project (Accommodation of Regional Diversity in Ukraine), funded by the Research Council of Norway, project number 287620.

S. Kropp (✉)
Otto-Suhr-Institut für Politikwissenschaft, Freie Universität Berlin, Berlin, Germany
e-mail: sabine.kropp@fu-berlin.de

© The Author(s), under exclusive license to Springer Nature Switzerland AG 2022
S. Keil, S. Kropp (eds.), *Emerging Federal Structures in the Post-Cold War Era*, Federalism and Internal Conflicts,
https://doi.org/10.1007/978-3-030-93669-3_5

system, or it seems at least 'custom-made for far-reaching regionalization' (Wolczuk, 2002, 65).

Yet, the mismatch between the societal and the political-administrative structure in Ukraine is noteworthy. Theoretical predictions and the empirical situation seem to diverge. Different from other large-area countries that accommodate various language and ethnic groups and political camps, Ukraine has not introduced a federal system. Instead, a decentralization reform was adopted in 2014, which itself entails a number of unsolved problems (Aasland & Lyksa, 2016; Romanova & Umland, 2019b; Shelest & Rabynovich, 2020). Considering the tensions between the institutional setting and its underlying societal make-up, this chapter argues that Ukraine can be studied as a crucial case (Gerring, 2008, 660), although this position might appear counterintuitive at first glance. The basic questions of this chapter are: Why then, is there no federal system in Ukraine, and are there signs of federal practices which herald the emergence of federal structures? (Map 5.1).

The subsequent analysis starts with a critical assessment of theories which suggest that some kind of federal order will possibly emerge in Ukraine. Thereafter, it is debated whether Ukraine's mix of fluid identities matches a federal system. Looking into the history of Ukrainian statehood, it is argued that there is little to justify 'federal' path dependence. Particular attention will be paid to the complicated geopolitical context, which makes federalism a securitized issue in Ukraine. Then, the process and current stage of the ongoing decentralization are outlined, which is considered a means to avoid federalization in Ukraine. Special emphasis is placed on the question whether Ukrainian parties exercise federal practices, which 'frequently reflect the underlying social structure' (Erk, 2007, 9; see also Livingston, 1952, 929), while the institutional setup is still unitary. Furthermore, the role informal practices and (non-)federal constitutional politics play is discussed. We conclude that although Ukraine needs consociational institutions integrating the diverse social groups and political camps, a full-fledged federal system might even exacerbate the problems which it is deemed to solve.

J. Holm-Hansen
Norwegian Institute for Urban and Regional Research, Oslo Metropolitan University, Oslo, Norway
e-mail: Jorn.Holm-Hansen@oslomet.no

5 WHY NO FEDERALISM? THE CHALLENGES OF INSTITUTIONALIZING... 97

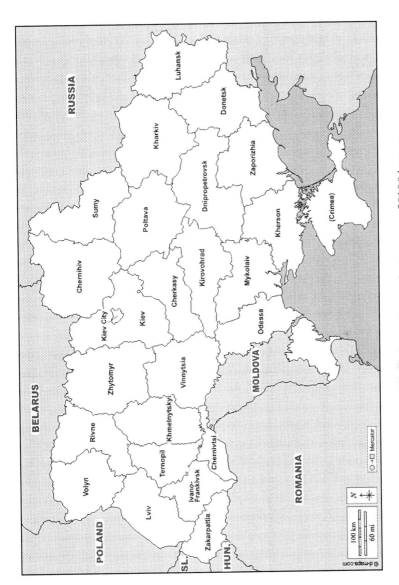

Map 5.1 Ukraine. *Source*: https://d-maps.com/carte.php?num_car=5010&lang=en

The Relevance of Federalism for Ukraine—Theoretical Perspectives

The current Ukrainian Constitution states that the country is a unitary state. Hence, political analysts might demur that looking at Ukrainian territorial politics through the lens of federal studies is futile. We do not share this view because elements of federalism may be alive even in unitary systems. Ronald Watts' (1998, 120) concept of 'federal political systems' covers this grey zone between unitary and federal models. As for the Ukrainian case, we would see a variety of reasons why elements of federalism might be present.

The first argument (see Kropp and Keil, this volume) is that federal elements may develop gradually into a federal setup. The country may therefore follow the path of incremental, 'devolutionary federalism' (Marlin, 2016, 279). Asymmetrical federalism may be the result when once established, single federalized institutions are insulated in an otherwise unitary order. Such asymmetries are deemed typical for multilevel systems that must accommodate linguistic and ethnic diversity (Stepan, 1999, 29–32). The Ukrainian government, for example, had already granted some autonomy to Crimea before the peninsula was annexed by Russia in 2014, while the other regional entities were still subordinated to the center. Similar solutions would be obvious if Ukraine and Russia were able to settle the hybrid war in Donbass.

Secondly, the concept of a 'federal society' (Livingston, 1952, 85, 88; Stein, 1968) expects institutions to achieve congruence with the underlying social structure in the long run. A 'federal society' is considered one in which the most politically salient aspects of identification and conflict are related to specific territories (Erk, 2007, 4). In Ukraine, such change would entail a direction of development corresponding to its ethno-linguistic heterogeneity. Recent studies assume a dialectical relationship between underlying social structures and overarching institutions (Erk & Koning, 2010). Such adaptation processes are mediated by the concrete choices of actors and their strategies and framed by (federal) attitudes and norms (March & Olsen, 2004; Peters, 2005, 31). One should note, however, that especially in Ukraine, which is reckoned among the 'hybrid' regimes (Freedom House, 2018), domestic political elites are less responsive to citizens than to full-fledged democracies. They tend to neglect issues like the accommodation of societal diversity, act in favor of their own clientele, and consider regional identities as a political project, which can be deliberately construed, rather than a social fact. Hence, it is everything but sure that the assumed adaptation materializes.

Thirdly, a country may feature a formally unitary setup, but its underlying federal practices make it federal in operation (Livingston, 1952). In a 'hybrid regime' like Ukraine, formal institutions do strongly interplay with informal rules that are not supportive to the formal rules, but tend to undermine the Constitution (Helmke & Levitsky, 2004). Patronalism and clientelism (Hale, 2015; Sakwa, 2010) are textbook examples of informal institutions. A crucial question related to center-periphery relations in Ukraine is whether such informal practices feature quasi-federal elements. In general, clientelism may help accommodate or conflict with regional diversity or add routes to power for territorial groups. That said it should be considered that these practices thwart the democratic quality, which is why researchers emphasizing the nexus between federalism and democracy (Burgess, 2017) would deny genuine 'federal' traits in such informal practices.

Why Federalism Is Rejected in Ukraine— Empirical Findings

Regional Diversity as a Driving Force?

The debate on federalism versus unitarianism in Ukraine bears the imprint of belated nation-building. It evolves around rivalling interpretations of the country's regional diversity and fluid identities. Those who have supported the idea of a federal model for Ukraine emphasize its regional diversities to justify their claim. The same holds true for proponents of milder versions of regional autonomy, for example, on the status of minority languages. The opposite stance is one of unitarianism. Its proponents tend to portray not only the diversity of identities and linguistic practices but also their fluidity as a result of undue foreign influence throughout history but also of the present. This goes, in their view, notably for Russian but also Hungarian and Romanian influences. The unitarianists aim at making one homogenous nation out of the Ukrainian population, aptly summed up in the pre-election slogan of former president Petro Poroshenko: 'One army, one tongue, one faith'.

Recent surveys seem to corroborate that Ukraine features some kind of federal society. Living in Western Ukraine, for example, significantly increases the likelihood of identifying with Ukrainian language compared to the other parts of the country (Sasse & Lackner, 2018, 5–6). Ethnic, religious and language identities are overlapping and fuzzy, with language use being the strongest predictor of political attitudes (Pop-Eleches & Robertson, 2018, 114–115; Onuch & Hale, 2018). Ukrainian Greek Catholics, concentrated in the West, identify Ukrainian language as their main identity fifteen times as much as people of other confessions, whereas followers of the Moscow Patriarchate are 'more as three times as likely to indicate that Russian was their native language' (Sasse & Lackner, 2018, 12). Citizens in Central Ukraine, again, are twice as likely to choose citizenship as their main identity marker, compared to people in Western Ukraine, who more frequently identify themselves as 'ethnic Ukrainian' (ibid., 5). Considering the complicated geopolitical context, a majority of Ukrainians still reject any autonomy status for the Donbass, but the willingness to accept some kind of autonomy has increased significantly within just one year (ibid., 8). After the Euromaidan in 2014, surveys reported a broadly shared acceptance of Ukraine as a nation state, while ethnolinguistic divisions still shape political attitudes and dynamics (Pop-Eleches & Robertson, 2018, 116; Aasland et al. 2021). Yet, even more than two-thirds of ethnic Russians accept Ukraine as their homeland (ibid., 111).

Correspondingly, Sasse and Lackner (2018, 13) argue that regional identities are more nuanced than the official state rhetoric, language and education policies. Momentous events like the Euromaidan, the annexation of Crimea and the war with Russia in Donbass have shifted identity in favor of Ukrainian citizenship (Kuzio, 2018, 342; Matsiyevsky, 2015, 4) and relaxed the tensions between the East and the West (Torikai, 2019, 14; Way, 2016, 55; Kuzio, 2018, 344). After Ukraine had lost control over Crimea and parts of Donetsk and Luhansk as *de facto regimes* during Poroshenko's term in office, a considerable share of the Russophile electorate departed (Way, 2016, 55). The underlying social structure of Ukraine, therefore, is definitely one of regional diversity along economic, linguistic and identity lines. If the 'federal society' assumption of congruence (Livingston, 1952) or a dialectical relationship between social structures and institutions (Erk & Koning, 2010) holds true, one would expect some kind of federal practices to develop (see below).

Obstacles to achieve such congruence accrue from the blurred and fluid character of most Ukrainian citizens' cultural identities and linguistic practices. Linguistic and ethnic groups are not territorially concentrated (Erk, 2017). Macro-social factors of regional diversity are not clearly cut along territorial-regional lines unless one juxtaposes the 'extremes', for example, Lviv and Donetsk. Therefore, constructing federal subunits based on territory would miss out on securing ethno-linguistic rights. This is a factor that hampers the drive for federal solutions in Ukraine.

A Path-Dependent Development of Federalism?

This disagreement can only be understood by taking the genesis of the Ukrainian state into consideration. Ukraine gained statehood only recently, at first in the aftermath of World War I and the Russian revolution, and then finally as a result of the dissolution of the Soviet Union in 1991 (Holm-Hansen & Kropp, 2021). The territories included in present day Ukraine have belonged to highly divergent neighboring states. The Eastern ones have been deeply integrated in mainstream Russian culture and economy since the mid-seventeenth century and the Southern parts were so since the second half of the eighteenth century. Donbass in the East was mainly populated by new arrivals from other parts of Russia since the late nineteenth century.

Most of the Western parts were included in Ukraine only as a result of World War II and bore traces of a Habsburgian past and Polish and Hungarian cultural and economic domination. The mainly rural Ukrainians in the region gained status as the titular nation only after the inclusion in Soviet Ukraine. The fact that this took place (following the genocide on the Jews and the transfer of local Poles to post-WWII Poland) facilitated the Ukrainification of the newly incorporated areas. After 1945, in particular Galicia, with Lviv as its main city, became a center of Ukrainian nation-building based on ethnicity, language, geopolitical orientation and memory politics.

In states with a Soviet past, path dependency has a bearing on how federalism is perceived. Soviet policies on the nationality issue consisted in assigning formal autonomy to ethno-linguistically defined peoples. These territories from union republics down to federal entities within the republics were set up to enable the protection but also control of cultural and linguistic identities. Such arrangements were turned to even in cases where the titular nationality was in minority numerically. Ethnic delineations were frequently made on political grounds. Nonetheless, the Soviet ethno-territorial subdivisions have by and large survived 30 years after the dissolution of the Soviet Union. Different from Russia, however, Soviet Ukraine was not composed of ethnically defined sub-territories. The only exception was the left bank of Dniestr (today's Transdnistria) that between 1924 and 1940 had status as a Moldovan autonomous republic within Ukraine. This lack of prior ethno-territories in Ukraine has been an obstacle to the proponents of federal models.

Federalism as a Securitized Issue

The path-dependent unfamiliarity with a federal model, however, is most likely less significant than the here-and-now concern about what would happen if Ukraine were federal. A recurrent theme in the Ukrainian debate is the fear of Russian influence. A federal model would entail that Russia might get a veto power on Ukrainian policies through regional authorities that possibly would be close to Russian positions, for example, on NATO membership or language issues. In other words, the issue of federalizing Ukraine is highly securitized. The rejection of federal models arises from the fear that Russia would be able to split up a Ukrainian federation (Romanova & Umland, 2019b).

Since 2014, federalism has been a no-go zone in Ukraine, but prior to that, the concept formed part of the political debate (Barbieri, 2020). The attraction to the concept proved to be highly situational. In the early 1990s proponents of Ukrainification and de-Sovietization, and not least de-Russification, saw a federal model to be conducive to their ends. The argument was that a more autonomous Galicia would serve as a springboard to strengthen ethno-linguistic Ukraine-ness in the entire republic and facilitate a geopolitical orientation toward the West. Countering this, leaders of Ukraine's regions where Lviv-based Ukrainifaction enjoyed little support, notably Crimea, Zakarpattia, and East and South Ukraine, supported a unitary model for Ukraine.

In a few years, positions changed diametrically. Having their electoral support primarily in the East and South, presidents Leonid Kuchma (1994-2005) and Viktor Ianukovych (2010-2014) were proponents of more autonomy to the regions. President Viktor Iushchenko (2005-2010) and Petro Poroshenko (2014-2019) with their voter bases mainly in the Center and West, were proponents of unitarianism.

With the marginalization of the regionalist political forces after 2014 and the loss of the territories on which voters traditionally supported them (Crimea and parts of the Donbass), the pressure from below to federalize has been considerably weakened. External initiatives, however, continue to assert themselves. Officially, Russia is still suggesting a federal model to secure the rights of Russian speakers, which generally is interpreted in Ukraine as an attempt to institutionalize Moscow's influence on Ukrainian politics through regional leaders.

Incitements to make exceptions to the unitary model—in addition to the special status Crimea had before 2014—have come from the 'Steinmeier Formula' to solve the crisis in the Donbass (Lachowski, 2020). The formula is a peace plan proposed by former German Foreign Minister Frank-Walter Steinmeier in 2016 to sequence the measures under the Minsk Agreement set to solve the problems in Ukraine's Eastern Donbass regions. According to this plan the two Donbass regions of Luhansk and Donetsk would have widened autonomy after having returned in their entirety to Ukraine. This issue, which would introduce asymmetries, is highly controversial in Ukrainian politics and constitutes a sharp dividing line between the current Zelenskyi administration and the political forces around the former president Petro Poroshenko. Zelenskyi's willingness to comply with the Steinmeier Formula may be seen as an illustration of *elements* of a federal model being introduced to accommodate for underlying societal circumstances despite federalization being rejected.

Decentralization as a Countermeasure to Federalization

As federalization is widely rejected, reforms of multilevel arrangements in Ukraine focus on decentralization. Decentralization is regarded as a tool to weaken the regional level and to prevent Russia-leaning regions from becoming bridgeheads for Russian influence (Barbieri, 2020). At the same time, it is regarded as a measure to reduce the power of oligarchs and other regionally and district-based groups.

Ukraine's complex and asymmetrical three-tier system of sub-national government consists of 27 regions,[1] sub-regional districts and local communities. Until 2014, the system continued to be highly centralized in spite of several, mainly rhetorical reform initiatives (Aasland & Lyksa, 2016). The only exception was a partly successful fiscal decentralization, mainly to the benefit of cities with the status of being of regional (oblast) significance (Romanova & Umland, 2019a).

Only after the Euromaidan events in 2014, decentralization reforms have been introduced with some effect. Legislation is still in the making,

---

[1] In addition to the 24 'ordinary' regions, the *oblasti*, they include the Republic of Crimea and two cities with special status—Kyiv and Sevastopol.

and progress is slow. After the landslide victories of Volodymyr Zelenskyi and his party *Sluga Narodu* in the 2019 elections, signals on how to proceed have been contradictory.

The reform's main component so far has consisted in voluntary merger of small and rural local communities (*hromady*). The aim has been to strengthen the local level and keep the regional and sub-regional levels weak. This is in line with one of the explicit objectives of the reform, which has been to pre-empt the strengthening of regionalism and federalist claims. Therefore, the decentralization reform has aimed at redefining, that is, weakening, the prerogatives of the regions. Today, Ukraine has 27 regions.

Also, the sub-regional level between oblast and local community has been targeted by the reform. This affects the districts (*raiony*) of which there are 290. Their number will be reduced as part of the reform, and they will be renamed into *okrugi*, another word for district in Ukrainian. Unlike regional and local levels, *okrugi* will not have elected councils. Just like at the regional level, they are deconcentrated state agencies at district level, functioning as agents of the central government districts. As part of the reform, the deconcentrated state administrations have been reorganized to cover several districts.

As for the local level of government, the *hromady* have been encouraged, among others through financial incentives, to amalgamate into entities big enough to build up their own institutional and social infrastructures. These new local units are called 'amalgamated territorial communities' (OTG). They are envisaged as the basic unit of territorial self-government and have direct links to the central government, bypassing the administrative levels of *oblast* and *raion*. This will reduce the risk that *hromady* come under control of regional and district level 'power cliques', often referred to as 'neo-feudals', in the Ukrainian debate; but decentralization has, at the same time, provided opportunities for local elite capture (Bader, 2020, 260).[2] Moreover, the OTGs often include former *hromady* with divergent linguistic practices, for example, Russian and Ukrainian in the East and Romanian and Ukrainian in the region of Chernivtsy.

By spring 2019, 26% of Ukraine's inhabitants lived in an OTG. Together with the 43.5% of Ukraine's population living in cities of so-called 'oblast significance', this means that 69.5% reside in municipalities with some

---

[2] See, for example, op-ed by Anatolii Tkachuk, scientific director of the Kyiv-based Institute for Civil Society, "Decentralizaciia—strategiia meniaetsia?" Zerkalo Nedelii, June 9, 2020.

degree of real local self-government (Romanova & Umland, 2019b). By summer 2020, Ukraine had around 1300 *hromady*.

Unlike the un-amalgamated *hromady*, the OTGs are envisaged as self-sustaining, local self-governments in charge of local development and basic public services. They are also responsible for primary and secondary schools in their territories and have considerable autonomy to collect taxes. About 60% of income tax collected stays in the local OTG. Moreover, they enjoy privileged access to funding from the central state. The international community, primarily the EU, has invested financially and prestige-wise in the success of OTGs.

One of the institutional features of Ukraine's centralized system has been the absence of executive organs under the locally and regionally elected bodies of self-government. The implementation of the decisions made by the self-government bodies have been delegated to executives that are staffed by the central authorities, but these local state administrations also form part of a strict hierarchy under the central government. This is generally considered to hamper local self-government (Aasland & Lyksa, 2016). The reform will place the administrative apparatus under locally and regionally elected bodies. The function of control and harmonization with central policies will be safeguarded by prefects at regional and okrug levels of government, who are appointed by the president and government. The introduction of prefects, however, still awaits the necessary constitutional amendments. The assessment of the reform is ambivalent: Responsibilities are not clearly separated but are duplicated.

Federal Practices? The Role of the Party System and Party Organization

Even in constitutionally unitary states, institutions may be operated *as if* they were federal. A 'truncated' party system that peripheralizes power and parties which are organized in a federal way are key factors in this respect. An overview of the Ukrainian parties' characteristics reveals that their role is not one as agents adapting the societal to the political structure in line with the 'federal society' assumption.

Although the party system has been in flux and has had highly volatile voters at all times since the early 1990s, Ukrainian parties have reflected rather stable cleavages. As noted by Chaisty and Whitefield (2018), these cleavages have been shaped by the geopolitical so-called Russian question and a geocultural divide between Westward-leaning and Russia-leaning voters. The latter have had their strongholds in the East (particularly in Donbass) and South and were mainly represented by the Communist Party in the 1990s, the centrist Party of Regions until 2014, and the weaker opposition bloc and platform 'For Life' party thereafter. These parties oppose the unitarianist policies pursued by the Ukrainian authorities since 2014, albeit in a more moderate version since the victories of Zelenskyi and his party in 2019.

Voters in West (most noticeably in Galicia) and Central Ukraine have voted primarily for the so-called nationalist democratic parties, like Our Ukraine and Fatherland. Chaisty and Whitefield (2018) show that the 2014 events did not undo the cleavages, but the Russian-leaning parties ended up almost unrepresented due to the fact that their voters emigrated or lived in regions outside Ukrainian state control.[3]

Ukrainian politics has been a back and forth between politicians and parties belonging to either an 'Eastern' or a 'Western' pole. In parliamentary elections the Eastern pole has dominated (Kudelia & Kuzio, 2015). Presidential elections have been won by the East and West more or less every other time. Volodymyr Zelenskiy's landslide (73.2% in the second round) in the 2019 presidential elections, followed by the unprecedented large majority (43.2%) won by his party *Sluga Narodu* in the elections to the Verkhovna Rada has been interpreted as a defeat of the Western pole, but not necessarily as a victory of the traditional Eastern pole, even though *Sluga Narodu* and Zelenskiy got its strongest support from voters in the East. It was Zelenskyi's signaling of a less ethno-nationalist Ukraine and more inclusive style that made him draw the large majority of voters in the East and South. It is still too soon to conclude that this marks the end of institutionalized regional diversity through parties, but it is evident that the role of Ukrainian parties is not one of agents adapting the societal to the political structure in line with the 'federal society' assumption.

A caveat has been made earlier in this chapter that the 'federal society' concept should be made with caution if taken out of the analysis of established democracies. Ukrainian political parties do not form a 'truncated' party system, representing regional interests within particular parties; rather, they operate nationwide. Because half of the deputies in the Verkhovna Rada are elected on national lists, it makes sense to try and

---

[3] The population of Crimea and the two secessionist proto-republics in Donbass constituted together 16% of the voters in the 2010 presidential elections and 12% in the 2012 parliamentary elections (D'Anieri, 2019).

attract voters from outside the party's core regions. Moreover, the possibility that parties could be agents of federal practices is made less likely by the fact that regional branches only play a minor role.

In addition to being short-lived, the political parties' institutional clout is weakened by high voter volatility. Moreover, all parties are strongly permeated with patronalism and clientelism. They are personalized, and with a possible exception for Tymoshenko's Fatherland party, they have developed little in terms of active membership bases. Kudelia and Kuzio (2015, 252) analyze these parties 'primarily as coordination devices intended to encourage cooperation between political and business elites seeking access to or continued control over the government's policy-making and distribution of private goods'. This applies particularly for the parties in the East, largely facilitated by the economic and industrial strength of Eastern Ukraine. Here, former political and enterprise nomenklatura and the financial and economic conglomerates and oligarchs became symbiotic and formed the Party of Regions. Attempts by the West-leaning president Viktor Iushchenko to halt the Party of Regions' oligarchic clientele could easily be framed as a nationalist attack on Russian speakers in the East aimed at attracting a wider electorate.

The two larger West-leaning, national democratic parties—Viktor Iushchenko's Our Ukraina and Juliia Tymoshenko's Fatherland—have a less clear-cut regional basis for their oligarch support and an overall less solid composition of their networks (Kudelia & Kuzio, 2015), but have had a clear regional profile as to their voter base. The same holds true for Petro Poroshenko's party. These parties are even more personalistic and less based on the composition of its networks and network members' strengths.

Ukrainian parties have weakly elaborated policy positions and hardly distinguishable programs. However, as Ukraine is politically more pluralist than other large post-Soviet states, parties include some programmatic positions and also undertake some attempts to balance regional interests. Among the distinguishing positions are the stances on mono- versus bilingual models for the country and Euro-Atlantic versus post-Soviet integration. Such issues encourage regionalist profiles of political parties, whereas the downplayed left-right issues on distribution of wealth and influence or liberal-conservative issues on traditional versus modern lifestyles and family patterns would cut across all regions.

Not all top politicians automatically belong to one or the other regional poles. Poroshenko, for instance, joined Iushchenko only after having failed to become the leader of the Party of Regions (Kudelia & Kuzio, 2015). Also, as we have seen above, regional identities among Ukrainians are more like a continuum than a Galicia-Donbass dichotomy, which makes vote-maximizing parties with a regional basis likely to moderate their regional profile. Some of the political dynamics resulting from the rivalries and balancing between East and West have changed as a result of Russia's annexation of Crimea and the establishment of the two Donbass proto-republics. Both D'Anieri (2019) and Dreyfus and Jeangène Vilmer (2019) argue that the loss of voters in these regions changes the political landscape significantly because regional balancing is now less needed than before. The forces pushing for closer ties with Russia and an official status for the Russian language are weakened, while the 'Ukrainification' forces are strengthened, even though they have not overcome their internal rivalries.

Informality and (Non-)federal Constitutional Politics

Cooperativeness of political elites, also described as federal 'comity' (Burgess, 2017), is a highly important prerequisite of federalism. It is not hyperbolic to state that not even rudiments of this principle are existent in Ukraine. Throughout the post-Soviet period, the Ukrainian Constitution has remained a battleground. Short-time calculi of antagonistic elites have taken priority over fundamental ideas on how to develop a proper constitution (Hale, 2015, 325–342; Fisun, 2016, 106). The center-regional relations have always been a sideshow of struggles between the two branches of government (Fisun, 2016, 110).[4] Patronal networks, including practices like vote buying, revolved around central formal institutions like the president and the premier (Matsiyevsky, 2018, 352–354; Hale, 2015, 332) and stretched upon the regional and local levels. Until today these networks link to 'oligarchs', businesspeople with resources acquired during post-Soviet privatization and who are able to capture the state

[4] In 2004, after the Orange Revolution, a constitutional amendment significantly lowered the power of the president (V. Iushchenko), who experienced serious confrontation with the Verchovna Rada under the premierships of Tymoshchenko and Ianukovich (Pleines, 2016, p. 111; Torikai, 2019, p. 13). After V. Ianukovich (2010-14) had been elected president, the presidential-parliamentary system of the Kuchma period (1994-2005) was reinstalled. In the course of the Euromaidan in 2014, after V. Ianukovich had been ousted, the presidential system was finally discredited (Kuzio, 2018, p. 344), and the constitutional reforms of 2004 were re-enacted.

(Pleines, 2016, 107; Kuzio, 2016). Up to the Orange Revolution of 2004, three regionally based clans existed: one represented in Dnipro, the other in Donetsk, while the third network was located in Kiev. The incumbents' attempts to secure their authority in the regions have differed according to the party structure and the variant of the system of government in place (Torikai, 2019). The formation and configurations of these informal networks changed several times, but most oligarchs survived despite frequent government turnovers (Matsiyevsky, 2018). Although these patronal networks have regional roots, one can assume that they do not create federal practices in the sense of representing territorial interests informally at the central level. The *appointment of governors* and the issue of a bicameral parliament are textbook examples illustrating the instrumental manner in which actors cope with potentially federal institutions. Ukrainian governors are not directly elected by the citizens or by a regional parliament. The Constitution rather empowers the president to appoint and dismiss the regional governors, a mode which substantially counteracts the federal spirit and the principle of self-rule. Governors are expected to mobilize voters in favor of the president's camp and to secure his or her victory in elections. Correspondingly, electoral performance has been the primary determinant of the governors' fates (Torikai, 2019, 8). The reshuffling of governors was a widespread practice after each government turnover, and as a rule, more or less all governors were replaced by the respective successor. This enables the president to award his satellites with lucrative positions and to intervene in local autonomy. It is important to note that the incumbent president has to repay the governors' loyalty. For this reason, all presidents aimed to strengthen the affiliation of the governors and tried to avoid agency loss by establishing a hegemonic party. Control over the 'regional barons' is essential for them, as the following examples reveal. Iushchenko's lack of authority in the central government, which was weakened by the parliament that nominated the prime minister after 2004 (Hale, 2015, 326–327), forced him to 'appoint some governors based on considerations other than his own self-interest' (Torikai, 2019, 13). His position remained too fragile to install all his satellites in the east or in the central parts of Ukraine. The organizational capacity of Ianukovich's 'Party of Regions', by contrast, was strong enough to 'ensure the continuous rent distributions to its members' and to absorb and control the regional elites. Nonetheless, he failed to impose a 'Donbas political machine' on the entire country (Kuzio, 2018, 343), and was forced to make some concessions to the elites in the West (Torikai, 2019, 14). His administrative network finally collapsed in the course of the 2014 protests. Taking office in 2014, Poroshenko dismissed 22 out of 24 heads of regional state administrations and replaced them mainly by members of the Vinnytskyi clan (from his native region; Matsiyevsky, 2018, 354). The installation of 'prefects' who are destined to exert presidential control over the decentralized territories (see above) may increase the president's opportunities to establish verticalized patterns of patronal politics. Some presidents tried to increase their power by establishing a *bicameral parliament*. In 2003 and 2009 Kuchma and Iushchenko aimed at drafting corresponding constitutional reforms. Significantly, the second chamber was neither planned as a body representing strong and independent regions, nor was it seen as an institution to accommodate the diverse ethno-linguistic groups. It was rather perceived as a tool to enlarge the president's power base and to counter the premiers' increasing influence within the dual executive. The debate about the second chamber illustrates that it was at no time guided by the idea to create a 'federal' institution. Actors' priorities were purely instrumental. Similar to Kuchma, Iushchenko intended to establish the senate (upper house) as his support base and to grant former presidents a life-long membership (Fisun, 2016, 113, 115). Especially eastern Ukraine feared that the equal representation of all regions (*oblasti*) in a senate could withdraw national policymaking away from the East (D'Anieri et al., 2018).

Concluding Discussion

At the outset of this chapter, it was argued that Ukraine may serve as a crucial case in comparative research to understand why there is no federalism, although the territorial setup is underlain by some kind of a federal society. At present the dynamics of territorial politics are not federal in Ukraine, and there is no evidence indicating a truly federal model in the near future. Several empirical observations corroborate this view. The above analysis has shown that identities in Ukraine are more blurred than often described. By now, they are geared toward Ukrainian citizenship as the main identity marker, even though linguistic and ethnic diversity is still relevant. This finding implies that the 'federal society' argument matches the macro-societal context partially at best. As regional diversity is not clearly cut but blurred, a federal model would probably fail to accommodate Ukraine's ethno-linguistic groups or even exacerbate given tensions. Moreover, different from Russia, which inherited a federal structure from the Soviet past, Ukraine lacks similar path-dependent institutions, which is why corresponding arguments of historical institutionalism do not match this case. One should also bear in mind that federalism is a highly securitized issue in the Ukrainian constitutional debate. Hence, the concept stirs the fear that particularly Russia—as a neighboring kin-state in the East—would be able to institutionalize its influence on regional leaders and fuel centrifugal developments (Brubaker, 1996, 55–69). In this respect the objective of 'holding-together' (Stepan, 1999, 22) Ukraine's statehood suggests *not* a federal but a unitary, albeit decentralized, polity. At this point one might demur that if federalism is not conceptualized as a static order but as a dynamic process, it seems possible that a decentralized setup may gradually change into a federal one over time. In this view a country may move on a continuum ranging between the poles of merely to full-fledged federal states. Even then, however, currently nothing suggests that the unitary system of Ukraine will transform into a federal one in the near future. To substantiate this finding federal practices which might herald federalization were investigated. In comparative research the party system is considered the most important factor. Ukrainian parties, however, are weakly rooted in society. They do not peripheralize politics, but operate nationwide. Informal institutions, like patronalism and clientelism that are widespread in Ukraine, do not have a federal 'flavor' either, but are by no means conducive to represent territorial interests at the central level. The examples given above revealed that 'comity' and elite cooperativeness, which are deemed necessary ingredients to make federalism work, are not engrained in Ukraine's constitutional politics; elites appreciate proto-federal institutions, like a second chamber or the function of the governor, mainly as an instrument to extend their patronal networks to the regions. Although consociational institutions might help to rehearse cooperative elite behavior, it seems most questionable whether federalism would be the adequate institutional choice to achieve that goal. Altogether, a federal model currently does not resonate with the preferred concept of Ukrainian statehood. Pressure to introduce asymmetrical responsibilities and widened regional autonomy for Luhansk and Donetsk as *de facto states* (Lachowski, 2020, 146) rather comes from outside (see the Steinmeier Formula), as international initiatives aim to solve the violent conflict in Donbass. This indicates that it is not impossible that single, albeit imposed, proto-federal elements emerge. The Russian invasion of Ukraine in February 2022, which was initiated a few days before the submission of this chapter to the printshop, however, changed the outlined original conditions. Most likely post-war Ukraine will see regional conflict lines and Russian entry points that differ from the ones presented in this chapter. Therefore, a possible future debate on federal elements in Ukraine's territorial make-up will probably take place within new parameters.

References

Aasland, A., & Lyksa, O. (2016). Local democracy in Ukrainian cities: Civic participation and responsiveness of local authorities. *Post-Soviet Affairs, 32*(2), 152–175.

Aasland, A., Deineko, O., Filippova, O., & Kropp, S. (2021). Citizens' perspectives: reform and social cohesion in Ukraine's border regions. In A. Aasland & S. Kropp (Eds.), The accommodation of regional and ethno-cultural diversity in Ukraine (pp. 237–272). Palgrave Macmillan.

Bader, M. (2020). Decentralization and the risk of local elite capture in Ukraine. In H. Shelest & M. Rabynovich (Eds.), *Decentralization, regional diversity, and conflict* (pp. 259–282). Palgrave Macmillan.

Barbieri, J. (2020). The dark side of decentralization reform in Ukraine. Deterring or facilitating Russia-sponsored separatism? In H. Shelest & M. Rabynovich (Eds.), *Decentralization, regional diversity, and conflict* (pp. 211–256). Palgrave Macmillan.

Brubaker, R. (1996). *Nationalism reframed: Nationhood and the national question in the new Europe.* CUP.

Burgess, M. (2017). "Federalism and federation: Putting the record straight", In *50 Shades of Federalism.* Retrieved April, 4, 2020, from http://50shadesoffederalism.com/theory/federalism-federation-putting-record-straight/.

Chaisty, P., & Whitefield, S. (2018). Critical election of frozen cleavages? How voters chose parties in the 2014 Ukrainian parliamentary election. *Electoral Studies, 56*, 158–169.

D'Anieri, P. (2019). Gerrymandering Ukraine? Electoral consequences of occupation. *East European Politics and Societies and Cultures, 33*(1), 89–108.

D'Anieri, P., Kravchuk, R., & Kuzio, T. (2018). *Politics and society in Ukraine.* Routledge.

Dreyfus, E., & Jeangène Vilmer, J.-B. (2019). A people-oriented peace formula for the Donbass. *The Washington Quarterly, 42*(2), 115–132.

Erk, J., & Koning, E. (2010). New structuralism and institutional change: Federalism between centralization and decentralization. *Comparative Political Studies, 43*(3), 353–378.

Erk, J. (2007). *Explaining federalism. State, society and congruence in Austria, Belgium, Canada, Germany and Switzerland.* Routledge.

Erk, J. (2017). 'Nations, nationalities, and peoples': The ethnopolitics of ethnofederalism in Ethiopia. *Ethnopolitics*, *16*(3), 219–231.

Fisun, O. (2016). Ukrainian constitutional politics: Neopatrimonialism, rent-seeking, and regime change. In H. Hale & R. Orttung (Eds.), *Beyond the Euromaidan: Comparative perspectives on advancing reform in Ukraine* (pp. 105–123). Stanford University Press.

Freedom House. (2018). *Nations in transit 2018: Ukraine country report*. Retrieved July 3, 2019, from https://freedomhouse.org/report/nations-transit/2018/ukraine.

Gerring, J. (2008). Case selection for case study analysis: Qualitative and quantitative techniques. In J. Box-Steffensmeier, H. E. Brady, & D. Collier (Eds.), *Oxford handbook of political methodology* (pp. 645–684). Oxford University Press.

Hale, H. E. (2015). *Patronal politics: Eurasian regime dynamics in comparative perspective*. Cambridge University Press.

Hale, H. E., & Orttung, R. W. (Eds.). (2016). *Beyond the Euromaidan. Comparative perspectives on advancing reform in Ukraine*. Stanford University Press.

Helmke, G., & Levitsky, S. (2004). Informal institutions and comparative politics: A research agenda. *Perspectives on Politics*, *2*(4), 725–740.

Holm-Hansen, J., & Kropp, S. (2021). The regional diversity in Ukraine: Can federalization be achieved? In A. Aasland & S. Kropp (Eds.), *The accommodation of regional and ethno-cultural diversity in Ukraine* (pp. 23–51). Palgrave Macmillan.

Kudelia, S., & Kuzio, T. (2015). Nothing personal: Explaining the rise and decline of political machines in Ukraine. *Post-Soviet Affairs*, *31*(3), 250–278.

Kuzio, T. (2016). Oligarchs, the partial reform equilibrium, and the Euromaidan Revolution. In H. E. Hale & R. W. Orttung (Eds.), *Beyond the Euromaidan. Comparative perspectives on advancing reform in Ukraine* (pp. 181–203). Stanford University Press.

Kuzio, T. (2018). Russian and Ukrainian elites: A comparative study of different identities and alternative transitions. *Communist and Post-Communist Studies*, *51*, 337–347.

Lachowski, T. (2020). The reintegration of Donbas into Ukraine exercised through the means of post-violence reconstruction and accountability. An international law perspective. In H. Shelest & M. Rabynovich (Eds.), *Decentralization, regional diversity, and conflict. The case of Ukraine* (pp. 145–183). Palgrave Macmillan.

Livingston, W. S. (1952). A note on the nature of federalism. *Political Science Quarterly*, *67*, 81–95.

March, J. G., & Olsen, J. P. (2004). *The Logic of Appropriateness*, ARENA Working Papers 9 (9), Oslo.

Marlin, M. (2016). Concepts of 'decentralization' and 'federalization' in Ukraine: Political signifiers or distinct constitutional approaches for devolutionary federalism? *Nationalism and Ethnic Politics, 22*(3), 278–299.

Matsiyevsky, Y. (2015). "Breaking out of an institutional trap. Ukraine's survival and the role of the West", *PONARS Eurasia Memo*, No. 406.

Matsiyevsky, Y. (2018). Revolution without regime change: The evidence from the post-Euromaidan Ukraine. *Communist and Post-Communist Studies, 51*, 349–359.

Onuch, O., & Hale, H. E. (2018). Capturing ethnicity: The case of Ukraine. *Post-Soviet Affairs, 34*(2-3), 84–106.

Peters, G. B. (2005). *Institutional theory in political science. The new Institutionalism* (2nd ed.). Continuum.

Pleines, H. (2016). Oligarchs and politics in Ukraine. *Demokratizatsiya: The Journal of Post-Soviet Demokratization, 24*(1), 105–127.

Pop-Eleches, G., & Robertson G. B. (2018). "Identity and political preferences in Ukraine–before and after the Euromaidan", *Post-Soviet Affairs* (online).

Romanova, V., & Umland, A. (2019a). *Ukraine's decentralization reforms since 2014—Initial achievements and future challenges*, Research Paper, The Royal Institute of International Affairs.

Romanova, V., & Umland, A. (2019b). Decentralising Ukraine: Geopolitical implications. *Survival, 61*(5), 99–112.

Sakwa, R. (2010). The dual state in Russia. *Post-Soviet Affairs, 26*(3), 185–206.

Sasse, G., & Lackner, A. (2018). "Public perceptions in flux. Identities, war, and transnational linkages in Ukraine, 2017-2018", *ZOiS Report* 4/2018, Berlin.

Shelest, H., & Rabynovich, M. (2020). *Decentralization, regional diversity, and conflict. The case of Ukraine.* Palgrave Macmillan.

Stein, M. (1968). Federal political systems and federal societies. *World Politics, 20*(4), 721–727.

Stepan, A. (1999). Federalism and democracy: Beyond the U.S. model. *Journal of Democracy, 10*(4), 19–34.

Torikai, M. (2019). The electoral logic of governor rotations in Ukraine: Rulers' authority, party strength, and regional polarization. *Post-Soviet Affairs*, 258–276.

Watts, R. L. (1998). Federalism, federal political systems, and federations. *Annual Review of Political Science, 1*, 117–137.

Way, L. (2016). Democracy and governance in divided societies. In H. E. Hale & R. W. Orttung (Eds.), *Beyond the Euromaidan. Comparative perspectives on advancing reform in Ukraine* (pp. 41–60). Stanford University Press.

Wolczuk, K. (2002). Catching up with 'Europe'? Constitutional debates on the territorial-administrative model in independent Ukraine. *Regional & Federal Studies, 12*(2), 65–88.

CHAPTER 6

The Emergence of Complex Federal Political Systems in the Western Balkans

Soeren Keil

I would like to thank Jens Woelk for helpful discussions on the first structure for this chapter.

S. Keil (✉)
Institute of Federalism, University of Fribourg, Fribourg, Switzerland
e-mail: Soeren.keil@unifr.ch

© The Author(s), under exclusive license to Springer Nature
Switzerland AG 2022
S. Keil, S. Kropp (eds.), *Emerging Federal Structures in the Post-Cold War Era*, Federalism and Internal Conflicts,
https://doi.org/10.1007/978-3-030-93669-3_6

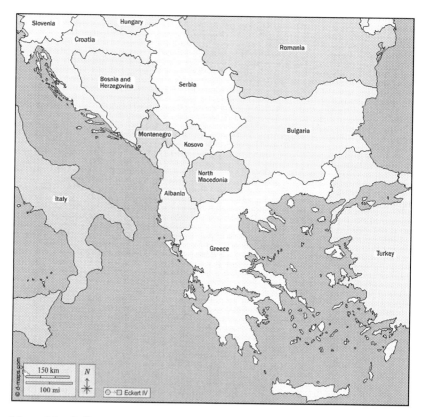

Map 6.1 Balkans region. *Source*: https://d-maps.com/carte.php?num_car=69052&lang=en

Introduction

The Western Balkans have rightly been identified as a laboratory of power-sharing and territorial autonomy (Bieber, 2005; Bieber & Keil, 2009; Keil, 2015; Hulsey & Keil, 2021). What can be seen when looking at the states that emerged from the breakup of Socialist Yugoslavia is a complex net of consociational power-sharing practices mixed with different forms of territorial autonomy,[1] including full federalization (in Bosnia and

---

[1] I use the terms territorial autonomy and federal political system interchangeably. I am aware that only Bosnia is a full-fledged federal system amongst the case studies, but North

Herzegovina, BiH) and different forms of regional and local autonomy (in North Macedonia and Kosovo). It is in light of this complexity and institutional diversity that this contribution aims to compare and contrast three different forms of territorial autonomy in the countries mentioned above. What will become visible is a multifaceted set of institutional provisions that have been applied in the case studies. The mechanisms often link territorial autonomy with group power-sharing through consociationalism, as has been applied most strictly in Bosnia, but can also be found in North Macedonia and Kosovo. While Bosnia is often considered a paralyzed state in which a high degree of decentralization (through full federalization) mixed with ethnic power-sharing has disabled any effective governance at the central level, Kosovo's key challenge is one of statehood. The country remains contested by Serbia (and its allies), and Kosovo Serbs interact with Kosovar institutions only sporadically, making an effective decentralization impossible to implement. North Macedonia is often seen as the success story in the Balkans, as a country where both ethnic power-sharing and local decentralization have not only defused ethnic tensions after 2000 but also opened the door for a re-democratization after 2017, following a period of authoritarian backsliding. What is more, in Bosnia, North Macedonia and Kosovo, autonomy and power-sharing institutions were preceded by interethnic violence, as seen in Bosnia's and Kosovo's full-blown civil conflicts between members of different ethnic groups. These conflicts, and their solution through international involvement, provided the background and the starting point of the power-sharing and territorial autonomy provisions we find in the three countries. This is not to say that these systems have not evolved over time, but it is important to highlight that the peacemaking aim of these provisions cannot be overstated—and has, until today, set in motion certain path dependencies which the three countries and their political elites have found hard to overcome. These include increased ethnic distance, the reduction of political competition to interethnic issues and an ongoing conflictual rhetoric between the members of different groups.

Macedonia, and Kosovo include key features of federal political systems, including substantial elements of regional and local self-rule, and forms of shared-rule in which minority communities and territorial units can influence decision in central state. institutions. For the use of terms, we follow the wider frameworks on autonomy, as outlined by Lapidoth (1997) and Watts (2008).

The chapter proceeds in three main steps. The first part assesses the evolution of the territorial autonomy and power-sharing regimes in the three case studies, looking particularly at similarities and differences. As already mentioned, international actors played a key role in the installment of interethnic power-sharing (and territorial autonomy) in Bosnia, North Macedonia and Kosovo—and this legacy plays an important role in the functioning and problems of these systems today.

What is more, as will be discussed in Part 2 of the chapter, there is a huge variety of functionality and operationality in the three autonomy regimes in the three Western Balkan case studies under examination. When comparing the systems in Bosnia, North Macedonia and Kosovo, substantial differences in functionality and effectiveness can be observed.

Finally, Part 3 of this contribution looks at the remaining challenges for all three case studies. Europeanization—referring to the process of integration into the European Union (EU) and the adaptation of relevant EU laws in the process—is the biggest challenge for all three case studies, as they have all committed to EU integration as their main foreign policy objective (Keil & Stahl, 2015). However, EU integration is not the only challenge these countries face. The territorial status of Kosovo is still not finalized, Bosnia's borders are continuously challenged from the inside (and occasionally from the outside as well), and North Macedonia's slow progress toward EU membership has also increased tensions within the country. While the territorial autonomy regimes in the Western Balkans might be seen as laboratories, we should not make the mistake and see them as static and inflexible political arrangements. These emerging federal systems very much evolve, change, move and develop. This does not mean that we can always identify a clear path in the development of the different countries and their federal political systems, but it does provide clear indication that Carl Friedrich's (1968) assumption that federal and decentralized systems evolve over time, and federalism and territorial autonomy should be seen as processes rather than fixed constitutional frameworks, holds very true when looking at and evaluating the emerging federal political systems in the Western Balkan states.

The Origins of New Models in the Western Balkans

The origins of the three models of territorial autonomy in Bosnia, North Macedonia and Kosovo are complex and go beyond traditional discussions on the origins of federal state. While more traditional scholarship on the origins of federal systems focuses on coming-together and holding-together federal systems (Stepan, 1999) or the process of statebuilding and economic development in a country (Ziblatt, 2006), in the case of the Western Balkans, imposition and external involvement played a major role in the constitutional implementation of different forms of territorial autonomy (Bermeo, 2002). In a further conceptual development of William Riker's initial assumptions that economic integration and external threats are key preconditions for the evolution of a federal political system (Riker, 1964), it can be argued that both the legacy of the Socialist system and political framework provided by Yugoslavia, and the experience of war and intergroup conflict were major factors in the evolution and eventual implementation of territorial autonomy and ethnic power-sharing provisions (Bunce, 1999; Ramet, 2006; Hulsey & Keil, 2021).

When looking at the origins of the different autonomy regimes in the Western Balkans, it is pivotal to focus on the historical legacy of the strange mixture of Socialist dictatorship and ethnic power-sharing, coupled with increased territorial autonomy for its different parts, that has developed in Socialist Yugoslavia after the Second World War. In what Sabrina Ramet (1992) labeled a "balance of power" system after the constitutional changes of 1974, a process of both decentralization toward the Republics (Slovenia, Croatia, Bosnia and Herzegovina, Serbia, Macedonia and Montenegro) and the two autonomous provinces (Kosovo and Vojvodina), and an increased requirement for leaders representing the different ethnic communities of the Republics and autonomous communities to cooperate and reach decisions by consensus can be observed (Djordjević, 1975; Denitch, 1997; Lampe, 2000). This is not to say that Yugoslavia over time became either more democratic or less contested; indeed, Aleksa Djilas' (1991) claim that Yugoslavia is better considered the "Contested Country"—where contestation is based not only on ideological grounds, as was common in most of Eastern Europe after the Second World War, but also on ethnopolitical groups because of the different priorities of the various ethnic communities and their elites in the country—remained a key feature of Socialist Yugoslavia until its final dissolution in 1992.

Yugoslavia employed a system of ethnic federalism within an authoritarian framework—after 1974, the Republics and autonomous provinces had a high degree of autonomy and self-governance, while in the central institutions in Belgrade, unanimity and cooperation between the different (Communist) representatives from each of the Republics and autonomous provinces was the norm after the death of long-term dictator Josip Broz Tito in 1980.

Most contemporary scholarship on federalism assumes that a functional federal political system requires basic democratic qualities, namely the rule of law, free and fair elections and the protection of human and fundamental rights (Watts, 2008; Burgess, 2006; Hueglin & Fenna, 2006; Burgess & Gagnon, 2010). This claim may be true, and deserves further examination in the three case studies later in this chapter—however, when looking at Yugoslavia, the absence of functional democracy clearly limited the nature of federalism as a form of self-rule and shared rule at the same time. It did, nevertheless, not prevent the emergence of important federal-like dynamics between the Republics and autonomous provinces and the center in Belgrade. What is more, despite its one-party political framework, there is a clear development toward asymmetry and ethnification visible; in other words, after 1985 political elites saw themselves less as representatives of the Communist League of Yugoslavia and much more as representatives of their specific ethnic group (Ramet, 1992). Furthermore, asymmetric arrangements and growing tensions between the center and the periphery help to explain the beginning process of the dissolution of the country, but they also allow for wider observations into the operations and inability of a decentralized power-sharing system that is based on one-party rule (Grgic, 2017). One should not forget that in the breakup of Yugoslavia, it was the Yugoslav League of Communists that collapsed first, further paralyzing the already struggling central state institutions in the process before the state began to disintegrate with the independence declarations of Slovenia and Croatia in June 1991 (Silber & Little, 1996). The legacy of Yugoslavia, namely, the accommodating of ethnic diversity through the provision of (increasing) territorial autonomy, the provision of asymmetric autonomy for different groups, and the focus on power-sharing between ethnic elites, would remain with the new political elites in the post-Yugoslav states, many of which were politically socialized in the former Yugoslavia.

Yet, it is not only the operation of Yugoslavia, and its reliance on autonomy and power-sharing as tools of holding this multinational country together, that substantially impacted the territorial autonomy regimes in Bosnia, North Macedonia and Kosovo. In fact, the 47 years (1945–1992) of membership in an ever-more decentralizing Yugoslavia were as important for the countries under examination as the period from 1992 to 1999, in which the state, initially formed as the Kingdom of Serbs, Croats and

Slovenes in 1918, fell apart and resulted, by 2008, in seven post-Yugoslav states (in addition to the six former Republics, Slovenia, Croatia, Bosnia and Herzegovina, Serbia, Montenegro and (North) Macedonia, Kosovo unilaterally declared its independence from Serbia in February 2008). When Yugoslavia dissolved, violence was a key element in the majority of Republics and territories aspiring for independence, although the degree of interethnic conflict differed substantially. While Bosnia suffered 3.5 years of full-blown civil conflict with approximately 100,000 deaths (Burg & Shoup, 2000), Croatia witnessed conflict in 1992 and early 1993 before fighting resumed in 1995, when Croatian government forces retook territory held by Serb rebels (Tanner, 2010). Fighting in Kosovo initially erupted in the early 1990s as well, but with international attention focused on Bosnia, it was only the widespread ethnic cleansing practiced by Serb forces in 1999 that resulted in NATO military actions (Bieber & Daskalovski, 2003). In North Macedonia, tensions have remained high between the Macedonian majority and the Albanian minority, exploding in 2000 and 2001, first in the capital Skopje and later in other parts of the country. However, swift action by international actors, in particular the EU and the US, prevented the outbreak of a full-blown civil conflict in the country (Koneska, 2014).

Despite a number of differences between the scale, timing and intensity of the fighting in the different Western Balkan countries, there are a number of similarities, which had an important impact on the evolution of territorial autonomy and power-sharing regimes in the aftermath of these conflicts. First, for most observers, and certainly for key international actors, all these conflicts, whether in Bosnia, in Croatia or later in Kosovo and Macedonia, were seen as ethnic conflicts between different groups with contradicting agendas and similar claims to the same territory which they called their natural homeland. While this strict focus on ethnic conflicts has been widely criticized (Gagnon, 2004; Piacentini, 2020), as it both undermines the complexity of identities (and their shifting nature) and relieves political elites from their responsibility as social engineers of identity and conflict, it has had a major impact on the solutions to these conflicts, which are all focused on accommodating different groups and ensuring their buy-in and participation in the state. Second, certainly in Bosnia and Kosovo, and to a lesser extent also in Macedonia, the legacy of conflict is visible in the geographic population distribution. In other words, ethnic cleansing campaigns and territorial ethnic homogenization were key elements of the conflicts, and indeed, continued even after they were officially concluded, as the violence against Serbs in Kosovo in 2004 demonstrates. The result of all of this are population settlement patterns, which make the use of territorial autonomy much easier as a solution for substantial group autonomy and protection. The introduction of a federal political system based on territorial autonomy for specific groups is therefore a legacy of violence, war crimes and ethnic conflict—a legacy that has substantially undermined the legitimacy of these arrangements. Third, as will be demonstrated below, the legacy of conflict and violence in our case studies has also ensured that key groups were included in autonomy and power-sharing provisions and were given substantial access to major state institutions through proportional representation, veto rights and reserved seats. This in turn, however, has also meant that other groups remain marginalized. The territorial autonomy and power-sharing provisions implemented in the cases under examination have provided accommodation for some groups, but have left out other groups and, as can be seen in Bosnia, have indeed disenfranchised certain smaller groups (Agarin et al., 2018).

One cannot understand the evolution of the territorial autonomy provisions in the Western Balkans without discussing the role of major international actors, both in the direct ending of violent conflict and in the process of state-rebuilding and democratization after the end of violence (Woodward, 1995; Keil, 2014). In these three case studies, international actors intervened diplomatically, and militarily, to end the ongoing conflicts before establishing long-term military and civilian missions in order to support these countries in their transition to functional democracy within a post-conflict setting.

The first of these interventions occurred in 1995 in Bosnia when NATO used its supreme air power to attack Bosnian Serb positions, while American leadership paved the way for the Dayton Peace Agreement (DPA) in late 1995 (Holbrooke, 1999), which includes in Annex IV the current Constitution of Bosnia and Herzegovina. NATO's intervention and American leadership in reaching a peace agreement had a major impact on Bosnia—not only did it provide the framework of a decentralized federal system that would be implemented in post-war Bosnia, but American leadership in years after 1995 would also push for major reforms in the country, from education to elections and security sector reform (Daalder, 2000; Coles, 2007; Kudlenko, 2017). After 1997, when the powers of the international High Representative were extended to include imposition of decisions and the dismissal of elected officials if they obstructed the peace agreement, a full-scale international statebuilding exercise was implemented in Bosnia. Key decisions, such as military reform and constitutional changes in the territorial units (called entities), symbolize a process of internationally imposed centralization in what was one of the most decentralized federal systems in the world after 1995 (Keil, 2013, 95–124). Since 2006, more emphasis has been paid to "local ownership," and the EU has become the major actor in the country; yet, the process toward the consolidation of what remains a very fragmented and unstable political system has since been mainly absent (Keil & Kudlenko, 2015).

In Kosovo it was also American leadership that resulted in NATO's military campaign against the forces of the Federal Republic of Yugoslavia (Serbia and Montenegro) in 1999. NATO's military action resulted in the establishment of a de facto international protectorate in Kosovo, where key international actors implemented autonomy provisions first through the provisions of the Constitutional Framework for Self-Governance in 2001, and later through the Ahtisaari Plan and the Constitution of Kosovo, which was implemented after the unilateral declaration of independence in February 2008 (Krasniqi, 2013; Skendaj, 2014).

Finally, in North Macedonia—the only Republic of Yugoslavia to come out of the dissolution processes in the 1990s without violent conflict—witnessed increased tensions between Macedonian government forces and Albanian paramilitaries in 2000 and 2001. While this did not result in large-scale conflict due to quick political interventions by leading American and European diplomats, it nevertheless laid the foundations of a new power-sharing agreement, which also included a commitment to decentralization—the Ohrid Framework Agreement (OFA) of August 2001 (Brunnbauer, 2002). The appointment of an EU Special Representative and the deployment of both NATO and EU military missions in the country further highlight the international nature of the conflict and the internationalized nature of the implementation of the OFA. What emerges, then, when looking at the reasons for these emerging federal systems in the three Western Balkan countries is a common thread. Ethno-nationalist tensions, often connected with interference by neighboring states, resulted in violence and required international intervention to pacify the countries. In the aftermath of intervention, international actors, first led by the US and later by the EU, also supported the post-conflict implementation of peace agreements, transitional frameworks and power-sharing systems in the three countries discussed above. These frameworks were meant to lay the foundation for peaceful intergroup relations in the first place, but they were also designed to ensure inclusion of different groups without highlighting minority rights per se, as specific groups were oftentimes excluded from these arrangements (as will be discussed below), and they were meant to support the countries' democratization and statebuilding (and strengthening) capacities as well. Territorial autonomy, which can be found in all three agreements, was a major tool of achieving this, but it was not the only tool. As will be discussed in the next section, the different forms of territorial autonomy that can be found in the Western Balkans have been accompanied by varying degrees of ethnic power-sharing provisions.

Implementing Territorial Autonomy

This section looks at the implementation of the different territorial autonomy regimes in the three case studies. While the three countries are different in the degree of territorial autonomy, as Bosnia is a federal system, while North Macedonia and Kosovo have implemented local autonomy, they also share a number of important features, most notably the link of territorial autonomy with elite power-sharing in the center on the one side, and the involvement of international actors in the setup and implementation of the post-war institutional arrangements on the other side.

Bosnia and Herzegovina

Bosnia has received many labels in academic literature, from asymmetric confederation (Kasapovic, 2005, 3) to consociational confederation (Bose, 2002, 21), and from a decentralized state (Kurtćehajić & Ibrahimagić, 2007, 185) to a "loose multinational federation" (Bieber, 2006, 60–62). Keil (2013) specified Bosnia's federal features by highlighting its nature as a system based on imposed federalism, which has resulted in an internationally administered federation.

Bosnia's current federal system is the result of the 3.5-year-long war in the country between 1992 and 1995 and the subsequent intervention by Western powers under the leadership of the US. Because war and international intervention framed Bosnia's constitutional discussions in the wake of peace negotiations in 1994 and 1995, it is no surprise that the result remains heavily contested in the country. For some, the Dayton Peace Agreement, which ended the war and included Bosnia's current Constitution, only froze the conflict lines of 1995 by manifesting the dominance of ethnic engineers of Bosnia's population (Perry, 2019), while for others it laid the foundations for a complex political system that has evolved over time (Bieber, 2006; Keil, 2013).

In the Constitution of 1995, Bosnia is not described as a federal country, unlike, for example, the designation of a democratic state. Instead, Article 1.3 states:

> Bosnia and Herzegovina shall consist of the two Entities, the Federation of Bosnia and Herzegovina and the Republika Srpska. (hereinafter "the Entities")

However, Article 1.3 only allows for the conclusion that Bosnia is a federal state if it is read together with Article 3, which provides a limited list of competences for the institutions of Bosnia and Herzegovina—all other (competences not listed) powers remain with the entities. These include, beyond the typical federal unit competences of education, local infrastructure and economic development, equally surprising competences such as defense and all aspects of social welfare and taxation. Indeed, after 1995 Bosnia was one of the most decentralized states in the world—the central level only featured three ministries in 1996, thereby demonstrating the weakness of the center. This degree of decentralization explains why some authors refer to Bosnia as a confederation, highlighting the dominant role of the entities in the political system. Indeed, until today and despite a process of centralization between 1997 and 2006, the entities remain important actors, and the central level requires the cooperation from the entities for the system to work. That is not to say that the entities are organized in the same way—while the Republika Srpska (RS) is centralized and mainly inhabited by Bosnian Serbs, the Federation of Bosnia and Herzegovina (FBiH) is further decentralized, and powers are given to ten cantons, three with a Croat majority, five with a Bosniak majority and two mixed cantons. Certainly, ethnic criteria and homogeneity of territory play a key role in Bosnia's federal system, which is the direct result of substantial population movements and ethnic cleansing during and shortly after the war in the country (Map 6.2).

The decentralized and ethnic territorial organization has been mixed with a complex power-sharing system, which requires Bosniak, Serb and Croat elites to work together. Literally all institutions at the center require cooperation of elites from parties representing the three "constituent peoples," while both central and entity institutions have important veto

Map 6.2 Bosnia and Herzegovina, territorial and ethnic organization. *Source*: https://reliefweb.int/map/bosnia-and-herzegovina/federation-bosnia-and-herzegovina

powers (Bahtic-Kunrath, 2011; Hulsey & Keil, 2021). The power-sharing system in Bosnia links territorial criteria (e.g., for the composition of the House of Representatives and the Constitutional Court) with ethnic criteria (e.g., for the composition of the House of Peoples and the Bosnian Presidency). However, these ethnic criteria have been declared as discriminatory by the European Court of Human Rights, as they are seen to exclude those that do not identify as Bosniak, Serb or Croat (European Court of Human Rights, 2009). Bosnia was ordered by the Court to change its Constitution to remove the discriminatory passages, but despite a lot of international pressure, this constitutional revision has not taken place until today. Bosnia remains a classical example of a power-sharing system in which non-majoritarian groups such as Roma, Jews and those that refuse to identify as Bosniaks, Serbs and Croats are excluded from important offices in the country, and they face discrimination both in the political and in the social and economic spheres (Agarin, 2020).

What is more, in Bosnia we can observe the evolution of a variety of informal and clientelistic networks. Kapidzic (2019) has highlighted how ethnic parties have been able to establish their own networks at entity and cantonal levels, including important control over publicly owned businesses, private businesses (through licenses and financial support) and through financial support (including public-private partnerships). While clientelism and state capture has been more visible at the central level in North Macedonia and Kosovo (Keil, 2018), Bosnia's real decision-making powers and financial autonomy can be found at the entity and cantonal level, and this is where state capture can be observed. As Dzankic (2018) has pointed out, the fact that Bosnia, Kosovo and North Macedonia are contested states, in which differing nation-building projects (and state-building projects) are going on at the same time, has also increased the space for clientelism and state capture.

Bosnia has undergone some important reforms since 1995. The number of central ministries has more than tripled, and the country today has an integrated military, a border force under the control of the center and a tax system, which provides direct income both for the center and at the local level, in addition to the dominance of the entities in taxation. Having said this, it is important to point out that the majority of these centralizing reforms took place between 1997 and 2006 as a result of international intervention through the Office of the High Representative (OHR). The OHR was created as part of the Dayton Peace Agreement in 1995 to oversee the civilian implementation of the peace agreement. Its powers were substantially expanded in 1997 when the High Representative was given the power to impose laws and dismiss Bosnian officials that obstruct the peace agreement. As a result, different High Representatives played a key role in political engineering, strengthening the central level in Bosnia at the expense of the entities and removing officials who were seen undermining the peace treaty or counteracting international statebuilding efforts in the country (Merdzanovic, 2019; Keil, 2020). Yet, despite this impressive international involvement in post-war reconstruction and international statebuilding, Bosnia remains a weak democracy, in which both the federal system and the state as a whole remain contested internally (by elites representing Bosnian Serbs and Croats particularly, but also by Bosniak elites) and sometimes also externally (as exemplified by Serbian elites who have claimed that if Kosovo can become independent from Serbia, then the RS should have a right to become independent from Bosnia). The strict power-sharing system mixed with a high degree of decentralization have ensured that ethnic parties have dominated Bosnian post-war politics with completely diametrically opposed agendas and interests (Hulsey, 2015).

North Macedonia

When North Macedonia declared its independence as the Republic of Macedonia in 1992, it became the only post-Yugoslav state that managed to become independent without violent conflict in the 1990s. However, this does not mean that Macedonian independence was not contested. Internally, ethnic Albanians were worried about the new state and its commitment to becoming the nation-state of Macedonians, while externally neighboring Greece blocked recognition by the EU and the United Nations (UN) due to a name dispute, which would only be solved in 2018 when the Republic of Macedonia would adopt the name North Macedonia (Niemetz, 2020). The internal contestation after Macedonia's independence would be further fueled by developments in Kosovo, where Kosovo Liberation Army fighters were able to cross the border into Macedonia and supply arms to Albanian paramilitaries in Macedonia. This resulted in a series of extensive fighting between Macedonian security services and Albanian paramilitaries. The clashes ended in 2001, once US and European diplomats mediated talks between the Albanian and Macedonian elites in the country, paving the way for the Ohrid Framework Agreement (OFA).

Unlike the other case studies in this chapter, territorial autonomy played less of a role in Macedonia. In fact, the OFA in Article 1.2 clearly states that "Macedonia's sovereignty and territorial integrity, and the unitary character of the State are inviolable and must be preserved. There are no territorial solutions to ethnic issues" (OFA, 2001, Art. 1.2). This remarkable section can be explained by a number of factors. First, the conflict in Macedonia was not about territorial control and ethnic homogenization. Unlike the conflict in Bosnia, and in Kosovo as well, settlement patterns in Macedonia would not allow for ethnically homogenous territorial units, and this was not on the political agenda in 1992 or in 2001. Instead, Albanian guerrillas and many Albanian parties complained about the treatment of Albanians as second-class citizens. They were clearly discriminated against in the civil service and the security apparatus, and their language and culture were not recognized explicitly by the state. Hence, the OFA focuses substantially on cultural autonomy for the Albanians, including the right to use the Albanian language as an official language in areas where at least 25% of the populations speak Albanian, as well as promoting access for Albanians to the public administration and the different civil services. In many respects, aspects related to representation and recognition have been considered success stories of the OFA (Bieber, 2015).

However, the OFA's denial of territorial autonomy's contribution to peacebuilding is not reflected in the practical reality of implementation. In fact, Article 3 of the OFA (2001, Art. 3.1) provides a new decentralization framework, one which is focused on:

> [r]einforc[ing] the powers of elected local officials and enlarges substantially their competencies in conformity with the Constitution (as amended in accordance with Annex A) and the European Charter on Local Self-Government, and reflecting the principle of subsidiarity in effect in the European Union. Page 2 of 14 Enhanced competencies will relate principally to the areas of public services, urban and rural planning, environmental protection, local economic development, culture, local finances, education, social welfare, and health care. A law on financing of local self-government will be adopted to ensure an adequate system of financing to enable local governments to fulfill all of their responsibilities.

In addition, it was agreed that a new boundary commission would redraw local municipality borders and a finance commission would establish an updated financial framework for local municipalities. The implementation of these provisions had two major effects. First, it provided particularly Albanian majority municipalities with substantial policy autonomy and access to more public finances (Lyon, 2011). Second, while strengthening the autonomy of Albanians, it did not improve the situation of other minorities such as Roma, who are more dispersed and smaller in number. What is more, the provision of autonomy mainly for Albanians and the majority Macedonian ethnic group further deepened the divisions between the main communities in the country (Piacentini, 2019). Overall, therefore, it can be summarized that territorial autonomy in the case of Macedonia focused mainly on municipal autonomy. The decentralization reforms implemented after the OFA, and agreed upon through a referendum in 2004, have nevertheless been generally seen as a success story in public policy making and have contributed to the easing of tensions between Macedonians and Albanians (Koneska, 2014, 97–118).

What we can find, instead of strong territorial autonomy provisions in the case of Macedonia, is a focus on power-sharing in parliament and the executive. While informal power-sharing between Macedonian and Albanian parties was implemented after 1992, it became more enforced after 2001 because the requirements for certain parliamentary majorities in questions related to culture, education and decentralization make cooperation between parties representing different ethnic groups necessary. This focus on executive power-sharing (McEvoy, 2015) can also be found in Bosnia, and to a lesser extent in Kosovo. For Albanian elites, the conflict of 2000 and 2001 was not one over controlling a certain territory or getting their own territorial unit. Instead, the focus was on inclusion in the state, representation and Albanian state co-ownership. In this regard, consociational power-sharing (Lijphart, 1969, 1977, 2005), which focuses on representation in parliament and in government through formal and informal arrangements on grand coalitions, representation in parliament and veto rights based on, was the preferred method by American and European mediators during the Ohrid negotiations (Koneska, 2014, 59–78). Territorial autonomy is an extension of consociationalism, although its application to Macedonia is rather weak, especially when compared to Bosnia and Kosovo. While municipalities are important decision-makers in key local affairs, their financial framework and their overall functioning often depends on the support they get from the central government in Skopje. What is more, for most political elites, national politics, not local politics, is the primary arena of decision-making in Macedonia, which further weakens the role of municipalities in the wider constitutional setup of the country. While decentralization has been considered a success story of the Ohrid Framework Agreement, it was always meant to be limited to mainly cultural and linguistic autonomy for areas in which minorities form a majority. It was conceived in a relatively weak fashion, not least as a lesson learned from the Bosnian system, where substantial decentralization has continued to fuel ethnic separatism. It is also important that the conflict structure was different in Bosnia and Macedonia—Albanians raised arms because they wanted to be included into Macedonia and have their language and culture recognized, while Serbs and Croats fought in Bosnia to secede from the state.

Finally, with no input into central decision-making, and a continued dependence on financial contributions from the center, municipalities are not veto players in Macedonia's power-sharing system. Unlike Bosnia, where territorial units have a lot of autonomy, including their own fiscal affairs, often remaining autonomous and decoupled from central politics, Macedonian politics in the center trump any local politics, leaving little room for maneuver, including policy innovation at municipal level. A good example for this lack of local power is the development of the Skopje 2014 project, which was engineered by then Prime Minister Nikola Gruevski and included substantial investments in redeveloping the capital city against local resistance, particularly from Albanian municipal leaders (Vangelov, 2019).

Kosovo

Kosovo's commitment to territorial autonomy stems from its internationally supervised and mediated independence, which remains contested both internally by Kosovo Serbs and externally by Serbia, Russia and five EU member states. The first element of territorial autonomy in Kosovo dates back to the UN's Constitutional Framework for Provisional Self-Governance, which was implemented in 2001, two years after the UN Mission in Kosovo (UNMIK) took control over the former Serbian province. In the Framework, Article 1.2 and 1.3 (UNMIK, 2001, Arts. 1.2 and 1.3) are of particular interest, as they introduce the idea of territorial autonomy:

> 1.2 Kosovo is an undivided territory throughout which the Provisional Institutions of Self-Government established by this Constitutional Framework for Provisional Self-Government (Constitutional Framework) shall exercise their responsibilities.
> 1.3 Kosovo is composed of municipalities, which are the basic territorial units of local self-government with responsibilities as set forth in UNMIK legislation in force on local self-government and municipalities in Kosovo.

While municipalities were clearly identified as the units of local self-governance within the Constitutional Framework, their role remained undefined. Instead, the Framework only defined the role of Kosovo's provisional institutions (Chap. 5) and how they need to assist municipalities in the implementation of decisions and capacity building. This weakness was the result of several developments—for once, the Constitutional Framework was, as the name suggests, only a framework. It was not designed to replace a constitution or in any way imply that the UN was moving toward independent governance for Kosovo. Instead, it was framed as a series of constitutional provisions, which would enable the establishment of Kosovar institutions within a democratic framework under international supervision, while major powers and Kosovo and Serbian officials would start negotiations on the future of Kosovo. When Martti Ahtisaari, the UN Special Envoy, published his recommendations for the future of Kosovo, the protection of Serbs and other minorities in the territory was at the heart of several conditions for his recommendation of supervised independence; these included a commitment to multiethnic democracy and special protections for the different minorities in Kosovo (Ahtisaari, 2007). In his proposal, Ahtisaari (2007, Art. 8) was much more specific than the Constitutional Framework, when he laid out:

> With regard to local self-government in Kosovo, the Constitution shall inter alia provide that: 8.1 Kosovo shall be composed of municipalities, which shall enjoy a high-degree of local self-government and which encourage and provide for the active participation of all citizens in democratic life.
> 8.2 Competencies and boundaries of municipalities shall be set by law.
> 8.3 Municipalities have the right to local sources of revenue and the receipt of appropriate funding from central authorities.
> 8.4 Municipalities have the right to inter-municipal and cross-border cooperation in the areas of their own and extended competencies.

Annex III of the Ahtisaari Plan outlines the framework in more detail, highlighting the importance of decentralization as part of any status settlement and providing a long list of competences for municipalities, including public health, housing, environmental protection and education.

The Ahtisaari Plan would become the basis for Kosovo's independence, which was declared in February 2008 unilaterally, after international discussions on the future of the former Serbian province stalled and failed to reach a consensual agreement among the EU, the US and Russia. This set in motion the contentious post-independence development of Kosovo, which includes external contestation by Serbia, Russia and five EU member states (Spain, Cyprus, Greece, Slovakia and Romania). In addition, internal contestation, especially by the Kosovo Serb community, resulted in the de facto establishment of independent and autonomous institutional structures in Northern Kosovo, with heavy financial and logistical support from Serbia, thereby also undermining the territorial integrity of Kosovo (Krasniqi, 2015).

Nevertheless, the provisions of the Ahtisaari Plan became an integral part of Kosovo's post-independence Constitution, which has a strong commitment to decentralization and municipal autonomy. In particular, Article 12 highlights (Constitution of the Republic of Kosovo, 2008, Art. 12):

> 1. Municipalities are the basic territorial unit of local self-governance in the Republic of Kosovo.
> 2. The organization and powers of units of local self-government are provided by law.

Yet, despite this commitment to decentralization, and further guidance on local self-governance in Article 124 and in a later decentralization law, it has remained a contentious issue in Kosovo's politics. This is because on one side there is North Kosovo, which is controlled by local Kosovo Serbs and where Kosovo authorities have failed to establish and enforce the rule of Kosovo's institutions, despite several attempts over the years that have all ended in violence and fatalities. The ongoing direct contestation of Kosovo's territory has had substantial consequences for the dialogue between Kosovo's and Serbia's elites on a normalization of relations, as even an exchange of territory has at one point been discussed as a possible solution.

Second, decentralization has not been properly implemented because Kosovo, like Macedonia, remains relatively centralized. Municipalities, despite their status in the Constitution and their autonomy provided for in the decentralization law, remain dependent on transfers from the center, with their activities being limited by central interference and dominance of major policy areas, including those that are technically reserved for municipalities such as economic development, infrastructure and tourism.

Third, even where decentralization has been reasonably successful, as seen in those Serb municipalities located in central Kosovo, contestation remains. Despite constitutional provisions and support by Kosovo's elites for municipalities forming "Associations of Municipalities," ongoing arguments remain about what the legal status of this Association would be, especially if it brings Serb municipalities in central Kosovo together with municipalities in the North, which are currently outside of the legal control of Kosovo's institutions (Baliqi, 2018). The lack of implementation of the decentralization framework and its contestation by Serbs in the North therefore highlight key weaknesses in the territorial autonomy structures in Kosovo. Finally, it should also be added that Kosovo, like Macedonia, focuses more strongly on minority inclusion and representation in central institutions through power-sharing. Serbs and other minorities are guaranteed seats in Parliament, and they also have to be represented in the Kosovar government. This has in recent years resulted in the paradoxical situation that the Serb party, which acts as an ally to different Kosovar parties in the ruling competition, is the same party that controls the institutions in North Kosovo and contests the Kosovar state's authority there (Hulsey & Keil, 2021).

Conclusion: Challenges and Opportunities

The previous sections demonstrated how different forms of territorial autonomy have been used in the Western Balkan states to contribute to peacebuilding, support democratization and establish functional states in which minority rights would be respected and different groups would be integrated within the main institutions of the state. Yet, the success of these different strategies has been mixed at best, and fundamental challenges remain.

While all three countries remain peaceful and comply with basic democratic standards, they are by no means consolidated functional democracies (Hulsey & Keil, 2021). Indeed, authoritarian tendencies have been visible in all three countries (Bieber, 2019), and contestation to the integrity of the state has played a major role in establishing semi-authoritarian regimes in Macedonia (under Gruevski until 2017) and at entity level in Bosnia and Herzegovina (Dzankic, 2018; Kapidzic, 2019). Additionally, it is also important that Bosnia's and Kosovo's territorial integrity remains contested, and debates about secession continue both from internal actors and from outsiders. What is more, the complex power-sharing structures in all three countries have, at times, proven hard to make the systems work. While Bosnia has seen a near complete paralysis of its central institutions due to Croat demands for a third entity, ongoing tensions between Albanians and Serbs in Kosovo at times also limit the functionality of the power-sharing framework, although with less drastic consequences for the overall state. In Macedonia, there has been a re-democratization and consolidation of the system after the change of government in 2017, demonstrating that despite power-sharing and ethnic animosity, change is possible. The electoral victory of Vetëvendosje in Kosovo in early 2021 and the rise of Albin Kurti as a major politician in the country further highlight the potential for change. In Bosnia, we are yet to witness any fundamental changes as attempts to form alliances beyond the major ethnic parties have usually been short-lived and without major impact.

Despite ongoing challenges to consolidate the state and democratic institutions, all three countries have committed to European integration as their main foreign policy goal. Many of the challenges that these countries face will need to be addressed in the context of their EU integration—for example, the distribution of competences in the context of negotiating with the EU is a fundamental question in Bosnia and Herzegovina, while Kurti has already announced that he is much less sympathetic and supportive of the EU's Rule of Law Mission in Kosovo than previous governments have been. What is more, North Macedonia's slow progress toward EU membership, despite a substantial number of reforms implemented since 2017, might send a signal to other Balkan capitals—reforms do not pay off, and the countries will integrate much slower and much later than many have predicted.

Notwithstanding the opportunities of EU integration and the many challenges listed above, the different forms of territorial autonomy have been key to establishing peace and ensuring interethnic cooperation in Bosnia, Macedonia and Kosovo. Bosnia's federal system with confederal elements remains in search of functionality and overall stability, and it is substantially contested from internal actors as well as from external spoilers. In Kosovo, the situation is similar when it comes to contestation and threats to the territorial integrity of the country. Especially the situation in Northern Kosovo will remain a key bone of contestation between Kosovo, Serbia and the EU as a mediator. It remains to be seen if a solution can be found and if EU integration of Serbia (and of Kosovo) can provide the framework for the reconciliation that is needed. Finally, North Macedonia had seen a substantial decrease in the functionality of its power-sharing system and its democratic credibility under the previous Prime Minister Gruevski. However, with the change of government in 2017, there has been a new focus on stabilizing democracy internally and making progress toward membership in the EU externally.

Bosnia remains the only full-fledged federation in the country. Yet, its dysfunctionality has prevented the use of federalism in other cases, so instead, Macedonia and Kosovo opted for local decentralization. This has been much more limited, both in terms of actual local decision-making competences and in its impact on the overall functioning of the countries in question. Federalism remains associated either with dysfunctionality as a result of the situation in Bosnia or with state dissolution as witnessed in the former Socialist Yugoslavia—the common state that all three countries shared once upon a time. In addition, external actors have played a key role in promoting federalism and decentralization in the region, which has further weakened their appeal. Instead of a local discourse on the benefits of a territorial division of power, it is still seen as a foreign tool to divide countries and weaken them. The discussions and numerous failed attempts about meaningful decentralization in Serbia are a good example for this. As long as local elites do not see the benefits of federalism and decentralized decision-making, it is unlikely that we will see the emergence of further federal countries across Southeastern Europe. The first step to change this would be an overhaul of the Bosnian system to demonstrate that federalism and ethnic power-sharing can actually work in the region and can contribute not only to peacebuilding but also to democratization and state consolidation.

References

Agarin, T. (2020). The limits of inclusion: Representation of minority and non-dominant communities in consociational and liberal democracies. *International Political Science Review, 41*(1), 15–29.

Agarin, T., McCulloch, A., & Murtagh, C. (2018). Others in deeply divided societies: A research agenda. *Nationalism and Ethnic Politics, 24*(3), 299–310.

Ahtisaari, M. (2007). Comprehensive proposal for the Kosovo status settlement. Retrieved 19 October 2020, from http://pbosnia.kentlaw.edu/Comprehensive%20Proposal%20for%20the%20Kosovo%20Settlement.pdf

Bahtic-Kunrath, B. (2011). Of veto players and entity voting: Institutional gridlock in the Bosnian reform process. *Nationalities Papers, 39*(5), 899–923.

Baliqi, B. (2018). Promoting multi-ethnicity or maintaining a divided society: Dilemmas of power-sharing in Kosovo. *Journal on Ethnopolitics and Minority Issues in Europe, 17*(1), 49–71.

Bermeo, N. (2002). A new look at federalism: The import of institutions. *Journal of Democracy, 13*(2), 96–110.

Bieber, F. (2005). Power sharing after Yugoslavia: Functionality and dysfunctionality of power-sharing institutions in post-war Bosnia, Macedonia, and Kosovo. In S. Noel (Ed.), *From power sharing to democracy—Post-conflict institutions in ethnically divided societies* (pp. 85–103). McGill-Queen's University Press.

Bieber, F. (2006). *Post-war Bosnia. Ethnicity, inequality and public sector governance*. Palgrave Macmillan.
Bieber, F. (2015). Partial implementation, partial success: The case of Macedonia. In I. O'Flynn & D. Russel (Eds.), *Power sharing—new challenges for divided societies* (pp. 107–122). Pluto Press.
Bieber, F. (2019). *The rise of authoritarianism in the Western Balkans*. Palgrave Macmillan.
Bieber, F., & Daskalovski, Z. (Eds.). (2003). *Understanding the war in Kosovo*. Frank Cass.
Bieber, F., & Keil, S. (2009). Power-sharing revisited: Lessons learned in the Balkans? *Review of Central & East European Law, 34*(4), 337–360.
Bose, S. (2002). *Bosnia after Dayton. Nationalist partition and international intervention*. Oxford University Press.
Bosnia and Herzegovina – Constitution. (1995). Full text retrieved 3 March 2021, from https://www.wipo.int/edocs/lexdocs/laws/en/ba/ba020en.pdf
Brunnbauer, U. (2002). The implementation of the Ohrid agreement: Ethnic Macedonian Resentments. *Journal on Ethnopolitics and Minority Issues in Europe, 1*, 1–24.
Bunce, V. (1999). *Subversive institutions—The design and the destruction of socialism and the state*. Cambridge University Press.
Burg, S., & Shoup, P. (2000). *The war in Bosnia and Herzegovina—Ethnic conflict and international intervention*. M. E. Sharpe.
Burgess, M. (2006). *Comparative federalism—Theory and practice*. Routledge.
Burgess, M., & Gagnon, A. (2010). Introduction: Federalism and democracy. In M. Burgess & A. Gagnon (Eds.), *Federal democracies* (pp. 1–26). Routledge.
Coles, K. (2007). *Democratic designs—International intervention and electoral practices in postwar Bosnia-Herzegovina*. The University of Michigan Press.
Constitution of the Republic of Kosovo. (2008). Full text retrieved 19 October 2020, from http://www.kushtetutakosoves.info/repository/docs/Constitution.of.the.Republic.of.Kosovo.pdf
Daalder, I. (2000). *Getting to Dayton—The making of America's Bosnia policy*. Brookings Institution Press.
Denitch, B. (1997). The evolution of Yugoslav federalism. *Publius: The Journal of Federalism, 7*(4), 107–117.
Djilas, A. (1991). *The contested country—Yugoslav unity and Communist revolution 1919–953*. Harvard University Press.
Djordjević, J. (1975). Remarks on the Yugoslav model of federalism. *Publius: The Journal of Federalism, 5*(2), 77–88.
Dzankic, J. (2018). Capturing contested states—Structural mechanisms of power reproduction in Bosnia and Herzegovina, Macedonia and Montenegro. *Southeastern Europe, 42*(1), 83–106.

European Court of Human Rights. (2009). *Judgement Sejdić and Finci v. Bosnia and Herzegovina* (27996/06 and 34836/06).
Friedrich, C. (1968). *Trends of federalism in theory and practice*. Frederick A. Praeger Publishers.
Gagnon, V. P. (2004). *The myth of ethnic war—Serbia and Croatia in the 1990s*. Cornell University Press.
Grgic, G. (2017). *Ethnic conflict in asymmetric federations—Comparative experience of the former Soviet and Yugoslav regions*. Routledge.
Holbrooke, R. (1999). *To end a war*. The Modern Library.
Hueglin, T., & Fenna, A. (2006). *Comparative federalism—A systematic inquiry*. Broadview Press.
Hulsey, J. (2015). Electoral accountability in Bosnia and Herzegovina under the Dayton Framework Agreement. *International Peacekeeping, 22*(5), 511–525.
Hulsey, J., & Keil, S. (2021). Power-sharing and party politics in the Western Balkans. In S. Keil & A. McCulloch (Eds.), *Power-sharing in Europe—Past practice, present cases and future directions* (pp. 115–140). Palgrave Macmillan.
Kapidzic, D. (2019). Subnational competitive authoritarianism and power-sharing in Bosnia and Herzegovina. *Southeast European and Black Sea Studies, 20*(1), 81–101.
Kasapovic, M. (2005). Bosnia and Herzegovina: Consociational or liberal democracy? *Politička misao, XLII*(5), 3–30.
Keil, S. (2013). *Multinational federalism in Bosnia and Herzegovina*. Ashgate.
Keil, S. (Ed.). (2014). *State-building in the Western Balkans—European approaches to democratization*. Routledge.
Keil, S. (2015). Power-sharing success and failures in the Western Balkans. In S. Keil & V. Perry (Eds.), *State-building and democratization in Bosnia and Herzegovina* (pp. 193–212). Ashgate.
Keil, S. (2018). The business of state capture and the rise of authoritarianism in Kosovo, Macedonia, Montenegro and Serbia. *Southeastern Europe, 42*, 59–82.
Keil, S. (2020). Imposed unions and imperfect states: The State Union of Serbia-Montenegro and Bosnia and Herzegovina in comparative perspective. *Irish Political Studies, 35*(3), 473–491.
Keil, S., & Kudlenko, A. (2015). Bosnia and Herzegovina 20 years after Dayton: Complexity born of paradoxes. *International Peacekeeping, 22*(5), 471–489.
Keil, S., & Stahl, B. (Eds.). (2015). *The foreign policies of post-Yugoslav states—From Yugoslavia to Europe*. Palgrave Macmillan.
Koneska, C. (2014). *After ethnic conflict—Policy-making in post-conflict Bosnia and Herzegovina and Macedonia*. Ashgate.
Krasniqi, G. (2013). 'Quadratic nexus' and the process of democratization and state-building in Albania and Kosovo: a comparison. *Nationalities Papers, 41*(3), 395–411.

Krasniqi, G. (2015). Foreign policy as a constitutive element of statehood and statehood prerogative: The case of Kosovo. In S. Keil & B. Stahl (Eds.), *The foreign policies of post Yugoslav states—From Yugoslavia to Europe* (pp. 198–222). Palgrave Macmillan.

Kudlenko, A. (2017). Security sector reform in Bosnia and Herzegovina. A case study of the Europeanization of the Western Balkans. *Südosteuropa, 65*(1), 56–76.

Kurtćehajić, S., & Ibrahimagić, O. (2007). *Politički sistem Bosne i Hercegovine.* Magistrat.

Lampe, J. (2000). *Yugoslavia as history—Twice there was a country.* Cambridge University Press.

Lapidoth, R. (1997). *Autonomy—Flexible solutions to ethnic conflicts.* United States Institute of Peace Press.

Lijphart, A. (1969). Consociational democracy. *World Politics, 21*(2), 207–225.

Lijphart, A. (1977). *Democracy in plural societies—A comparative exploration.* Yale University Press.

Lijphart, A. (2005). Constitutional design for divided societies. *Journal of Democracy, 15*(2), 96–109.

Lyon, A. (2011). Municipal decentralisation in the Republic of Macedonia: Preserving a multi-ethnic state? *Federal Governance, 8*(3), 28–49.

McEvoy, J. (2015). *Power-sharing executives—Governing in Bosnia, Macedonia and Northern Ireland.* University of Pennsylvania Press.

Merdzanovic, A. (2019). 'Imposed consociationalism': External intervention and power sharing in Bosnia and Herzegovina. *Peacebuilding, 5*(1), 22–35.

Niemetz, M. (2020). The Macedonian 'name' dispute: The Macedonian question—resolved? *Nationalities Papers, 48*(2), 205–214.

Ohrid Framework Agreement (OFA). (2001). Full text retrieved 19 October 2020, from https://www.osce.org/files/f/documents/2/8/100622.pdf

Perry, V. (2019). Frozen, stalled, stuck, or just muddling through: The post-Dayton frozen conflict in Bosnia and Herzegovina. *Asia-Europe Journal, 17,* 107–127.

Piacentini, A. (2019). State ownership and 'state-sharing': The role of collective identities and the sociopolitical cleavage between ethnic Macedonians and ethnic Albanians in the Republic of North Macedonia. *Nationalities Papers, 47*(3), 461–476.

Piacentini, A. (2020). *Ethnonationality's evolution in Bosnia Herzegovina and Macedonia—Politics, institutions and intergenerational dis-continuities.* Palgrave Macmillan.

Ramet, S. (1992). *Nationalism and federalism in Yugoslavia 1962–1991* (2nd ed.). Indiana University Press.

Ramet, S. (2006). *The three Yugoslavias—State-building and legitimation, 1918–2005.* Indiana University Press.

Riker, W. (1964). *Federalism—Origin, operation and significance*. Little, Brown and Company.
Silber, L., & Little, A. (1996). *The death of Yugoslavia*. Penguin Books.
Skendaj, E. (2014). *Creating Kosovo—International oversight and the making of ethical institutions*. Woodrow Wilson Center Press.
Stepan, A. (1999). Federalism and democracy: Beyond the US model. *Journal of Democracy, 10*(4), 19–34.
Tanner, M. (2010). *Croatia—A nation forged in war* (3rd ed.). Yale University Press.
UN Mission in Kosovo (UNMIK). (2001). *Constitutional framework for provisional self-governance*. Retrieved 19 October 2020, from http://constitutionnet.org/sites/default/files/kosovo_constitutional_framework_for_provisional_self-government_2001-2008.pdf
Vangelov, O. (2019). The primordialisation of ethnic nationalism in Macedonia. *Europe-Asia Studies, 71*(2), 203–224.
Watts, R. (2008). *Comparing federal systems* (3rd ed.). McGill-Queen's University Press.
Woodward, S. (1995). *Balkan tragedy—Chaos and dissolution after the Cold War*. The Brookings Institution.
Ziblatt, D. (2006). *Structuring the state—The formation of Italy and Germany and the Puzzle of Federalism*. Princeton University Press.

CHAPTER 7

Federalism and Conflict Resolution in Nepal and Myanmar

Michael G. Breen

Nepal and Myanmar are part of a new generation of emerging federal systems, built to hold together an ethnically divided state after conflict. This chapter discusses some of the reasons behind the emergence, or non-emergence, of federalism and some of the challenges in its establishment. It reveals the importance of agency and timing in the transformation of a political structure to better reflect a federal society, and it outlines some of the distinct features that have arisen as a result of the processes, the societal features and the path-dependent nature of the initial structure of the modern (post-war) state in those countries. The fledgling nature of political institutions, including political party systems and the simultaneous democratization process, means that the center has been slow to devolve power, with capacity in provincial and local levels lacking and many outcomes remaining uncertain. The military in Myanmar remains autonomous and continues to impede federalization and democratization. But if

M. G. Breen (✉)
University of Melbourne, Melbourne, VIC, Australia
e-mail: michael.breen@unimelb.edu.au

© The Author(s), under exclusive license to Springer Nature Switzerland AG 2022
S. Keil, S. Kropp (eds.), *Emerging Federal Structures in the Post-Cold War Era*, Federalism and Internal Conflicts, https://doi.org/10.1007/978-3-030-93669-3_7

successful, Nepal and Myanmar will be showcases for both simultaneous federalization and democratization, and new approaches to the management of ethnic diversity through federal design.

A Brief History of Federalism Discourse in Nepal and Myanmar

Ethnic Diversity and Federal Societies

Nepal and Myanmar have a high degree of ethnic diversity, each officially comprising more than 100 ethnic groups (including caste groups). Nepal scores at 0.663 and Myanmar at 0.506 on the index of ethnic fractionalization (Alesina et al., 2003). Ethnic groups are often clustered and have, more or less, maintained their own languages, religions and cultural practices, and in some cases, autonomous political structures (Breen, 2018c, 60–63, 65–67). Though there is much intermingling and dispersal, overall, Nepal and Myanmar can be characterized as federal societies. However, in each case, political and economic structures have been dominated by the largest ethnic group. Maps 7.1 and 7.2 shows the provincial (Nepal) or state and region (Myanmar) boundaries for each country.

Map 7.1 Nepal. Source: https://d-maps.com/carte.php?num_car=5522&lang=en

7 FEDERALISM AND CONFLICT RESOLUTION IN NEPAL AND MYANMAR   143

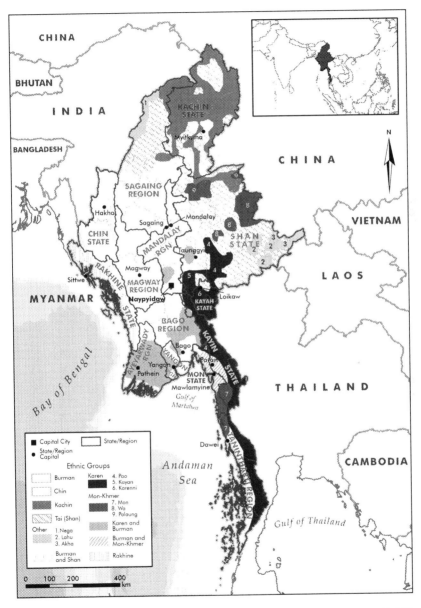

Map 7.2 Myanmar. *Source*: https://d-maps.com/carte.php?num_car=4164&lang=en

In Nepal the hill-based high-caste Hindu group (Bahun and Chhetri—herein referred to as Khas Arya), while comprising only around 28% of the population, have made up a majority of the executive, all of the prime ministers during the pre-2008 democratic eras (Ghai, 2011; Lawoti, 2005) and the former king and predecessors. In Myanmar, the 136 officially recognized ethnic groups have been categorized into eight national races (herein "ethnic nationalities"). The largest ethnic nationality (Bamar, or Burmese) comprise about two-thirds of the population and dominate political structures and the military (Smith, 1991; Taylor, 2009, 62, 92; Walton, 2013). Table 7.1 provides an overview of the major categories of ethnic groups for each case.

Federalism has been a longstanding demand of non-Bamar ethnic nationalities in Myanmar, dating back to before independence, whereas it only emerged into popular discourse relatively recently in Nepal (Breen, 2018c, 68–73). In each case the driving forces of federalization have been conflict and ethnic exclusion. In the post-World War II (WWII) period, states across the world sought to implement the idea of a *nation-state*, whereby the state would be of and for one particular ethnic group. This "nation-building" agenda was taken up with great enthusiasm by many

Table 7.1 Categories of Ethnic Groups in Nepal and Myanmar, and Proportion of Population

Nepal*		Myanmar**	
Category	Proportion of Population (%)	Category	Proportion of Population (%)
Khas Arya	28.8	Bamar	69
Janajati	37.0	Shan	8.5
• Magar	7.3	Karen (Kayin)	6.2
• Tharu	6.6	Rakhine	4.5
• Newa	5.9	Mon	2.4
Madhesi	20.5	Chin	2.2
Dalit	12.7	Kachin	1.4
Muslim	4.4	Karenni (Kayah)	0.4

*Based on categories used for the design of the electoral system, including the three largest Janajati groups, and using data from the 2011 census.

**Based on the national race categories that are officially recognized by the government, using data from the 1983 census, which is the most recent official data on ethnicity.

states in Asia, which sought to consolidate the borders that were externally imposed and an outcome of decolonization, but which otherwise housed a great diversity of ethnic groups (Reid, 2010). Nepal and Myanmar are no exceptions.

Nation-building and the Revival of Authoritarian Rule

Nepal and Myanmar established *modern nation-states* after WWII. I have shown elsewhere that this critical juncture resulted in a path-dependent institutionalization of ethnic domination (Breen, 2018c, 68–77, 83–102). But it also created a simultaneous reactive sequence that would undermine this otherwise reproductive path dependence and leave it vulnerable to transformative change. Ethnic domination was met by resistance from minority ethnic groups, who built their own systems of governance and established armed organizations. Concessions made by ethnic elites at the center stabilized the level of conflict at times, but left the discontent to fester and periodically erupt, weakening the central state and leaving it unable to deal with converging crises or disruptive random events, such as economic crises, or in the case of Nepal, the fallout from the "Royal massacre" of 2001. These interacting path dependencies have led to federalization in both cases, but it is ongoing and contingent on agency and timing. A convergence of conditions (a moderate secession risk and a peripheral infrastructural capacity) incentivizes and enables such agency and an associated alliance-building toward federalization, but does not determine it. In Nepal the late 1940s and 1950s saw the end of an authoritarian oligarchy and the introduction of democracy. At the time only one ethnic group sought federalism, and the idea was barely considered by the political elite, which included democrats and monarchists. The monarchists and the democrats could not agree on much, but they both saw Nepal as a state for the Khas Arya. Democracy lasted only until 1960, and during that time there were six different governments and just one election. The then king, who seized power in 1960, acted to reinforce Khas Arya privilege and the identity of the state. For example, he promulgated a slogan "*eutai bhasa, eutai bhes, eutai raja, eutai desh*" ("one language, one dress, one king, one country") (Malagodi, 2013, 32). The caste system, which entrenched ethnic inequality, discrimination and exclusion, had formal legal status, and each group was specifically ranked. The next attempt at democracy, from 1990, fared little better, with the (new) king seizing power in 2002 and later proceeding to arrest political parties. This democratic period failed to address the issues of the marginalized ethnic groups, and in response a Maoist insurgency rose up in 1996, waging a civil war until the 2005 ceasefire and subsequent (2006) Comprehensive Peace Agreement, which committed the signatories to *state restructuring* to address issues of discrimination and marginalization (Lawoti, 2008). In Myanmar (then Burma) an agreement between a representative of the majority Bamar ethnic group, General Aung San and representatives from three ethnic nationalities to establish federalism was a precursor to independence from British colonial rule. However, before it could be established, Aung San was assassinated. The new leader, U Nu, was not a supporter of federalism, and the eventual constitution substantially watered down the intent of that agreement. It established a federal system, but not one that was satisfactory to any of the supposed beneficiaries. Conflict broke out at independence and continued largely unabated. For the military the final straw was the threat by one group (Shan) to exercise a secession right it had been granted in the constitution (exercisable after ten years), subject to its federal reform demands being met. The military seized power, abolished the existing federal institutions and ruled (under one guise or another) for the next 50 years. According to the new prime minister at the time, General Ne Win, "federalism is impossible, it will destroy the Union" (cited in Smith, 1991). But the ethnic nationalities' fight for federalism, or independence, continues. The military did not hand over power until after it established a new constitution in 2008 and held an election in 2010. But under the new constitution, the military retained a guarantee of its role in state governance and established a political party (United Solidarity and Development Party, USDP), initially comprising mostly ex-military men. The USDP easily won the 2010 election, thanks in large part to a boycott by the National League for Democracy (NLD) (which was the winner of the non-recognized 1990 election). In 2015 the NLD competed and won a large majority on the back of its promise to establish genuine democratic federalism. As discussed below, it has made some but limited progress toward this goal.

Internal Conflict and Key Actor Interests

In both cases, insurgents—or ethnic armed organizations as they prefer to be called in Myanmar—have been key actors (herein referred to as EAOs for both cases). Political parties are also key actors in both cases and have, at times, sided with EAOs against a common opponent. But the nature of this common opponent has been a key difference between the cases. In Nepal the political parties and the Maoists aligned against the former king to usher in substantial reforms to the structure of the state. Although the Maoists and the political parties had different interests, they were able to find a common ground (and a common enemy) that created mutual gain (Breen, 2018b). The Maoists prioritized the establishment of a republic, secularism, presidentialism and federalism. The political parties wanted a multiparty parliamentary democracy. The Maoists compromised in agreeing to the multiparty and parliamentary systems, and the political parties compromised on federalism and secularism. They both gained access to power from which they were previously excluded (the Maoists transformed themselves into a political party). In Myanmar the common opponent of many EAOs and political parties is the military (Tatmadaw), which has led the state directly or through proxy political parties from 1962 up until the NLD took power in 2016, following a large election victory. Under the 2008 constitution the military retains a place in the governance of the state, including guaranteed seats in all legislatures and executives, and a veto right over constitutional change. But unlike Nepal, neither the EAOs nor the political parties' interests have been in alignment, and they have remained internally divided on several key issues. The military supports political parties (most notably the USDP) and has a range of agreements with EAOs that have the effect of sometimes pitting one against another. This "divide and rule" strategy—perhaps learned from the British colonialists—has been one effective approach to maintaining the military's grip, or at least foothold, on power. There is also a proliferation of ethnic political parties, which mostly compete for power at the provincial level but are critical to the success or failure of the federalization process.

HOLDING-TOGETHER FEDERALISM AND DEMOCRATIZATION

Federalization in Nepal

Federalization in Nepal was guided by the Comprehensive Peace Agreement (2006). It committed the state to the progressive restructuring of the state (Item 3.5) through a constituent assembly. It is generally accepted that the restructuring referred to federalization, but the absence of the word reflected the reluctance of many of the ruling class (i.e., the Khas Arya leaders of the two major political parties at the time [Nepali Congress and CPN(UML)]). In the South of the country, which is home to most Madhesis, there was an uprising against the absence of a commitment to federalism in the resulting Interim Constitution, under which a constituent assembly was to be elected. Many Madhesis protested on the streets, Madhesi political parties formed and armed groups caused havoc (Miklian, 2009). In the end the protests were quelled by the commitment of the major political parties to amend the constitution. Accordingly, in its very first sitting, the Constituent Assembly amended the Interim Constitution and declared Nepal to be a secular, democratic, federal republic. Federalism was seen as a means to end discrimination, support democratization and guarantee decentralization (Karki, 2014). Federalism was preferred to decentralization under a unitary constitution in part because of the failure of the decentralized policies of the past. In particular, there was meant to be substantial decentralization under the 1990 democratic constitution, but it was never properly implemented, and from 2002 until 2017, elected local government seats were left entirely vacant. Nevertheless, the "reluctant federalists" in the major parties would privately prefer decentralization only and were at times obstructionist toward the federal agenda (author interviews; Jha, 2014; Karki, 2014). They feared what else might come from federalism. Specifically, they feared secession and disintegration of the country and the future of the identity of the state which was, and remains, centered around the Khas Arya. Royalist parties remained competitive and campaigned for a return to a Hindu state. The election for the Constituent Assembly was held in 2008. A mixed parallel electoral system was used, with 60% of the seats decided by a proportional representation formula. The results were a major surprise in that the Maoists' party (CPN-Maoist) won the most seats. The Assembly was itself perhaps the most inclusive institution in Nepal's political history, with almost all ethnic groups represented. The Assembly established committees to develop sections of the constitution, including one on the restructuring of the state. This committee could not reach an agreement on the form of federalism or the basis of the provinces, which became the most contentious issue (Breen, 2018a; Hachhethu, 2014). Eventually, a second Constituent Assembly was elected (2013), which changed the balance of power toward the more traditional Khas Arya-dominated parties. There was little dialogue in the Assembly by this point, and most major decisions were made by the political parties in another place. Though they may have been reluctant federalists, they were committed and in too deep. Further, in the meantime the parties had become more multiethnic and were subject to significant internal pressure to accommodate diversity through federal reform. In the face of a reconstruction effort following devastating earthquakes and further protests in the South of the country, the main political parties passed a new federal constitution in September 2015. It includes seven provinces, a local government level and a bicameral parliament at the center. The first provincial elections were held in 2017, along with elections to the new constitutionally empowered local tier. Many remain dissatisfied (there are still periodic protests in the Southwest of the country), but the scale of transformative change attempted make this inevitable.

Federalization in Myanmar

In Myanmar the current federalization process centers around the twenty-first-century Panglong Conference, also known as the Union Peace Conference, held since August/September 2016. This conference is meant to be a national political dialogue, and it includes representatives from the government and political parties, the military, EAOs and civil society. However, its progress has stalled. It has met four times and agreed around 50 principles to guide reform. Discussions are still quite superficial and focus on concepts and meanings rather than on substance. For example, agreements have been reached to ensure the separation of religion and politics, ensure the equality of ethnic nationalities and establish a constitutional division of powers, but without any detail (Union Peace Conference, 2020). Further, it remains stuck on the issue of secession and constitutions for ethnic states (see Breen & He, 2020). The other key process is the negotiation of a National Ceasefire Agreement (NCA). The NCA, among other things, commits the signatories, which include the military, to "establish a union based on principles of democracy and federalism" (NCA, 2015 item 1a). The signing of the NCA triggered the requirement to commence the dialogue toward a democratic federal union. However, only ten EAOs, and none of the most important EAOs, have signed the agreement. Non-signatories have observer status only at the twenty-first-century Panglong Conference. The federalization process in Myanmar is very much a work in progress. The election in November 2020 resulted in another overwhelming victory for the NLD. Ethnic parties, many of which merged, had seemed likely to increase their vote share thanks to the widespread dissatisfaction with the lack of progress on federalism. However, with some exceptions, they—and the USDP—performed poorly. The NLD won 83% of the elected seats in the combined houses of parliament and the most seats in every state and region, with one exception. In Rakhine State the Arakan National Party won 7 out of 15 elected seats, though still not enough to form a majority. In Shan State most elected seats were split among the NLD (31%), the Shan National League for Democracy (25%) and the USDP (23%). However, the military has the most seats overall in that state. The NLD has reiterated its commitment to establishing federalism and commenced consultations with ethnic parties to form a "national unity government" (Nyein, 2020). In fact, Myanmar has a kind of federal system already, specifically a constitutionally decentralized union (according to Watts', 1999, 8 criteria). Under its 2008 constitution, there is a federal division of powers among the center, the 14 states and regions and the six self-administered areas, and each is accountable to its electorate. The military itself has admitted the federal features of the current constitution (see Breen, 2018a, 130–1). However, the autonomy of the states and regions is severely curtailed, and there are no issues on which a state or region can be assured a final and decisive say. For example, the chief ministers of states and regions are appointed by the president (Article 261, 2008 Constitution) while economic powers are to be exercised "in accord with law enacted by the Union" (Schedule 2, Item 2). Furthermore, the courts are not independent and are, in practice, "consigned to the margins of political and legal influence" (Crouch, 2019, 174). Myanmar falls well short of the standards of a democratic federation.

Federalism in Practice

Holding-together Federalism

Nepal, like the other federal states in Asia, is a "holding-together" federal system. In particular, the decision to commit to federalism in the Constituent Assembly is a response to a secession risk that was heightened by the Madhesi uprising (Breen, 2018b). Many international actors, such as the United Nations Development Programme and the Swiss and German development agencies, played an important role in supporting the transition and, in many cases, were advocates for federalism. Neighbors like China and India were influential, but the final decision, and the form of federalism, was made on the basis of domestic interests and pressures (Breen, 2018a).

In particular, one of the key debates was whether to have one or more provinces in the *Terai*, along the southern border with India. India sought to exert considerable pressure on the Nepali people, even allegedly orchestrating border blockades in order to goad the Constituent Assembly into accepting India's preferred federal structure (Karki, 2015). But the fear of secession prevailed, and two provinces, plus an intersecting trade route, were established. Furthermore, the constitution establishes what can be called an hourglass type of federalism, where the provinces were kept relatively weak and local governments were empowered as one way to keep a check on secessionist tendencies and maintain central supremacy (Payne, 2020). Myanmar's federal choices are also based on a "holding-together" imperative, particularly in the management of a secession risk (Breen, 2018b). The federal project in Myanmar has, since independence, been about maintaining the colonial borders. The 1947 Panglong Agreement whereby certain ethnic nationality representatives agreed to "join" the union was really about securing their agreement, not to leave. The threat by representatives of the Shan State in 1962, to exercise its right to secession, led directly to the military intervention and the abolition of its previous federal structure. Since then, two more constitutions have been produced. One, in 1974, provided for a federal structure with a one-party system and established hierarchy. The current constitution, established in 2008, also has a federal structure, though the center remains dominant. These processes are so important because the process of federalization, as discussed in the Introduction, in many respects determines or confines the scope of possible choice, the type of federal system and the parameters of operational practice. In both cases, the process is devolutionary. The question during such a federalization process is what powers should be reallocated from the central level to the provincial and local levels. It is no surprise that central authorities seek to maintain strong powers. On the other hand, a "coming-together" federalization will almost inevitably result in strong provincial-level governments, which aim to keep as much of their autonomous powers as possible. One reason that the federalization process in Myanmar has so often stuttered is the gulf between the expectations of ethnic nationalities and the present-day realities that sees real power in the hands of the central state and (its) military. Prior to 1947, the main ethnic areas (Frontier Areas) were indirectly governed by the British and had substantial autonomy over their internal affairs. They saw—and still see themselves—as independent nations who joined the union by consent. Today, in lieu of independence, some advocate for a confederal arrangement, or at least the kinds of powers and security that are enjoyed by constituent units in coming-together federations like the US and Switzerland (see the discussions at the twenty-first-century Panglong Conference, for example). But the center has held all or almost all of the powers for nearly 60 years. Federalization in Myanmar is now well and truly a holding-together process.

Diversity and Accommodation

As mentioned both Nepal and Myanmar have a very high diversity with well over 100 ethnic groups. There are many substantially clustered communities, but there has also been significant internal migration, meaning most parts of the country contain a mixture of different ethnic groups. Accommodating this diversity has been one of the main drivers of federalization and a necessary response to internal conflict. Hence, Nepal and Myanmar have both established a form of ethnic federalism. In Myanmar there are seven states, seven regions and six self-administered areas. The states are all ethnically based and named accordingly. They have a majority or plurality of the titular ethnic nationality. The regions are all nominally territorially based and have a majority Bamar. States and regions have symmetrical powers and no language rights (Breen, 2019). The self-administered areas were allocated to smaller ethnic groups that comprise a majority in at least two adjacent townships, while also being related to ceasefire agreements (Crouch, 2019, 140–148). In Nepal there are seven provinces. Only one has a majority of a minority ethnic group, however, a further three have a plurality or majority of Janajati (author's calculations based on census data). Provinces can select their own official languages, names and capitals. One controversy is whether their names should reflect ethnicity or geographical features. The Constituent Assembly could not agree on names for the provinces, which were left to their legislatures. Over three years after provincial elections and the formation of provincial legislatures, two provinces remain unnamed. The other five have been given names that are based on geographical features or regions. Obviously, these provincial-level structures are not able to adequately reflect the enormous diversity in either case, so each country has established further processes and structures by which minority ethnic groups might secure autonomy and representation. The self-administered areas in Myanmar are one such structure. Additionally, Myanmar has established 29 non-territorial ethnic ministries ("national race affairs ministries") that provide representation to groups that are a minority in a given state or region, but have a population of at least 0.1 per cent of the total population of the country. The ministers have responsibility to represent the interests of their ethnic group in the respective state or region and have also been active in mediating between government and EAOs (Thawnghmung & Yadana, 2017). Nepal's new constitution enables, but does not establish, autonomous regions as well as non-territorial identity-based commissions, such as for Tharu, Muslims, Dalits and others (Articles 252-65, Constitution of Nepal). The initial drafts of the constitution, released in 2010, included the names and locations of 23 autonomous regions (Committee on the Restructuring of the State and Distribution of State Power, 2010), while the State Restructuring Commission recommended a non-territorial province for Dalits (low-caste Hindus) (High Level State Restructuring Commission, 2011). Although these sub-state structures were not included in the final constitution, substantive local autonomy was, in the form of a constitutionally empowered third tier of government. This local layer, comprising 753 multilevel authorities, is (at an aggregate level) more inclusive than the provincial or central levels. The local level has important powers allocated to it by the constitution, including for local or basic health, education and police (Schedule 8, Items 1, 8–9, Constitution of Nepal 2015), and has been active in legislating, providing services and investing in local development.

Political Parties and Informal Institutions

Nepal and Myanmar both have fledgling federal political systems and there is still a great deal of informal and evolving practice. The rule of law is frequently abrogated as the military and governments often act as they please or find backdoor ways to direct and control the activities of the constituent units. This compounds the challenges of the holding-together process that relies on the transfer of authority and resources from the center. The center can find a way to maintain control, such as through political parties, delegitimize other levels of government by "setting them up to fail," or just straight up not devolve power, irrespective of the constitutional requirement. In Myanmar the constitution has allocated 41 distinct powers, plus taxation and concurrent powers, to states and regions. However, through the political party system and the permissive constitutional framework, the central government has assumed effective control of all of the states and regions—even those where it is not a majority. The constitution provides that the chief ministers are appointed by the president. Following its 2015 election victory, the NLD selected the president and the chief ministers from amongst its own members. In Shan State and Rakhine State, the NLD was not the largest party and the appointment of the chief minister was made against the wishes of the majority of the respective legislatures (Lwin & Lone, 2016). The NLD is a highly centralized and personality-based party. On paper the NLD is structured similarly to many other large parties with decentralized committee structures and voting procedures. But in practice, the state, regional and local branches have little autonomy, and party discipline is strictly enforced. State and region ministers (including chief ministers) regularly act on the direct and explicit instructions of the central government, including NLD leader Aung San Suu Kyi (Batcheler, 2018, 32). Practices in other parties vary widely, but most are quite centralized. In interviews with this author, party members talked about the difficulty of finding local candidates and members and the financial costs, which makes it difficult to decentralize the parties in accordance with federal structures. These findings have been echoed elsewhere (Tan et al., 2020, 19–32). The NLD government has thus given little real opportunity to the states and regions to build their legitimacy. The proportion of overall expenditure that is by the states and regions stands at under 12% (2018), and the majority of this is subject to the direction and control of the center (Batcheler, 2018, 75). By most accounts most chief ministers have not been up to the task, and they have been mired in controversies from major corruption, incompetence and the backlash associated with their support for the central government's plans to erect statues of Aung San in ethnic minority areas (Moe, 2020). The most prominent powers are those that remain subject to federal law (e.g., economic powers). The courts have been subject to the influence of the president and the NLD dominated legislature, such that it is unable to provide an adequate check on the rights of states and regions (Crouch, 2019). For self-administered areas the situation is even more stark. The head of the Danu Self-Administered Zone concludes that, "to put it bluntly, these are self-administered areas in name only" (cited in S. Lwin, 2018). It took more than five years for any self-administered area to pass a law, and the influence and direction of the state and regional governments, and the central government via its control of the civil service (see below), have undermined their autonomy, which was minimalist in the first place. In such a situation it is difficult for the constituent units to obtain the legitimacy and backing of the people. But progress is positive.

Since 2013, the proportion of revenue allocated to states and regions in Myanmar has more than doubled. They have become more active with expanding roles and responsibilities, and reforms to the structure of the civil service are increasing its accountability to states and regions (Batcheler, 2018). In Nepal the major political parties are also highly centralized and personality based. During the constitution-making process, there were three major parties—Nepali Congress, CPN(UML) and CPN-Maoist— with the latter more representative of the interests of minority ethnic groups. However, following the 2017 elections, the Maoists and CPN(UML) merged to form the Nepal Communist Party (Centre) (NCP). The former CPN(UML) faction and its leader KP Oli have become dominant, and the new party controls six out of seven provinces and 400 of the 753 local governments. Hence, although the constituent units in Nepal have substantial autonomy on paper, in practice most important decisions, including candidates for the national assembly and chief ministerial appointments in provinces, have been made by central-level leaders (e.g., Republica, 2020; Sharma & Kharel, 2015). The informal patronage politics of Nepal enables the center to retain power over key areas, contrary to the constitutional allocation of power. Provincial chief ministers have complained that the "federal government is showing no signs of devolving power" (Pradhan, 2019). In addition, the constitution established an intermediate district-based coordinating structure. This "quasi-tier" comprises a district assembly that consists of local government mayors/chairs, deputy mayors/chairs and an executive district coordination committee. It is meant to be an arm of local government, but it is staffed by federal civil servants who answer to and, at times, undermine the role and decisions of the local governments themselves (Bhusal, 2020). It has become one backdoor way for the federal government to retain control or influence over the local governments. Notwithstanding, the governing party in Nepal does not have control over all the provinces or local governments. Province 2 (which has a majority of Madhesi and has not yet been named) is governed by a smaller ethnic party and has been a leader in asserting its provincial powers. It has pressed ahead, legislating and implementing its police powers against the express wishes of the central government and taken the federal government to court for "usurping the provincial government's powers" regarding forestry (Kamat, 2019). At the local level approximately 47% of governments are run by a further nine parties plus six by independents. Local governments have multiparty executives, so they are also less susceptible to capture by central-level politicians.

Another major issue in the operation of both Myanmar's and Nepal's federal systems relates to the civil service. Myanmar does not have a federalized civil service, and until last year (2019), the civil service was responsible to the military (specifically, the Minister for Home Affairs). Many civil servants remain loyal to the military and the central government, and their cooperation is required in order to implement the decisions of state and region governments. Directives issued by state and region ministers tend to be sent to central departments and ministers for amendment and approval (Nixon, Joelene, Saw, Linn, & Arnold, 2013, 28–35; Batcheler, 2018, 47–64). "In effect, the state and region government has ministers but does not yet have its own ministries" (Nixon et al., 2013, viii). In Nepal the civil service has not been fully deployed to the new structures, and capacity remains the biggest obstacle to full implementation of the constitution's devolutionary elements (Acharya, 2018; Democracy Resource Centre, 2018). The role of civil servants in the districts' structures is also problematic, as discussed above.

Democratization and Sequencing

Nepal and Myanmar may have had a federal society within a modern nation-state, but it has taken decades for that federal society to start to be reflected in the institutions of the state. As discussed in the Introduction, institutional choices are less likely to reflect social structures in non-democratic regimes (Erk, 2008). Indeed, throughout much of their modern histories, Nepal and Myanmar have not been democratic, and at present, Myanmar is a hybrid regime. Yet federalization is associated with democratization in both Myanmar and Nepal.

Contrary to the sequenced approach to federalization in the coming together federations of the West (Burgess, 2012, 253), in these cases federalization comes at the same time as democracy and is mutually reinforcing. There are several overlaps between federal and democratic institutions such as an independent judiciary, constitutionalism and the separation of powers. Federalism enables easier and more direct access to, and participation in, democratic institutions, bringing government closer to the people and making it more accountable. But as outlined in the Introduction, there is no inevitability about the federalization or the democratization of each country. It is true that both Myanmar and Nepal have a "federal society," but there are other conditions that must be in place, and political parties and EAOs both have significant agency. To elaborate the federalization process in these cases, the federal society, or high extent of ethnic diversity, is subject to an assimilating nation-building agenda, which leads to internal conflict and a secession risk. One response of states to this risk has been repression (such as through military conflict or exclusion). This tends the central state toward authoritarianism because of the high costs of control. When the secession risk is moderate and combined with a high "infrastructural capacity" within restive regions or groups (as applicable), there are incentives for the ethnic minority groups who are demanding—fighting—for autonomy and democratic forces from the dominant group to make alliances to achieve mutual objectives. In other words, they agree to a federal democracy and avoid zero-sum outcomes. But it is one thing to make an agreement, and another to implement it. The 2015 election in Myanmar saw the NLD make an alliance with ethnic political parties and EAOs in that the NLD committed to federalism, and the ethnic parties and EAOs committed to democracy. But the NLD won an overwhelming majority and did not make good on its promise. One thing that held it back was the role of the military, which maintains a veto right over constitutional change and autonomy over its own budget and operations. The military is fearful of federalism because it considers that it is a step toward secession (Breen & He, 2020). Following the 2020 election the NLD reiterated its commitment to federalism and sought to establish a national unity government by the inclusion of ethnic parties. However, the USDP has disputed the election result, and many ethnic parties feel betrayed by the NLD, which has not prosecuted its federal agenda adequately, nor acted in accordance with a "federal spirit." Indeed, the leader of the NLD Aung San Suu Kyi has reiterated that she will take a personal role in the selection of chief ministers (Waitan, 2020).

Like in Nepal, we can characterize the NLD as reluctant federalists. Despite its multiethnic membership, the senior leaders of the party are Bamar and have demonstrated their nationalist tendencies, such as through the establishment of a series of race and religion laws, which have proved electorally popular. It remains fixated on first establishing a fuller democracy by removing the military from its role in the governance of the state. The NLD has openly stated that democracy should come first as it will then allow the people to participate in a federalization process. But once (if) democracy is fully established, the prevailing majoritarianism is likely to make federalization more difficult (see Breen, 2018c, 128, 133–4).

Further, federalism can cause problems for newly established democracies. As systems become more complex through multi levels of governance, achieving democratic principles can become challenging (Benz, 2015). It has been argued that such a challenge is too much for a fledgling democracy because governments and elites do not have the tradition of resolving conflicts through competition and compromise, and instead, the center reverts to restrictions (Filippov & Shvetsova, 2013). However, in these cases the absence of one or the other is what has resulted in a restrictive and repressive stance from the center. Nepal made two attempts to institutionalize a unitary democracy, but the political exclusion of minority ethnic groups, among other things, led to its abandonment and the reinstatement of authoritarianism (Lawoti, 2005). Myanmar sought to establish some kind of "putting-together" federal system within a one-party state. This federalism without democracy was unsurprisingly not accepted by ethnic groups in conflict, and it too collapsed under the weight of its own all-encompassing repression (following an economic crisis, the people's uprising and a coup in 1988), only to be replaced by another 20 years of military rule. Myanmar's and Nepal's processes are both transformative (especially Nepal). As argued by Stepan (1999) more than 20 years ago, in the context of a large, modern and highly diverse state, democracy needs to be federal just as much as federalism needs to be democratic.

Concluding Discussion

Nepal has established itself as a democratic federation, though much remains to be done to fully implement and embed in the new structures and systems. Myanmar remains a constitutionally decentralized union and a hybrid regime that is debating further reform. Nepal and Myanmar are part of what I have called the third generation of federalism in Asia. Their deliberations and reforms are part of an emerging federal model to manage diversity in divided societies in Asia. Several of the features are a result of the process of formation, including the holding-together process and its association with democratization and conflict resolution. Other features are partly derivative of social structures, such as the political party systems and the makeup of the constituent units. Finally, the balance of power between the three sets of actors, in a path-dependent context, is also critical (e.g., electoral systems).

Specifically, Nepal and Myanmar's federal systems are ethnic, multilevel and designed to balance imperatives to accommodate diversity and maintain national unity (manage a secession risk). They both have some provinces based on ethnicity, with others based more on territorial factors and having the effect of splitting the dominant group across several provinces. Further, these large and mostly heterogeneous structures are supplemented by lower-level autonomy that targets autonomy to smaller groups. Nepal has a third tier of government, plus a constitutional provision to establish autonomous regions. Myanmar has self-administered areas for small ethnic groups. Perhaps most uniquely, each has a form of non-territorial autonomy: Myanmar in the form of ethnic ministries and Nepal through identity based constitutional commissions.

They also have similar political party systems and majoritarian electoral systems. Both Nepal and Myanmar have at least two major multiethnic parties (albeit ones that are still mostly in the control of the respective dominant ethnic groups), plus a number of relevant ethnic and regional parties, some of which join coalition governments at the center and hold a majority of seats in certain provinces and states. These party and electoral systems, which are neither consociational or centripetal, are key to finding and maintaining the balance between the aforementioned imperatives. It is notable, however, that in Nepal the preceding transition process was consociational and included a grand coalition (Breen, 2018c, 121–127). The NLD has also tried a reconciliation-type executive in Myanmar, including in the Cabinet members from the main opposition, the military and ethnic parties. But many ethnic parties refused to be part of that executive, and it is far from a grand coalition. There are no veto rights for any group or state/region, with the exception of the military.

The prospects for further federalization in Myanmar declined drastically early in 2021. The military, which together with the USDP had raised allegations of electoral fraud in the November 2020 election, staged a coup. On 1 February 2021 the military arrested the leaders of the NLD and others, declared a year-long state of emergency and allocated all powers of the state to the Commander-in-Chief Min Aung Hlaing. The military claims it will hold a new election once the allegations of electoral fraud have been addressed. Although it is far too early to make any reasonable prediction, the dramatic and wide reaching action has demonstrated how tenuous the processes of federalization and democratization can be and the depth of dispute regarding the very character and identity of the state.

In Nepal federalism is also still tenuous. The central government is regularly not acting in the federal spirit, and local governments remain understaffed. However, elections at all three levels have been successfully held, and the legislatures, executives and local authorities have all been established. The decentralized institutions are more inclusive than those of the past and more powerful and secure. There is discontent within many in the community about the slow pace of change, but this can be partly attributed to the expectations raised during the reform process, which promised to "end discrimination," "ensure equality" and accelerate regional development. Further, as of December 2020, NCP has split along its two factions, and the president, on the advice of the prime minister, dissolved parliament and called for a new election in mid-2021. This decision is subject to a ruling of the Supreme Court. The governing party holds a large majority, but is internally fractured. Ultimately, both Myanmar and Nepal are test cases for simultaneous democratization and federalization and of transformative versus incremental federalization. If Myanmar can complete its process and establish "genuine federalism" that finally ends the violent civil conflicts between armed organizations, and Nepal can embed its transformation by finally devolving real power and resources to the provinces and local levels, they will provide evidence for the viability of a parallel transformation for conflict resolution. Political party reform is central to these objectives. Major parties need to become more decentralized to allow for constituent units to be more autonomous in practice and more inclusive to support the development of moderate policies and interethnic cooperation and dialogue. Myanmar (specifically its military) needs to find ways to manage the risk of secession, rather than seeing it as an inevitable outcome of federalization. In particular, the military needs to quickly restore democratic institutions, following its coup of February 2021, and address its concerns through the existing institutions and processes (i.e., the courts and the peace process). After all, if there is no risk of break-up, there is no "holding-together." Ultimately, (ethnic) federalism is a middle ground between independence and assimilation, which has been the perpetual pendulum of Myanmar's modern history. And there is no federalism without democracy.

References

Acharya, K. K. (2018). Local governance restructuring in Nepal: From government to governability. *Dhaulagiri Journal of Sociology and Anthropology, 12*, 37–49.

Alesina, A., Devleeschauwer, A., Easterly, W., Kurlat, S., & Wacziarg, R. (2003). Fractionalization. *Journal of Economic Growth, 8*(2), 155–194.

Batcheler, R. (2018). *State and region governments in Myanmar, New edn.*.Retrieved from Yangon

Benz, A. (2015). Making democracy work in a federal system. *German Politics*, 24(1), 8–25.

Bhusal, T. (2020). *District coordination committees in Nepal: What are they? Why do we need them?* Online: Medium.

Breen, M. G. (2018a). Nepal, federalism and participatory constitution-making: Deliberative democracy and divided societies. *Asian Journal of Political Science*, 26(3), 410–430.

Breen, M. G. (2018b). The origins of holding-together federalism: Nepal, Myanmar and Sri Lanka. *Publius: The Journal of Federalism*, 48(1), 26–50. https://doi.org/10.1093/publius/pjx027

Breen, M. G. (2018c). *The road to federalism in Nepal, Myanmar and Sri Lanka: Finding the middle ground*. Routledge.

Breen, M. G. (2019). Asymmetry or equality? Ethnic nationalities in a Bamar-dominated state. A country study of constitutional asymmetry in Myanmar. In P. Popelier & M. Sahadzic (Eds.), *Constitutional asymmetry in multinational federalism*. Palgrave Macmillan.

Breen, M. G., & He, B. (2020). Do people really want ethnic federalism anymore? Results from deliberations on the role of ethnic identity in federal institutions. In J. Chalmers, C. Galloway, & J. Liljeblad (Eds.), *Living with Myanmar* (pp. 289–314). Singapore.

Burgess, M. (2012). *In search of the federal spirit: New comparative empirical and theoretical perspectives*. Oxford University Press.

Committee on the Restructuring of the State and Distribution of State Power. (2010). *Report on Concept Paper and Preliminary Draft*. Retrieved from Kathmandu.

Crouch, M. (2019). *The Constitution of Myanmar: A contextual analysis*. Hart Publishing.

Democracy Resource Centre. (2018). *Findings on functioning of local and provincial governments in Nepal*. Retrieved from Kathmandu.

Erk, J. (2008). *Explaining federalism: State, society and congruence in Austria, Belgium, Canada, Germany and Switzerland*. Routledge.

Filippov, M., & Shvetsova, O. (2013). Federalism, democracy and democratization. In A. Benz & J. Broschek (Eds.), *Federal dynamics: Continuity, change, and the varieties of federalism*. Oxford Scholarship Online.

Ghai, Y. (2011). Ethnic identity, participation and social justice: A constitution for new Nepal. *International Journal on Minority and Group Rights*, 18(3), 309–334.

Hachhethu, K. (2014). Balancing identity and viability: Restructuring Nepal into a viable federal state. In B. Karki & R. Edrinsinha (Eds.), *The federalism debate in Nepal: Post peace agreement constitution making in Nepal, 2* (pp. 35–54). United Nations Development Programme Support to Participatory Constitution Building.

High Level State Restructuring Commission. (2011). "*Recommendation report of the high level commission for state restructuring*", Majority Report, Retrieved from Kathmandu http://www.spcbn.org.np/index.php?action=resources

Jha, P. (2014). *Battles of the new republic: A contemporary history of Nepal*. Hurst and Co.

Kamat, R. K. (2019). "Province 2 sues federal government", *The Himalayan Times*, Retrieved from https://thehimalayantimes.com/nepal/province-2-sues-federal-government/

Karki, B. (2014). State restructuring and federalism discourse in Nepal. In B. Karki & R. Edrisinha (Eds.), *The federalism debate in Nepal: Post peace agreement constitution making in Nepal* (Vol. 2, pp. 1–23). United Nations Development Programme Support to Participatory Constitution Building Nepal.

Karki, R. (2015). "India's demands grind Nepal to a standstill", *Australian Outlook*, Australian Institute of International Affairs. Retrieved from https://www.internationalaffairs.org.au/australianoutlook/indias-demands-grind-nepal-to-a-standstill/

Lawoti, M. (2005). *Towards a democratic Nepal: Inclusive political institutions for a multicultural society*. SAGE Publications.

Lawoti, M. (2008). Exclusionary democratization in Nepal, 1990–2002. *Democratization*, 15(2), 363–385.

Lwin, E. E. T., & Lone, W. (2016). "NLD control over chief ministers riles ethnic parties", *The Myanmar Times*. Retrieved from http://www.mmtimes.com/index.php/national-news/19694-nld-control-over-chief-ministers-riles-ethnic-parties.html

Lwin, S. (2018). "New self-administered areas struggle to assert authority", *Myanmar Times*. Retrieved from www.mmtimes.com/national-news/9589-new-self-administered-areas-struggle-to-assert-authority.html

Malagodi, M. (2013). *Constitutional nationalism and legal exclusion: Equality, identity politics and democracy in Nepal (1990-2007)*. Oxford University Press.

Miklian, J. (2009). *Nepal's Terai: Constructing an ethnic conflict*. Retrieved from Oslo: http://file.prio.no/Publication_files/Prio/Nepals%20Terai%20(South%20Asia%20Briefing%20Paper%201).pdf

Moe, K. Z. (2020). "Ex-regional chief minister jailed for 30 years in landmark Myanmar corruption case", *The Irrawaddy*. Retrieved from https://www.irrawaddy.com/opinion/commentary/myanmars-ruling-nld-must-address-achilles-heel-choosing-wrong-people.html

Nixon, H., Joelene, C., Saw, K. P. C., Linn, T. A., & Arnold, M. (2013). *State and region governments in Myanmar*. Retrieved from Yangon: https://asiafoundation.org/resources/pdfs/ConflictTerritorialAdministrationfullreportENG.pdf

Nyein, N. (2020). "NLD reaches out to Myanmar's ethnic parties seeking federal union and an end to civil war", *The Irrawaddy*, 13 November 2020. Retrieved from https://www.irrawaddy.com/elections/nld-reaches-myanmars-ethnic-parties-seeking-federal-union-end-civil-war.html

Payne, I. (2020). *Transition in crisis: COVID-19 and federalisation in Nepal*. Asian Law Centre, University of Melbourne. Retrieved from https://law.unimelb.edu.au/centres/alc/engagement/asian-legal-conversations-covid-19/alc-original-articles/transition-in-crisis-covid-19-and-federalisation-in-nepal

Pradhan, T. R. (2019). "Federal government is showing no signs of devolving power, chief ministers say", *The Kathmandu Post*, Retrieved from kathmandupost.com/national/2019/04/28/federal-government-shows-no-signs-of-devolving-power-chief-ministers-say.

Reid, A. (2010). *Imperial alchemy: Nationalism and political identity in Southeast Asia*. Cambridge University Press.

Republica. (2020). "PM Oli races to save his hold on power as Nepal-Dahal alliance seeks his ouster", *myRepublica, 29 April 2020*, Retrieved from https://myrepublica.nagariknetwork.com/news/pm-oli-races-to-save-his-hold-on-power-as-nepal-dahal-alliance-seeks-his-ouster/.

Sharma, B., & Kharel, P. (2015). "NC-UML coalition will continue until the constitution is written", *eKantipur*, 12 January 2015, Retrieved from http://www.ekantipur.com/2015/01/12/interview/nc-uml-coalition-will-continue-until-the-constitution-is-written/400222.html

Smith, M. J. (1991). *Burma: Insurgency and the politics of ethnicity*. Zed Books.

Stepan, A. C. (1999). Federalism and democracy: Beyond the US model. *Journal of Democracy, 10*(4), 19–34.

Tan, N., Minoletti, P., Bjarnegard, E., & Tun, A. L. (2020). *Party building and candidate selection: Intraparty politics and promoting gender equality in Myanmar*. Retrieved from Yangon.

Taylor, R. H. (2009). *The state in Myanmar*. National University of Singapore Press.

Thawnghmung, A. M., & Yadana. (2017). "Citizenship and minority rights: The role of 'National Race Affairs'", Ministers in Myanmar's 2008 Constitution. In A. South & M. Lall (Eds.), *Citizenship in Myanmar: Ways of being in and from Burma* (pp. 113–139). ISEAS – Yusof Ishak Institute.

Union Peace Conference. (2020). *Union Peace Accord Part III*. National Reconciliation and Peace Centre. Retrieved from http://www.nrpc.gov.mm/en/index.php/node/470

Waitan. (2020). "State counsellor to lead team to form region, state governments", *Myanmar Times*, 17 November 2020. Retrieved from https://www.mmtimes.com/news/state-counsellor-lead-team-form-region-state-cabinets.html

Walton, M. J. (2013). The 'Wages of Burman-ness': Ethnicity and Burman privilege in contemporary Myanmar. *Journal of Contemporary Asia, 43*(1), 1–27.

Watts, R. L. (1999). *Comparing federal systems* (2nd ed.). Published for the School of Policy Studies, Queen's University by McGill-Queen's University Press.

CHAPTER 8

India: An Emerging or Fragile Federation?

Wilfried Swenden

W. Swenden (✉)
The University of Edinburgh, Edinburgh, UK
e-mail: w.swenden@ed.ac.uk

© The Author(s), under exclusive license to Springer Nature
Switzerland AG 2022
S. Keil, S. Kropp (eds.), *Emerging Federal Structures in the Post-Cold War Era*, Federalism and Internal Conflicts,
https://doi.org/10.1007/978-3-030-93669-3_8

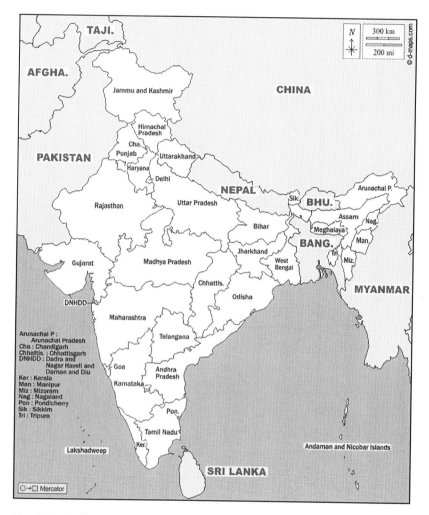

Map 8.1 India. *Source*: https://d-maps.com/carte.php?num_car=4184&lang=en

INTRODUCTION

This chapter charts the trajectory of federalism and democracy in India. India is not a "robust federation" (Bednar, 2008). The lived experience of federalism and democracy has been punctuated by periods of centralized and authoritarian disruption. Given that India's constitution privileges the center, state-favorable practices are more likely when parties in control of the central government are ideologically committed to democracy *and* subnational autonomy. We argue that this is more likely under a multi-party system than a one-party dominant system. Furthermore, the chapter posits that the flexibility of India's federal arrangement has both facilitated and threatened the survival of the country's federal (and democratic) order. The ability to redesign the federal order from above has enabled the redrawing of India's federal structure to make it more responsive to "societal" or bottom-up demands, thus implementing "societal federalism" (Erk, 2007). However, the absence of strong subnational checks has also provoked instability and left sub-state autonomy vulnerable to state capture by a centrist and majoritarian-inclined party in central command (Sharma & Swenden, 2018; Tillin, 2019).

As the chapter will illustrate, India flirted with centrist authoritarianism under the leadership of Indira Gandhi, especially during her Premiership between 1971–1977 and 1980–1984, and again, under Narendra Modi as Prime Minister, particularly so since the reelection of his Hindu nationalist government in May 2019 (Jaffrelot & Verniers, 2020). Yet, even in periods when the national party system threw up results that were more conducive to territorial accommodation, India has encountered difficulties in integrating its so-called boundary regions adjacent to Pakistan (Jammu and Kashmir, Punjab) or China (Northeast India), many of which hold non-Hindu majorities, speak languages that are far detached from the Hindi family mainstream or house large tribal populations. The discrepancy between constitutional sub-state autonomy (often asymmetry), democracy and their "lived experience" is often at its widest in these regions.

The chapter proceeds as follows. In the first section, it analyzes the process of state formation in colonial and postcolonial India and how this informed India's constitutional territorial design. Subsequently, the chapter focuses on center-state dynamics and the quality of subnational democracy in the so-called Hindu "mainland." In the final section, we focus on "boundary opening" strategies of the center in relation to the borderlands and its complicity in creating or at the very least tolerating "authoritarian subnational enclaves."

Colonial Legacies and the Making of the Postcolonial State and Territorial Constitution

The process of state formation in India (and South Asia more generally) does not follow a familiar (West) European pattern (Poggi, 2017). The ordered but heterogeneous nature of Indian society, in which distinct groups (in Hinduism often revolving around *jatis* or caste subgroups) accepted their cultural differences, interaction and interdependence constrained the ability of state institutions to impose a singular or dominant understanding of community (Rudolph & Rudolph, 2008, 10). The process of state formation in the subcontinent was more comparable to that of "Russia or China, in which empires became 'multinational' states (my parentheses), than of Western Europe, where regional kingdoms were transformed into absolute monarchies, and then into nation states" (Rudolph & Rudolph, 2008, 50). This is not to say that a certain centralization of rule was not attempted by some of these rulers, especially the Mughal emperors, but always with the cooperation and mediation of local chieftains or zamindars (Metcalf & Metcalf, 2012, 20).

With British colonization, more serious efforts to establish an interventionist state were made. Although colonization established "direct control" over most of Indian territory, about a third of its landmass and a quarter of its population were made up of more than 550 so-called princely states, which the British controlled only indirectly (Bates, 2007, 82). In the directly controlled territories, colonial government provided a limited degree of indigenous local and provincial self-rule, albeit on a limited franchise (not more than 12% in the 1937 provincial elections). The British also engaged in "categorizing" the population of the subcontinent based on caste, language, religion, tribe and race ("martial races"), through the implementation of decennial censuses. These generated new collective identities (such as backward castes) which hitherto had remained fragmented. Occasionally, they also informed "territorial policy choices," for instance, when entrusting hill tribes in the Northeast with special rights (see further) or when seeking to divide opposition voices to colonial rule along religious lines by (briefly) splitting Bengal into a Muslim-majority and Hindu-majority state in 1905.

The piecemeal and incomplete opening of local and provincial institutions to indigenous politics since the late nineteenth century enabled the formation of an organized opposition to British colonial rule. Since assuming its leadership, Mahatma Gandhi transformed the Indian National Congress from a cadre party into a broad-based movement and mass party with a wide territorial coverage except for much of the Northeast and Jammu and Kashmir (Adeney & Wyatt, 2004; Tudor, 2013). The Congress even gained sympathy in many of the princely states, although no elections were held there until after independence (Bates, 2007).

Apart from galvanizing opinion for an independent Indian dominion and later state, Congress and its senior leaders such as Gandhi, Nehru and Patel gave shape to Indian nationalism. They "turned what previously had been a cultural unit (as summarized by the concept of 'Indian civilization') into a cultural-political unit—a *nation*" (Varshney, 1998, 35). Indian nationalism was not built on a singular identity but embraced the notion of "unity in diversity." For Gandhi, this notion was built on a multicultural, often syncretic understanding of Indianness, though others placed a stronger emphasis on unity (Varshney, 1993). Some minority voices within Congress (and civil society more widely) even supported the construction of the Indian nation around a Hindu-dominant religious core. This view, which echoes Jinnah's "two nation theory" (Muslim-Pakistan; Hindu-Hindustan), was key to the ideology of the Hindu Mahasabha, the Jan Sangh and its contemporary successor, the Bharatiya Janata Party (BJP) (the Indian People's Party).

Muslim-Hindu tensions became more pronounced in the decades leading up to independence and shaped the proposed territorial constitution for an independent India. Muslims, representing about 25% of the population but a minority group with a traditionally high cultural status, were fearful of becoming second-class citizens in an independent Hindu-majority state (Adeney, 2007). The Muslim League developed into a separate Muslim party and leading voice of the Muslims of British India. Although the Government of India Act (1935) proposed a relatively centralized constitution for British India, the closer India approached independence, the more it veered toward a consociational, federal settlement in which Muslims were promised a veto right at the center (in addition to separate electorates which they already acquired earlier), and Muslim-majority and Hindu-majority provinces were promised a large degree of provincial self-rule (Adeney, 2007; Swenden, 2017). The Cabinet Mission Plan (1946), which proposed such a scheme as a last measure to hold British India together as a single separate state, failed. Partition left India divided in two state-nations: Hindu-dominant India and Muslim-dominant Pakistan (until 1971 also comprising Bangladesh).

Partition made India less multireligious but scarcely less divided on the basis of language, caste or tribe (Swenden, 2017). However, the death of about a million citizens and the displacement of around 10 million pushed India and the Congress much closer toward an integrationist understanding of the nation (Talbot & Singh, 2009). This was made visible in two important aspects. First, in the process of territorial consolidation, where the chief aim was to secure the territorial integrity of the Indian state against a hostile external environment (principally from Pakistan, but also from China). Second, in the distribution of competencies between the center and the provinces (now renamed as "states" or "union territories") and the ability of the center to intervene in state politics when deemed "in the national interest." I touch upon both aspects in turn.

First, although in post-independent India the provinces of British India located on Indian territory mostly became "states," this was not true for the more than 550 princely states, all but 9 of which shared territory contingent to India. Small, and often led by leaders with limited popular legitimacy, the princely states lacked a credible exit threat which undermined their bargaining power with the new "parent" state. In their territorial integration, the Indian state practiced what Stepan and Linz referred to as "putting-together" federalism (Stepan et al., 2010). All but three of the princely states that were territorially contingent to India were "persuaded" to join India and merge with erstwhile Indian provinces (now referred to as states). As sweeteners, princely rulers were allowed to hold on to their privy purses and retain a ceremonial role.

Junagadh, Hyderabad and Jammu and Kashmir provided stronger resistance. Junagadh joined in 1948 after its pro-India population rose up against its Nawab (princely ruler) and affirmed its desire to join India in a plebiscite. In the case of Hyderabad, the Indian state intervened militarily in 1948, after it had become clear that the Nizam (princely ruler), aided by a radical paramilitary Muslim organization, prepared for a military confrontation against the wishes of its population (Chandra et al., 2008, 91). The princely state of Jammu and Kashmir could have opted either way: its territory also bordered Pakistan and its Muslim-majority population was led by a Hindu princely ruler. The incorporation of Jammu and Kashmir by India was made possible after the intrusion of Pashtan tribesmen led by Pakistani officers into its territory in October 1947. This prompted the state's Hindu ruler to seek military assistance from India (Bose, 2007). In return for acceding to India, Jammu and Kashmir was offered a unique constitutional status and the prospect of a UN-monitored referendum on staying with India or joining Pakistan.

Second, following Partition, the Indian Constituent Assembly opted for a territorial constitution which more strongly resembled the Government of India Act (1935) than the consociational federal blueprint of the Cabinet Mission Plan (1946). India adopted a parliamentary model, which concentrated powers in a central parliamentary cabinet, based on the support of a parliamentary majority in the Lok Sabha elected under the first-past-the-post (simple plurality) electoral system. To secure the territorial integrity of the newly born state, it introduced a system of multilevel governance, which empowered the center politically, financially and militarily (Austin, 1966; Singh, 2019). Reflecting its centralist bias, the constitution refers to this as a "union" rather than a "federal" model (Saéz, 2002; Saxena, 2006; Swenden, 2016; Tillin, 2019). Apart from Jammu and Kashmir, no states could have their own constitution or flag, and only the Indian center is responsible for citizenship and immigration. The center has acquired a long list of exclusive or concurrent legislative competencies, the latter with central "paramountcy" in case of conflict between both levels. Residual powers also remain with the center. There is an integrated judiciary and elite civil service (Indian Administrative, Forest and Police Services), modeled after the colonial Indian Civil Service. The center controls most direct taxes, excise and duties and shares most indirect taxes (especially after the introduction of the Goods and Services Tax in 2017) with the states. Amending constitutional provisions in relation to territorial finance or the distribution of legislative competencies requires the parallel consent of the central government and a majority of state legislatures, but unlike in other federations, redrawing the country's internal state boundaries only needs central parliamentary majority (Tillin, 2013, 2015).

Next to limited fiscal and legislative self-rule, states also have limited shared rule. The federal second chamber, although elected indirectly by state legislatures, is subordinate in power to the popularly elected parliamentary lower house, the Lok Sabha. It has only suspensive veto powers on a majority of issues and no right to initiate money bills. States are roughly represented according to population in both houses. Until the creation of a (heavily underused) Inter-State Council in the 1990s, there were no constitutionally mandated procedures for channeling intergovernmental relations. The creation of a Planning Commission in 1950 (active until 2015) linked to the Prime Minister's Office and tasked with crafting five-year national development plans and annual state development plans added to the centralization of India. Although state leaders (Chief Ministers and head of union territories) were represented in the National Development Council, its role in sanctioning or developing five-year plans has been quite limited (Swenden & Saxena, 2017).

Most significantly, the center acquired important emergency provisions (once more frequently carried over from the colonial regime) such as the power to suspend the autonomy of a state (under so-called President's Rule as specified in Article 356) or to overrule a state bill if considered in the national interest. A key role in overseeing the interests of the center in state politics is played by the governor, a centrally appointed official. Some of these provisions have been abused from time to time for party-political ends. Overall then, the Indian constitution, to cite B.R. Ambedkar, the prominent chairman of the Drafting Committee of the Indian constitution, could be considered "federal or unitary, according to the requirements of time and circumstance" (Constituent Assembly Debates, Vol. VII, 34 (Raju, 1991, 160)).[1]

In spite of these centralizing features, some key policies were placed in the exclusive state list, most notably health, policing (law and order) or land. Education (except from central universities) was featured in that list as well, but under Indira Gandhi's premiership, it was moved into the concurrent list. Some of these "welfare-oriented" policies acquired more visibility in the twenty-first century, especially during a period of accelerated growth in state income between 2004 and 2009 (Manor, 2011). The states also play an important role in the administration of welfare schemes in which the central government has invested significantly (so-called national development programs or centrally sponsored schemes). Not unlike in Germany, the implementation of many central legislative policies requires the administrative support of the states.

---

[1] To cite Ambedkar in full: "In normal times it [the constitution] is framed to work as a federal system. But in times of *war* it is designed to make it work as though it was a unitary system. Such a power of converting itself into a unitary state, no federation possesses." With regard to the abuse of the central emergency powers, Ambedkar argued that "the proper thing we ought to expect is that such Articles will never be called into operation [sic] and that they would remain a dead letter" (Constituent Assembly Debates, Vol. IX, p. 177).

Federalism and Democracy: How the State of National Democracy Affects Center-State Interactions in Mainstream India

In general, democracy and federalism have reinforced each other. Yet, there are temporal and spatial variations in the quality of democracy (across both levels) in India (Swenden & Adeney, 2021). This section focuses on variations in the quality of *national* democracy and what this means for center-state interactions in relation to what we may call "mainstream India." Apart from the Hindi-speaking states in the North of India (frequently referred to as the Hindi-belt), mainstream India comprises the key states of West, South and East India. All of them are predominantly Hindu in character.

By and large, India's relatively centralized territorial constitution operates in a more "decentralized" way when it is supported by a pluralized (or as some have argued "federalized") party system. Conversely, the centralized dimensions of India's federal constitution are amplified under national one-party dominance. Under such conditions, the center is more likely to engage in "clientelist" practices to reward politically loyal subnational governments or to punish state governments controlled by parties in national opposition. Rewards can take the form of *discretionary* grants (Sharma, 2017), especially during the state-led economy (1952–1991). Punishments may result in the allocation of a disproportionately lower share of discretionary grants or—at its most invasive—the sacking of state governments through the imposition of the President's Rule for party-political ends (made harder due to judicial safeguards post-1994). Furthermore, the territorial ideology of the ruling party at the center and its organizational properties influence the extent to which one-party dominance leads to centralized authoritarianism. Centralization is more likely where the party in national government ideologically opposes state self-rule; authoritarianism is more likely where the party itself is highly centralized organizationally around a single national leader.

Given the conditions set out above, subnational autonomy was more widely respected during the sustained period of minority and/or coalition government, which started around 1989 and lasted until 2014 (Singh & Verney, 2003). This period also coincided with a substantial reduction in the unwarranted suspension of state autonomy through the political abuse of President's Rule. In this states found partners in a more assertive Supreme Court, which used the favorable party-political opportunity structure to start policing such abuses (something it, until its *S.R Bommai* ruling in 1994, had considered a political prerogative). Although led by polity-wide parties with a centralizing outlook, such as Congress or the Bharatiya Janata Party, coalition governments cushioned their centralizing tendencies as they included parties with a specific state-based following (regional parties) or with specific interests linked to regional culture, language or traditions (regionalist parties) (Kailash, 2014; Schakel et al., 2019; Ziegfeld, 2016).

However, in the nearly 70-year electoral history of post-independent India, national elections threw up fewer coalitions than one-party governments. Given the nature of the electoral system (first past the post), single-party governments in India have frequently been built on less than 40% of the popular vote. For instance, the current BJP government headed by Prime Minister Narendra Modi had the support of 37.1% of the voters in the 2019 general elections. The extent to which said governments pursue a (de)centralizing agenda then hinges on the ideological openness of that party to federalism, its ability to adopt or accommodate regionalist challengers and its organizational properties.

For instance, in relation to Congress party dominance (1952–1989), useful distinctions can be made between Congress under the leadership of Jawaharlal Nehru (1947–1964) and (his almost immediate successor) Indira Gandhi (1966–1977; 1980–1984). Nehru was steeped in democratic politics and had been at the forefront of a broad-based Congress national movement. Nehru and the central party leadership tolerated different voices within and gave considerable autonomy to Congress Pradesh (state) committees in organizing their own affairs (Kothari, 1964). This influenced the structure and working of Indian federalism. For instance, despite reorganizing the party units on the basis of vernacular languages in the 1930s, post-independence Congress initially shied away from implementing linguistic federalism and stuck with the multilingual state boundaries it inherited from the British (albeit in different shape due to the absorption of princely states as discussed above). It feared the centrifugal pressures linguistic reorganization might provoke in a subcontinent which had already been divided on the basis of religion. As a tool of integration, Congress also proposed a gradual transition toward Hindi as a national language (and a diminished role for English).

Yet in 1952, a hunger strike (and subsequent death) of a Congress activist in Madras and more widespread mobilization *within and outside* the party kickstarted linguistic state reorganization (Gupta & Dasgupta,

1970; Chandhoke, 2007; Sarangi, 2009). Although restructuring the Indian states along linguistic lines strengthened their significance as territorial political communities, it also defused a threat of subnational violence and potentially secession, especially in combination with the eventual retention of English as an associate official language.

Congress developed more authoritarian and centralizing tendencies under the leadership of Nehru's daughter, Indira Gandhi. Faced with a split within her party in 1969, many of the erstwhile state party leaders left, leaving Gandhi in control of the central parliamentary party. Gradually, the parties' local and state party organizations fell in disuse, intra-party elections were abolished and Gandhi built up a party image centered around her personality and populist politics ("eradicate poverty") (Kochanek, 1976; Swenden & Toubeau, 2013). Clientelist exchanges, in the form of state sources to placate Congress-ruled states and the recurrent imposition of President's Rule against opposition-ruled states (Sharma, 2017), cemented her centralized and authoritarian leadership. When opposition against her leadership ran out of control in 1975, she imposed an 18-month-long nationwide emergency during which all national and state assembly elections were suspended, opposition party leaders were jailed and freedom of the press was curtailed.

Similarly, the return of one-party dominance in 2014, this time under the control of a Hindu nationalist government, strengthened the centrist and authoritarian tendencies in the Indian state. The 2014 elections were the first in which the BJP could muster an absolute parliamentary majority. The broader association of Hindu organizations ("Sangh Parivar"), to which the party is organizationally and ideologically aligned, has traditionally been hostile to federalism, propagating a Hindu majoritarian cultural nation instead (Jaffrelot, 2011). During earlier periods in which the BJP led national coalition governments (1998 and 2004), little of this vision was realized, however. The party was headed by a more pragmatic leader (Vajpayee), suitable for keeping together a broad coalition in which regional(ist) parties participated. Key BJP territorial demands (such as the abrogation of Kashmir's special status) were shelved as a result (Adeney, 2005). Freed from such party systemic constraints, more evidence of state centralization has emerged since 2014, alongside the centralization of the BJP party structures. Although the Supreme Court has continued to halt political abuses of President's Rule (Sharma &

Swenden, 2018), centralization is apparent in the running (naming and administering) of centrally sponsored welfare programs, many of which intrude into state exclusive competencies such as health (Aiyar & Tillin, 2020). This can be seen, for example, in attempts to undo the rather state-favorable recommendations of the XIV Finance Commission for the allocation of shared tax revenue to the states and in curtailing the role of the states in areas in which they had shown more assertiveness during the coalition era, most notably para-diplomacy (Sharma et al., 2020). The BJP government is also seeking (thus far unsuccessfully) to realign state assembly and general elections, assuming this would "center"' state politics and, given the popularity of Narendra Modi, nationalize the result (although the BJP won a large number of state assembly elections between 2014 and 2017, it has performed comparatively poorly in subnational elections thereafter).

Critics also argue that, unlike Congress in the 1970s and 1980s, the BJP does *not need* to resort to President's Rule or emergency provisions as much to keep the states under control. A change in party finance laws (with the introduction of anonymous "electoral bonds") has provided the party with a massive electoral war chest. Corporate houses stand to benefit from supporting a dominant party, given that even in India's marketized setting, the center holds significant powers in areas such as the regulation of product and labor standards, environmental clearances, competition or land acquisition (Jaffrelot et al., 2019). The BJP has used its resources to dominate election campaigns or poach opponents before or after the elections (provoking the toppling of opposition-led governments in Karnataka and Madhya Pradesh since 2018). It has used further mechanisms to selectively "disarm" political opponents, for instance, by using the Income Tax Department, the Central Bureau of Intelligence or the Enforcement Directorate to intimidate senior opposition figures in central and state politics. It has tried to "expose" corruption scandals implicating senior judges (of the Supreme Court of State High Courts) to facilitate government-friendly court rulings (Jaffrelot & Verniers, 2020). It (as well as state governments) can withhold lucrative government advertisements from newspapers or withhold licenses to TV or radio channels (Reddy, 2019). These measures contributed to a recent slippage in India rankings as a "liberal" democracy, even though elections remain (heavily) contested at the national, state and local levels (The Economist Intelligence Unit, 2019).

FEDERALISM AND DEGREES OF SUBNATIONAL DEMOCRACY IN MAINSTREAM INDIA

If we define *national* "democratic consolidation" as the "alternation in power in which an erstwhile opposition serves a full term in power," then India approximated that status in 1980, even though the period in which the Janata Party displaced the Congress from power lasted fewer than three years (1977–1980). In fact, the first non-Congress government to complete a full four-year legislative term was the BJP-led National Democratic Alliance (1999–2004). Yet, in India's multilevel polity, *subnational* democratic consolidation was accomplished ahead of national democratic consolidation in some states but after in others (Tudor & Ziegfeld, 2016, 56).

For long, democracy at the subnational level (state level) in "mainstream India" followed the national pattern. Congress dominated most of the state governments (Yadav & Palshikar, 2008; Palshikar et al., 2014). Yet, Kerala, Tamil Nadu and West Bengal were among the first states to elect non-Congress governments. Appropriating the "centralized" features of Indian federalism, the Congress-led government imposed President's Rule on Kerala in 1959, just two years after it had elected a Communist government into power. In the 1967 general and state elections, Congress was displaced from power in a majority of the states, while facing a reduced majority in the Lok Sabha (national parliament). Although the 1970s and 1980s coincide with the most frequent abuse of the "power-vertical" (the inappropriate sacking of state governments in control of national opposition parties), vertical power incongruence has become a more recurrent feature of Indian politics since then and, at least since the 1990s, has generally been tolerated.

Despite the recurrence of President's Rule under one-party dominance, subnational autonomy has resulted in territorial variations in subnational democracy, both in procedural terms (procedural democracy) and in substantive terms. In a recent comparative study, Imke Harbers (2019, 1159–1163) and a team of researchers have sought to map (variations) in the former on the basis of four key indicators. Their democracy index is based on *election outcomes* (turnover or alternation in government); *electoral contestation* (measured by the strength of the opposition and the effective number of parties in the state legislature, with extreme pluralism *and* extreme concentration boding poorly for democracy); *autonomy* (the application of President's Rule to the state) and *clean elections* (based on news reports about election fraud, booth capturing, violence at the polls and voter intimidation—possibly including boycotts by armed groups). Based on data between 1985 and 2015, Harbers and her team report 2 states with a high democracy index between 1.5 and 2 (Uttarakhand and Kerala), 9 states and the union territory of Puducherry scoring moderately high between 1.0 and 1.5 (in decreasing order: Maharashtra, Puducherry, Haryana, Mizoram, Himachal Pradesh, Odisha, Rajasthan, Madhya Pradesh, Assam and Tamil Nadu), a large group of 13 states and the union territory of Delhi traversing the full spectrum between 0.5 and 1 (in decreasing order: Delhi, Andhra Pradesh, Punjab, Sikkim, Karnataka, Meghalaya, Gujarat, Goa, Manipur, Uttar Pradesh, Jammu and Kashmir, West Bengal, Chhattisgarh and Bihar), whereas 4 states score very low (Arunachal Pradesh, Tripura, Nagaland and Jharkhand).

Social scientists have not yet systematically linked Harbers' useful index, which is based primarily on measuring "input" or procedural democracy to *substantive* democracy. However, recent studies abound which map territorial policy divergence in India (Tillin et al., 2015; 2022; Mundle et.al, 2016; Kohli, 2012). The impact thereof on national politics requires further consideration. Some states (such as Tamil Nadu or Maharashtra) have piloted welfare schemes such as free midday meal schemes or rural employment welfare schemes, which subsequently developed into national cost-sharing programs. At the same time, the Hindi-belt states of Uttar Pradesh, Rajasthan, Madhya Pradesh and Bihar weigh heavily on national politics but are open to more clientelistic practices and marked by lower development and growth figures. Given their demographic size, they weigh heavily on national politics. In this context, the relatively developed states of the Dravidian South are keen to protect their subnational policy autonomy, especially because they are marked by distinctive party systems in which the polity-wide parties (apart from the BJP in Karnataka) hold limited sway.

Territorial Management and Subnational Democracy in the Borderlands

Unlike in mainstream India, center-state relations and the quality of subnational democracy have been more fraught in the so-called borderlands. These make up a group of eight relatively small states (with the exception of Assam, which is medium sized) of the Northeast plus Jammu and Kashmir and Punjab. Among this group are several states *without* Hindu majorities (Jammu and Kashmir—which, since August 2019, is no longer a state—has a Muslim majority; Punjab is predominantly Sikh; Nagaland, Meghalaya and Mizoram are predominantly Christian). Some of the remaining states in the Northeast are composed of significant tribal and/or Muslim-minority populations. The integration of these border states into the Indian union raised peculiar challenges and was accommodated by special provisions, which often were carried forward from the late colonial period. Although relatively numerous, these nine states and two union territories (since 2019, Jammu/Kashmir and Ladakh) constitute a small share of the overall population. The Northeast has a combined population of around 45 million, just 3.7% of India's population; Jammu and Kashmir holds a population of 12.5 million, less than 1% of India's total, and Punjab has just about 28 million, approximately 2.2% of India's total. Collectively, they have limited weight in the national parliament where they represent just 25 (of which Assam alone has 14), 6 and 13 Lok Sabha seats, respectively (thus 44 seats in total), out of a total of 545.

Three consequences derive from this. First, the distortion of "federalism" (due to the imposition of central rule or heavy central interference in the running of some of these states) must be put into perspective when assessing federalism and democracy in India as a whole. Second, their limited parliamentary representation has worked against their accommodation through specific shared rule provisions at the center. Instead, asymmetric self-rule mechanisms were worked out (or inherited) from the past for several of the Northeastern states and Jammu and Kashmir (until 2019) but not for Punjab. At times, these mechanisms have been honored more often in the breach than in the observance. Third, their strategic location, below-average levels of development and small population have made these border regions amenable to "boundary opening strategies" (Gibson, 2012) by the center. At the same time, several factors facilitate elements of sub-state national "pushback" or "boundary control" against central incursions: (1) the peripheral and mountainous terrain of their territories; (2) the comparatively speaking still limited capacity of the Indian state (Ganguly & Thompson, 2017) in a context where it seeks to control multiple boundary regions adjacent to Pakistan, China, Myanmar and Bangladesh at the same time; (3) the distinctive ethnic profile (several Northeast states have Christian majorities, while Jammu and Kashmir and Punjab have majority Muslim and Sikh populations, respectively) of some states, underpinned by a distinctive party system, which nurtures a regional political identity; (4) the presence of constitutional asymmetries, often carried forward from colonial times, which render a special status to some territories of the Northeast and until 2019 also to Jammu and Kashmir (but NOT to Punjab) (Manor, 1998, 25–28; Tillin, 2016; Baruah, 2020, 25–33).

In terms of assessing the strategies of the center, we find that the center has sought to limit the scope for subnational "boundary control" by ruling out certain political options. First, the constitutional and legal framework declares the territorial integrity of India as sacrosanct; no groups can openly entertain the idea of secession. The constitution contains an antisecession clause and requests allegiance of public servants to the Indian flag and constitution, while the Representation of the People Act identifies parties with an openly independentist agenda as "anti-national" and therefore beyond the law (Swenden, 2016).

Second, despite the previous point, the Indian state has not been averse to negotiating with insurgent factions and signing peace agreements (Manor, 1998; Stepan et al., 2011). In such accords, the center may pledge more development aid to these regions. Indeed, as (formerly) "special category states," all of the above states (apart from Punjab) have benefited from larger per capita support from the center in the way of grants for national development programs (though these scarcely make up for disproportionately low levels of private investment here).

Third, in seeking to bind these states to the union, the center has shown greater commitment to stability than to subnational democracy. With the exception of Assam and Mizoram, post-1985, all of the states in the above group score low or very low in Harbers et al.'s subnational democratization index. Security concerns have often led to the imposition of large interludes of President's Rule. For instance, Jammu and Kashmir experienced a sustained period of 2455 days under President's Rule between 1987 and 1996, following violence after the 1987 state assembly elections, which were widely perceived as rigged (Harbers et al., 2019, 1162; Adeney, 2007; Swenden, 2016, for a summary of pan-India applications of President's Rule). Alternatively, the center has been complicit in the making and sustenance of subnational authoritarian enclaves in exchange for nonviolence against the Indian state (Lacina, 2017; Baruah, 2020). In some of these states, the center has faced various warring insurgent factions; some with irredentist claims in relation to other Indian states and/or neighboring countries (e.g. Myanmar in the case of the Nagas, Pakistan for some of the Muslim insurgent groups in the Kashmir valley). In Nagaland, some insurgent groups (most notably the NSCN-IM) have operated a "shadow state" within the "state", that is, they extract taxes and provide services *alongside* the regularly elected state government, with the latter operating as a bridge between the central government and NSCN-IM (Baruah, 2020, 114).

Fourth, all of these states have been subject to intense securitization. This implies the presence of a large number of "boots" on the ground. For instance, the Indian military has stationed about 210,000 soldiers in Jammu and Kashmir alone, of which 150,000 are regular army and 60,000 are counterinsurgency units. Added to these are 100,000 soldiers manning the Central Armed Police Force and the Border Security Force. Erstwhile, state-controlled police forces as well as special police officers and intelligence agencies added 130,000 personnel (since the demotion of Jammu and Kashmir to a union territory in August 2019, these forces are now directly answerable to the central government), plus 30,000 personnel of the Indo-Tibet border force to secure the border with China. Hence, collectively there are about 470,000 security personnel in a (former) state of just 12.5 million inhabitants, making Kashmir one of the most militarized zones in the world (Shukla, 2018). Furthermore, securitization implies that central and state authorities can invoke security laws to suspend civil liberties or preventively incarcerate suspects of terrorist or "anti-national" activities. Collectively, such policies have led some scholars, such as Baruah (Baruah, 2005), to describe federalism in the border states as predominantly "cosmetic" or, as Singh asserts (Singh, 2000; Singh & Kim, 2018), subservient to the interests of an ethnic Hindu core.

Although the borderland states have always challenged India's commitment to territorial diversity, the degree to which this was honored is influenced by factors which have shaped center-state relations in mainland India. By and large, violent disruptions and insurgencies tend to be more associated with periods of one-party dominance. In contrast, multiparty coalition government at the center, especially since 1996, has helped to stabilize democratic instability in Punjab, much of the Northeast and even Jammu and Kashmir (where between 2002 and 2015 elections were more strongly contested, less boycotted and more free). Regionalist parties from Kashmir, the Northeastern states and Punjab found their way in one of the two main party alliances vying for national power: the Congress-led United Progressive Alliance or the BJP-led National Democratic Alliance.

The Hindu cultural-nationalist vision of the BJP, which since 2014 has had an absolute parliamentary majority and is led by a hard-line Hindu Prime Minister, challenges India's commitment to "unity in diversity."

This has become most obvious in relation to Jammu and Kashmir, which, until August 2019, was India's only Muslim-majority state. By 2019, successive central governments had already hollowed out most of Kashmir's special status. What was left was largely symbolic (own flag, own constitution), except for provisions limiting property to resident Kashmiri citizens (Noorani, 2014). In August 2019, the BJP took the unprecedented step to abrogate the state's special status and bifurcate it into two union territories instead: Jammu and Kashmir (with the prospect of an autonomous assembly) and Buddhist-majority Ladakh (without assembly). Union territory status also puts the police (a "state power") under direct central control. The way in which sections of Article 370 were made inoperative is contentious and has been challenged in the Supreme Court (Nair, 2019). Timing in this matter is crucial. Although a five-member Supreme Court bench is expected to rule on the validity of revoking key provisions of Article 370 in the future, the Attorney General K.K. Venugopal, representing the center, argued in March 2020 that "the abrogation of provisions of Article 370, has now become a 'fait accompli' leaving sole option to accept the change" (India Today, 2020).

The same level of assertiveness has not been on display in the Northeast, where the BJP-led center has signed a framework peace agreement with the *National Socialist Council of Nagaland*, Isak-Muivah (NSCN-IM), in 2015 while upholding the concept of "shared sovereignty." It remains to be seen whether the NSCN-IM is willing to cede its demands for a separate flag and a separate constitution. In January 2019, the Union Cabinet even approved a constitutional amendment to Article 280 and the Sixth Schedule to grant more powers and financial resources to the ten autonomous councils in Assam, Tripura, Manipur, Sikkim, Nagaland, Mizoram, Arunachal Pradesh and Meghalaya. On July 25, 2019, the BJP formed a missionary cell in Mizoram to assist Christian missionaries if they face religious persecution. The politics of Hindutva appears to operate in softer ways, as the BJP realizes that unlike in Jammu (but not Kashmir) and Punjab, the party did not have a foothold in these states until recently (Longkumer, 2019). By working with and not against some of the regionalist parties (2019), the BJP is playing the long game, seeking to pull the region into the party's religious-cultural nationalism project. The financial dependence of the Northeast on central grants and the relative weakness of its indigenous industrial sector has helped to nurture this unlikely alliance between the Northeast's indigenous politicians and the BJP. That said, considerable strains have become visible after the BJP sought to roll out a Citizen Amendment Bill (December 2019) in conjunction with a National Register of Citizens (Assam) (Jaffrelot & Laliwala, 2019). While the Hindu nationalists and the indigenous groups are united in their aim to keep unwanted Muslims (who are mainly "framed" as immigrants from Bangladesh) out of the region, many of the Northeastern political elites see the BJP's push for the Citizen Amendment Bill as a means to regularize Hindu citizens who are not indigenous to the region. Thus, the Hindu-first approach of the BJP is pitted against the "sons—and daughters—of the soil approach" of the indigenous Northeastern communities.

Conclusion: The Fragile Federation Under a Politics of "Vishwas" (Sircar, 2020)

This chapter analyzed center-state relations and the state of national and subnational democracy in India. It showed how state formation produced a centralized, yet also flexible constitution which was cast intently as a union, not as a federation. This made center-state relations vulnerable to central overreach, especially during periods of one-party dominance. In contrast, coalition government protected (though did not constitutionally expand) subnational autonomy. Indeed, the chapter demonstrated the vibrancy of subnational electoral competition (in the mainland), the ability of states to craft different policies tied to their competence portfolio and their role in implementing central policy. Indeed, it was between 1989 and 2014 that Indian federalism was most emergent.

Center-state relations have been more fraught in the border regions where the Indian state's commitment to "unity in diversity" has been put strongest to the test. Here, too, the nature of central power (one-party dominance versus coalition government) has influenced the willingness of the center to accommodate. "Boundary opening strategies" have often come at the cost of subnational democracy, sometimes even abetting in the creation of subnational authoritarian enclaves. The willingness to accommodate these regions is also influenced by the ideology of the party in central power: for example, to make Article 370 (and Article 35) inoperative deprives India's only Muslim-majority state (subsequently demoted) of a meaningful form of symbolic recognition. It underlines the BJP's project to center the Indian nation along Hinduness, closer to unity than diversity.

The fragility of Indian federalism is also underpinned by the paradoxes of the Indian population at large in their commitment to both federalism and democracy. Voters have turned out in higher numbers in state rather than general elections, and consecutive election surveys confirm their strong levels of identification with the region or the state. However, in the build up to the 2014 BJP electoral victory voters have shown a steep rise in individual religiosity and a penchant for strong and decisive leadership (Sircar, 2020). This, Sircar argues, has led to the replacement of a politics of vikas (development) with a politics of vishwas (a politics of belief built on "the linking of an individual's personal character and decision-making with defending a singular national [Hindu] identity for India") (Sircar, 2020, 184). He shows how Modi, media, money and a well-oiled BJP party machine pushed voters away from voting retrospectively (punishing the BJP for lackluster economic development between 2014 and 2019) and into voting for Modi "because of their vishwas" (belief) in him. The extent to which this belief can be sustained (which necessitates using state resources to "disarm" national and subnational opposition) is likely to affect the state of Indian democracy for years to come and push Indian federalism closer toward its "unionist" features.

References

Adeney, K. (2005). Hindu nationalists and federalism in an era of regionalism. In K. Adeney & L. Lawrence Saéz (Eds.), *Coalition politics and Hindu nationalism, Routledge advances in South Asian Studies* (pp. 97–115). Routledge.

Adeney, K. (2007). *Federalism and ethnic conflict regulation in India and Pakistan*. Springer.

Adeney, K., & Wyatt, A. (2004). Democracy in South Asia: Getting beyond the structure-agency dichotomy. *Political Studies, 52*, 1–18.

Aiyar, Y., & Tillin, L. (2020). 'One nation,' BJP, and the future of Indian federalism. *India Review, 19*, 117–135.

Austin, G. (1966). *The Indian constitution: Cornerstone of a nation*. Clarendon Press.

Baruah, S. (2005). *Durable disorder*. Oxford University Press.

Baruah, S. (2020). *In the name of the nation: India and its Northeast*. Stanford University Press.

Bates, C. (2007). *Subalterns and the Raj. South Asia since 1600*. Routledge.

Bednar, J. (2008). *The robust federation. Principles of design*. Cambridge University Press.

Bose, S. (2007). *Contested lands. Israel-Palestine, Kashmir, Bosnia, Cyprus and Sri Lanka*. Harvard University Press.

Chandhoke, N. (2007). Negotiating linguistic diversity: A comparative study of India and the United States. In K. S. Bajpai (Ed.), *Democracy and diversity. India and the American experience* (pp. 107–143). Oxford University Press.

Chandra, B., Mukherjee, A., & Mukherjee, M. (2008). *India since independence*. Penguin Books India.

Erk, J. (2007). *Explaining federalism*. Routledge.

Ganguly Sumit and Thompson W.R (2017). Ascending India and its State Capacity. Extraction, Violence and Legitimacy. New Haven: Yale University Press.

Gibson, Edward L. (2012). Boundary Control. Subnational authoritarianism in Federal Democracies. Cambridge: Cambridge University Press.

Gupta, J. D., & Dasgupta, J. (1970). *Language conflict and national development: Group politics and national language policy in India*. University of California Press.

Harbers, I., Bartman, J., & van Wingerden, E. (2019). Conceptualizing and measuring subnational democracy. *Democratization, 26*, 1154–1175.

Jaffrelot, Christophe (2011). Religion. Caste and Politics in India. London: Hurst

Jaffrelot, C., Kohli, A., & Murali, K. (Eds.). (2019). *Business and politics in India, modern South Asia*. Oxford University Press.

Jaffrelot, C., & Laliwala, S. (2019). Citizenship Law, proposed nation-wide NRC will revise conception of group rights in India. *Indian Express*.

Jaffrelot, C., & Verniers, G. (2020). A new party system or a new political system? *Contemporary South Asia, 28*, 141–154.

Kailash, K. (2014). Regional parties in the 16th Lok Sabha elections: Who survived and why? *Economic and Political Weekly, 49*, 64–70.

Kochanek, S. A. (1976). Mrs. Gandhi's pyramid. In H. Hart (Ed.), *Indira Gandhi's India* (pp. 93–124). Westview Press.

Kohli, Atul (2012). Poverty Amid Plenty in the New India. Cambridge: Cambridge University Press.

Kothari, R. (1964). The Congress 'system' in India. *Asian Survey, 4*(2), 1161–1173.

Lacina, B. (2017). *Rival claims: Ethnic violence and territorial autonomy under Indian federalism*. University of Michigan Press.

Longkumer, A. (2019). Playing the waiting game: The BJP, Hindutva and the Northeast. In A. P. Chatterji, T. B. Hansen, & C. Jaffrelot (Eds.), *Majoritarian state: How Hindu Nationalism is changing India* (pp. 281–296). Oxford University Press.

Manor, J. (1998). Making federalism work. *Journal of Democracy, 3*, 21–35.

Manor, J. (2011). Government and opposition in India. *Government and Opposition, 46*, 436–463.

Mathur, A. (2020). Supreme Court refuses to refer Article 370 cases to larger bench. *India Today*.

Metcalf, B. D., & Metcalf, T. R. (2012). *A concise history of modern India.* Cambridge University Press.

Mundle, Sudipto, Chowdhury Samik and Sikdar Satadru (2016). 'Governance performance of Indian states 2001–2002 and 2011–2012' NIPFP Working Paper Series, Delhi.

Nair, B. (2019). Abrogation of Article 370: Can the president act without the recommendation of the constituent assembly. *Indian Law Review, 3,* 254–279.

Noorani A. G. (2014). *The Kashmir Dispute 1947–2012.* New York: Oxford University Press.

Palshikar, S., Suri, K., & Yadav, Y. (2014). *Party competition in Indian states: Electoral politics in post-Congress polity.* Oxford University Press.

Poggi, G. (2017). The Nation-state. In D. Caramani (Ed.), *Comparative politics* (pp. 67–82). Oxford University Press.

Raju, K. H. C. (1991). Dr. B. R. Ambedkar and the making of the constitution: A case study of Indian federalism. *Indian Journal of Political Science, 52,* 153–164.

Reddy, C. R. (2019). Media in contemporary India: Journalism transformed into a commodity. In C. Jaffrelot, A. Kohli, & K. Murali (Eds.), *Business and politics in India.* Oxford University Press.

Rudolph, L. I., & Rudolph, S. H. (2008). State formation in India: Building and wasting assets. In L. I. Rudolph & S. R. Rudolph (Eds.), *The realm of institutions. State formation and institutional change* (pp. 46–98). Oxford University Press.

Saéz, L. (2002). *Federalism without a centre: The impact of political and economic reform on India's federal system.* Sage Publications.

Sarangi, A. (2009). *Language and politics in India.* Oxford University Press.

Saxena, R. (2006). *Situating federalism: Mechanisms of intergovernmental relations in Canada and India.* Manohar Publishers.

Schakel, A. H., Kumar Sharma, C., & Swenden, W. (2019). India after the 2014 general elections: BJP dominance and the crisis of the third party system. *Regional and Federal Studies, 29*(3), 1–26.

Sharma, C. K. (2017). A situational theory of pork-barrel politics: The shifting logic of discretionary allocations in India. *India Review, 16,* 14–41.

Sharma, C. K., Destradi, S., & Plagemann, J. (2020). Partisan federalism and subnational government's international engagements: Insights from India. *Publius, 50*(4), 566–592.

Sharma, C. K., & Swenden, W. (2018). Modi-fying Indian federalism? Center–state relations under Modi's tenure as Prime Minister. *Indian Politics and Policy, 1*(1), 51–82.

Shukla, A. (2018). India has 700,000 troops in Kashmir? Retrieved July 15, 2020, from https://www.rediff.com/news/column/india-has-700000-troops-in-kashmir-false/20180717.htm

Singh, A. K. (2019). Dynamic de/centralization in India, 1950–2010. *Publius, 49*(1), 112–137.

Singh, G. (2000). *Ethnic conflict in India: A case-study of Punjab*. Springer.

Singh, G., & Kim, H. (2018). The limits of India's ethno-linguistic federation: Understanding the demise of Sikh nationalism. *Regional and Federal Studies, 28*, 427–445.

Singh, M. P., & Verney, D. V. (2003). Challenges to India's centralized parliamentary federalism. *Publius, 33*, 1–20.

Sircar, N. (2020). The politics of Vishwas: Political mobilization in the 2019 national election. *Contemporary South Asia, 28*, 178–194.

Stepan, A., Linz, J. J., & Yadav, Y. (2010). The rise of 'State-Nations'. *Journal of Democracy, 21*, 50–68.

Stepan, A., Linz, J. J., & Yadav, Y. (2011). *Crafting state-nations: India and other multinational democracies*. JHU Press.

Swenden, W. (2016). Centre-state bargaining and territorial accommodation: Evidence from India. *Swiss Political Science Review, 22*, 491–515.

Swenden, W. (2017). Governing Diversity in South Asia: Explaining Divergent Pathways in India and Pakistan. *Publius, 48*, 102–133.

Swenden, W., & Adeney, K. (2021). Federalism and democracy in India. Mutually reinforcing? In Benz, A. and Sonnicksen, J. (eds.) Federalism and democracy at work. Varieties of complex government. University of Toronto Press, 218–38.

Swenden, W., & Saxena, R. (2017). Rethinking central planning: A federal critique of the Planning Commission. *India Review, 16*, 42–65.

Swenden, W., & Toubeau, S. (2013). Mainstream parties and territorial dynamics in the UK, Spain, and India. In A. Benz & J. Broschek (Eds.), *Federal dynamics. Continuity, change and the varieties of federalism* (pp. 249–273). Oxford University Press.

Talbot, I., & Singh, G. (2009). *The partition of India*. Cambridge University Press.

The Economist Intelligence Unit. (2019). A year of democratic setbacks and popular protest. *Democracy Index 2019*.

Tillin, L. (2013). *Remapping India: New states and their political origins*. Hurst Publishers.

Tillin, L. (2015). Explaining territorial change in federal democracies: A comparative historical institutionalist approach. *Political Studies, 63*, 626–641.

Tillin, L. (2016). Asymmetric federalism. In S. Choudhry, M. Khosla, & P. B. Mehta (Eds.), *The Oxford handbook of the Indian Constitution* (pp. 540–559). Oxford University Press.

Tillin, Louise, Deshpande, Rajeshwari and Kailash K.K (2015) eds. The Politics of Welfare. Comparisons across Indian States. Delhi: Oxford University Press.

Tillin, L. (2019). *Indian federalism*. Oxford University Press.

Tillin, Louise (2022). Does India have subnational welfare regimes?, Territory, Politics, 10, 1, 1–11.
Tudor, M. (2013). *The promise of power: The origins of democracy in India and autocracy in Pakistan.* Cambridge University Press.
Tudor, Maya and Ziegfeld Adam. (2016). "Sunational Democratization in India: The Role of Colonial Competition and Central Intervention." In Laurence Whitehead and Jacqueline Behrend, eds. Illiberal Practices: Territorial Variance within Large Federal Democracies. Baltimore, MD: Johns Hopkins University Press, 49–86.
Varshney, A. (1993). Contested meanings: India's national identity, Hindu nationalism, and the politics of anxiety. *Daedalus, 122,* 227–261.
Varshney, A. (1998). India defies the Odds. Why democracy survives. *Journal of Democracy, 9,* 36–50.
Yadav, Y., & Palshikar, S. (2008, November 14–22). Ten theses on state politics in India. *Seminar,* 591. https://www.india-seminar.com/2008/591/591_y_yadav_&_s_palshkar.htm
Ziegfeld, A. (2016). *Why regional parties?* Cambridge University Press.

CHAPTER 9

Learning from Iraq? Debates on Federalism and Decentralization for Post-War Syria

Eva Maria Belser and Soeren Keil

E. M. Belser • S. Keil (✉)
Institute of Federalism, University of Fribourg, Fribourg, Switzerland
e-mail: evamaria.belser@unifr.ch; Soeren.keil@unifr.ch

© The Author(s), under exclusive license to Springer Nature
Switzerland AG 2022
S. Keil, S. Kropp (eds.), *Emerging Federal Structures in the
Post-Cold War Era*, Federalism and Internal Conflicts,
https://doi.org/10.1007/978-3-030-93669-3_9

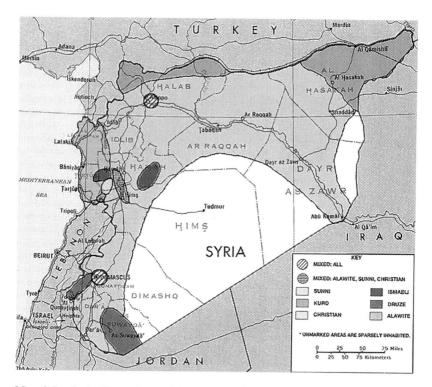

Map 9.1 Syria. *Source*: https://commons.wikimedia.org/w/index.php?search=syria+ethnic+groups&title=Special:MediaSearch&go=Go&type=image

9 LEARNING FROM IRAQ? DEBATES ON FEDERALISM... 191

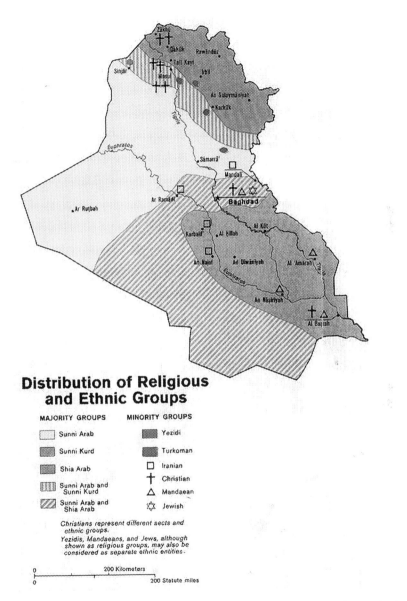

Map 9.2 Iraq Ethnic groups. *Source*: https://commons.wikimedia.org/w/index.php?search=iraq+ethnic+groups&title=Special:MediaSearch&go=Go&type=image

Introduction

The ongoing war in Syria has resulted in one of the largest humanitarian crises in the period after the Second World War; more than ten years after fighting started in the wake of the Arab Spring, the conflict continues to increase suffering and create new victims. Over the course of the war, UN-led peace talks and numerous other peace initiatives have been launched only to have been stalled, postponed or blocked by geopolitics and politics tout court.

The Syrian conflict, the root causes and dynamics, and the complex and ever-changing network of transnational alliances are context-specific and unique. Yet, Syria is not the only country in the Middle East suffering from conflict and ongoing inter-group violence (Anderson, 2018). The ongoing tragedy in Yemen as well as continued unrest between Israel and the Palestinian territories highlight the fragility of the region and its exposure to violence, group conflicts and state weakness. Iraq is no exception in this regard, for despite over 15 years of international involvement, peacebuilding and democracy promotion in the wake of the American-led intervention in 2003, the country is de facto a failed state (Cordesman, 2019; Fürtig, 2011). Instead of a stable federal democracy pacifying and developing the country, conflicts between the different ethnic, religious and political groups as well as interventions by groups supported from Iran and Saudi Arabia are common. The lack of state functionality became particularly visible in 2014 when the Islamic State (ISIS) launched offensives on Mosul, Tikrit and other cities and, at some point, held 40% of Iraq's territory. It was called to mind again in 2017 when the Kurdish Autonomous Region held a unilateral independence referendum and prepared to secede from the rest of the country, only to backtrack once the Iraqi army had conquered the oil-rich city of Kirkuk from Kurdish forces.

This contribution looks at the current discussion on a post-war political order in Syria and asks what the country can learn from Iraq. In doing so, we are particularly interested in questions of federalism, decentralization and inter-ethnic power-sharing in the two countries. While both Iraq and Syria evidently show numerous idiosyncratic features, they also share a number of important similarities, which make such a comparison particularly useful. First, both countries are multi-ethnic and multi-religious countries in the Middle East, a region characterized by the legacies of colonialism, geopolitical relevance and ongoing instability. Indeed, it is also important to highlight that in both countries, Kurds form the second largest ethnic groups (after Arabs) (Romano & Gurses, 2014), while the Shia-Sunni split among Arabs is also visible in both countries. In both countries, federal debates are simultaneously fueled and impeded by the so-called Kurdish questions due to Kurdish territories claiming autonomy or independence—or being suspected of doing so—or establishing de facto self-governance. Second, both countries have seen long periods of military and connected to this, Baath Party dictatorships and have weak traditions of democracy and separation of powers. In Iraq, Saddam Hussain came to power in the 1970s, but Iraq was far from democratic governance before his formal ascension to power. Likewise, Syria never functioned as a proper democratic state before Hafez al-Assad, the father of current President Bashir al-Assad, came to power through a coup d'état in 1971 (Lesch, 2019). His son formally became president in 2000 after Hafez passed away and continued the decades-long family rule through the Baath Party. Third, both countries have a long history of inter-group cooperation and peaceful multi-ethnicity and -religiosity but also of inter-group conflict, including between Arabs and Kurds, between Shia and Sunni Muslims and between Muslims and non-Muslim populations in their territory. Both countries have gone through long and often violent nationalization and Arabization processes denying and banning non-Arab languages and other cultural expressions. The oppression of the Kurds is the most drastic example of inter-group violence in both countries, where chemical weapons were used against Kurdish civilians in Iraq, while in Syria a campaign of resettlement and oppression targeted the Kurdish community specifically. Both countries are heavily burdened by these legacies of suppression of cultural and linguistic diversity. Finally, in both countries international actors played and still play a key role in constitutional and territorial politics. In Iraq, internationally orchestrated democratization took place as a result of the American-led military intervention in 2003, while Syria's civil war, erupting after protests against President Assad in 2011, has rapidly become highly internationalized (Jaeger & Tophoven, 2013), with Iran, Russia and Turkey as direct participants in the conflict and the USA and Saudi Arabia also involved. The consequences of the conflict have been felt not only in the region but also in Europe and worldwide through an influx of refugees which reached and destabilized Europe in 2015. Furthermore, the rise of the so-called Islamic State in Iraq and Syria (ISIS), as well as its cruel treatment of groups such as the Yezidi population and its support for terrorism globally, have additionally highlighted the global implications of the conflict in Syria. The rise of ISIS further contributed to the internationalization of the Syrian crisis and laid the foundation for Russia's involvement in the country, which has since resulted in changing fortunes in the conflict and the revival of the Assad regime with Russian and Iranian support (Abboud, 2018).

This contribution will assess which lessons Syria can learn from Iraq when thinking about a future democratic framework in a post-war era and mitigating inter-group conflicts; it will also consider the (deterrent) effect the Iraqi experiences have on debates about federalism and decentralization in Syria. While it looks likely today that the Assad regime will win the ongoing civil war thanks to its support from Iran and Russia, the regime will need to undergo constitutional and political reforms if it is interested in creating stability in post-war Syria. This will require finding some common ground with opposition groups, particularly with the leaders of the de facto autonomous northern and eastern regions of the country. Working with European and American countries and the international community, not least to access urgently needed support for the post-war recovery of the country, will also call for political solutions to the conflict. It is therefore not surprising that democratic governance and decentralization play an important role in the ongoing negotiations between representatives of the regime and the opposition. Both topics are neither prioritized nor wanted by the regime but can hardly be avoided in the long run. Syria is unlikely to see an enforced democratization (and federalization) as has been witnessed in Iraq, but basic democratic norms, minority rights and a process of political decentralization will be needed in order to provide a framework for internal peace and access to international support. In this context, it becomes vital for the different actors in Syria to look at the process in Iraq and assess which lessons can be learnt from it and which mistakes should be avoided.

We will do this throughout this paper and structure our discussion around four core areas. In the next section, we will look at why federalism and decentralization, along with ethnic power-sharing, were an obvious option in Iraq and might be useful for Syria. We will start by recalling the democratization process in Iraq and assess the current Iraqi framework of ethnic diversity accommodation before discussing its relevance in Syria. In a second step, we will look at the current situation in both countries. While Iraq is formally federal, its federal system is heavily flawed and dysfunctional. Syria remains a fractured, divided and, at the same time, highly centralized country; further steps to decentralize decision-making are desperately needed, not least to coordinate the post-war rebuilding and economic recovery of the country. In the third section, we will assess the functionality of any agreement. While minority protection and decentralization were at the heart of the debates in Iraq, the mechanisms chosen have been poorly (or not at all) implemented. The system remains weak, and conflicts persist, largely because of a flawed institutional framework and a lack of commitment among key political elites. In other words, Iraq is a failed federal system, in which federal principles, while mentioned in the Constitution, have never been fully implemented. In Syria, on the other side, federalism is being discussed as a solution to the ongoing civil war and as a key element of any democratization of the country. Yet, this is a minority discussion in Syria, driven mainly by the Kurds and certain international actors. The questions discussed in this section focus on the intertwinement of emerging federal structures in the Arab region: How does the failed federal experiment in Iraq affect the debates in Syria, where the future of the country does not only remain politically contested but also continues to be fought over on the battleground? In the final section of this contribution, we will look at the prospects of functional federal and decentralized democracy in the two countries. What are the key obstacles on the road to inclusive democracy in Iraq and Syria and are there any indications that these could be overcome?

The Unsurprising Nature of Federal Debates in Iraq and Syria

Federalism and decentralization are important aspects in the wider debates about democratization and pacification in the two countries. While Iraq became federal particularly to accommodate the needs and aspirations of the Kurdish population in the North (see Map above), in Syria, the existence of compact settlements of the Druze population in the South of the country, as well as Kurdish majority territories in the North around the cities of Afrin, Kobane and Qamishli (see Map above), demonstrate that ethnic and religious diversity does not only exist but is also territorialized in both cases. Hence, a solution that focuses on some kind of federal political system[1] seems appropriate for these countries, in which different ethnic, linguistic and religious groups claim certain parts of the territory as

---

[1] We follow the use of a federal political system as suggested by the editors in the Introduction, which may refer to a fully functional federation or to any other decentralised system, with several key federal elements as highlighted by Ronald Watts (2008).

their homeland, and increasingly rival (and hostile) nationalisms competing with each other can be observed. As Burgess (2006) pointed out, in multinational, multi-religious states, federalism can serve as a tool to tame and moderate competing nationalisms and provide a framework for accommodation and reconciliation as well as a way forward to live together peacefully.

In the cases of Iraq and Syria, however, historical legacies, particularly the role of colonial and postcolonial developments, are of importance. In Syria, France as a colonizing power left behind a centralized, and Arab-dominated, system, despite Kurdish and Christian attempts to promote autonomy arrangements (Tejel, 2009; Savelsberg, 2021). In Iraq, the British united three previously autonomous provinces after World War I and implemented a policy of 'divide and conquer' with consequences that would affect discussions on federalism and state-building until today. They focused on a process of state-building by establishing institutions for tax collection and local administration, while at the same time trying to form a united Iraqi nation, simply ignoring local divisions and pushing for a nation-state, which would be able to take care of its own affairs (Dodge, 2006). Instead, the British mandate failed to unite the Iraqi people or to forge a common identity that would overcome existing ethnic, cultural and religious divides. Iraq remained a fragmented state, with ongoing intra-group tensions and an Arabization project, which did not overcome but deepened the divisions we see today (Kirmanj, 2013).

Federalism and decentralization today are not just discussed (and constitutionalized in the case of Iraq) in order to manage ethnic and religious diversity that has developed over centuries and has significantly impacted on the state- and nation-building experiences in both countries. Instead, they are also used as tools of conflict resolution, as mechanisms to hold the countries together and deal with enduring challenges to the territorial integrity of these states. In Iraq, constitutional ambiguities inviting extra-legal political power plays, regular flaring up of conflicts in different parts of the country, blockages and provocations in the relations between Baghdad and Erbil and the abovementioned Kurdish referendum of 2017 demonstrate the ongoing need to redefine and renegotiate the country's constitutional arrangement and how it accommodates the different groups within it. Meanwhile in Syria, we find a country that is highly fractured, with the majority of the territory under the control of the government and its Iranian and Russian allies, while the major city Idlib is still controlled by rebels and opponents of the regime and key territories in the North of Syria by Turkey. The preservation of territorial integrity, the management of de facto fragmentation of the country and the use of federalism to overcome ongoing tensions between different groups are therefore at the heart of the federal debate in both countries (Brancati, 2009; Anderson, 2013; Keil & Anderson, 2018).

In line with these considerations about federalism as a tool of conflict resolution, it is also important to consider the wider regional and geopolitical implications for the choice of federalism in the two cases. In particular, the accommodation of the Kurds in the North of Iraq set an important and highly controversial precedent for similar demands in Syria (as well as for Iran and Turkey). Moreover, the ongoing Sunni-Shia conflict that dominates current politics in the Middle East (and the wider Arab world) and the regional confrontations between Saudi Arabia as the leader of Sunni Muslims and Iran as the leader of Shia Muslims heavily reflects on inter-group relations and internal conflicts in Iraq and Syria. Therefore, any suggestions for federalism or a decentralized system have wider regional implications, as seen through the creation of the Autonomous Kurdistan Region in Iraq. Yet, these regional implications may also disincentivize the use of federalism. The developments in the Kurdish autonomous region particularly in Northern Iraq have set a negative example that elites in Syria will want to avoid. Likewise, the failure to properly implement the federal settlement in Iraq (Belser, 2020), limiting its ability to accommodate ongoing conflicts, has also resulted in more hesitation toward federal and decentralized solutions in other countries in the Middle East (Aboultaif, 2021). Federalism is still seen as an organizational principle that leads to chaos and state disintegration, and the evidence from the regional federal experiments in Iraq and Yemen strengthens these negative stereotypes, especially among the Arab majority.

In addition to these negative assumptions about federalism, notably among the majority population, there is another reason for continued suspicion toward any federal solution in the region. This has to do with the role of international actors, who are seen as the key drivers of federalism and decentralization reforms in the two countries. Indeed, without pressure from the Americans, federalism would probably not have been chosen for Iraq after 2003 (Eklund et al., 2005; Dingley, 2011; Danilovich & Pineda, 2019; Belser, 2020). Likewise, the current debates about federalism and decentralization in Syria are driven by international actors (though not exclusively as discussed below) (see, e.g. Yazidi, 2016). Despite the fact that the highly centralized regimes operating for decades are mainly the result of colonial interventions (and in Syria, legacies of French influences), a study in 2016 confirmed that most citizens saw federalism as an alien theory that is not suitable for their country, though the results differed substantially among Arabs and Kurds, who were more supportive of a federal solution (The Day After Project, 2016). In Iraq, survey data also indicate that the majority of the population does not identify with the dysfunctional federal system and instead supports greater integration (and even centralization) (Al-Mawlawi, 2018). There is, in other words, a feeling by local populations in Iraq and Syria that federalism is an imposed solution which is based neither on domestic consensus nor on historical experience. This lack of a federal political culture (Burgess, 2012) does not necessarily mean that the implementation of federalism is unlikely to succeed, but it will certainly make any future federal arrangement in Syria, and any adjustments toward more functionality in Iraq, more difficult (Keil & Alber, 2020). At the same time, it raises the question of local ownership in any federal bargaining and agreement (Riker, 1964), while also indicating the growing links between external democratization and imposed federalism as witnessed in countries such as Bosnia (Keil, 2013).[2]

What we find in both countries is an absence of deep-rooted democratization and a lack of support for federal and decentralized solutions to conflict resolution. This is particularly important, as it is unlikely that Iraq's federal system will ever work (or any decentralized solution for Syria will ever become reality) without at least basic support from the Arab majority (see O'Leary, 2001). Federal and decentralized governments are still seen by many as tools of external powers (most notably the USA) to promote their interests and contribute to further disintegration in the region. The general suspicion toward any form of external (especially Western) involvement is linked to historical experience of colonization and continued anti-American sentiments across the region (Hetou, 2019). This has also tarnished federalism's reputation, as the USA remains the most important federal country in the world, and those promoting federalism in other parts of the world are often seen as neo-colonialists who are pushing for the installation of Western models of democracy in the Middle East.

---

[2] See also Soeren Keil's contribution on the Balkans in this volume.

Iraq and Syria Today: Between Dysfunctional Statehood and State Dissolution

While a case for the usefulness of federalism to manage the ongoing conflicts and inter-ethnic and inter-religious tensions in Iraq and Syria can certainly be made (as outlined above), in order to understand the current hesitancy, and at times hostility, it is important to assess the political situation in both countries and the role that federalism plays in the ongoing constitutional debates.

Iraq formally became a federal country in 2005, when a new Constitution was passed which states in Article 1 that 'The Republic of Iraq is a single federal, independent and fully sovereign state in which the system of government is republican, representative, parliamentary, and democratic, and this Constitution is a guarantor of the unity of Iraq' (Iraq Constitution, 2005, Article 1). Iraq's federal system is on paper at least relatively decentralized, giving a number of key responsibilities to regions (and also governorates (Articles 116–123)). However, in practice only one region exists in the country, namely, the Kurdish Autonomous Region in the North, which is made up of three governorates. Other attempts to form a region have failed, partially as a result of the non-respect of constitutional rules by the central government (Belser, 2020). While the Constitution provides for a distribution of competences between the center, regions and governorates, in practice this has only been applied in the Kurdish Region. Other governorates have been prevented from forming Regions or even claiming the competences that are assigned to them by the Constitution. In fact, both the territorial arrangement and the allocation of powers in Iraq are substantially incomplete—a fact that is also visible when looking at the institutional provisions. Both the second chamber of parliament (called the Federation Council in Article 65) and the Federal Supreme Court (Article 93) have not been established through the Constitution but rely on additional legislation from the Council of Representatives, the first chamber of parliament. In the absence of such legislation, more than 15 years after the acceptance of the Constitution, Iraq continues to function as a unicameral federal system. And while a Federal Supreme Court was established in 2005, it still lacks the legal basis of an agreed law in the Council of Representatives, thereby seriously challenging its proper functioning as a neutral arbiter. What further negatively affects the perception of federalism in Iraq and in the entire region is the fact that the constitutional arrangement did not allow for the re-integration of the Kurdish region into the Iraqi state after the war. In the absence of joint institutions, robust shared rule and intergovernmental relations, Iraqi Kurdistan continues to operate as a quasi-independent entity not concerned by Iraqi rules. In the eyes of most observers, therefore, federalism stands for allowing a disintegrated region to go its own way.

The incompleteness of Iraq's federal model (Kane et al., 2012) goes back to a flawed process of federal bargaining. While key aspects of Iraq's federal design were negotiated in the aftermath of the US-led military intervention between the major stakeholders in the country (Shakir, 2017, 50–77), serious questions about the inclusiveness of these negotiations were raised when major Sunni groups (previously associated with the Saddam Hussein regime) boycotted the constitutional process (Belser, 2020). Furthermore, the nature of negotiations, which became more and more sectarian and moved the debate away from a purely territorial solution to one that would suit the major ethnic and religious groups, also caused concerns and explains some of the ongoing challenges today (Al-Qarawee, 2010). Iraq's federal bargaining, that is, the initial discussion on federalism as a solution to some of the major issues of the country, can be described best as a mix of local bargaining between some (but not all) of the major stakeholders in the country, in which particularly the representatives of the Kurds pushed for a federal solution and for far-reaching autonomy. Their demands were supported by the USA, who at the time remained the main occupying force and security provider, thereby giving a distinctly international dimension to the federal solution in the country (Danilovich, 2014). It is therefore not surprising that we only find the Kurdish Autonomous Region (Article 117) recognized in the Constitution, while the power-sharing system implemented between Shia, Sunni and Kurdish elites is relatively weak and informal (Dodge, 2020). In fact, the power-sharing arrangement in place, which ensures that the three groups have to work together to form the government and ensures the even representation of all groups in the highest offices of the states, has been strongly linked to accommodating the existing diversity in the country and promoting a form of inclusive democracy in post-Saddam Iraq (McCulloch, 2014, 1–10; Bormann, 2017; McEvoy & Aboultaif, 2020). Yet, neither the democratization nor the implementation of federal arrangements can so far be considered as a success story. Instead, Iraq remains a conflict-prone country, with the Kurds focused on the autonomy of their region and paying little attention to the developments in Baghdad, while Shia elites in Baghdad have pushed for more majoritarian visions of the state. In particular, during the different premierships of Nouri al-Maliki (2007–2009, 2010–2014), there was a substantial push to promote Shia representation in the civil service and the armed forces, thereby limiting the representation and influence of both Kurds and Sunni. Dodge (2013) has labeled Iraq under al-Maliki as a 'new authoritarian regime,' and despite his departure in 2014 (as a result of increased internal and external, especially American, pressure), there is still an imbalance between the main groups in the country. Freedom House lists the country in 2020 as not free, summarizing that 'Iraq holds regular, competitive elections, and the country's various partisan, religious, and ethnic groups generally enjoy representation in the political system. However, democratic governance is impeded in practice by corruption and security threats' (Freedom House, 2020a). The party system is deeply fragmented, representing mainly the three main communities, that is, Shia, Sunni and Kurds. The parties mainly serve as interest representation of certain elites; they are not vertically integrated and lack proper democratic structures (Khalilzad, 2010). State weakness and ongoing inter-ethnic and inter-religious tensions continue to weaken the Iraqi state and the democratization process.

The situation is even bleaker in Syria. Here, Freedom House (2020b) summarizes its report as follows:

> Political rights and civil liberties in Syria are severely compromised by one of the world's most repressive regimes and by other belligerent forces in an ongoing civil war. The regime prohibits genuine political opposition and harshly suppresses freedoms of speech and assembly. Corruption, enforced disappearances, military trials, and torture are rampant in government-controlled areas. Residents of contested regions or territory held by non-state actors are subject to additional abuses, including intense and indiscriminate combat, sieges and interruptions of humanitarian aid, and mass displacement.

Syria remains a deeply divided, war-torn country. While the majority of the territory is now under the control of the Assad regime and its Iranian and Russian allies, there are still territories held by Syrian rebels around the city of Idlib, as well as pockets of territories controlled by Turkey and the Kurdish People's Protection Units (YPG). With half the population displaced and more than 600,000 deaths, it is no exaggeration to claim that Syria's civil war has been one of the worst humanitarian catastrophes since the Second World War (Syrian Observatory for Human Rights, 2021).

While the situation on the battlefield has been frozen in recent months, and a likely final resolution will depend on an agreement between Russia, Turkey and Iran, ongoing constitutional negotiations in Geneva highlight the need for an inclusive solution that cannot just provide a short-term ending to the ongoing violence, but also a long-term solution that brings stability and opens the path to democratic reforms (Heydemann, 2020).

Despite the ongoing violence and the substantial destruction across Syria, discussions about federalism and decentralization have been on the agenda for a number of years now. In 2015, the Kurdish Democratic Union Party (PYD) announced the creation of a democratic confederation in the North of Syria, consisting of Afrin, Jazira and the Euphrates regions, which were categorized as cantons for a future federal Syria (Sabio, 2015). While this project seems to have failed with the Turkish intervention in Afrin in 2018, and Russian and Syrian forces conquering territory in the other parts of North Syria, it has nevertheless mobilized the Kurdish population in Syria to demand a federal arrangement in which their rights would be protected. In 2016, the Kurdish National Council (KNC) developed a draft Constitution for Kurdistan in Syria, which foresaw far-reaching autonomy for a Kurdish autonomous region in the North of Syria—thereby very much following the example of Iraq (ARA News, 2016). This draft Constitution laid the foundation for wider debates among members of the Syrian Opposition and resulted in the drafting of a constitution, which foresaw the federalization of the country in 2018 (EZKS, 2020).[3] Article 3 of this draft states that 'Syria shall be a federal state which shares power and resources equitably between the federal, regional and municipal levels.' In addition to the federal principle, the Constitution also emphasizes the importance of power-sharing and the inclusion of different ethnic and religious groups. Article 80.2, for example, states that 'Half of the members of the government shall comprise representatives of the Sunni-Arab people and the other half shall comprise representatives of other groups.' Likewise, Articles 62 and 64 establish the principle of bicameralism, but, unlike Iraq, highlight how the second chamber is established (independently from the first chamber) and how it functions as a body of territorial representation. The constitution also deals with the controversial matter of designing regions by, on the one hand, making transitional arrangements for the initial formation of regions

---

[3] Both authors have worked as advisors to the Syrian opposition and contributed to and commented on the Draft Constitution discussed here.

(Article 6 Appendix) with a view of rapidly establishing federal institutions, and, on the other hand, allowing for later border adjustments (Article 2). Further, Article 90 establishes a Constitutional Court as the neutral arbiter both for conflicts between the different chambers and for conflicts between the federal level and the regions. Overall, it is clearly visible that the drafters of this Constitution have learnt from the mistakes in Iraq. The Constitution is more detailed and specific, and both the principle of federalism and the power-sharing system between the different ethnic, linguistic and religious groups are stronger and more visible in the draft. While the draft has not been endorsed by all members of the Syrian opposition, major representatives of minority communities, including the Kurds, the Druze and the Assyrian groups, have supported this constitutional draft, and members of the Arab community use elements of this draft as the basis of their political demands in the ongoing negotiations with the Assad government in Geneva. While the constitutional future of Syria remains uncertain, demands for a more inclusive federal system in which major groups are protected and included in state institutions will be vital for long-term stability (Kahf, 2021).

Making Federalism and Decentralization Work: The Question of Functionality

In their discussion on power-sharing systems in Europe, Keil and McCulloch (2021a) highlight the importance of functionality as a key element of any solution to managing diversity within a democratic framework. Functionality refers simply to 'the ability to get things done' (McCulloch, 2021, 5), which may sound simple and easy, but often poses key challenges for post-conflict societies (Martin, 2013). As the discussion above has demonstrated, the functionality of any agreement is of key importance—a lesson learnt from the current dysfunctionality of the Iraqi system.

When looking at the question of functionality, it is important to return to the discussion of federal bargaining. While the labels of 'holding-together' and 'coming-together' might offer useful descriptive terms to assess the evolution of federal and decentralized systems (Stepan, 1999), the reality is often more complicated, as the mixed nature of coming-together, holding-together and external imposition of the Iraqi Constitution highlights (Danilovich, 2014; Sharif, 2017; Belser, 2020).

Indeed, as Ziblatt (2008) and Riker (1964) have demonstrated in their respective discussions on the evolution of federal systems, there are a variety of factors at play—history, the party system, the focus on common defense and commercial benefits of any federal system and the wider economic, social and political situation at the time of federal bargaining. These complex factors also played a role in Iraq, yet externally enforced time pressure and historical antagonism between major actors severely limited the inclusiveness of the bargaining in the first place. The fact that these federal negotiations took place in the aftermath of enforced regime change (and excluded any members of the old regime) further contributed to the specific outcome we see today—a system that is incomplete and that has emphasized ethnic and religious identities more than historically pre-existing identities (Vissar & Stansfield, 2008). In other words, the ills of the current political system in Iraq were created at the beginning; while federalism had the potential to hold the country together and provide an umbrella uniting self-rule and shared rule for the different groups in the country (Brancati, 2004), its flawed implementation and the incompleteness of the state-building and democratization process have severely limited this potential.

This is an important lesson for the current discussion about federalism and decentralization in Syria. Any solution that includes federal elements needs to be built on the inclusion of all major actors and must evolve through a series of complex negotiations in which all sides will need to be willing to compromise. While political regime changes can be designed by the majority in a supreme law, federal power-sharing arrangements, in order to be sustainable, must result from group negotiations and be based on the consensus (or *foedus*) of all groups powerful enough to spoil the process. The current Baath-regime has followed an ideology that emphasized the Arab identity of the country (Wieland, 2013) and ensured strong centralized control by installing pro-regime leaders at the different levels of government (Gerlach, 2015). The continuation of such strategies is unacceptable to most minority groups and does not promise peaceful perspectives in the long run, not even when supported by important majorities. The making of compromises thus seems as unavoidable as it is unattractive to those holding power. Yet, there are alternative historical scenarios for Syria's constitutional organization (Lange, 2013). As highlighted by Jordi Tejel (2009) and Eva Savelsberg (2021), there are historical demands for federalism and autonomy which did not just come from the Syrian Kurds but also included Christian and other minority representatives. Hence, it is generally wrong to assume federalism and decentralization as an alien ideology for Syria (rather French-style centralism is), and it is hard to see that representatives from the different Kurdish groups will accept any post-war solution that does not include the provision of autonomy for them. Whatever the post-war situation will be in Syria, and despite the Assad regime's aim to renew its legitimacy by installing a new Constitution in 2012 which provided a form of democratic façade, any future solution will need to have a much more inclusive definition of 'who the people are' and for whom the constitution is written (Gluck & Bisarya, 2020).

It is also interesting to recall that the very first short-lived constitution of Syria, adopted in 1920, showed numerous federal features, in particular a bicameral parliament ensuring the representation of the Syrian people and the governorates, and a constitutional distribution of competences limiting the center and empowering the governorates. While it is true that the 'Faisal-Constitution' was monarchic and not lived after, it is still notable that the first Syrian constitution centered around the protection and accommodation of the country's diversity.

Among the most relevant lessons that Syria can learn from Iraq is that any federal arrangement must not only be negotiated but its implementation also carefully planned. It is important to highlight that any future solution for Syria needs to provide for a transitional stage. During this time, when the war memories are still fresh, refugees return home and the post-war recovery, rebuilding and reconciliation process begins, new institutions and processes must be carefully built. Yet, at the same time, any transitional arrangements must be strong enough to bind the different actors and interests and ensure their buy-in to any agreement, while allowing for the evolution of more permanent solutions over a period of time. As Keil and McCulloch (2021a) highlighted, 'functional adaption' is key in the democratization process of post-conflict societies. Any solution must be allowed to evolve, adapt and change (Du Toit, 2003). While the Iraqi Constitution does allow this, for example, through the creation of new regions, in practice this has not happened as this has been blocked by key interests in the center. No constitutional mechanism has been put in place to guarantee the implementation of the constitution, help overcome blockages at the center, conquer blockages between Baghdad and Erbil or solve conflicts between the center and governorates. As a result of this, we see an incomplete state that is not allowed to progress further due to opposing interests from its main actors.

Indeed, the scholars of federalism, decentralization and power-sharing have spilled a lot of ink discussing the importance of institutions and structures (Steiner & Dorff, 1985; Bakvis, 1985; Schneckener, 2015). However, there is an increasing recognition in the academic literature that actors play an equally important role and that any constitutional framework implemented in societies such as Iraq and Syria needs to consider the different preferences and long-term interests of a variety of actors. McEvoy (2014), for example, highlights that external actors can play a major role, not only through incentivizing the installation of power-sharing and minority rights in post-war situations but also by supporting the different local actors to reach consensus and agreement in times of crises. Keil and McCulloch (2021b, 10) also highlight:

> a general recognition that both scholars of power-sharing and those promoting power-sharing institutions in different countries need to pay more attention to the role of actors in these systems. In this regard, it is particularly important to assess the interests of different actors—both those articulated publicly and those underlining interests that explain certain policy and institutional preferences for group representatives.

The examples of Iraq and Syria demonstrate the need to include actor preferences in any potential discussions about the future of federalism and decentralization. It is unlikely that any future constitutional settlement does not include a federal solution or a strong provision of autonomy in both countries, as a return to a centralistic regime would be unacceptable for the Kurdish communities and their elites (Gunter, 2011; Allsopp & van Wilgenburg, 2019). Likewise, there are strong pressures from both the Sunni and the Shia communities for centralized solutions that would emphasize the Arab nature of these countries, thereby negating the existence of other ethnic, linguistic, cultural and religious groups. Any viable solution hence must seek to make concessions to both seemingly irreconcilable views. It is no surprise, then, that the main 'federalists' in Iraq are the Kurds that have pushed for autonomy for decades, including through violent struggle; more recently, however, their claims have shifted from autonomy to secession. Likewise, the Kurds, together with a number of other minorities, have favored a federal solution for Syria (The Day After Project, 2016). Yet, the vast majority of Arabs in both countries oppose federalism and see it as a tool of division and a step to the breakup of the state. Will federalism be able to bring these opposing views together and provide autonomy on the one hand, while safeguarding territorial integrity on the other? This remains to be seen, but the actions of the Kurdish elites in Iraq in 2017 have further increased opposition to any federal discussions among the Arab majority in Syria. Likewise, the inability to implement a functional federal state has frustrated Kurdish elites in Iraq and explains the shifts toward secessionism. In many respects, what we see in the two countries is the worst of both worlds: where centralization is implemented, it substantially oppresses minorities and is used to hold an authoritarian regime in power (in Syria), while the implementation of an unfinished, undemocratic federal system in Iraq has also left majority and minority communities dissatisfied.

Finally, to assess the functionality of any agreement and make any federal and decentralized solutions work, it is important to consider the issue of sustainability. In Iraq, a rushed and exclusive constitutional process, pushed for by a major external actor (the USA), has resulted in a flawed constitutional framework, which has not been sustainable. Kurdistan's 2017 unilateral independence referendum and the resulting conflict between Kurdish troops and the Iraqi army, as well as the intervention and subsequent success of ISIS in Iraq before 2014 (which included taking control of the second largest city of Mosul), all demonstrate the weakness of the Iraqi state, the ongoing conflicts between different ethnic and religious groups and the fragility of the post-intervention constitutional order. Iraq remains one of the weakest states in the world, as confirmed by the Fragile State Index (The Fund for Peace, 2020), where it was ranked the 17th most unstable country in the world between Mali and Ethiopia in 2020. Despite the 2005 Constitution's commitment to federalism and democracy, Iraq is neither a functional federation nor a functional democratic state. A new constitutional settlement is desperately needed, not only to deal with the aftermath of Kurdistan's unilateral push for independence but also to provide accommodation for Sunni Arabs and other groups that have been left out of the 2005 settlement.

In this respect, Iraq offers important lessons for Syria. Any settlement, in order to have a chance at providing a sustainable solution, needs to be inclusive, accommodative and able to adapt over time as actor preferences change and other issues become more salient. While it might seem unlikely that any such solution could emerge anytime soon with military victory for the Assad regime only being a question of time in the decade-long civil war, a comprehensive solution will nevertheless be needed for sustainable peace. In addition, the UN Security Council Resolution 2254, adopted in 2015 and still widely regarded as the blueprint to normalization in Syria, requires a 'Syrian-led and Syrian-owned political transition in order to end the conflict in Syria' (para. 1), urges representatives of the Syrian government and the opposition to engage in formal negotiations on such political transition process 'with a view to a lasting political settlement of the crisis' (para. 2) and makes it clear that 'a new constitution' must be drafted as its basis (para. 4). Such a political settlement addressing the root causes of the conflict will necessarily include elements of decentralization (and potentially federalism). The Kurdish population, the second largest ethnic group in the country, is unwilling to accept any long-term constitutional framework that does not offer them substantial autonomy, inclusion in central decisions and accommodation in the wider state structures. Other minorities and opposition leaders, while not officially demanding federalism or political decentralization, still recognize over-centralization and power abuse by the center as one of the governance problems the new constitution must deal with. While Assad's victory is likely to spark renewed authoritarian and totalitarian control, the oppression of different ethnic, religious, cultural and linguistic groups will—if unaddressed—create continued instability and remain a source of conflict across the country. Assad's reliance on his external allies (Russia and Iran most notably) might have opened his eyes about his own internal weakness and might provide a window of opportunity for a more inclusive solution—however unlikely this might seem today.

Conclusion: Federalism in the Middle East: Doomed to Fail?

There is still a lot of skepticism and even hostility toward the federal idea in the Middle East. Federal experiments such as the United Arab Republic between Egypt, Syria and Yemen (1958–1961), the federal system in Yemen (which was foreseen as an outcome of the National Dialogue Conference 2013–2014), the confederal and undemocratic regime in the United Arab Emirates and the flawed federal system in Iraq have all contributed to this critical perspective on federalism and decentralized governance.

Yet, decades of instability and in some cases open conflict, long-term Arabization policies and renewed minority demands for recognition, rights and representation and accommodation within a multicultural state have kept thoughts and constitutional discussions on federalism and decentralization alive. The region hence is confronted with a practical and political dilemma. While federalism and decentralization are widely perceived as foreign concepts which are unwanted and unsuccessful in the Middle East, no other option presents itself as offering real chances to overcome legacies of cultural and political oppression as well as social and economic marginalization. In fact, countries like Iraq and Syria, both confronted with the de facto disintegration of the state and the loss of unity between Arab and Kurdish territories, could see a negotiated federal arrangement as the best option to preserve territorial integrity in the long run. Opening the federal toolbox and reluctantly agreeing on a federal power balance indeed seems the best alternative to frozen territorial conflicts and long-term instability. As other contributions in this volume have highlighted, federalism is not a static process, it is an evolving system (Friedrich, 1968; Popelier, 2021) and one, as Burgess (2012) has pointed out, that needs to be learnt and appropriated. Constitutions are born in a political momentum; federations are not. Rather, they slowly come into being while continuously adapting to new aspirations and power relations. Are we witnessing such an emergence of federal thinking and acting in Iraq or Syria? Unfortunately, the lessons learnt are rather deterrent. While the federal experiments in the region have been substantially flawed, undemocratic and lacked proper self-rule and shared rule elements in their design, they have nevertheless tainted the idea of federalism and the possibility of decentralization. Moreover, local practices of party politics and informal decision-making between elite networks have proven in Iraq to undermine rather than support federal structures and processes.

This is not to say that federalism cannot provide an answer to some of the most common challenges across the region of the Middle East more generally, particularly, in Iraq and Syria. Ongoing state weakness and the inability of the center to enforce its rule can easily be counteracted by strong decentralized rule, which enables decision-making at a regional and local level. Likewise, the quest for minorities to seek autonomy and find recognition in the wider state can also be addressed through a federal system, as it would allow those groups that are territorially concentrated to exercise a substantial amount of autonomy over their own affairs, while at the same time increasing state capacity through shared rule mechanisms and cross-group cooperation. Smaller minorities often find inclusion through specific minority rights and forms of power-sharing that provide for their inclusion at local, regional and central levels. In a region where borders were drawn by colonial powers and different groups have been forced to share the same state as a legacy of colonialism, it is easy to say that the long-term alternative to proper accommodation and inclusion can only be continued instability and increased conflict. However, this form of inclusion will also need to address the legacies of Arab domination, the feeling of exclusion and oppression by many minority groups (Georges, 2020) and wider regional dynamics, symbolized, for example, by the existence of Kurdish people across four countries in the region. The wider conflicts between Shias and Sunnis, between Muslims and non-Muslim minorities and the interest of international actors will continue to influence debates about federalism and decentralization in Iraq and Syria. The transnational characteristics of the conflicts and tensions in both countries are so decisive that the question arises whether they can at all be mitigated by a country acting on its own. The Iraqi experience has demonstrated that imposed and short-term solutions are not an answer to the complex challenges of the individual countries and that more sophisticated and consensual provisions are needed in order to ensure stability and a successful democratic transition. This is not to say that international actors should play no role in the future of the countries in the region. Instead, Western countries can provide incentives for inclusive negotiations and expert input and suggestions, without imposing solutions. In short, rather than giving the floor to Russia and China to push for their authoritarian versions of political stability in the region (Abboud, 2018; Dimond, 2019), what is needed is a wider, inclusive dialogue and new constitutional foundation which break the cycle of oppression and dominance of centralization and authoritarian rule and open the door for processes of inclusive transformation focused on decentralization and democracy.

References

Abboud, S. (2018). *Syria* (2nd ed.). Polity.
Aboultaif, E. W. (2021). The federal question in Lebanon—Myths and illusions. *50 Shades of Federalism*. Retrieved June 7, 2021, from http://50shadesoffederalism.com/case-studies/the-federal-question-in-lebanon-myths-and-illusions/
Allsopp, H., & van Wilgenburg, W. (2019). *The Kurds of Northern Syria—Governance, diversity and conflicts*. I.B. Tauris.
Al-Mawlawi, A. (2018). 'Functioning federalism' in Iraq: A critical perspective. *LSE Blog*, 11 March. Retrieved June 7, 2021, from https://blogs.lse.ac.uk/mec/2018/03/11/functioning-federalism-in-iraq-a-critical-perspective/

Al-Qarawee, H. (2010). Redefining a nation: The conflict of identity and federalism in Iraq. *Perspectives on Federalism*, 2(1), 32–41. Retrieved June 7, 2021, from http://www.on-federalism.eu/attachments/061_download.pdf

Anderson, L. (2013). *Federal solutions to ethnic problems—Accommodating diversity*. Routledge.

Anderson, S. (2018). *Zerbrochene Länder—Wie die Arabsiische Welt aus den Fugen geriet*. Bundeszentrale für Politische Bildung.

ARA News. (2016). Kurdish National Council announces plan for setting up "Syrian Kurdistan Region". Retrieved June 7, 2021, from http://aranews.net/files/2016/08/kurdish-national-council-announces-plan-setting-syrian-kurdistan-region/

Bakvis, H. (1985). Structure and process in federal and consociational arrangements. *Publius—The Journal of Federalism*, 15(2), 57–69.

Belser, E. M. (2020). A failure of state transformation rather than a failure of federalism? The case of Iraq. *Ethnopolitics*, 19(4), 383–401.

Bormann, N.-C. (2017). Ethnic power-sharing coalitions and democratization. In A. McCulloch & J. McGarry (Eds.), *Power-sharing—Empirical and normative challenges* (pp. 124–147). Routledge.

Brancati, D. (2009). *Peace by design: Managing intrastate conflict through decentralization*. Oxford University Press.

Brancati, D. (2004). Can federalism stabilize Iraq? *The Washington Quarterly*, 27(2), 5–21.

Burgess, M. (2006). *Comparative federalism—Theory and practice*. Routledge.

Burgess, M. (2012). *In search of the federal spirit—New theoretical and empirical perspectives on comparative federalism*. Oxford University Press.

Cordesman, A. (2019). *Iraq as a failed state*. Working Paper, Center for Strategic & International Studies.

Danilovich, A. (2014). *Iraqi federalism and the Kurds—Learning to live together*. Ashgate.

Danilovich, A., & Pineda, P. (2019). Kurdish interests and US foreign policy in the Middle East. In A. Danilovich (Ed.), *Federalism, secession, and international recognition regime—Iraqi Kurdistan* (pp. 201–215). Routledge.

Dimond, L. (2019). *Ill winds—Saving democracy from Russia rage, Chinese ambition, and American complacency*. Penguin Books.

Dingley, J. (2011). Kudistan zwischen Autonomie und Selbstverantwortung. *Aus Politik und Zeitgeschichte*, 61(9), 31–36.

Dodge, T. (2006). The British Mandate in Iraq, 1920–1932. *The Middle East Online Series 2: Iraq 1914–1974, Cengage Learning EMEA Ltd*, Reading. Retrieved July 15, 2021, from https://www.gale.com/binaries/content/assets/au-resources-in-product/iraqessay_dodge.pdf

Dodge, T. (2013). State and society in Iraq ten years after regime change: The rise of a new authoritarianism. *International Affairs*, 89(2), 241–257.

Dodge, T. (2020). Iraq's informal consociationalism and its problems. *Studies in Ethnicity and Nationalism, 20*(3), 145–152.

Du Toit, P. (2003). Why post-settlement settlements? *Journal of Democracy, 14*(3), 104–118.

Eklund, K., O'Leary, B., & Williams, P. (2005). Negotiating a federation in Iraq. In B. O'Leary, J. McGarry, & K. Salih (Eds.), *The future of Kurdistan in Iraq* (pp. 116–142). University of Pennsylvania Press.

European Center for Kurdish Studies (EZKS). (2020). *Draft constitution for Syria—Commented version*. Retrieved June 7, 2021, from https://power-sharing-syria.ezks.org/wp-content/uploads/2020/10/Syrian-Constitution-Draft_EN.pdf

Freedom House. (2020a). *Freedom in the World 2021—Iraq*. Retrieved June 7, 2021, from https://freedomhouse.org/country/iraq/freedom-world/2021

Freedom House. (2020b). *Freedom in the World 2021—Syria*. Retrieved June 7, 2021, from https://freedomhouse.org/country/syria

Friedrich, C. (1968). *Trends of federalism in theory and practice*. Frederick A. Praeger Publishers.

Fund for Peace. (2020). The Fragile States Index 2020. Retrieved June 7, 2021, from https://fragilestatesindex.org/data/

Fürtig, H. (2011). Der Irak als demokratischer "Musterstaaat" in Nahost? *Aus Politik und Zeitgeschichte, 61*(9), 3–10.

Georges, N. (2020). *Minorities in the Syrian legal system and the principle of state neutrality*. European Center for Kurdish Studies. Retrieved June 7, 2021, from https://power-sharing-syria.ezks.org/wp-content/uploads/2020/11/Study_Nael-Georges_Minorities-and-State-Neutrality_En.pdf

Gerlach, D. (2015). *Herrschaft über Syrien—Macht und Manipulation unter Assad*. Bundeszentrale für Politische Bildung.

Gluck, J., & Bisarya, S. (2020). Federal constitution-making processes and the stable cessation of conflict. In A. Griffiths, R. Chattopadhyay, J. Light, & C. Stieren (Eds.), *The forum of federations handbook of federal countries 2020* (pp. 385–404). Palgrave Macmillan.

Gunter, M. (2011). *The Kurd ascending—The evolving solution to the Kurdish problem in Iraq and Turkey* (2nd ed.). Palgrave Macmillan.

Hetou, G. (2019). *The Syrian conflict—The role of Russia, Iran and the US in a global crisis*. Routledge.

Heydemann, S. (2020). The Syrian conflict: Proxy war, pyrrhic victory, and power-sharing agreements. *Studies in Ethnicity and Nationalism, 20*(2), 153–160.

Iraq Constitution. (2005). Retrieved June 7, 2021, from https://www.constituteproject.org/constitution/Iraq_2005.pdf?lang=en

Jaeger, K., & Tophoven, R. (2013). Internationale Akteure, Interessen, Konfliktlinien. *Aus Politik und Zeitgeschichte, 63*(8), 23–30.

Kahf, A. (2021). Decentralization as an entry point to peacebuilding in Syria. In D. Khatib (Ed.), *The Syrian crisis—Effects on the regional and international relations* (pp. 213–233). Springer.

Kane, S., Hilterman, J., & Alkadiri, R. (2012). Iraq's federalism quandary. *The National Interest, 118*, 20–30.

Keil, S. (2013). *Multinational federalism in Bosnia and Herzegovina*. Ashgate.

Keil, S., & Alber, E. (2020). Introduction. Federalism as a tool of conflict resolution. *Ethnopolitics, 19*(4), 329–341.

Keil, S., & Anderson, P. (2018). Decentralization as a tool for conflict resolution. In K. Detterbeck & E. Hepburn (Eds.), *Handbook of territorial politics* (pp. 89–106). Edward Elgar.

Keil, S., & McCulloch, A. (2021a). Conclusion: The past, present and future of power-sharing in Europe. In S. Keil & A. McCulloch (Eds.), *Power-sharing in Europe—Past practice, present cases and future directions* (pp. 257–274). Palgrave Macmillan.

Keil, S., & McCulloch, A. (2021b). From plural democracy to conflict resolution…and back again: Revisiting the consociationalism-federalism debate. *Unpublished Manuscript*, pp. 1–19.

Khalilzad, Z. (2010). Lessons from Afghanistan and Iraq. *Journal of Democracy, 21*(3), 41–49.

Kirmanj, S. (2013). *Identity and nation in Iraq*. Lynne Rienner Publishers.

Lange, K. (2013). Syrien: Ein historischer Überblick. *Aus Politik und Zeitgeschichte, 63*(8), 37–43.

Lesch, D. (2019). *Syria*. Polity.

Martin, P. (2013). Coming together: Power-sharing and the durability of negotiated peace settlements. *Civil Wars, 15*(3), 332–358.

McCulloch, A. (2014). *Power-sharing and political stability in deeply divided societies*. Routledge.

McCulloch, A. (2021). Introduction: Power-sharing in Europe—Form adoptability to end-ability. In S. Keil & A. McCulloch (Eds.), *Power-sharing in Europe—Past practice, present cases and future directions* (pp. 1–18). Palgrave Macmillan.

McEvoy, J. (2014). The role of external actors in incentivizing post-conflict power-sharing. *Government and Opposition, 49*(1), 47–69.

McEvoy, J., & Aboultaif, E. (2020). Power-sharing challenges: From weak adoptability to dysfunction in Iraq. *Ethnopolitics*. Retrieved June 7, 2021, from https://www.tandfonline.com/doi/pdf/10.1080/17449057.2020.1739363?casa_token=HHo5MsR8cjkAAAAA:PPGqiskNBbGhujcEmSkN1qqCFJwD9BaTTrcpnOiRB6LuihH1VuxOzVaFS7fTYqaYW_oGZUth7PLD

O'Leary, B. (2001). An iron law of nationalism and federation?: A (neo-Diceyian) theory of the necessity of a federal *Staatsvolk*, and of consociational rescue. *Nations and Nationalism, 7*(3), 273–296.

Popelier, P. (2021). *Dynamic federalism—A new theory for cohesion and regional autonomy*. Routledge.

Riker, W. (1964). *Federalism—Origin, operation, significance*. Little Brown and Company.

Romano, D., & Gurses, M. (2014). Introduction: The Kurds as barrier or key to democratization. In D. Romano & M. Gurses (Eds.), *Conflict, democratization and the Kurds in the Middle East—Turkey, Iran, Iraq and Syria* (pp. 1–16). Palgrave Macmillan.

Sabio, O. (2015). *Rojava—An alternative to imperialism, nationalism and Islamism in the Middle East*. Lulu Press.

Savelsberg, E. (2021). *Die Entstehung des Kurdischen Nationalismus in Syrien zur Zeit des französischen Mandats: Die Autonomiebewegung Hajo Aghas von den Haverkan*. Unpublished PhD Thesis, University of Erfurt.

Schneckener, U. (2015). *Auswege aus dem Bürgerkrieg—Modelle zur Regulierung ethno-nationalistischer Konflikte in Europa* (2nd ed.). Suhrkamp.

Shakir, F. (2017). *The Iraqi federation—Origin, operation and significance*. Routledge.

Steiner, J., & Dorff, R. (1985). Structure and process in consociationalism and federalism. *Publius—The Journal of Federalism, 15*(2), 49–55.

Stepan, A. (1999). Federalism and democracy—Beyond the US model. *Journal of Democracy, 10*(4), 19–34.

Syrian Observatory for Human Rights. (2021). *Over 606,000 people killed across Syria since the beginning of the "Syrian Revolution", including 495,000 documented by SOHR*. Retrieved June 7, 2021, from https://www.syriahr.com/en/217360/

Tejel, J. (2009). *Syria's Kurds—History, politics and society*. Routledge.

The Day After Project. (2016). *Syria—Opinions and attitudes on federalism, decentralization, and the experience of the democratic self-administration. Survey results*. Retrieved June 7, 2021, from https://tda-sy.org/wp-content/uploads/2020/03/Syrian-Opinions-and-Attitudes-on-Decentralization.pdf

Vissar, R., & Stansfield, G. (Eds.). (2008). *An Iraq of its regions. Cornerstones of the federal democracy?* C. Hurst and Co.

Watts, R. (2008). *Comparing federal systems* (3rd ed.). McGill-Queen's University Press.

Wieland, C. (2013). Das politisch-ideologische System Syriens und dessen Zerfall. *Aus Politik und Zeitgeschichte, 63*(8), 55–62.

Yazidi, J. (2016). No going back: Why decentralisation is the future for Syria. *European Council on Foreign Relations Policy Brief*. Retrieved June 7, 2021, from https://ecfr.eu/wp-content/uploads/ECFR185_-_NO_GOING_BACK_-_WHY_DECENTRALISATION_IS_THE_FUTURE_FOR_SYRIA.pdf

Ziblatt, D. (2008). *Structuring the state—The formation of Italy and Germany and the puzzle of federalism*. Princeton University Press.

CHAPTER 10

Federalism in Ethiopia: Emergence, Progress and Challenges

Yonatan Tesfaye Fessha and Beza Dessalegn

Y. T. Fessha (✉)
University of the Western Cape, Cape Town, South Africa

B. Dessalegn
Hawassa University, Awassa, Ethiopia

© The Author(s), under exclusive license to Springer Nature Switzerland AG 2022
S. Keil, S. Kropp (eds.), *Emerging Federal Structures in the Post-Cold War Era*, Federalism and Internal Conflicts, https://doi.org/10.1007/978-3-030-93669-3_10

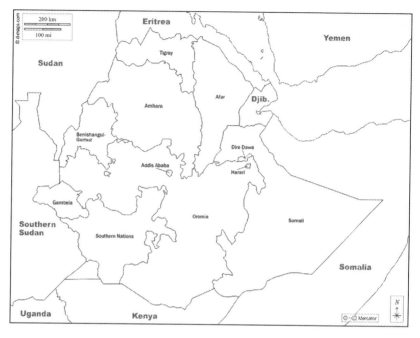

Map 10.1 Ethiopia. *Source*: https://d-maps.com/carte.php?num_car=4259&lang=en

Introduction

Ethiopia wrote a new constitution and emerged as a federation in 1995. But the road to a federal polity began in 1991, when ethnic liberation movements assumed political power and implemented a highly decentralized ethnic-based system of government. The 1995 constitution codified the same by reorganizing the country on the basis of ethnicity. Thirty years down the line, however, no other issue remains as divisive as the subject of federalism itself and the role ethnicity has assumed in the federal project. The dispute on the nature of the federal arrangement reached new heights when the country was engulfed by mass anti-government protests in late 2015, forcing a leadership change in 2018. The country is again at crossroads, pulled in different directions. On the one hand are those that want to continue to territorially empower ethnic communities, believing that the ethno-territorial model is the only road leading toward peace and stability. On the other hand are those that agree on the establishment of federal polity but argue that its strong link with ethnicity is not only a recipe for communal tension but also an incentive for disintegration. This chapter examines the intractable challenges of the Ethiopian polity by retracing the emergence of the federal model, its progress and its impending deadlocks. The chapter proceeds in four interrelated parts. First, it describes the making of the Ethiopian state, focusing on how the state is transformed from a highly centralized state to an ethnic federation. This is followed by a section that examines the major features of the federation as well as the political practice that has affected the functioning of the federation. The focus then shifts to the challenges of the federal experiment and, in particular, the interaction between mobility and autonomy rights that has bedeviled the federal experiment. This is followed by a section that briefly mentions the emerging challenges of the federation. The chapter finally offers brief concluding remarks.

The Road to Federalism

Ethiopia is a country of diverse ethnic, linguistic and religious groups, although this character of the state has not been explicitly recognized until recently. Arguably, the ethnically and religiously diverse modern state of Ethiopia was essentially created in the second half of the nineteenth century (Mengisteab, 1997), with the centralization of state power reaching its peak in 1974 (ibid.). In 1991, ethnicity was introduced as the principal basis of political competition and cooperation, something that was considered as a political taboo in pre-1991 Ethiopia. This, however, does not mean that ethnicity was never used as a basis for political mobilization before 1991.

In fact, the first public debate on ethnicity goes back to 1969 when Walelign Mekonen, a student of Addis Ababa University and one of the public faces of the Ethiopian Student Movement (ESM), published a piece that described Ethiopia as a "prison house of nationalities" (Gudina, 2006; Markakis, 2003). The ESM, in a bid to remove the last emperor from power, articulated what, up until today, remains the most controversial question of the century—"the question of nationalities". The ESM was highly inspired by the Marxist-Leninist ideology of the time, which advocated for national and ethnic equality. Even though the early periods of student movement presented the national question within the broader theme of class struggle, the class question, as time went by, was subsumed by the national question. Ethnic-based political forces assumed prominence and, as a result, the country's tribulations were reduced to the singular problem of ethnic justice. The military success of ethnic-based liberation movements in the 1980s meant that the ethnic question emerged as the major problem that needed to be addressed (Gudina, 2006). The popular revolution of 1974 ousted the last emperor and abolished the feudal foundations of imperial Ethiopia. The student-led revolution against the monarchy was, however, hijacked by the military that actually deposed the Emperor in 1974 and established a military council. A military Junta, known as *Derg* (meaning committee), assumed state power and effectively ruled the country for 17 years. Derg continued with the centralization of state power under the guise of maintaining the territorial integrity of the state. While Derg spent much of its time trying to quell ethnic and secessionist armed movements, it introduced measures that appeared to respond to the question of nationalities. It decreed the nationalization of land, which dismantled the economic foundation of imperial Ethiopia (Markakis, 2003).[1] It also promised the equality of all nationalities. Yet, it is during this period that ethnic-based armed movements proliferated in the country. Derg, as much as possible, tried to push ethnicity away from the public spotlight. Yet, the intensification of ethnic (civil) wars in the country, the increasing resistance to military rule and the rise of militant ethnic-based armed movements compelled it to introduce some kind of constitutional reform that appeared to respond to ethnic concerns (Ayenew, 2002). It established the Institute of Nationalities, whose main task was to draft a constitution and reorganize the country into new viable administrative divisions that reflected the ethnic makeup of the country (Abbink, 1998).[2] A new constitution that granted autonomy to carefully selected provinces distressed by ethnic conflict was adopted in 1987.[3] However, this was too late to reverse the ethnic insurgencies and counter the political instability. Derg was removed from power in 1991 by a coalition of ethnic-based liberation movements, just four years after the adoption of the new constitution.

---

[1] Equality at the time meant the end of cultural subordination and the freedom to exercise one's culture but not territorial autonomy and self-government of the nationalities.

[2] The Institute for the Study of Ethiopian Nationalities was a political research bureau that did research under the military regime. Most of the results from the Institute's work have been directly included into the post-1991 restructuring of the country via ethnicity.

[3] For a discussion of the administrative divisions, their powers and boundaries at the time, see Fiseha (2007).

The Federation

The Ethiopian People's Revolutionary Democratic Front (EPRDF), a coalition of ethnic liberation fronts, was the force that assumed power by ousting Derg. The coalition quickly identified the unresolved question of nationalities as the country's major political problem. Hence, there was no confusion about the system of governance that needed to be established in post-1991 Ethiopia. Ethnicity was to take center stage. This was codified with the adoption of the 1995 constitution that declared the adoption of a federal form of government that is grounded in ethnicity and recognizes the "Nations, Nationality and Peoples of Ethiopia" as the constituent communities of the federation (FDRE Const, Preamble, Art 8, 39 and 47). The Ethiopian federal dispensation is unique in many aspects. Although its commitment to the protection of ethnic communities (what the constitution calls "nations, nationalities and peoples") stands out as its distinctive feature, the fact that it recognizes these ethnic communities as the authors of the constitution (FDRE Const, Preamble, Para 1), ultimate holders of sovereign power (FDRE Const, Art 8) and exclusive holders of the right to self-determination, including the unconditional right of secession (FDRE Const, Art 39), sets it apart even from multinational federations that are committed to the protection of diversity. The constitution's conspicuous grant of the power to interpret the constitution (FDRE Const, Art 62(1)) to the representatives of ethnic communities, as opposed to a judicial organ, is another indication of the prominent place the constitution has given to ethnic communities. The federal arrangement has territorialized ethnicity, according to which an ethnic group or a combination of ethnic groups are deemed to own territory to the exclusion of others (Clapham, 2002). Of the ten states that constitute the Ethiopian federation, seven of them are explicitly linked to a single ethnic group, while each of the remaining three is linked with a select few ethnic groups. Although not the only ones,[4] the latter have, in particular, further divided

---

[4] Amhara and, to an extent, the Afar regions while reserving the lion's share of ownership of their regional territory to the respective dominant Amhara and Afar identities, very jealously share portions of their territories to select recognized native minorities. Somali, Sidama and Oromia have jealously guarded the ownership of their regional territory, thereby extending the privileges only to the dominant ethnic identities of Somali, Sidama and Oromo, respectively. The Tigray region, even though it follows a similar approach, has de facto permitted some sort of territorial sharing to the recognized indigenous minorities of Irob and Kunama—although this is done outside the regional constitutional architecture. The city-

their respective territory into ethnically defined local government units, further deepening the link between territory and ethnicity (Van der Beken, 2013). The state of Southern Nations and Nationalities People (SNNP), for instance, is divided into dozens of ethnic zones and special districts (*liyu woredas*); the states of Gambella and Benishangul Gumuz have established local units (i.e. nationality administrations) for the specific ethnic communities that are regarded by the state constitutions as indigenous and, thereby, owners of the states (Benishangul Gumuz Region Const, Art 2: Gambella Region Const, Art 46). While Benishangul Gumuz and Gambella explicitly declare particular communities as founders or owners of the state, some of the other states have done the equivalent by vesting sovereign power and the right to self-determination only on the community on whose behalf the state is apparently established for. One important discernible development in the Ethiopian federal structure since its introduction is the increasing prominence ethnicity has achieved, in both private and public spaces. By territorializing ethnicity and making it the single most important and singular political identity—trumping all other identities (Fessha, 2017)—ethnic federalism has dichotomized citizens, both legally and politically, into natives and settlers (Van der Beken, 2012). On the one hand are those that belong to the nations, nationalities and peoples, who are assumed to be the owners of a certain territory. On the other hand are those that happen to find themselves in a territory that is deemed to be owned by an ethnic group they do not belong to and, as a result, have little or no right over the territory.[5] While those considered native are regarded as the sole beneficiaries of political empowerment and territorial autonomy, non-native communities remain on the margins, often sidelined from access to political power and self-government rights.[6] These developments have now proven to be one of the most intractable chal-

---

state of Harar, founded for the Harari identity, probably because its entire territory is located within the region of Oromia, has somehow tried to share its regional territory with ethnic Oromo, but not with others, even to those like the Amhara, with sizeable numerical presence.

[5] Because these constitutional dispensations focus on empowering natives in their defined territories, its adverse impact upon the rights of non-members has been immense. For instance, since ethnic groups are bestowed with the right to own land, an individual inevitably has to trace membership to an ethnic group to access and use land. In an ethnic federation, this could result in the understanding that access to land is not extended to all as a matter of citizenship rights but only to individuals who can trace their belonging to the respective nations, nationalities, and peoples (Behailu, 2015).

[6] This, among others, has led to the proliferation of identity-based claims and ethnic autonomy conflicts.

lenges of the federal dispensation. It is these increasingly worrying developments that form the central focus of the next section.

Mobility: An Impending Tension Between "Natives" and "Settlers"

In the context of the native/settler dichotomy, one area that has demonstrated an impasse is the issue of mobility. As apparent and unproblematic as it might seem, the exercise of freedom of movement in plural societies could become very difficult when it is perceived as threatening the self-government rights of communities that are considered "native" to the territory in question. This is the case when there is migration to ethnically defined territories, which minorities consider as their homeland. Under certain circumstances, the unchecked migration of people into designated "ethnic homelands" has the capacity to alter the demographic balance of these territories. And this, through time, might affect the political status of ethnic communities, in turn, potentially affecting the political, social and cultural self-determination rights of those ethnic communities (Côté, 2008). The ensuing tension, therefore, creates a fierce competition for resources, employment and political power. In Ethiopia, the interplay of internal movement and the autonomy of ethnic communities controlling state governments have posed serious challenges. Constitutionally speaking, the FDRE Constitution includes a chapter on fundamental rights, which provides for a number of individual rights, including the rights of an individual to liberty of movement and freedom to choose residence (FDRE Const, Art 34(1)). The same constitution also provides for a bundle of group rights that provides ethnic communities with extensive non-derogable self-rule rights. Balancing the two sets of rights is not an easy task. As already outlined, the envisaged federal setup in Ethiopia has given disproportionate and unusual attention to ethnic rights. Ethiopia is basically a prime example of what is widely known as ethnic federalism (ethno-federation), a model of federalism that is deliberately designed to respond to ethnic concerns.[7] The political and constitutional decision to solely empower "native groups" has encouraged the latter to consider themselves as the only owner of a given territory and the only group entitled to exercise the right to self-determination over it. They do not only exercise operational control of ethnic territories and their public

---

[7] See also the preamble of the FDRE constitution in this regard.

institutions (Fiseha, 2016), but they also believe that they own the territories and institutions in the proprietary sense of ownership (Assefa 2014), thereby threatening the basic rights of those considered as settlers. The impression given by the constitutional design is further strengthened by the political practice that has promoted nativist sentiments, leaving the so-called "settlers" at the mercy of empowered native identities. As Lavers noted, people are increasingly asking for a very strict interpretation of ethnic federalism which will "differentiate between ethnic groups depending on whether they are in their 'home' region or not, even justifying the removal of ethnic minorities to their 'home' regions to preserve resources for the dominant ethnic group" (Lavers, 2018, 469–470). Under a political and constitutional system that attaches territories to ethnicities, it is no surprise that forced expulsion of those considered non-native, mainly from farming plots, has become a daily occurrence.[8] In fact, since the reorganization of the political and geographical landscape of the country in 1991, there were numerous reports of tensions and conflicts that have ensued between citizens exercising their freedom of internal movement and communities that are concerned with the threat such a movement poses to their demographic and political supremacy. The State of Benishangul Gumuz, which is home to an almost equal population of native and non-native communities, witnessed, on more than few occasions, the mass eviction of non-natives (Gedamu, 2018; Gerth-Niculescu, 2021). Similar disturbing developments including forced expulsions have been witnessed in the states of Amhara, Oromia and SNNP (Human Rights Council, 2016). Disturbingly, state and local authorities usually have a hand in the forced evictions of non-natives, and at times, the forced evictions seem to be sponsored by the state and local authorities themselves (Abbink, 2011).On the other hand, citizens who happen to find themselves in ethno-states not named after them or that do not recognize the ethnic group they belong to as native are made to feel as guests and sometimes as unwelcome. They have suddenly found themselves on the losing side of the federal experiment (Assefa, 2008). The end result has been a federation that has separated its citizens, as mentioned earlier, into indigenous and non-indigenous, guests and owners, native and non-natives. This dichotomization of

---

[8] This was disturbingly witnessed, among others, in the *Guraferda* district of the SNNP region, *Kamashi, Assosa and Metekel* zones of Benishangul Gumuz region, and in various parts of Oromia region.

citizens and its devastating consequences have continued unabated despite the major political developments that saw Abiy Ahmed come to power in 2018. Non-natives continue to face mass and orchestrated removal from their homes and farming plots. Given its emphasis on empowering native communities, the Ethiopian federalism experiment is notable in its absence of explicit constitutional protection to the mobility rights of non-natives. Of course, the constitution places no restriction on freedom of movement, including in the name of protecting self-governing rights of "native communities." That, however, does not seem to be sufficient in a constitutional architecture that gives disproportionate attention to ethnic communities and their rights. Under such circumstances, it is more likely that such communities and their government might engage, directly or indirectly, in acts that undermine the mobility rights of individuals that do not belong to the empowered communities. For instance, constitutions of the States, like the regions of Benishangul Gumuz, SNNP and Oromia (Benishangul Gumuz Region Const, Art 33; SNNP Region Const, Art 33; Oromia Region Const, Art 33), have subjected the right to work to a language proficiency requirement of the respective states. It is not evident whether these states have inserted this provision as part of the effort to curb internal migration, but these are states that are home to millions of individuals that do not belong to the empowered communities. It is not clear how these states determine language proficiency, ensuring that the language requirement is not used as a basis to engage in discriminatory practices. In any way, such a requirement has a clear impact on individuals that want to move between states and establish their livelihoods, especially those seeking employment in the civil service. An opportunity presented before the House of the Federation (HoF), the body that is tasked with the duty of interpreting the constitution and resolving constitutional disputes, also proved futile as it displayed a strong institutional favoritism for the rights of native communities, as seen in the case involving the State of Benishangul Gumuz. The decision, however, of a group of residents of the State that do not belong to the communities that are regarded by the State Constitution as native to run for a seat in the State Parliament was objected by some on the ground that they do not speak any of the languages spoken by the indigenous communities. The objection was accepted by the National Electoral Board of Ethiopia that relied on an electoral proclamation of 111/95. The individuals petitioned the HoF, arguing that the mandatory language proficiency requirement violates their constitutional right to be elected, which is guaranteed without any restriction (Decision of the HoF, 2008). The case involved a tension between an individual right to stand as a candidate and the right of ethnic communities to self-determination. The House validated the law that requires proficiency in the working language of the state as a condition to stand for election. It argued that effective representation of the electorate requires the candidate to be proficient in the language of the state parliament. The decision of the HoF to solve the case on pragmatic grounds meant that the decision has little contribution to the jurisprudence on mobility rights or self-government rights and, therefore, can and should be reconciled (Fessha & Dessalegn, 2020). The resolution of the dispute on pragmatic grounds was unfortunate as the House missed an opportunity to elaborate on how the commitment of the constitution for the equal enforcement of both individual and group rights can be realized and how both rights can be implemented in a mutually inclusive way. The HoF was given another opportunity to deal with a similar situation when victims of the Guraferda incident mentioned above took the matter to the HoF to complain about violation of their freedom of movement, freedom to choose residence and freedom to pursue a livelihood of their choice (Petition to the HoF March 9, 2009). The HoF did not give a formal response to the petition. This is unfortunate, as the HoF should have used this opportunity to clarify the relationship between mobility rights and the self-determination rights of communities. The HoF could have used this case to clarify whether justifiable limitations could be placed on mobility and self-rule rights, if so, who has the power to legislate on those limitations and whether the federal or regional government can regulate inter-regional migration. From the foregoing, it is clear that the federal constitution, though enshrined for both individual and group rights, does not seem prepared to address apparent tensions between group and individual rights. The subnational constitutions, as mentioned above, are not different in this regard. Of course, it is also naive to think that the ensuing trends of illegal evictions are mere spontaneous actions that can quickly be remedied by strictly adhering to the constitutional right of free movement. The mere declaration that every Ethiopian has the right to move anywhere in the country would be a very light response to a very complicated problem. After all, in one way or another, these unqualified actions of restricting the mobility rights of those that are regarded as non-native seem to be propelled, among others, by the unrectified historic inequalities, unfair distribution of wealth and inequitable utilization of resources, lack of good governance and derailed social and ethno-cultural justice. Addressing these issues will require a broader policy and legal framework, negotiated between federal and regional authorities.[9]

THE ROAD AHEAD: EMERGING ISSUES

The first two decades of Ethiopian federalism, to use Lenin's famous words, were "decades nothing happened." By contrast, "decades happened" in the last three years. One even might dare to opine that federalism came to life in Ethiopia after the political events that unfolded following the mass protests that began in 2015. It was and continues to be a difficult and painful labor. In the meantime, ethnic divisions have deepened further. The current state of the Ethiopian federation reveals that the situation would have been worse had it not been for the fact that, for the first two decades (until 2015), the Ethiopian federation was operating under a dominant party system (Fiseha, 2006, 2012; Gudina, 2011). As noted elsewhere, Ethiopia is a federal country that, for too long, operated with little federal credentials (Fessha, 2019). Since 1991, EPRDF's command on power has been absolute as it controlled both federal and all nine state governments. It acted in a manner that is indifferent to the federal system, making the federation function as a centralized unitary state. Key political decisions, including nomination, election and appointment of state officials, were made by the party, and the principle of democratic centralism ensured that both federal and state officials implement those decisions. Until very recently, intergovernmental relations (IGR), as mentioned above, was a non-issue. Intergovernmental matters were managed through the party channel, where decisions were made by high-ranking officials and implemented through the party's chain of command based on the principle of democratic centralism (Van der Beken, 2012). Ethnic tensions that are now spiraling into intergovernmental disputes were managed through party channels, giving an impression of cordial

---

[9] For instance, see Smith and Hiden (2012) on the use of the "personality principle" to address the often competing demands between territorial federalization and internal migration.

intergovernmental relations.[10] With the slow death of democratic centralism, the days of a coherent and cohesive ruling party seem to have gone. The relationship of the states with each other and the federal government has increasingly become antagonistic, so much so that it has led to military confrontations. The needs for institutions and processes of intergovernmental relations have never been so urgent. Intergovernmental relations might have become more complicated by the issue of equitable fiscal decentralization. While this subject has remained an open secret in the past, no state government had the audacity to openly assert that they are not receiving a fair share and that others are disproportionately benefiting, contrary to their contributions to the national economy. Now, almost all states have publicly expressed their dissatisfaction with their share of revenue, which they receive from the federal government in the form of grants (Ezega News, 2019). In the meantime, members of ethnic communities have intensified their demand for the implementation of the rights enshrined under the constitution. In this regard, the most prominent of certain groups was the demand for their own "ethnic state". In just one state (i.e. the SNNP), some 13 ethnic communities invoked the constitutional right for their own state and submitted petitions for the establishment of their own states. Although a demand for an own subnational unit is not a new phenomenon, one can note two major developments with respect to the demands that started to emerge beginning from 2018. Prior to 2018, a request for an independent state was discouraged or suppressed (Aalen, 2011). Using the arresting power of democratic centralism, the ruling party kept a very tight grip on those agitating for the formation of new states. As a result, with the exception of the Sidama, which itself ended in a bloody suppression, little or no effort was made by members of ethnic communities to rely on the constitutional provisions and seek the establishment of new states. With the withering away of democratic centralism in 2018 and thereafter, ethnic elites adopted the "ethnic free for all approach" and pursued a request for new states with more vigor and determination. Although the petitioners heavily relied on constitutional provisions, some of the agitations were accompanied by violent and

---

[10] It must, however, be noted that, even under those circumstances, the ruling party chose to empower native identities, perpetuating the exclusion of the so-called settlers from the political process. However, the empowerment extended to the natives, as alluded above, was nominal as real decision-making power remained with the center (Fiseha, 2007).

gruesome tactics of holding minorities hostage (Abdu, 2018a, 2018b). The demand for self-rule did not only come in the form of a request for their own state. Ethnic communities that are not numerically big requested for the establishment of their own local government, especially in states like the SNNP, where ethnic minorities are found in sizable numbers. Others have sought for a re-demarcation of state or local government area boundaries, so that they can join their ethnic kin across the border. The language policy of the federal government has also emerged as another area of contention. In a country with more than 100 languages and twice that in the form of dialects, it is unavoidable that the use of language becomes a thorny issue. The constitution chose to manage the challenge by more or less adopting the territorial model of language policy whereby states and local governments have designated the language of the majority as the working language. That has allowed communities to promote their language and culture. At the same time, it has, among others, restricted movement across the states, disrupting existing patterns and networks of exchange and communication between different areas and people. What has rather been more contentious is the decision of the constitution to pick Amharic as the only working language of the federal government (FDRE Const, Art 5(2)). For some time now, Oromo nationalists have been demanding the recognition of Oromiffa, the language of the largest ethnic group in the country, the Oromo, as an additional working language of the federal government (Seyoum 2020). Under huge pressure from Oromo nationalists, the ruling party declared its intentions to introduce some four more languages as additional working languages of the federal government (ibid.).[11]

Conclusion

The relevance of federalism as the appropriate response to the challenges that the country is facing continues to dominate constitutional and political debates. Undeniably, however, the nature of the debate has notably evolved through the years. During the initial years, the introduction of federalism faced fierce opposition as an unsuitable solution for the country's ills. This position is now significantly weakened. Today, it is hard to

---

[11] This has raised a constitutional dilemma as to whether additional working languages for the federal government can be recognized without a constitutional amendment or not.

find a political formation that, at least, openly challenges or campaigns against the relevance of federalism. The nature of the debate has shifted from the relevance of federalism per se to the nature and character of the federal arrangement and, more specifically, to the ethnic-based nature of the current arrangement—whether it should be tied to ethnicity or mere geography.[12] The emergence of a federal setup in Ethiopia has sought to respond to ethnic-based demands. Although it has secured important achievements in recognizing the legitimate question of nationalities and has gone some way in responding to those concerns, it has also created some serious challenges. The federal setup, without an adequate legal framework, is struggling to address the competitive demands of the so-called natives and settlers, which is a problem of its own creation. Because both citizen and ethnic rights have not been adequately qualified in Ethiopia, the uncontrolled exercise of one has easily become an encumbrance on the other. What is also notable is the reluctance on the part of constitutional interpretation organs, at both federal and regional levels, to develop a solution that enhances the possible implementation of the two constitutionally guaranteed rights in a mutually inclusive manner. More critical is the lack of political commitment on the part of both federal and regional authorities to protect the rights of those considered "outsiders" without jeopardizing the rights of "native" communities. Things are changing quickly in the Ethiopian federation, although not always for the better. We are no longer dealing with a federation that was ruled by a coherent and cohesive ruling party that, as a result, turned the country into a federation in name only. A cacophony of competing voices is coming from the state governments, often accompanied by deadly violence. Although the ruling party has transformed itself into a single national party, raising the hope that it might eliminate the cacophony of voices coming from the state governments, that has not translated into less conflictual intergovernmental relations. The country has not seen the level of intergovernmental disputes that it is currently witnessing even during the days when the ruling party was, at least formally speaking, a coalition of four parties that control four state governments. With intergovernmental disputes becoming more frequent, louder and even deadly, the need for institutions and processes to manage intergovernmental disputes is more

---

[12] The two political forces that stand back to back to each other currently are those that advocate for federalism on ethnic attributes and those that advocate for federalism on civic grounds.

evident than ever. A few years ago, hopes were high that true federalism might finally arrive in Ethiopia. The government introduced a series of political and legislative reforms that suggested that the days of pseudo federalism might be a thing of the past. That may no longer be evident. Today, it is not clear whether the country is capitalizing on the early reforms of 2018 or relapsing to its days of governance without the rule of law, constitutionalism and democratization. As we are busy completing this chapter, the country is mired in a devastating civil war and preparing for an election that does not include major political forces. The "spring of hope" might be giving away to "the winter of despair."

References

Aalen, L. (2011). *The politics of ethnicity in Ethiopia: Actors, power and mobilization under ethnic federalism.* Brill.

Abbink, J. (1998). New configurations of Ethiopian ethnicity: The challenge of the South. *Northeast African Studies, 5*(1), 59–81.

Abbink, J. (2011). Ethnic based federalism and ethnicity in Ethiopia: Reassessing the experiment after 20 Years. *Journal of Eastern African Studies, 5*(4), 596–618.

Abdu, B. (2018a). Sidama zone detains 226 in relation to deadly conflict. *The Reporter.* Retrieved July 11, 2019, from https://www.thereporterethiopia.com/article/sidama-zone-detains-226-relation-deadly-conflict

Abdu, B. (2018b). Sidama zone head, Hawassa mayor resign. *The Reporter.* Retrieved July 1, 2019, from https://www.thereporterethiopia.com/article/sidama-zone-head-hawassa-mayor-resign

Assefa, G. (2008). Federalism and legal pluralism in Ethiopia: Reflections on their impacts on the protection of human rights. In G. Alemu & S. Alemahu (Eds.), *The constitutional protection of human rights in Ethiopia: Challenges and prospects.* Ethiopian Human Rights Law Series.

Assefa, G. (2014). Constitutional protection of human and minority rights in Ethiopia: Myth v. Reality. PhD Thesis, University of Melbourne.

Behailu, B. (2015). *Transfer of land rights in Ethiopia: Towards a sustainable policy framework.* Eleven International Publishing.

Benishangul Gumuz Region Constitution. (2002). Proclamation No. 31 2002, The Revised Constitution of the Benishangul Gumuz Regional State, Lisane Hig Gazeta of the Benishangul Gumuz Regional State.

Clapham, C. (2002). Controlling space in Ethiopia. In W. James (Ed.), *Remapping Ethiopia: Socialism and after* (pp. 9–30). James Currey.

Côté, I. (2008). Autonomy and ethnic diversity: The case of Xinjiang Uighur autonomous region' in 'Decision of the HoF on the Benishangul Gumuz Election Case. The House of the Federation of the Federal Democratic Republic of Ethiopia. *Journal of Constitutional Decisions, 1,* 14–33.

Decision of the HoF on the Benshangul Gumuz Election case. (2008). The House of Federation of the Federal Democratic Republic of Ethiopia. *Journal of Constitutional Decision, 1*, 14–33.

'Ezega News'. (2019). Ethiopian house of federation to revise budget subsidy to regions. *Ezega News*. Retrieved May 5, 2021, from https://www.ezega.com/News/NewsDetails/7093/Ethiopian-House-of-Federation-to-Revise-Budget-Subsidy-to-Regions

FDRE Constitution. (1995). Proclamation No. 1/1995, Proclamation of the Constitution of the Federal Democratic Republic of Ethiopia, Federal Negarit Gazeta, 1st Year No.1, Addis Ababa-21st August.

Fessha, Y. (2017). The original sin of Ethiopian federalism. *Ethnopolitics, 16*(3), 232–245.

Fessha, Y. (2019). A federation without federal credential: The story of federalism in a dominant party state. In N. Stytler & C. Charles Fombad (Eds.), *Decentralization and Constitutionalism in Africa* (pp. 133–150). Oxford University Press.

Fessha, Y., & Dessalegn, B. (2020). Internal migration, ethnic federalism and differentiated citizenship: The case of Ethiopia. In A. Gagnon & A. Tremblay (Eds.), *Federalism, democracy and national diversity in the 21st century: Opportunities and challenges* (pp. 269–288). Palgrave Macmillan.

Fiseha, A. (2006). Theory versus practice in the implementation of Ethiopia's ethnic federalism. In D. Turton (Ed.), *Ethnic federalism: The Ethiopian experience in comparative perspective* (pp. 131–159). James Currey.

Fiseha, A. (2007). *Federalism and the accommodation of diversity in Ethiopia: A comparative study*. Artistic Printing Enterprise.

Fiseha, A. (2012). Ethiopia's experiment in accommodating diversity: 20 years' balance sheet. *Regional and Federal Studies, 22*(4), 435–473.

Fiseha, A. (2016). Intra-unit minorities in the context of ethno-national federalism in Ethiopia. *Ethiopian Journal of Federal Studies, 3*(1), 39–79.

Gambella Region Constitution. (2002). Proclamation No. 27/2002, Proclamation of the Revised Gambella People's Constitution.

Gedamu, Y. (2018). Persecution of Ethnic Amharas will harm the reform agenda. *The conversation*. Retrieved May 5, 2001, from https://theconversation.com/persecution-of-ethnic-amharas-will-harm-ethiopias-reform-agenda-98201

Gerth-Niculescu, M. (2021). Anger, fear run deep after months of ethnic violence in western Ethiopia. *The New Humanitarian*. Retrieved May 5, 2021, from https://www.thenewhumanitarian.org/news-feature/2021/2/23/fear-runs-deep-after-ethnic-violence-in-western-Ethiopia

Gudina, M. (2006). Contradictory interpretations of Ethiopian history: The need for a new consensus. In D. Turton (Ed.), *Ethnic federalism: The Ethiopian experience in comparative perspective* (pp. 119–130). James Currey.

Gudina, M. (2011). *Ethiopia: Competing ethnic nationalisms and the quest for democracy, 1960s–2011.* Chamber Printing House.

Human Rights Council. (2016). Stop immediately the extra-judicial killings, illegal detentions, beatings, intimidation and harassment committed by government security forces!!. 140th Special Report, Addis Ababa.

Lavers, T. (2018). Responding to land based conflict in Ethiopia: The land rights of ethnic minorities under federalism. *African Affairs, 117*(468), 462–484.

Markakis, J. (2003). Ethnic conflict in pre-federal Ethiopia. Paper presented at the 1st National Conference on Federalism, Conflict and Peace Building, .

Mehret Ayenew. (2002). Decentralization in Ethiopia: Two case studies on devolution of power and responsibilities to local government. In B. Zewde & S. Pausewang (Eds.), *Ethiopia: The challenge of democracy from below* (pp. 13–148). Nordiska Afrikainstitutet; Forum of Social Studies.

Mengisteab, K. (1997). New approaches to state Building in Africa: The case of Ethiopia's ethnic-based federalism. *African Studies Review, 40*(3), 111–132.

Oromia Region Constitution. (2001). Proclamation No. 46/2001, Oromia Regional State Revised Constitution Proclamation.

Petition to the HoF by the Victims of Expulsion in Guraferda District Dated. (2009). (Yekati 30, 2001 E.C.), on File with the Secretariat of the HoF, Addis Ababa.

Seyoum, A. (2020). Solving the Language puzzle. *The Reporter.* Retrieved May 4, 2020, from https://www.thereporterethiopia.com/article/solving-language-puzzle

Smith, D., & Hiden, J. (2012). *Ethnic diversity and the nation state: National cultural autonomy revisited.* Routledge.

SNNP Region Constitution. (2001). Proclamation No. 35/2001, A Proclamation to Ratify the Revised Constitution 2001, of the Southern Nations, Nationalities and Peoples Regional State.

Van der Beken, C. (2012). *Unity in diversity-federalism as a mechanism to accommodate ethnic diversity: The case of Ethiopia.* Lit Verlag.

Van der Beken, C. (2013). Federalism in a context of extreme ethnic pluralism: The case of Ethiopia's southern nations, nationalities and peoples region. *Verfassung und Recht in Übersee VRÜ, 46*(1), 3–17.

CHAPTER 11

The 'Federal Solution' to Diversity Conflicts in South Africa and Kenya: Partial at Most

Nico Steytler

I would like to acknowledge the support provided by the South African Research Chairs Initiative of the Department of Science and Technology and National Research Foundation, through the South African Research Chair in Multilevel Government, Law and Development.

N. Steytler (✉)
Dullah Omar Institute of Constitute Law, Governance and Human Rights, University of the Western Cape, Cape Town, South Africa
e-mail: nsteytler@uwc.ac.za

© The Author(s), under exclusive license to Springer Nature Switzerland AG 2022
S. Keil, S. Kropp (eds.), *Emerging Federal Structures in the Post-Cold War Era*, Federalism and Internal Conflicts,
https://doi.org/10.1007/978-3-030-93669-3_11

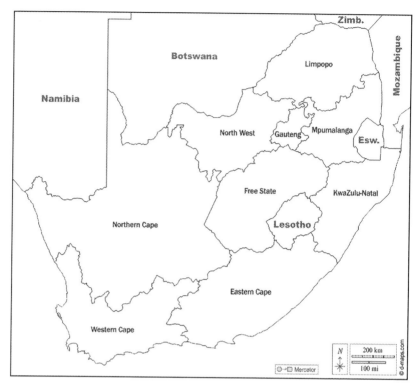

Map 11.1 South Africa. *Source*: https://d-maps.com/carte.php?num_car=4415&lang=en

11 THE 'FEDERAL SOLUTION' TO DIVERSITY CONFLICTS IN SOUTH AFRICA... 235

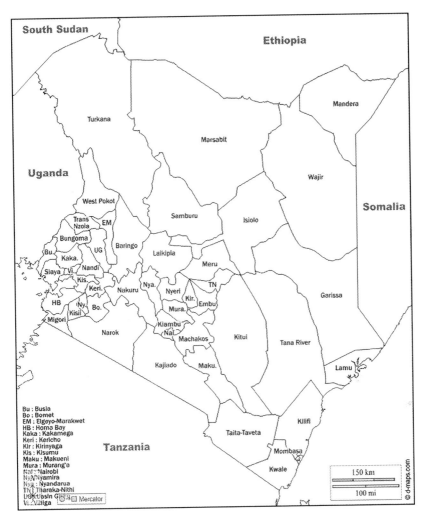

Map 11.2 Kenya. *Source*: https://d-maps.com/carte.php?num_car=239&lang=en

Introduction

There are at least four federations or federal-type countries in Africa which may be categorized as being partially successful in managing or containing conflict—Nigeria, Ethiopia, South Africa and Kenya. But conflict remains not far from the surface, as events in Ethiopia show; there have been violent protests in the region since 2018 and open warfare broke out in November 2020 between the Federal Government and Tigray. The question is whether the federal arrangements, which were designed to deal with those conflicts, have indeed contributed to their containment.

Of the four countries, South Africa and Kenya are most alike since the latter borrowed heavily from the former's federal features. There are also a number of other commonalities: multi-ethnic and multiracial societies and, of course, being patrimonial states. There are inevitably also important differences in their colonial histories and stages of economic development.

As two of the few examples of functioning non-centralized states in Africa, South Africa and Kenya lead to the question of whether the 'federal solution' has been successful in managing or mediating diversity conflicts and then why and how federal arrangements have helped to manage or mediate internal conflicts and alleviate tensions within these two countries. In answering this overarching question, four subsidiary questions are posed. First, whose interests did the federal idea serve as a conflict management tool? Second, what were the practical arrangements to give effect to the federal idea as a conflict resolution tool? Third, how successful have these federal arrangements been in addressing the underlying conflict? And fourth, what is the salience of the federal idea to address current and future challenges?

In answering these questions, it is argued that the federal idea served various objectives during the course of each country's constitutional trajectory—from a tool for minority supremacy to minority protection. Because the federal idea was contested, the resultant practical arrangements established highly centralized federations. In both countries, the federal arrangements have been only partial solutions, with both countries still facing major conflicts. While for the black/white conflict in South Arica federalism provides no answer, the ethnic conflict in Kenya cannot be addressed by devolution alone and seems best to be complemented with power-sharing arrangements at the center.

South Africa

Background

In South Africa's population of 57 million people (2020), the primary cleavages are still racial: 80% of the population are African, 10% are colored, 9% are white, and 1% are of Asian origin.[1] In the African component, nine different languages are officially recognized, while among the other three racial groups, the main languages are Afrikaans and English. South Africa is a middle-income country but displays one of the highest levels of inequality, which is particularly pronounced between the white and black groups (African and colored).

The modern state of South Africa emerged after the coming together of four British self-governing colonies in 1910—the Cape, Transvaal, the Orange River Colony and Natal. After a three-year-long war (1899–1902) between the British Empire and the two Boer Republics (Transvaal and the Orange Free State), the white population of the four colonies opted for a Union rather than a federation. The white minority government's goal from the start was the monopoly of power to the exclusion of the black majority. This goal was pursued at both a macro and a micro level. At the macro level, the National Party (representing white Afrikaner interests), after coming to power in 1948, sought to secure the separation of races by establishing ten ethnic homelands for the various African ethnic groups, setting them on a trajectory for secession and independence. After toying with the idea of creating a homeland for the colored community, a form of consociationalism was attempted in 1983, bringing the white, colored, and Asian communities together in one Parliament but with separate chambers. The exclusion of black South Africans from power from the 1910s led to resistance, at first non-violent, but after this strategy's failure to affect change, to an armed struggle in the 1960s, led by the principal black liberation movement, the African National Congress (ANC).

Together with internal armed resistance, an antagonistic international community, and a faltering economy as a result, the white minority regime, immediately after the collapse of the Soviet bloc, commenced negotiations in 1990 with the ANC for a democratic South Africa, which ultimately led

---

[1] These categories were creatures of the apartheid regime but are still used by the government for measuring progress made by previously disadvantaged communities.

to the first democratic non-racial elections in April 1994 and an ANC-led government. In the 26 years of democratic rule, violent conflict between groups has been successfully addressed, although the schism between the white and African communities is as palpable as before, now not on the question of democracy but on access to wealth, which still reflects the apartheid legacy.

Why the Federal Idea

In a country composed of various race, language, and ethnic groups, various power-sharing ideas have circulated since the foundation of the South African state until the present, all in attempts to resolve the deep cleavages in South Africa.

Federalism was keenly debated by the Convention on South Africa in 1909 as a way of bringing the four colonies together. Following earlier successful applications of the federal idea in Canada (1867) and Australia (1900), a federation was ardently supported by the Cape Colony and Natal, fearing dominance of the gold-rich Transvaal in a unitary state. In the end, an agreement was reached on a Union. The principal argument against a federation was the need to unite the two language groups—Afrikaners of the former Boer republics and the English-speakers from the other two colonies; a federation would have entrenched the divisions and enmity of the Anglo-Boer War. Also, there was unanimity that the mineral wealth of the Transvaal should be shared by the country as a whole (Steytler, 2005).

A provincial system of government was established with the responsibility for education, health, agriculture, and roads, but conflicting Union legislation would automatically override provincial laws. A measure of diversity was allowed; in the Cape Province and Natal, the pre-existing voters' roll containing black voters would be constitutionally protected.

The National Party's attempt to resolve the conflict between white and black was not a federal structure in theory but looked much like that in practice. The grand apartheid idea was that South Africa was a society of ethnic minorities (except the whites, which was regarded as a single group despite language and cultural divisions). In terms of a thinly veiled strategy of divide-and-rule, each black ethnic group should thus exercise their right to self-determination in an own 'homeland' which would mature into a fully-fledged independent state. This vision was implemented by seeking to squeeze 75% of the population into 13% of the land. Africans would thus be tolerated in the 'white' urban areas only to sell their labor. Since 1976, four homelands opted for 'independence' (although not receiving recognition from any country in the world), while the other six firmly rejected that goal, operating as 'self-governing territories'. They were all bound to white South Africa through the latter's purse strings; none of them had any economic base of note and were reliant on transfers. De facto there was an element of federalism present as there was a high level of political self-rule. However, they remained subservient to the financial control of the dominant white government and informal modes of shared rule through consultation.

The other two black racial groups—the colored and the Asian communities—did not fit the African ethnic model of a group with an own historical territory and were interspersed among the white community; a more explicit power-sharing model—a variant of consociationalism—was introduced by the 1983 Constitution.

The exclusion of Africans from any political accommodation at the center of power added a further spur of black resistance to apartheid in all its manifestations. The activities of the ANC's external military wing were complemented by civic uprisings in black townships, resulting in a low-intensity civil war.

As the fall of the Berlin Wall in November 1989 grandiosely signaled the end of communism, the National Party government moved swiftly to unban the ANC and its alliance partner, the South African Communist Party, and negotiations for a new non-racial democratic South Africa commenced. While the principles of non-racialism and majority government could be agreed upon, the form of the new state was highly contentious. The ANC, reflecting its own centrist ethos and communist vanguardism, insisted on a unitary state with centralized powers necessary to undo the ravages of apartheid. Any form of federalism, proposed by its negotiating partners, would merely perpetuate the old apartheid system of divide and rule. For the National Party, federalism offered the possibility of a weak center (they feared a strong center) and strong subnational governments. At first they toyed with the idea of Swiss cantons as small white enclaves in which they would protect their 'way of life'. When non-racialism became the founding premise for negotiations, they advanced the notion of provinces (dreaming of winning a couple of such structures). Buthelezi, from a Zulu nationalism perspective, also ardently advocated federalism, if not secession (Ellman, 1993).

A hard-won compromise had the following elements. First, federalism became the unspeakable 'f-word' because of its apartheid historical baggage. Although all the structures and trimmings of a federation were present, that label was avoided. Second, in demarcating provinces, ethnicity would be one among a number of other factors, economic integration the dominant. Although economic regional blocks were used, seven of the nine provinces nevertheless had a linguistic (ethnic) majority. The names of provinces should also have had no bearing to such an ethnic majority. Attaching KwaZulu to Natal to create the hyphenated KwaZulu-Natal was the only exception as it was a solution to entice Buthelezi to participate in the election. Third, a weak provincial system was established; provinces enjoyed only concurrent powers with the national government, but with a qualified override clause in favor of the latter. Fourth, the troublesome (and powerful) right-wing Afrikaners were placated by the promise of a *Volkstaat*, if they could establish any area where Afrikaners (now an ethnic group not based on race) were in the majority. Also, the recognition of the right to self-determination was conceded but expressed in such a convoluted manner that it was devoid of traction (Steytler & Mettler, 2001).

The deal articulated in the Constitution of 1993 and finally secured with three days to spare before the election was only an interim arrangement. Again, as a compromise, the final constitution was to be drafted by the duly elected people's representatives, but bound by a set of Constitutional Principles, which included the preservation of the provincial system.

Federal Arrangements

The 1996 Constitution was also a product of compromise, as the ANC did not get a two-thirds majority in the newly elected Parliament. The provincial system was explicitly modeled on the German federal system of executive federalism, in which the exercise of autonomy is contained through the principles of cooperative government via structures and procedures at both legislative and executive branches (Brand, 2006).

The dispersal of power to subnational governments is not a founding value listed in section 1 of the Constitution, but the emphasis falls on South Africa being 'one, sovereign' state. However, in section 40(1), the 'government' is described as 'constituted by a national, provincial, and local spheres of government' which are 'distinctive, interrelated and interdependent'. Unlike in the interim Constitution, local government was elevated to a sphere of government alongside the other two, in part to hollow out the provincial domain.

The powers of provinces are limited. In addition to a thin list of exclusive powers (which the national Parliament may trump on certain conditions), a list of concurrent powers with the national government gives some substance to its jurisdiction. The primary functions include primary and secondary education, health, social welfare, agriculture, and trade, but provincial legislation may be overridden by national legislation on certain conditions. In addition, provinces may adopt their own constitution but within strict confines.

Local government also has a list of powers—the usual municipal functions of water, electricity, sanitation, roads, health services, and so on—which may be regulated by both the national and provincial governments.

The straightjacketing of provinces is most pronounced in the area of taxing powers. Provinces have an undetermined scope for taxing powers, but all lucrative tax sources are excluded. Moreover, any provincial tax is premised on national regulations. In contrast, local government has the constitutionally guaranteed property taxes and surcharges on fees.

What the provinces lack in own powers, they may recoup through their participation in the national Parliament. The second chamber of Parliament, the National Council of Provinces, is modeled on the German *Bundesrat*; the nine provincial legislatures each send a delegation of ten members (comprising four provincial executive members and six elected by the legislature) with a mandate which may include vetoing legislation affecting provinces (but with a National Assembly two-thirds override), constitutional amendments (requiring six votes), co-ratifying international treaties, national states of emergency, and approval of national intervention in a province (and a provincial intervention in a municipality).

The basic principles of cooperative government are neatly articulated in the constitution, entailing respect for each other's autonomy, commitment against centrifugal actions, and the nitty-gritty of cooperation, including the avoidance of litigation to resolve intergovernmental disputes (chapter 3 Constitution, 1996).

The Success of Cooperative Government

The success of federal arrangements can only be measured if there was indeed an attempt to implement them. Unlike many other African countries where an initially reluctant compromise to adopt some form of federalism does not mature into an embrace, the first democratic government under the leadership of Mandela made every effort to give effect to the provisions of the Constitution (Steytler, 2019).

The immediate conflict between the IFP and the ANC in KwaZulu-Natal was addressed by the ANC not contesting the IFP's narrow win in the provincial elections of 1994. Allowing an IFP-led government of provincial unity immediately led to a rapid decline in violent conflict. The IFP was able to secure the premiership for the next ten years in a continuation of the government of provincial unity. Also, the former ruling party, the National Party, would not be left empty-handed; it won the Western Cape in 1994.

With peace established in the troublesome KwaZulu-Natal, and most provinces proving poor in delivering development, the Mbeki government (1999–2008) sought to both recentralize power and put the abolition of provinces on the agenda (Steytler, 2014). At the same time, the ANC hollowed out the substance of provinces by ruling them politically from the center. For example, premiers were appointed by the ANC president and not by party rank and file. The question was posed whether the strong party hierarchy would hollow out the structures to such an extent that they simply imploded or whether the formal political structures would have a reciprocal impact on politics (Steytler, 2014). At their fifth yearly conference in 2007 (which elected Zuma as ANC President), the ANC placed three options on the table: maintain the status quo, reduce their role, or abolish them. A major government policy review was initiated in 2007, focusing on the necessity for the future existence of provinces, but it petered away with the demise of President Mbeki at the hands of his successor Jacob Zuma.

The politics changed. The politics of the ANC was provincialized, and Zuma defeated Mbeki because provinces brought out block votes. The ascendency of Zuma and his predatory coterie of rent-seeking officials and private sector also reverberated throughout the provinces, and they too became lucrative troughs to feed from.[2] Over 38% of the national budget is expended by provinces. Building on elites that coalesced around

---

[2] See, for example, the well-documented corrupt regime under the then Free State Premier Ace Magashule (Myburg, 2019), the latter (who was elected Secretary-General of the ANC in 2017) appearing in court on November 13, 2020, on charges of corruption and racketeering.

provinces, savoring the spoils of government, the debate within the ANC about the future of provinces slowly fizzled away. By the 2017 ANC elective conference, provinces were no longer a burning issue and the election of the ANC president was again conducted along provincial block votes (which, this time, brought Cyril Ramaphosa to power).

Current and Future Challenges

The main conflict in South Africa has been, and still is, the racial division between white and black. The federal arrangements could not, and thus did not, seek to address this cleavage. 'White monopoly capital' is now the focused enemy to unite Africans around common action. Politics has also radicalized on both sides of the racial divide. The Economic Freedom Fighters, an Africanist party on the left, demand expropriation without compensation (a demand to which the ANC has acceded), while the 2019 national and provincial elections saw the resurgence of the right-wing Afrikaner party, the Freedom Front Plus.

The state, through employment policies and the procurement of goods and services, has played a major role in slowly affecting transforming the racial composition of the economy. During the Zuma years (2009–2018), the state, under the cover of transformation, also became predatory. While corruption at the national level benefitted the few, fiscal decentralization has opened up opportunities on a wider scale for predation. When the COVID-19 pandemic struck in March 2020, the country was already in recession. With the economic contraction of the GDP in 2020 by an estimated 8–10%, and a loss of a million jobs, the economic divide and contestation in the country are bound to get more intense.

While ethnicity will remain a factor, the provincial system, with its access to (shrinking) state wealth, may provide an important antidote to tension among African ethnic groups. Provinces provide an unarticulated safety net for ethnic groups, catering for both identities and material well-being (Fessha, 2010).

KENYA

Background

Kenya's population of nearly 50 million (2017) is also ethnically fragmented: Kikuyu 22%, Luhya 14%, Luo 13%, Kalenjin 12%, Kamba 11%,

Kisii 6%, and Meru 6%, with the remainder made up by 30 smaller groups (15%) and non-Africans (Asians and whites—1%) (Index Mundi, 2019).

The colonial state of Kenya was 'an artificial entity' created by agreement among Great Britain, Germany, Italy, and Ethiopia in the late nineteenth century. Kenya as a British colony was formally established in 1905 and was governed directly by the Colonial Office through a resident governor, while internally the colony was centrally governed through a system of provinces comprising a number of districts under the control of Provincial and District Officers, respectively. The boundaries of the provinces and districts based on tribes reinforced the tribal association to the land (Ghai, 2015, 60). With the settlement of Europeans on the fertile 'White Highlands', a bifurcated system of local authorities based on race emerged. Having the 'White Highlands' for exclusive white ownership, elected local councils for Europeans were largely financially self-sufficient. For Africans, tribal lands outside the White Highlands were governed by traditional authorities under the control of the district officers.

When African nationalism swept through Africa in the 1950s, Kenya's independence also became inevitable. The independence Constitution of 1964 contained strong federal provisions, but they did not survive for more than a year. A continuation of the centralized colonial system followed, which in 1982 resulted in one party rule. At the end of the Cold War a second wave of democracy swept across Africa, including Kenya, and multiparty democracy was again introduced in 1992. This change did not alter the nature of the 'imperial presidency', and by 2000, the Constitution of Kenya Review Commission was reintroducing the concept of devolution. After the 2007 contested presidential elections and the violence that followed, a new constitution was adopted in 2010 with devolution as one of its key pillars, a system that was implemented in 2013.

The Federal Idea

The federal idea has long been part of the constitutional debates and practices since at least the 1940s, drawing support from various interest groups at various times—at first European settlers in the 1940s and 1950s, then African ethnic minorities in 1964, and finally, devolution under the 2010 Constitution. Majimboism, the Swahili word for federalism, thus carried 'heavy emotional and political baggage' as each group advanced it for their own purposes (Maxon, 2017, 3, quoting Ghai, 2008, 213).

In his book *Majimbo in Kenya's Past: Federalism in the 1940s and 1950s*, Robert Maxon describes the emergence and eventual failure of a federal solution to the European settlers' political and material concerns. The first advocates for federalism came from the European settlers in the 1940s in response to the colonial policy of African paramountcy, already declared in 1923, and that a white minority government, as in South Africa, would not be countenanced. The 'federal solution' was inextricably coupled to racial segregation and the protection of valuable economic assets, namely, the land, and its exploitation, in the White Highlands. After World War II, federal schemes were advanced both by colonial officials and European settlers. For the latter group, the aim was partition and governance of the White Highlands as well as access to the sea and possible control of the central government. As an autonomous province of the White Highlands proved problematic for the Colonial Office, there was also a shift of emphasis toward powerful local authorities which would protect the Europeans' 'way of life' and land, institutions which were already functional. This emphasis continued in the 1950s.

In the face of decolonization already rolling out in India and Pakistan in 1947 (or because of it), the European settlers in the 1950s clamored for control of the White Highlands with full control of education and other social services, propounding a view of Kenya as a multiracial society which should be structured as such. But there were also other voices that sought refuge in strong local authorities. In a specific proposal, the Swiss cantonal model featured prominently: segregation through localization of all parts of the country, even using the terms of 'commune' and 'canton' (Maxon, 2017, 135–136).

Maxon argues that the Europeans advocated federalism because, fearful of the uncertain times, it was to be a defense against majority rule and a measure to protect their property and 'Western way of life', informed by racism, the belief in European superiority, and white supremacy. Their advocacy failed because the Colonial Office rejected the notion of white supremacy (as it did later in Southern Rhodesia). The view was also that such a 'federal solution' would not reduce racial and ethnic tensions but increase them by hindering national cohesion and integration. Moreover, the Colonial Office was skeptical of any break in the colonial tradition of centralized rule.

When the federal idea proved not a pragmatic solution to their concerns, Maxon notes that the Europeans quickly moved away for the idea, seeking other ways of protecting their material interests—emigration and securing compensation for their lands after independence. At the first Lancaster Conference in 1960 toward self-government for Kenya, federalism ideas were thus no longer on the table. However, by the second and third Lancaster Conferences in 1961 and 1962, there were new advocates for federalism, who had some success to entrench federal arrangements (see Ghai, 2015; Hornsby, 2013, 70 eff).

Once African political parties could appeal across district boundaries (before 1958 political activities were confined to districts, thus fostering ethno-centricity), the Kenyan African National Union (KANU), principally under the Kikuyu and Luo leadership with Jomo Kenyatta, a Kikuyu, as leader, sought independence as soon as possible. Minority ethnic groups feared the dominance of a Kikuyu-Luo central government, and particularly the loss of their land, and formed a rival party, the Kenyan African Democratic Union (KADU), under the leadership of Odinga Odinga and Tom Mboya. The Kalenjin leader Daniel Arap Moi argued that a very centralized system of government may lead to the abuse of political power. KANU pushed for regionalism, called majimboism, to protect their lands and rights and ensure a share of state power (Ghai, 2015, 63). Drawing on the earlier European proposals, the KANU advocated for strong regional governments and a weak center. The clash between KANU's position on centralism and KADU's position on regionalism was irreconcilable, resulting in the British government imposing a constitution reflecting both. Kenyatta accepted the proposed constitution on the ground that it would speed up the independence process but with no intent of implementing it (Mutakha Kangu, 2015, 73).

The 1963 Constitution established a two-level government: a national government and seven regions, composed of 41 districts, the boundaries of which were adjusted according to ethnic lines. The division of powers and functions has been described as 'complex, elaborate and confusing', but it did include regional police forces (Ghai, 2015, 72). A weak Senate, based on the House of Lords model, did not give the regions much say in central decision-making. Although regional elections were held, regional governments and administrations were not established, and Kenyatta dismantled the system constitutionally within a year and politically through the merger of KADU into KANU.

Although majimboism lasted not even a year, its legacy continued as the ethnic boundaries of the 41 districts remained for the next 40 years (Ghai, 2015, 74). As predicted, the concentration of power in the center, firmly located in the hands of an imperial presidency, soon led to its abuse.

After the death of Kenyatta in 1978 and the assumption of the presidency by Daniel Arap Moi, multiparty democracy was eventually a casualty when a one-party state became law in 1982.

The end of the Cold War and pressure from the West resulted in a return to multiparty democracy in 1992. But a more comprehensive constitutional change was required to deal with the imperial presidency. A Constitution of Kenya Review Commission (CKRC), appointed in 2000 under the chairpersonship of Yash Pal Ghai, had the mandate of investigating the structure of government, including federal and unitary systems. After extensive consultation with the people, the CKRC placed a draft constitution before the National Conferences (Bomas), which adopted it, with devolution as one of its key features. Ghai attributes the popular demand for devolution to the following: first, the widespread alienation from the central government because of the concentration of power in the center and in the president; the marginalization, neglect, and victimization on the basis of political or ethnic affiliation; and the abuse of power by the provincial administration, reporting directly to the president (Ghai, 2015, 75). Very different from the elite support for majimboism in the early 1960s, devolution now had a popular support base, and the fear of the abuse of power and tribal-based rule in 1960s was a reality now.

The government of President Kibaki, a Kikuyu who beat Moi's anointed candidate, Uhuru Kenyatta, the son of the Jomo, in the 2002 election, rejected the Bomas draft, and after key elements of devolution were removed (by the Attorney-General Wako), it was submitted to a compulsory referendum in 2005. The so-called Wako draft failed to get a majority endorsement, with support coming only from Kikuyu areas. Against this backdrop, the clinging to power by Kibaki against his rival Raila Odinga, a Luo and son of Odinga Odinga, in the rigged election of 2007, led to massive post-election violence at the beginning of 2008, sharply dividing the country along ethnic lines. The causes were the same as those that informed the Bomas draft—the excessive centralization in the imperial presidency resulted in ethnic partisanship in the distribution of resources.

After the formation of a government of national unity (Kibaki remained president and Odinga became the prime minister), a constitution (a harmonized text of the Bomas and Wako drafts) was adopted by Parliament and received a strong popular endorsement in the 2010 referendum, setting Kenya on a new devolution trajectory.

Devolution

Unlike South Africa's implicit 'federal framework', devolution is posited as a fundamental value and component of the new constitutional dispensation. The people's legislative sovereignty is exercised through 'Parliament and the legislative assemblies of county governments', and the same applies to the executive (art. 1(4) Constitution). The 'sharing and devolution of power' are again stated as a national value and principle, alongside 'patriotism [and] national unity' (art. 10(2)(a)). The articulated objects of devolution reflect the common goals of self-rule: democracy, accountability, participation, and self-governance; effective service delivery and development; equitable access to resources; and limited centralization (Mutakha Kangu, 2015, 111–121).

Unlike the Majimbo Constitution and the Bomas draft, only two levels of government are provided for: the national government and 47 counties. Shying away from regional structures which would align with the large ethnic groups, they were broken up, using the former 41 colonial districts (increased to 47 in 1992) with their ethnic-based boundaries, inevitably incorporating the ethnic dimension indirectly (Rugo Muriu, 2015).

The constitution's centralized bend is clear from the counties' limited powers. While a long list of exclusive national functions is provided, there is legal uncertainty whether the counties have any exclusive powers; all their listed powers may be held concurrently with the national government, with a South African-copied qualified override clause in favor of the national government (Mutakha Kangu, 2015, 189; Bosire, 2015, 183). In the main, the range of powers is limited, more reflective of a super-sized local authority. The powers include pre-primary education, roads, county health facilities, implementation of national agricultural policies, control of air and noise pollution, water and sanitation, electricity reticulation, housing, sport and cultural activities, and firefighting.

As for financing, the model is skewed toward reliance on national transfers, as own source revenue is constitutionally limited to property taxes, 'entertainment taxes', and fees for services rendered. Of the revenue raised nationally, not less than 15% of the national budget must be distributed equitably among the 47 counties according to a formula determined by the second house of Parliament, the Senate.

The Senate made a comeback, but now in a more federalist jacket; with one senator elected from each county, this second chamber of Parliament is designed to present the interest of the counties at the national legislative level.[3] Legislatively, the Senate has three functions: it must approve all constitutional amendments by a super majority; it must pass all legislation affecting counties; and it determines the five-year formula for the horizontal division of the counties' share of revenue raised nationally. Its oversight role includes the impeachment of the President or Deputy President and the final decision after the National Assembly has initiated proceedings. It also plays a peer-review role over counties: it 'exercises oversight over national revenue allocated to county governments' (art. 96(3) Constitution), and any impeachment of governors by county assemblies requires its endorsement.

Cooperative government and intergovernmental relations are further aspects borrowed from the South African Constitution: the two levels of government must 'conduct their mutual relations on the basis of consultation and cooperation' (art. 6(2) Constitution).

The Success of Devolution

With devolution being a compromise between the devolutionists and the centralists, its implementation would be contested terrain when Uhuru Kenyatta and his Jubilee party won the 2013 elections with a wafer-thin majority against Odinga. Resistance to implementation was apparent from its inception, but two institutional features proved vital for the establishment of counties: a constitutionally embedded transition process and an independent judiciary.

The expeditious implementation of the Constitution was provided for in the Constitution itself; it specified legislation that had to be enacted, including those related to devolution, also setting timelines for such enactment. The sanction for failing to meet such timelines would be the dissolution of Parliament itself. The Constitution also established the Commission for the Implementation of the Constitution (CIC), the task of which, as the name suggests, was to oversee, monitor, and advise on the implementation of the Constitution, including devolution (Wanyande, 2015).

---

[3] In addition to 47 directly elected senators, there are also 16 women senators, 2 for the youth, and 2 representing persons of disabilities, all of whom are nominated by the parties in the National Assembly according to the strength of the parties. In matters affecting counties, the nominated members do not have a vote. See Mutakha Kangu (2015, p. 350).

Right from the outset, the Supreme Court asserted the role of the Senate in law-making. When the National Assembly sought to pass the budget, including the vertical division of revenue, without the participation of the Senate, the Supreme Court invalidated the budget, noting that devolution was a fundamental pillar of the new constitutional dispensation (*Speaker of the Senate and another v Attorney-General and others* [2013] eKLR).

Has devolution been a success measured against the goals of restraining the imperial presidency, equitable development, and ethnic peace? The answer is only a partially yes.

First, the Jubilee government of Kenyatta did not embraced devolution fully, which meant that all the benefits of devolution could not be realized. National legislation that undermines devolution has been passed and old order legislation has not been reviewed (Mutakha Kangu, 2019). For example, the presidency has been reluctant to deconstruct the center's provincial administration system, which is at odds with devolution.

Second, the equitable sharing of national resources across the country has made some inroads in addressing uneven and under-development among counties. Over 20% of the national budget (in excess of the mandatory 15%) has been allocated to counties. The decentralization of funds has ensured that for the first time, services and infrastructure projects extend to the far reaches of the country. Because many counties are too small to perform major tasks, some are regrouping as 'regions' based on ethnicity to provide more comprehensive services. At the same time, devolution has also seen the decentralization of corruption.

Third, an ethnic peace dividend has not been firmly secured. When in 2017 Kenyatta once again won the presidential election but now with a putative better margin of votes against Odinga (54% for Kenyatta and 47% for Odinga), the ethnic cleavages emerged yet again. Odinga, once again cheated from victory, refused to accept the result on the basis of alleged 'computer-generated fraud'. This prompted violent protests by his supporters, which led to the loss of lives in clashes with security forces as well as a legal challenge to the Supreme Court. In a precedent-setting decision for Africa, the Court invalidated the election owing to widespread non-compliance with the electoral rules and ordered a new election within 60 days (*Railo Amolo Odinga and Another v Independent Electoral and Boundary Commission and Others*, Presidential Petition 1/2017, 27 August 2017 [2017] eKLR). The rerun of the election on October 26 was boycotted by Odinga because the demanded changes to the election management body were not affected, resulting in President Kenyatta drawing

98% of the votes cast by only 39% of the registered voters (the voter turnout in August was 80%).

Having been cheated for the third time at the polls (in 2007 as well), Odinga called for a People's Assembly which would endorse him as the legitimate leader of the country. He called on all governors and county assemblies to endorse this initiative, but in the end only 12 of the 47 counties supported it, although Kenyatta's Jubilee Party won only 29 counties. In the event, Odinga was sworn in publicly on January 30, 2018, as the 'People's President'. This coincided with calls for secession by non-Kikuyu counties.

The secession calls and the endorsement of Odinga as the 'People's President' have not deteriorated into open ethnic conflict for two principal reasons. First, devolution blunted the past winner-takes-all elections; counties for the first time provided opposition parties with a stake in government and the spoils it brings. Second, a national rapprochement emerged. To the astonishment and dismay of some of his followers, Odinga appeared on the steps of State House with Kenyatta on March 9, 2018, presenting a handshake that signaled a new initiative 'Building Bridges to Unity' (called BBI—Building Bridges Initiative). The newfound friends committed themselves to addressing the key issues confronting Kenya: ethnic divisiveness and a lack of a 'national ethos'; the lack of inclusivity in 'mainstream national development initiatives'; devolution (regarded as 'the most successful story in the recent process of building a strong nation') leading to exclusive practice in the counties; and corruption. To give effect to the 'handshake', Kenyatta on May 31, 2018, appointed a 'Building Bridges to Unity Advisory Taskforce', mandated to look at the 'national challenges' and 'make practical recommendations and reform proposals that build lasting unity', with a reporting period of one year to May 31, 2019. Odinga was also given the status of an elder statesman and represented Kenya internationally on several occasions. The Taskforce produced a comprehensive report in November 2019 dealing with an array of issues (Presidential Taskforce, 2019). Of importance for our study are the following: first, the winner-takes-all electoral competition should be replaced with a more consociational model. In a semi-return to a parliamentary system, the President should appoint the leader of the strongest party (or coalition) in Parliament as Prime Minister who would be responsible for the day-to-day running of the country, but at the pleasure of the President who can remove the person at any time. As the outcome of parliamentary elections usually track presidential elections, there is no requirement to appoint the leader of the opposition to any position in the national executive. However, the person who comes second on the presidential poll becomes ex officio a member of Parliament. Second, for the counties, the existence of which was lauded as a success, their share of national revenue should increase to a minimum of 35% of the national budget. In January 2020, the President appointed a Steering Committee to validate the Taskforce Report and to propose policy, statutory, and constitutional changes to implement the Taskforce's recommendations. Reporting in October 2020, it endorsed the Taskforce's findings and recommendations and proposed an extensive array of constitutional and statutory bills to that effect. It also added two additional executive positions: the President must appoint two deputy prime ministers from among his cabinet ministers (Steering Committee, 2020). Overall, the BBI increased the possibility for greater inclusivity without proposing a more structured consociational model; inclusivity would all depend on the politics of the day.

Current and Future Challenges

The challenge remains, as before, the ethnicization of politics, exacerbated by the centralization of power in the presidency. First, the splitting up of the main ethnic groups in smaller counties has not succeeded in diminishing the salience of ethnic identity. Although many argued that such identity is a construct, the salience lies in its ready mobilization for political purposes (Ghai, 2019). Already, there is the formation of informal blocks of counties, reconstituting the ethnic regions. Second, as the devolved county governments still decidedly play second fiddle to the dominance of the center, the presidency remains the ultimate polical prize. As noted, devolution has blunted the winner-takes-all paradigm but has not dented the omnipresence and omnipotence of the presidency. The future seems to lie in a combination of strengthening devolution as well as institutionalizing power-sharing as suggested by the BBI.

COMPARATIVE CONCLUSIONS

The comparison between two hybrid-federal African countries reveals some answers to the four questions posed.

Federalism as a Conflict Management Tool

First, it is striking in both countries that the federal idea was a pragmatic tool used to address an actual or perceived conflict. The notion of 'federalism' as a set of beliefs about its superiority as a form of governance had very few adherents. Supporters of the federal idea or tool shifted over time as the exigencies of time, place, and power changed. The two case studies illustrate Ronald Watts's view of federalism as a pragmatic way of dealing with governance challenges.

Second, as a pragmatic tool the federal idea could be used to various ends. The chequered career that it has had in both South Africa and Kenya suggests that at times the advocacy of the concept can be more divisive than achieving the ostensible goal of accommodation. This hangs together with the experience of federal arrangements used for narrow partisan interests. As a concept, it was contaminated in both Kenya and South Africa for the very same reason: a mechanism to preserve and protect white interests. Whereas Kenya's settlers reached a dead end with racial segregation after the Second World War, white South Africans' quest for racial supremacy, too, reached a dead end after the Cold War. These two tectonic shifts in world history changed the legitimacy of minority supremacy under whatever federal guise it may come.

The federal idea has mainly been put to use for the purpose of accommodating marginalized groups, usually in ethnic enclaves. Using the very same tools as the white supremacists in Kenya, ethnic groups clubbed together in KADU, propagating majimboism in the independence constitution, fearing their marginalization in a hegemonic political elite. So did the IFP in South Africa, seeking refuge in the promise of federalism.

Kenya is singular in that the return to devolution was not driven primarily by ethnic interests, but by a genuine desire, not for accommodation, but for bringing the presidential Leviathan to heel. This neglected object of federalism is as valid as the more run-of-the-mill ethnic accommodation purpose.

The Practical Arrangements Giving Effect to the Federal Idea as a Conflict Resolution Tool

As federalism was a contested paradigm, the practical arrangements exhibited a strong centralized dispensation. For South Africa, the German model of executive federalism, of cooperative government, provided a suitable compromise between the ANC's insistence on the centralization of power and the minority groups' claims for federalism. Following the lead of South Africa, in Kenya, the ruling Kikuyu elite could accept the diminution of power with a weak form of decentralization. The compromises that were reached in both countries have resulted in a specific model of non-centralism, which has been categorized as 'fragile federalism', a model not only applicable to the two countries under discussion but also in the federations of Nigeria and Ethiopia (Steytler & de Visser, 2015). The overall structure of government reflects very centralized federations. First, the powers allocated to subnational governments are weak and the central governments have strong override powers. Second, the fiscal powers are even more attenuated; the main tax sources are attributed to the central government, with an equalization system in place for sharing in the revenue raised nationally. Third, the legislative institution of shared rule—the second chamber of Parliament—may have the potential for being a counter-balance, but it is not so used in practice. Executive intergovernmental relations tend to be center-dominated. Fourth, the center has also overriding intervention powers.

How Successful Have These Federal Arrangements Been in Addressing Conflict?

In comparison to other attempts at decentralization in Africa, South Africa and Kenya are more or less functioning non-centrist states relatively at peace. The accommodation of the IFP in KwaZulu-Natal was the turnkey to peace in that region. Access to power for ethnic groups other than the ruling Kikuyu and Kalenjin alliance prevented ethnic conflagrations after both the contested 2013 and 2017 elections.

What would be the main causal factors that would explain the relative success? First, the federal compromises were actually implemented. Provinces and counties were established and funded. The political will (or necessity) was present to give effect to the federal arrangements. Second, the political will was at times coaxed by the courts, getting the central government to stick to the rules. A political commitment to constitutionalism and a functioning independent judicial system have thus been key. Third, although limited in powers, the subnational governments allowed for actual power-sharing among the various elites. Access to significant resources blunted the winner-takes-all paradigm. Moreover, the more government there was, the larger and more inclusive was the illegal market in government services. Devolution, operating within the socioeconomic mindset of the patrimonial state, entailed, among other things, the movement from the feasting by the few at the national table to the eating by regional elites of leftovers. Fourth, despite devolving power to territorial units, there were attempts at de-emphasizing ethnic divisions. Neither South Africa nor Kenya viewed itself as multinational societies, yet recognized its language and cultural diversity. The political history of South Africa made this project more realizable. In Kenya, despite proscribing ethnic parties and fragmenting the main ethnic groups in numerous counties, the political history and even the very boundaries of the counties militated against achieving this goal.

The Salience of the Federal Idea to Address Current and Future Challenges

Federal arrangements are, of course, territorially based governance structures that may or may not deal with deep-seated cleavages among groups. In South Africa, the major cleavage, deepened and entrenched by apartheid, remains race—the dominance of white wealth. The ethnic diversity among the black majority was not seen as being of great significance, as the anti-apartheid struggle was also a fight against 'tribalism'. While the 1994 first democratic elections brought a black majority government to power, the latter has not by any measure achieved the transformation of the economic dominance of whites, be it land or wealth ownership. After 26 years of democracy, the continued concentration of economic power in white hands remains the Achilles heel of South Africa. And federalism provides no solution.

In Kenya, the centralization of power (including over economic resources) in the hands of a Kikuyu minority (in alliance with any of the other ethnic groups) remains the primary source of conflict, as the 2017 election showed. Would making Kenya more federal by consolidating counties in larger units, bestowed with greater powers and funds, provide a more sustainable peace? This is unlikely as it may condemn most non-Kikuyu groups to permanent outsider status at the center of power. Within an ethnicized society, there are some ethnic winners and some ethnic losers. The handshake between Kenyatta and Odinga suggests again the need for ethnic power-sharing at the center. In the long run, however, an open political culture where parties organize on cross-cutting policies rather than on ethnicity would be a more sustainable option.

In summary, both countries' engagement with federalism illustrates that federalism provided only partial solutions to some causes of conflict. It is facile to say that federalism cannot solve many entrenched conflicts, but is worth saying it again, nevertheless. Other ways of sharing power (including economic power) are equally important.

References

Bosire, C. M. (2015). Powers and functions of county governments in Kenya. In N. Steytler & Y. P. Ghai (Eds.), *Kenya-South Africa dialogue of devolution* (pp. 181–200). Juta.

Brand, D. (2006). *Financial Constitutional Law: A comparison between Germany and South Africa*. KAS.

Ellman, S. (1993). Federalism gone awry: The structure of Government in the KwaZulu-Natal Constitution. *South African Human Rights Journal, 9*, 165–176.

Fessha, Y. (2010). *Ethnic diversity and federalism: Constitution making in South Africa and Ethiopia*. Ashgate.

Ghai, Y. (2019). Ethnicity, decentralisation and constitutionalism: A comparative perspective. In C. M. Fombad & N. Steytler (Eds.), *Decentralisation and constitutionalism in Africa* (pp. 53–69). Oxford University Press.

Ghai, Y. P. (2008). Devolution: Restructuring the Kenyan state. *Journal of East African Studies, 2*(2), 211–226.

Ghai, Y. P. (2015). Devolution in Kenya: Background and objectives. In N. Steytler & Y. P. Ghai (Eds.), *Kenya-South Africa dialogue of devolution* (pp. 56–80). Juta.

Hornsby, C. (2013). *Kenya: A History since Independence*. IB Tauris.

Index Mundi. (2019). *Kenya demographics 2019*. [online]. (Last update 7 December 2019). Retrieved April 6, 2019, from https://www.indexmundi.com/kenya/demographics_profile.html

Maxon, R. (2017). *Majimbo in Kenya's past: Federalism in the 1940s and 1950s*. Cambria Press.

Mutakha Kangu, J. (2015). *Constitutional Law of Kenya on devolution*. Strathmore University Press.

Mutakha Kangu, J. (2019). The Kenyan experience with implementation of devolution: Challenges and opportunities, presentation at Devolution Implementation Indaba, 26 March 2019, Harare, Zimbabwe.

Myburg, P. (2019). *The Gangster State: Unravelling Ace Magashule's web of capture*. Penguin Books.

Presidential Taskforce. (2019). *Building bridges to a United Kenya: From a nation of blood ties to a nation of ideals, Report of the Presidential Taskforce on Building Bridges to Unity Advisory*. Government of Kenya.

Rugo Muriu, A. (2015). Number, size and character of counties in Kenya. In N. Steytler & Y. P. Ghai (Eds.), *Kenya-South Africa dialogue of devolution* (pp. 102–117). Juta.

Steering Committee. (2020). *Report of the Steering Committee on the Implementation of the Building Bridges to a United Kenya Taskforce Report.* Government of Kenya.

Steytler, N. (2005). Republic of South Africa. In J. Kincaid & A. Tarr (Eds.), *Constitutional origins, structure, and change in federal countries* (pp. 311–346). McGill-Queen's University Press.

Steytler, N. (2014). The politics of provinces and the provincialisation of politics. In T. Maluwa (Ed.), *Law, politics and rights: Essays in memory of Kader Asmal* (pp. 191–214). Brill/Nijhoff.

Steytler, N. (2019). The dynamic relationship between devolution and constitutionalism in South Africa. In C. M. Fombad & N. Steytler (Eds.), *Decentralisation and constitutionalism in Africa* (pp. 151–182). Oxford University Press.

Steytler, N., & de Visser, J. (2015). 'Fragile Federations': The dynamics of devolution. In F. Palermo & E. Alber (Eds.), *Federalism as decision-making* (pp. 79–101). Brill/Nijhoff.

Steytler, N., & Mettler, J. (2001). Federal arrangements as a peacemaking device during South Africa's transition to democracy. *Publius: The Journal of Federalism, 31*(4), 93–106.

Wanyande, P. (2015). The implementation of Kenya's system of devolved government. In N. Steytler & Y. P. Ghai (Eds.), *Kenya-South Africa dialogue of devolution* (pp. 410–441). Juta.

CHAPTER 12

Institutional Instability and (De)federalizing Processes in Colombia

Kent Eaton

K. Eaton (✉)
University of California, Santa Cruz, CA, USA
e-mail: keaton@ucsc.edu

© The Author(s), under exclusive license to Springer Nature
Switzerland AG 2022
S. Keil, S. Kropp (eds.), *Emerging Federal Structures in the Post-Cold War Era*, Federalism and Internal Conflicts,
https://doi.org/10.1007/978-3-030-93669-3_12

Map 12.1 Columbia. *Source*: https://d-maps.com/carte.php?num_car=4095&lang=en

Colombia does not appear on the conventional list of established federations in Latin America, which identifies Argentina, Brazil, Mexico, and Venezuela as the region's only four federal systems. Instead, article 1 of the 1991 constitution explicitly labels Colombia as a "decentralized unitary republic with autonomy of its territorial units." Despite being endowed by the constitution with autonomy, these territorial units lack the "procedural safeguards protecting against excessive centralization" that Keil and Kropp emphasize as the critical difference between federal systems and systems that are merely decentralized. As a key example of the lack of such safeguards, Colombia's 1991 constitution can be amended by Congress, a Constituent Assembly, or by the people through a referendum (Article 374), but no role is envisioned for ratification mechanisms in the country's 32 departments (Nielson & Shugart, 1999, 321). Furthermore, the 1991 constitution shifted from the election of Senators in departmental districts—a form of shared rule—to their election in a single nationwide district. Thus, while we certainly see the operation of federal principles and federalizing processes in Colombia, the critical absence of meaningful protections for subnational prerogatives means that the country should not be considered a federation.[1]

Indeed, as I hope to show in this chapter, the absence of procedural safeguards for its territorial units helps explain the tremendous institutional instability that Colombia has experienced in recent decades as the result of multiple overlapping processes of territorial design and redesign. Specifically, in the 1980s and 1990s reformers at the national level embraced federal principles in the course of processes that were designed to build democracy, peace, and even the state itself. Subsequently, however, the displacement of these reformers from power led to the enactment of several de-federalizing processes over the past two decades. The pendulum has swung rapidly back toward the center. Although the existence of procedural safeguards by no means guarantees that they will be used, in their absence Colombia has oscillated dramatically between reforms that empowered and then disempowered its territorial units due to contradictory processes of institutional (re)design that enjoyed little input from the

---

[1] For a contrary view, see Wibbels' claim that the introduction of direct elections for governors in 1991 "pushes the nation from a fairly decentralized unitary system to a fairly centralized federal system" (2005, p. 91).

representatives of these units themselves. In this way, Colombia illustrates the merits of the processual approach to the study of emerging federal systems that is adopted in this volume.

The Driving Forces of Federalization in Colombia: Actors and Interests

Contemporary struggles over federal principles in Colombia have unfolded against a particular historical backdrop of intense earlier conflicts over the design of federal institutions. In the nineteenth century, Colombia was the site of one of Latin America's boldest experiments with federalism ever. In 1860 a successful rebellion by governors belonging to the Liberal party against the Conservative-dominated national government led not just to the promulgation of a new federal constitution in 1863 but to a new name for the country: the United States of Colombia (Mazzuca and Robinson 2009). In addition to cutting the president's term from four to two years and introducing the popular election of governors, the 1863 Constitution enabled states to write their own laws, maintain their own judicial systems, and even create their own armies (Morelli, 1997, 116). What followed was two decades of conflict between the Liberal defenders of this federal constitution and Conservative critics, who also opposed its anti-clerical and pro-free trade orientations. The memory of the turbulence of this federal period likely helps explain the depth of opposition to formal federalization thereafter, including in the late twentieth century when reformers were otherwise willing to debate and adopt quite radical institutional changes to boost subnational authority and resources.

In a more immediate sense, Colombia's volatile nineteenth-century experience with federalism generated a highly centralizing backlash in the form of the 1886 Constitution, which governed the country for nearly a century until its replacement in 1991 (remarkable in a region where constitutions have tended not to be so long lived). The 1886 Constitution converted sovereign states into mere departments, which lost their ability to act independently of the national government. The President appointed all governors, typically as the result of intra- and inter-party negotiations, and governors in turn appointed all the mayors in their departments. Although voters did elect municipal councils and departmental assemblies across this long century, both bodies were informally controlled by appointed mayors and governors who owed their position to political patrons at higher levels. Mirroring the centralism of the political order, the fiscal system was dominated by the use of congressional assistance funds (*auxilios parlamentarios*) through which subnational units depended on the intervention of individual members of congress to pull down resources from Bogotá, which were then exchanged for votes in pervasive clientelistic networks (Archer & Shugart, 1997). Despite the slogan attached to the 1886 Constitution of "political centralization with administrative decentralization," in reality capacity deficits in departments and cities reinforced the power of the center, especially with the onset of developmentalist models in the mid twentieth century that expanded the size of the national government (Restrepo, 2015).

Although for most of the twentieth century the centralizing logic of Colombian institutions appeared virtually unassailable, the confluence of three powerful processes drove the country rapidly toward federalization in the last two decades of that century. These processes, which were interwoven in practice and largely reinforcing, were also analytically distinct and can be conceptualized as state-building, democracy-building, and peace-building. In sociological terms, these three processes were shaped by stakeholder groups that frequently overlapped but also diverged, and the processes themselves unfolded in a number of institutional venues, including the national legislature, peace negotiations and dialogues, and most importantly the 1991 Constitutional Assembly. Rarely was federalism the explicit goal of any of these actors; instead, those who sought to build the state, or democracy, or peace, opted to employ federal principles as a means to these ends rather than out of any normative commitment to federalism itself (which among other obstacles would have had to overcome the negative association with the anarchic quality of Colombia's nineteenth-century experiment with federalism).

State-building was the first process to crystallize in the form of civic strikes (*paros cívicos*) that sought to draw attention to the poor quality of government-provided goods and services. Between 1970 and 1986, Colombia experienced over 200 of these strikes, which were "organized by local citizens' groups protesting poor service provision and the concentration of government expenditure in the largest cities" (Nickson, 1995, 146). According to Falleti, poor quality and unevenness in service delivery by parastatal institutions that were "attached to central agencies and ministries" generated a widespread demand for the direct election of mayors rather than their appointment by higher-level patrons, a system that had created high turnover, pervasive corruption, and so-called "'professional mayors' who would travel around all the municipalities of one department until they were discredited in all of them" (2010, 131, 132). Frustrated by the informal but widespread practice of clientelism, according to which legislators brokered goods and services only to their voters rather than to the citizenry at large, these civic strikers sought to build the state by embracing a core federal principle: meaningful policymaking authority for autonomous substate units.

Federal principles also animated those whose chief objective was to deepen democracy rather than to build state capacity. Although Colombia's political regime had been democratic since 1958, when the country experienced a pacted transition to democracy that put an end to its only period of military rule in the twentieth century (1953–1958), the National Front institutions adopted in that pact generated a corrosive effect on democracy (Bejarano & Pizarro, 2005). Ascribing to the view that inter-party violence had created the opening for direct military rule, the leaders of the Conservative and Liberal parties agreed to a power-sharing arrangement that would end the violence by lowering the stakes of inter-party competition and by offering each party institutional guarantees. These National Front institutions included a period of 16 years (1958–1974) in which the two parties would rotate in and out of the presidency, hold equal numbers of seats in the two legislative chambers, enjoy parity vis-à-vis bureaucratic spoils, and appoint similar numbers of subnational officials (Hartlyn, 1988). But when the country's two traditional parties continued to monopolize political life even after the formal end of the National Front in 1974, a whole host of actors locked out of the two-party system, including labor unions, church groups, and university students, mobilized to demand democratizing changes (and a new Constitution) that would open up the political system to new entrants. One of their chief demands was to resurrect the direct election of governors from the 1863 federal constitution and to go even further by introducing elections for mayors as well.

Useful as a means to build democracy and the state, federal principles were also taken up in the peace process by both sides in the country's long-standing internal armed conflict. By the mid-1980s, when the first decentralizing reforms were introduced, the Colombian state had already been at war for two decades with a range of guerrilla organizations, including the Cuban-inspired *Ejército de Liberación Nacional* (ELN), the Soviet-oriented *Fuerzas Armadas Revolucionarias de Colombia* (FARC), and the urban-focused *Movimiento 19 de Abril* (M-19). Insurgent groups demanded political decentralization and the direct election of mayors as a way to come to power "through the ballot box," either in lieu of armed struggle (as in the case of the M-19) or in combination with armed struggle (as in the case of the FARC). On the government side, the inability of the armed forces to defeat the insurgencies militarily encouraged a bipartisan coalition of politicians from both parties to endorse a number of reforms that would devolve authority and resources (Eaton 2006). Especially critical was the "pacification through decentralization" strategy most closely associated with Jaime Castro, a Liberal politician who served as the Minister of Government in the Conservative administration of President Belisario Betancur in the mid-1980s (Castro, 1998). The idea of ceding control over territory to build peace was also taken up by a subsequent Conservative President, Andrés Pastrana (1998–2002), who demilitarized four large municipalities to serve as the site of (unsuccessful) peace negotiations with the FARC (in the so-called *despeje*).

Thanks to the convergence of these three processes (state-building, democracy-building, and peace-building), Colombia at the turn of the twenty-first century still fell short of federalism, but nevertheless had significantly elevated the governing authority of its "autonomous territorial units." Just as important is the sequence of the decentralizing changes adopted. According to Tulia Falleti (2010), Colombia closely conforms to the sequence (political, then fiscal, then administrative decentralization) that is most likely to strengthen subsequent demands by subnational actors for additional prerogatives. Beginning with political decentralization as a reform associated with all three of the processes described above, Colombia introduced the direct election of mayors in 1986 and governors in 1991. Second, the direct election of mayors and governors enhanced the legitimacy of their demands for fiscal decentralization, which took the form of a generous new system of automatic revenue sharing with both departments (in the *situado fiscal*) and municipalities (via *participaciones*). Finalizing the sequence, administrative measures were then adopted that transferred responsibility for education and health care, both in the new Constitution and through landmark legislation passed in 1994 (Law, 60). A little over 100 years after the end of its last experience with federalism in 1886, Colombia in the 1990s appeared to have traveled far down the road back to federation.

Recentralizing Processes and the Current Stage of (De)federalization

Despite the reality that federal principles were enlisted in a number of transformative processes and embraced by a disparate set of important actors (ranging from traditional politicians to guerilla organizations), Colombia in the past two decades, nevertheless, has experienced a variety of recentralizing processes that directly challenged and displaced these principles. Colombia's reform window, forced open by a coalition of actors who were temporarily empowered by the politics surrounding the 1991 Constitutional Assembly, began to close just a few short years later. Decentralizing reforms that had strengthened Colombia's territorial units, and that appeared perhaps irreversible given the degree to which they dovetailed with the global zeitgeist at the turn of the century, actually proved to be quite reversible. Lacking the procedural safeguards characteristic of formal federalism, elected authorities in departments and municipalities were powerless to protect the reforms that had so recently brought them into being. As described in the paragraphs below, and similar to the federalizing dynamic of the 1980s and 1990s, the processes that led to de-federalization also came in a number of distinct forms, each with its own set of protagonists.

The first recentralizing process to emerge was set in motion by the country's powerful economic technocracy as early as 1994 (i.e. the very year that administrative reforms completed Colombia's sequence of decentralization). Located in three key institutions (the Ministry of Finance, the National Planning Department, and the Central Bank), Colombia's technocrats and their highly insulated approach to macroeconomic policymaking are credited with saving the country from the ravages of Latin American hyperinflation. As Dargent argues, many technocrats began their careers in the private sector think tank FEDESARROLLO, whose focus in the 1990s "turned to the new institutions adopted in the 1991 Constitution and their problematic effects on long-term economic stability" (2014, 258). Their first move in 1994 was to impose new restrictions on the rule changes that had made it easier for subnational governments to borrow from the private sector. Later in the 1990s, as Colombia experienced its greatest macroeconomic distress since the Great Depression of the 1930s, technocrats were able to use the economic crisis to delegitimize the fiscal decentralization that had just taken place. Thanks to reforms that were initially framed as temporary in 1998 but then became permanent in

2001, Colombia shifted from a system of percentage-based revenue sharing to a set of fixed-sum transfers that had the effect of cutting subnational revenues as a share of total revenues from 46.5% to 37.2% by 2005 (Dickovick & Eaton, 2013). Blamed for the economic crisis, subnational governments had no institutional mechanisms to limit, postpone, or even question fiscal recentralization—unlike in a truly federal system.

Just as technocrats were making the case that decentralization would undermine rather than promote Colombia's long-term development prospects, another key figure emerged to successfully oppose federal principles: President Alvaro Uribe. Despite having served as a governor prior to his rise to the presidency, Uribe's two terms in office (2002–2010) were disastrous for those seeking federal solutions to Colombia's problems. In contrast to those civic strikers in the 1970s who envisioned decentralization as a way to build the state's administrative capacity, Uribe's approach to state-building emphasized instead (and nearly exclusively) the urgency of strengthening the coercive capacity of the armed forces. When Uribe's strategy of militarization succeeded in beating back the guerrillas and restoring the territorial reach of the state (in the form of military and police outposts), his popularity soared to such an extent that he was able to change the constitution to run for and win a second term as president. In a country that long bucked the populist dynamics so salient elsewhere in the region (Bejarano, 2013), Uribe personalized power and undermined institutions in ways that were anathema to the logics of federalism. This can be seen most clearly in the case of the "mobile cabinets" (*gabinetes mobiles*) that Uribe used as an informal territorial device to govern the country. Every weekend during his long presidency, Uribe would travel to local governments in the company of select national ministers to directly receive, debate, and act on local requests for nationally mediated support. Ostensibly occasions where local actors could give national officials feedback and input vis-à-vis national policies and programs, the mobile cabinets in reality represented the encroachment of national officials into decisions that had been formally decentralized by the 1991 Constitution and associated legislation.

If Uribe in the executive branch and technocrats in the bureaucracy viewed federal principles as threats to state capacity and economic development (respectively), de-federalizing dynamics were also unleashed by the peace process set in motion by Uribe's successor as president, Juan Manuel Santos (2010–2018). What's striking here is that, while both sides in the internal armed conflict saw the strengthening of the country's territorial units as a possible solution in the 1980s and 1990s, neither side defended or promoted decentralization in the peace negotiations that began in Havana in 2012 and that culminated in the historic 2016 peace agreement. The very reforms once seen as holding the key to peace were now dismissed as either unnecessary or actually unproductive from the standpoint of building peace.

Among the government team that negotiated the Havana Accord, decentralization suffered from a bad reputation, largely because of the view that decentralizing reforms in the 1980s and 1990s had enabled the FARC to bolster its legitimacy as a governing actor in the municipalities that it came to control after the introduction of direct elections (Gutiérrez Sanín, 2010; Duncan, 2015). Others came to believe that, although decentralization was adopted in the hopes that it would sever clientelistic exchanges between national legislators and captive voters, it merely enabled mayors to build their own clientelistic networks (Eaton & Chambers-Ju, 2014). Military representatives on the government team had their own reasons for skepticism about subnational governments, fearing that the FARC would continue to try to challenge the state from their subnational bases of support. But the FARC on the other side of the negotiating table was no more keen on strengthening existing subnational governments, in part because they wanted to replace them with an alternative institutional modality (the so-called *Zonas de Reserva Campesina* or Peasant Reserve Zones). Just as importantly, having given up armed struggle as a means to achieve their transformative goals, FARC leaders came to believe that the non-violent pursuit of these same goals as a political party would require a national stage rather than control over diffuse subnational governments.

At a time when institutional engineering in virtually all post-conflict settings around the world now emphasizes federalizing or decentralizing designs, the 2016 Havana Accord deviates from this pattern by denying subnational governments meaningful roles in post-conflict reconstruction.[2] This design choice is most clearly at play in the first chapter of the Accord focusing on rural reform, through which negotiators sought to reduce rural inequality and reverse the concentration of land ownership

---

[2] For a copy of the final 2016 Accord see *Acuerdo Final para la Terminación del Conflicto y la Construcción de una Paz Estable y Duradera* at http://www.altocomisionadoparalapaz. gov.co/procesos-y-conversaciones/Documentos%20compartidos/24-11-2016NuevoAcuerdoFinal.pdf.

that had ignited the guerrilla insurgency in the 1960s—and worsened still further over the course of the war due to extensive land grabs by paramilitary forces (Duncan, 2015). In order to forestall FARC demands for the expropriation of large, unproductive landowners, government negotiators agreed to centralize control over land registries (*cadastros*) to ensure that landowners would have to pay taxes on the market value of their land. In addition to losing this important policy authority, subnational governments were also relegated to mere implementing roles in the Territorially-Focused Development Programs (*Programas de Desarrollo Territorial* or PDETs) that have been created by the Havana Accord in those zones most affected by the war. These nationally funded PDETs are designed to coordinate the national government's various sectoral interventions in 170 municipalities heavily impacted by the conflict, which are grouped into 16 Zones Most Affected by the Conflict (ZOMAC). Although the Accord stipulates that in no case will this infringe on the prerogatives of local authorities, most municipalities have opted to formally replace their own local development plans with the PDETs, representing a considerable loss of local autonomy.[3]

Rather than emphasize actions by separately elected subnational governments (e.g. decentralization), which had no formal seat at the table in the negotiations in Havana, the 2016 peace agreement instead emphasized the protagonism of a powerful and authoritative national government whose sectoral ministries would ramp up their presence in, control over, and direct financing of those subnational regions most affected by the conflict (e.g. deconcentration). In this way, Colombia's most recent peace-building process reflects the same centralizing logics and the same deep skepticism about federal principles that animated both the technocratic rollback of fiscal decentralization and the personalistic process of state-building directed by President Uribe.

Federal Institutions in Practice: Overawing Colombia's Territorial Units

Having analyzed the macro-level processes that propelled Colombia toward federal solutions in the 1980s and 1990s and then away from them in the years since 2000, this section zeroes in on some of the key

[3] Roundtable on the PDETs sponsored by the Woodrow Wilson Center, "Peace in Colombia: Challenges and Opportunities in the Post-Accord Era," October 7, 2019.

institutions that structure the relationship between national and subnational governments. Across this institutional landscape—which includes the Senate as well as a host of new participatory and planning institutions—we see evidence to support the claim that, as the editors write in the introduction, "habits and practices often do not keep up with institutional change." Even as formal institutions experienced significant change, Colombia witnessed considerable continuity with respect to the underlying tendency of the central government to overawe the country's territorial units, which continue to play the kinds of subservient roles that are incompatible with the federal ideal.

Consider, for example, the case of the Colombian Senate, an upper legislative chamber whose composition was targeted for reform by the same coalition that sought to use the 1991 Constitutional Assembly to fully democratize the country. According to the prior (1886) Constitution, Colombia's departments served as electoral districts for the election of Senators, with each department sending the same number of representatives (3) to the Senate. As Colombia urbanized over the course of the twentieth century, the Senate came to act as an important break vis-a-vis the kinds of progressive policy changes that presidents increasingly articulated in their attempts to appeal to the (urban) median voter (Nielson & Shugart, 1999)—unless they were accompanied by sufficient enticements from the pork barrel. Informal but deeply entrenched practices of patronage and clientelism served as the grease that lubricated Colombia's political system (Léal & Dávila, 2010). Since governors were not elected, senators played the dominant role as regional brokers who exchanged the political support of their clients for resources and privileges from the center, including the informal right to name those individual supporters who would be appointed as governors and mayors. Although ostensibly meant to represent their departments at the center, all senators had to do to perpetuate themselves in power was to maintain and nurture their highly personalistic networks of support.

Critical of these clientelistic practices in the Senate, and having themselves been elected in a single nationwide district, members of the 1991 Constitutional Assembly decided to increase its size to 100 senators but to end their election in departmental districts in favor of a single nationwide district. Senators, henceforth, would have a national rather than regional constituency in what might be considered an important setback with respect to federalism. However, while assembly members conceptualized this reform as an institutional change that would encourage candidates to develop and campaign on programmatic agendas that might appeal to diffuse sets of voters located in different departments, the reality is that most senators still win and retain their offices due to highly concentrated bases of support in a single department. According to Floréz (2008), in the first four elections held under the new rules, a great majority of winning candidates still concentrated their votes in a single department. Although the new system did enable a few non-traditional parties to win Senate seats, including demobilized guerrilla leaders on the left and church-affiliated parties on the right, many traditional politicians continued to be able to leverage Senate seats out of their roles as regional brokers. In the end, the bold attempt to limit the informal clientelistic networks that permeate the Senate failed to actually reduce clientelism—a practice that clearly undercuts rather than reinforces the autonomous authority of substate units to set their own policy course.

In addition to their attempt to reengineer the Senate, reformers in the 1991 Constitutional Assembly designed a new set of participatory institutions toward the same goal of undermining traditional politicians and the clientelistic networks that sustain their continued influence. In other words, while reformers saw decentralization as one of the best ways to consolidate democracy, as argued above, they also feared that decentralization alone might merely empower traditional politicians at the local level in the absence of additional changes that would extend and deepen political participation. In this sense, Colombia was no exception to the widespread experimentation that took place beginning in the 1990s across Latin American countries, most of which saw the introduction of a whole layer of participatory institutions that were designed to deepen if not challenge liberal representative models of democracy (Wampler, 2007; Goldfrank, 2011). Colombia's new constitution, for example, featured a new National Planning Council (NPC), which includes reserved seats for departmental and municipal governments in addition to civil society actors. Because the stated purpose of the NPC is to influence planning by the national government across the national territory, it could technically be considered a federalizing innovation. However, as Lindsay Mayka argues, planning councils in Colombia "are characterized by a weak institutional design, with only a consultative role in policymaking, considerable ambiguity about how they are to contribute to the planning process, and no clear enforcement mechanism" (2019, 185). In the three decades since its creation, the NPC has not functioned as a mechanism of influence for Colombia's territorial units.

A further institutional example of the continued ability of the national government to dominate what are formally inter-governmental mechanisms and to thereby "overawe" territorial units can be seen in the governance of Colombia's natural resources. In concert with the decentralizing spirit of the times, Colombia's 1991 Constitution incorporated rules that shared 80% of the royalties from natural resource extraction with "producer regions" (namely, the four departments of Arauca, Casanare, Guajira, and Meta). Thanks to a spike in prices from the global commodity supercycle, these royalties increased to nearly 2% of Colombian GDP by 2011, which is the same year the national government imposed a new General Royalty System (*Sistema General de Regalías* or SGR) that significantly gutted subnational autonomy. According to the new SGR, 50% of royalties are now kept at the national level to finance sectoral programs, while the remaining half are technically transferred to producer regions but subject to the control of new "administrative and decision-making collective organs" (*Organos Colegiados de Administración y Decisión* or OCADs). Although these OCADs include one representative each from municipal, departmental, and national governments (hence their official designation as "triangles of good government"), the reality is that the OCADs can only use royalties to finance projects that have already been successfully enrolled in a project database maintained by the powerful National Planning Department (Benítez, 2013).

While this survey paints a bleak picture of the institutional landscape facing subnational governments in Colombia, one partial exception to this pattern can be found in the new Constitutional Court (*Corte Constitucional* or CC) that the 1991 Constitution created to institutionalize the practice of judicial review. If contemporary Colombian politics can be described in part as a battle between progressive forces who have sought to defend the spirit of the 1991 Constitution against conservative forces who have resisted its innovations, the CC has emerged a hero for the former thanks to the role it has played in upholding the rights of labor unions, the LGBT population, and individuals displaced by the armed conflict (Rodríguez-Gavarito & Rodríguez Franco, 2015). As the national government under presidents Uribe and Santos have often questioned the prerogatives of subnational governments, the CC has frequently ruled in their favor. For instance, in 2013 the CC suspended an article in the new royalty system described above that would have let national ministers veto subnational projects (though these projects still must be approved in advance by the National Planning Department). More importantly, in 2016 the CC declared unconstitutional an article of the 2001 mining code that had stipulated that no subnational authority could establish zones in which extraction would be prohibited on a permanent or temporary basis, an important victory for territorial units (Bocanegra & Carvajal, 2019, 152).[4] The CC has begun to emerge as a potentially critical institutional ally for subnational governments, which they sorely need in the absence of a Senate that can defend territorial prerogatives, and in the presence of the powerful juggernaut formed by Colombia's economic technocracy (e.g. Finance Ministry, Central Bank, National Planning Department).

Prospects of Federalization: Institutional Instability and Ideological Contestation

The processual approach to the study of federal systems that is advocated in this volume and applied in this chapter brings into sharp relief the extent and severity of the contestation that surrounds federal principles in Colombia. The state-building process, for example, unleashed stark conflict between actors (i.e. the civic strikers) who advocated for decentralization as a way to build state capacity "from below" versus those who insisted on the need to build the state from the center out (i.e. Presidents Uribe and Santos). Likewise, whereas proponents of decentralization saw it as a mechanism to unleash economic development in Colombia's disparate regions, critics in the economic technocracy claimed it had directly imperiled the country's development prospects. Democratizers gathered together in the 1991 Constituent Assembly thought political decentralization would deepen democratization, while others claimed it would simply enable new forms of subnational authoritarianism (Eaton & Prieto, 2017). For peace negotiators in the 1980s and 1990s, the strengthening of territorial units seemed to hold the key for post-conflict reconstruction, but these same units were intentionally marginalized in the more recent round of negotiations that generated the historic 2016 Havana Accord.

This profound contestation over the desirability of federal principles, along with the institutional instability produced by this contestation, makes it difficult to assess the prospects of federalization in Colombia. On the one hand, two decades into the twenty-first century, there are few

[4] More recently, however, the Court also ruled that subnational governments must coordinate their actions with the national government. See "Claves del fallo sobre consultas para frenar actividades extractivas," *El Tiempo*, October 12, 2018.

signs of the resurgence of the type of pro-federalizing forces that held sway in the 1980s and 1990s. If subnational governments then were largely the passive beneficiaries of shifts in the balance of power that took place at the national level, that balance of power now favors institutions that are either hostile or indifferent to subnational prerogatives (e.g. the economic technocracy, the Senate) rather than institutions that are more sympathetic (like the Constitutional Court). On the other hand, what the last four decades would seem to predict is further volatility and perhaps shorter cycles of institutional change as the pendulum swings even more rapidly between national and subnational governments. Without the kinds of "procedural safeguards" that are the defining feature of a federal state, territorial units can do little to limit the destabilizing effects of these top-down institutional changes, either when they are suddenly and unrealistically seen as the answer to all of the country's ills (including the lack of development, democracy, and peace) or instead vilified as obstacles to the pursuit of security, state capacity, and economic growth.

Finally, while the Colombian case offers further support for the importance of the "procedural safeguards" that distinguish formally unitary from federal cases—a central touchstone in the literature on federalism—it also suggests that this literature would benefit from more sustained attention to ideology, partisanship, and ideational dynamics more generally. The Colombian case can be hard to easily classify vis-a-vis comparative research on federalism, and not just because it is not formally federal. While Colombia is an ethnically diverse society, it cannot be considered a "federal society" in the sense that its ethnic divisions do not overlap neatly with territorial identities, nor is its internal armed conflict an ethnic conflict but rather an ideological one. Thus, Colombia sits uneasily within the literature on peace-preserving federalism, which normally assumes that the conflict federalism is meant to ameliorate has been an ethnic one. Colombia reminds us that, yes, federal solutions deserve serious consideration in post-conflict cases but that, no, not all internal conflicts are ethnic in their structure.

Furthermore, ideology matters in the Colombian case in an additional sense, which is the reality that the parties in power at different levels of government (national and subnational) have increasingly come to occupy very different positions on the ideological spectrum. In a country where the left has never been able to make inroads at the national level, or won the presidency, recent decades have seen the election of progressive and left-leaning mayors and governors. The kinds of territorial conflicts over subnational prerogatives that are emphasized in this chapter have inevitably become entangled with ideological conflicts over the role of the Colombian state in the economy. How ideological struggles over economic liberalization interact with territorial struggles over federalization will likely become an increasingly salient question in other countries as well, especially wherever the experimentation with federal models takes place in the context of democratic regimes and/or competitive elections.

References

Archer, R., & Shugart, M. (1997). The unrealized potential of presidential dominance in Colombia. In R. Archer & M. Shugart (Eds.), *Presidentialism and democracy in Latin America* (pp. 110–159). Cambridge University Press.

Bejarano, A. (2013). Politicizing insecurity: Uribe's instrumental use of populism. In C. de la Torre & C. Arnson (Eds.), *Latin American populism in the twenty-first century*. Johns Hopkins University Press.

Bejarano, A., & Pizarro, E. (2005). From restricted to besieged: The changing nature of the limits to democracy in Colombia. In F. Hagopian & S. Mainwaring (Eds.), *The third wave of democratization in Latin America* (pp. 235–260). Cambridge University Press.

Benítez Ibagué, N. (2013). Caracterización del nuevo sistema general de regalías y su efecto fiscal. *Finanzas y Política Económica, 5*(1), 151–178.

Bocanegra, H., & Carvajal, J. (2019). Extractivismo, derecho, y conflicto social en Colombia. *Revista Republicana, 26*, 143–169.

Castro, J. (1998). *Descentralizar para pacificar*. Editorial Ariel.

Dargent, E. (2014). *Technocracy and democracy in Latin America: The experts running government*. Cambridge University Press.

Duncan, G. (2015). *Los señores de la guerra: de paramilitares, mafiosos y autodefensas en Colombia*. Penguin Random House.

Eaton, K. (2006). The downside of decentralization: Armed clientelism in Colombia. *Security Studies, 15*(40), 533–562.

Eaton, K., & Chambers-Ju, C. (2014). Teachers, mayors, and the transformation of clientelism in Colombia. In C. Chambers-Ju, D. Abente Brun, & L. Diamond (Eds.), *Clientelism, social policy and the quality of democracy*. Johns Hopkins University Press.

Dickovick, T. & Eaton, K. (2013). Latin America's resurgent center: National government strategies after decentralization. *Journal of Development Studies, 49*(11), 1453–1466.

Eaton, K., & Diego Prieto, J. (2017). Subnational authoritarianism in Colombia: Divergent paths in Cesar and Magdalena. In T. Hilgers & L. Macdonald (Eds.),

Violence in Latin America and the Caribbean: Subnational structures institutions, and clientelistic networks. Cambridge University Press.

Falleti, T. (2010). *Decentralization and subnational politics in Latin America.* Cambridge University Press.

Floréz Henao, J. A. (2008). 16 años de la circunscripción nacional para Senado en Colombia: dónde está el espacio de representación nacional? *Desafíos, 18,* 243–285.

Goldfrank, B. (2011). *Deepening local democracy in Latin America: Participation, decentralization, and the left.* Penn State University Press.

Gutiérrez Sanín, F. (2010). "Instituciones y territorio: La descentralización en Colombia," in 25 años de la descentralización en Colombia. Konrad Adenauer Stiftung.

Hartlyn, J. (1988). The Politics of Coalition Rule in Colombia. Cambridge University Press.

Léal Buitrago, F., & Dávila, A. (2010). *Clientelismo: el sistema político y su expresión regional.* Universidad de los Andes.

Mayka, L. (2019). *Building participatory institutions in Latin America: Reform coalitions and institutional change.* Cambridge University Press.

Mazzuca, S., & Robinson, J. (2009). Political conflict and power sharing in the origins of modern Colombia. *Hispanic American Historical Review, 89*(2), 285–321.

Morelli, S. (1997). La égida del centralismo en Colombia: dos ejemplos históricos. In Departmento de Publicaciones de la UEC (Ed.), *El federalismo en Colombia: pasado y perspectivas.* Universidad Externado de Colombia.

Nickson, R. A. (1995). *Local government in Latin America.* Lynne Rienner.

Nielson, D., & Shugart, M. (1999). Constitutional change in Colombia: Policy adjustment through institutional reform. *Comparative Political Studies, 32*(3), 313–341.

Restrepo, D. (2015). *Procesos de descentralización en Bolivia y Colombia.* Universidad Nacional de Colombia.

Rodríguez-Gavarito, C., & Rodríguez Franco, D. (2015). *Radical deprivation on trial: The impact of judicial activism on socioeconomic rights in the global South.* Cambridge University Press.

Wampler, B. (2007). *Participatory budgeting in Brazil.* Penn State University Press.

Wibbels, E. (2005). *Federalism and the market.* Cambridge University Press.

CHAPTER 13

Federalism in the European Union

Eva G. Heidbreder

E. G. Heidbreder (✉)
Otto von Guericke University Magdeburg, Magdeburg, Germany
e-mail: eva.heidbreder@ovgu.de

© The Author(s), under exclusive license to Springer Nature
Switzerland AG 2022
S. Keil, S. Kropp (eds.), *Emerging Federal Structures in the
Post-Cold War Era*, Federalism and Internal Conflicts,
https://doi.org/10.1007/978-3-030-93669-3_13

Map 13.1 The EU. *Source*: https://d-maps.com/carte.php?num_car=260684&lang=en

Introduction: The EU as a Federal System

Whether we see a European federation emerging and whether the European Union (EU) ought to become a federation has inspired political thinkers and actors throughout the twentieth century. Since the 1990s, the conceptualization of the EU as a multilevel governance system has gained predominance as an alternative to state-based definitions, causing increased attention on the EU as a case of non-state federal polity. The predominant questions of federalist EU research at the end of the first decades of the twenty-first century are therefore: to what extent does the EU qualify as a federal system, how do federal ideas shape the EU and what can we gain analytically from conceptualizing the EU as federal polity? By raising these questions, this contribution investigates how federalism informs our understanding of the EU and, inversely, how studying the EU promotes federalism in theory and practice. To capture both the evolution of the EU as a federal system and the implications for our understanding of the EU and federalism, I distinguish between two notions of federalism: a normative-teleological version and an empirical-analytical one. This analytical distinction relates to the often-cited juxtaposition of "federalism as ideology or philosophy and […] federation as institutional fact" (King, 1982, 146). However, while for King the normative values and principles represented *federal ideas* and *empirics* turned around the tangible organizations of *federations*, the relation between ideas toward federalization and actual federal organization get twisted when applied to the EU. In the following the normative-teleological perspective suggests a dynamic understanding of the EU as a federation in the making to explain or promote a European state-building process, while the empirical-analytical view distills defining dimensions of federal systems to explain the functioning logics of the EU as a specific case of a federal system which may serve as a model for a new, genuine type of federal governance. Following this theoretical distinction, section two outlines how personalities that shaped EU integration related to—and continue to follow or reject—a federalist agenda. Section three elaborates inside from empirical-analytical research. Drawing in particular from comparative federalism, this perspective allows us to bring crucial polity features and functioning logics of the EU to the fore. At the same time, differences between the EU and other federal entities enlighten our understanding of dysfunctionalities of non-state federal orders. As the conclusions pinpoint, normative questions are essential for both perspectives applied. However, while the normative-teleological view puts into question whether legitimate rule can occur in absence of a constituent act and a federalist finalité for the EU, the empirical-analytical view calls for a dynamic and constant balancing act between questions of shared rule and self-rule and therefore considers the EU as a role model for federal polity-building beyond the state.

The EU as a Federation-to-be: Integration as a Normative-Teleological Project

Before delving into the details of the two federal perspectives on the EU, the state-of-the-art in defining the EU as a federal system must be laid out. Most fundamentally, there is widespread agreement that the EU is not a federal state (for many Burgess, 2000, 2006; Elazar, 2001). There is less agreement whether this implies that the EU is a federation in the making or a genuine, new type of federal system (Elazar, 1996; Tömmel, 2011). A plethora of studies focuses on a wide range of federal features of the EU and offers a rich base to conceptualize federal aspects of the EU. Yet, this literature does not provide a clear-cut definition of the EU as a federal system. As the first access point, this section reviews the federalist ideas held by key figures in the actual EU integration process because these specific visions have a sustained impact on EU polity development and the theory development around it. Scrutinizing the driving forces of EU integration reveals a persistent contestation over what the EU ought to be. On the one hand, federalists claim that the EU needs to become a federation to legitimately perform its key functions. On the other hand, functionalists especially see the federal innovation of the EU in its multifaceted functional differentiation that defects from the concept of state-based rule. In addition to these two competing views, federal thinking continues to influence a third normative position. Proponents who aim to preserve or even "re-erect" the independent nation-state build their arguments in opposition to the ostensibly teleological imperative that drives the EU to become a proper federation. Arguably, opposition to alleged EU federalization has recently been most pertinent for the course of EU integration because it was a core motivation for the British exit from the EU and the rise of EU-skeptic and anti-EU organized opposition throughout the continent. The following reviews the three perspectives.

Actors and Their Models: Constituent and Functional Federalism

The first two perspectives, the normative and functional federal visions, have been formative from the inception of European integration until today because the underpinning federalist ideas continue to influence political elites. It is worthwhile to single out two key figures' understandings, objectives and strategies to contextualize the actual integration dynamics federalism has triggered: Altiero Spinelli and Jean Monnet. Both held a teleological-normative concept of European integration. At the same time, they disagreed vitally in their appreciation of constitutional-legitimizing versus output-producing values, therefore exposing a "fundamental strategic difference founded upon competing conceptions of a federal Europe" (Burgess, 2009, 32). Spinelli's understanding rested on three key assumptions (Glencross, 2010, 118). First, he contested the notion "that time was not ripe for implementing a federal blueprint". Second, he showed that following the non-federalist dominant path "produced various democratic shortcomings". And, third, "he was highly skeptical that the performance per se of supranational government could establish the legitimacy of a new polity" (Glencross, 2010, 118). This "radical strategy meant starting with the political institutions and a popularly endorsed treaty that would be quickly translated into the familiar statist language of a constitution" (Burgess, 2009, 32). In contrast to Spinelli's conviction that a federal constitutional moment authorized by the European citizens ought to be the first indispensable step, Monnet favored an incremental functional approach and was convinced that "the political strategy of small, concrete, economic steps would culminate in a federal Europe" (Burgess, 2009, 32).

Continuous Implications of Federal Ideas

The difference between Spinelli's and Monnet's positions is not of mere historical relevance. It continues to shape political objectives and strategies that oppose a functional path that promotes output legitimacy. At the heart of this opposition lies the argument that a constitutional moment is highly overdue and vital to overcome the EU's lack of input legitimacy (Scharpf, 1999). This question raised vivid debates in the context of the drafting of the *Treaty establishing a Constitution for Europe* (2002–2003) and its failed ratification due to negative public votes in France and the Netherlands (2005). Moving back from Spinelli's and the Convention's to Monnet's approach, the eventual passing of the Treaty of Lisbon scrapped all references that could evoke the notion of a constitutional moment in favor of a purely output-oriented EU image.[1]

---

[1] The shift from the constitutional-moment claim to the only slightly modified *Treaty of Lisbon* is clearly spelled out in the Council mandate for revising the original draft: "the term 'Constitution' will not be used [. ...] Likewise, there will be no article in the amended

To capture the continued relevance of the historical visions, it is paramount to want to elucidate their conceptual distinctiveness. Spinelli's radical-constitutional federalism endures to motivate federalists who argue for the building of a state-like EU federation, as seen in the civil society movement *Union of European Federalists*. More subtly, Spinelli's conception is inherent in a great number of claims about rendering the EU more democratic. At the center of the unsettled arguments lies the question about how the EU governance system can be legitimized and what kind of political community the EU is and should offer to its citizens. Does the EU create sufficient legitimacy through rights guaranteed in its quasi-constitutional treaties? Do the treaties lend themselves sufficiently to a new form of constitutional patriotism? And does the EU even offer a chance to replace the nation-state with a new form of cosmopolitan community (Habermas, 1995, 2012)? Or can such a legitimacy only be created in a constitutional moment which the EU cannot achieve due to its lack of proper demos (Grimm, 1995; Fabbrini, 2005)? Has the EU already "charted its own brand of constitutional federalism" (Weiler, 2001, 70) based on the Principle of Tolerance and voluntary obedience in applied constitutional pluralism (MacCormick, 1993)? Is a constituting demos necessary, or can a democracy defined as "Union of peoples who govern together but not as one" (Nicolaïdis, 2013, 351) resolve the conundrum of constitutional representation in the EU (Bellamy & Castiglione, 2013; Nicolaïdis, 2013; Lacey, 2016)? It is these ongoing debates about a federalization of the EU that reflect the EU-specific take on the central questions asked in this volume. With the EU conceived as a federation-in-the-making, these questions remain contested.

In contrast to Spinelli's radical-constitutional federalism, Monnet's functional-incremental vision appears to be a rather sober description of the EU's historical trajectory. It echoes not only in the course of stepwise treaty reforms but also in some of the major reforms of the past decade, particularly in response to the banking and sovereign debt crisis that led to the creation of the EU's Banking Union without substantive treaty changes (Howarth & Quaglia, 2014; Epstein & Rhodes, 2016; but seen as important qualification Schimmelfennig, 2016). Practically, evading the ultimate federal question creates the leeway for issue-specific agreements among the member states. A telling example is offered by the debate

Treaties mentioning the symbols of the EU such as the flag, the anthem or the motto" (Council of the European Union, 2007, *Annex: ICC Mandate*).

Commission President Jean-Claude Juncker attempted to start in 2017 by issuing his *White Paper on the Future of Europe* (European Commission, 2017). It offered no actual proposals but five ideal-type models, all referring to functionalist options for more or less EU. Unlike the German Foreign Minister Joschka Fischer, whose proactive federalist intervention was vital in starting the constitutional debate of the early 2000s (2000), both of Juncker's proposals and the response by French President Emmanuel Macron (Macron, 2017), arguing for more EU for a core group of states, did not set off a serious debate. Staying within elite circles, the long silence by Chancellor Angela Merkel let this debate trail off before it had started. It remains an open question if the subsequent installment of a new *Conference on the Future of Europe* in late 2019 will develop ideas in an intended inclusive process with citizens. In addition, the far-reaching redistributive measures in the 2020 COVID-19 response will mark a qualitative shift in the EU polity development that cannot be judged at the time of writing. For our purpose, what matters is that critical decisions have emerged from within the European Council and without any flaking decisions that would mark a boost in federalization.

Finally, the EU opponents' nihilistic-dystopian federalist vision contradicts the shared pro-integrationist approach of both Spinelli's and Monnet's followers. Whereas the perceived threat of an elite-driven federal teleology of the EU is by no means new, it has thrived with increasing politicization of EU integration since the 1990s (Hooghe & Marks, 2009; De Wilde, 2011; Hutter et al., 2016). How the federalist bugbear serves as driver of disintegration is best exemplified in the Brexit process. "The referendum was to be preceded by a reform deal, which should have made the EU more palatable to the British electorate by reducing its federalist impetus" (Auer, 2017, 42)—irrespective of the open question whether the EU was indeed becoming a federal state. The overriding motto of "taking back control" was formulated in opposition to the perceived integration dynamic and the specific federal shape the EU represented. Brexit exemplifies a type of politicization that activates the globalization winner-loser cleavage that has evolved as a new political dividing line across the Europe (Hobolt, 2016) and on which an EU federation in the making is perceived as the unwanted incarnation of globalization (Kriesi et al., 2008). It is this image of the EU on the new societal dividing line which is exploited both by anti-EU populists, such as the Polish PiS, Hungarian Fidesz or Italian Lega Parties who argue against the threat of federalization, and by promoters of EU integration, like Emmanuel Macron, to exploit EU images and normative stands in electoral competitions.

To sum up Altiero Spinelli's teleological federalist vision and Jean Monnet's functionalist approach represent two distinct positions that continue to shape political strategies and the actual course of EU integration. Both rest on the conceptualization of a federalization process leading to a federalist finalité, yet by decisively different means. Empirically, EU integration has predominantly followed Monnet's functional path, be it out of strategic consideration or the failure of federalist initiatives such as the so-called Constitutional Treaty and the earlier Spinelli-driven draft passed by the European Parliament (EP; European Parliament, 1984). The arguments Spinelli promoted throughout his life stay therefore acute. The question of whether the EU as a federal system can face non-democratic rule especially remains a matter of concern. Spinelli answered this quest unambiguously claiming "that only federal constitutionalism could solve the problems of democratic authorization and accountability that integration raises" (Glencross, 2010, 118). We will return to this argument at the end of the next section.

The EU as Comparable Case: Structure and Functioning of the Federal EU

How does an empirical-analytical perspective differ from the normative-teleological one? Most relevantly, it operates without assumptions about the final state of the EU. Accordingly, the federal perspective serves predominantly to describe, understand and explain dynamics of (dis)integration and the functioning of the EU. While these objectives are similar to key "classical" integration theories and share explanatory logics in particular with neo-functional theory (for overviews on the theories, Wiener et al., 2020), federalism differs in that it conceptualizes the EU as a case of a larger population of federal systems and, accordingly, offers ample room for comparative analysis (for key contributions see Nicolaïdes & Howse, 2001; Menon & Schain, 2006; Fossum & Jachtenfuchs, 2017). To do so, comparatists depart from the federation in the making expectation and instead perceive the EU as a specific federal entity based on an understanding of "federalism as a set of analytical principles, rather than a fixed form of government" (Keating, 2017b, 616; Burgess, 2009). However, federalism as an analytical device is not void of normative concerns. As Keating stresses, federalism "is an analytical device but also has a normative underpinning, based on values including shared rule, self-rule and solidarity" (Keating, 2017b, 622). Thus, in contrast to both the functional theory that aims at explaining why states integrate and the multilevel governance heuristic (Marks et al., 1996) that allows for systematic scrutinization of the division and sharing of authority, federalism theorizes the emergence and implications of divided and shared rule. In contrast to the normative-teleological variant, the normative dimension of the empirical-analytical perspective focuses on the positive substance of federal orders and leaves open whether legitimate rule can *only* be achieved through federation-building or if non-state federal orders provide a viable or even more desirable alternative. Based on this notion, the following applies key dimensions of comparative federalism as ordering principles to explore the type of polity at hand, the origins and dynamics of EU integration, the functioning logic of policymaking, and the defections and endogenous unintended dynamics the system produces. Specific attention is paid to the underpinning federal concerns for shared rule, self-rule and solidarity.

The EU Polity in Comparison: Confederation and Federation

The foundation of the European Union in the early 1990s set off dynamics that rendered federal theory in a comparative design increasingly attractive. First, the Treaty of Maastricht's motto of "an ever closer union" resonated with long-standing notions of federalization and stipulated comparisons with such processes in other federations. This type of comparison climaxed in the context of the Convention drafting the so-called Constitutional Treaty that triggered a great number of studies, especially on constituent moments in federalization processes. Second, the Treaty of Maastricht (1992) entailed an integration boost that raised far-reaching questions about legitimate rule in the EU and politicized EU policymaking to an unprecedented degree. As prominently argued by Hooghe and Marks, citizens' attitudes toward EU integration turned from a dominant "permissive consensus" to an ever-more virulent "constraining dissensus" (Hooghe & Marks, 2009). In EU studies this entailed the rise of normative questions about legitimacy in multilevel governance. In other words attention shifted to matters of shared rule, self-rule and solidarity, which integration theories and multilevel governance had previously successfully discarded to gain analytical impartiality. While the matter of legitimate rule triggered a great number of EU reforms leading, above all, to impressive power gains by the European Parliament (EP), the question of solidarity experienced additional thrust during the decade of poly-crisis. After the failure of the Constitutional Treaty had finally been resolved with the enforcement of the Lisbon Treaty (2009), the EU was hard-hit by the banking and sovereign debt crises in 2009, the pressing need for inner EU solidarity in matters of migration in 2015, the growing authoritarian and illiberal populism in the 2014 EP as well as national elections, and actual disintegration that climaxed in the British vote to exit the EU in 2016. The mere volume of the 2020 measures to counter the economic effects of the COVID-19 pandemic further spur the need for a normative underpinning for EU-wide solidarity and for instructions on how to legitimize such far-reaching budgetary decisions. Thus, due to the trajectory of EU integration, normative questions about the constituting features of the EU continue to gain relevance in the political and public realm, which explains the reentry of federalism on the EU agenda. Yet, in contrast to the federalists' agenda of the 1950s and 1960s, this time federalism is referred to predominantly as an empirical-analytical device. In a comprehensive survey of the rich body of comparative research that compares the EU with other polities (for a review of the large share of EU/USA comparisons, Tortola, 2014), Fossum and Jachtenfuchs observe accordingly a dominance of studies that scrutinize politics and policy rather than polity development (Fossum & Jachtenfuchs, 2017, 469).

What are the innovative findings on the EU as a federal system? Scholars who attribute federal features to the EU agree by and large on "the claim that the EU already constitutes a federal Europe. It is a new federal model" (Burgess, 2009, 39). While it remains legally based on an international treaty between independent states and thus resembles a confederation (a union among states not people), it has developed strong direct linkages and modes of direct influence-taking like a federation (a union between people). In essence the EU embraces both confederate and federal elements in its constituting treaties and practices. What does this mean in terms of shared rule and self-rule? Unlike states, the EU lacks a *Kompetenz-Kompetenz*, that is, the constituent power to endow itself with competences (Calliess & Schnettger, 2019, 353). At the same time the EU is above all a legal order that binds its member states to comply. Thus, "European federalism is constructed with a top-to-bottom hierarchy of norms, but with a bottom-to-top hierarchy of authority and real power" (Weiler, 2001, 57). In comparison to other federations, this means that the EU "continues to be marked by the inverse distribution of powers"

(Tömmel, 2011, 43). Elazar branded this a new model of self-rule and shared rule fit to respond to the challenges caused by growing global interdependence since the Second World War. Observing "a world of diminished state sovereignty and increased interstate linkages of a constitutionalized federal character" (1996, 417), he saw the EU's inverted power model as a possible federal role model because it offered an escape route for the nation-state in demise. The paradigm shift he identified in European integration was the development of functional instead of federalist solutions that allowed precisely for bottom-up distribution of actual power according to functional considerations and top-down hierarchy to enforce these "in new-style federal arrangements" (ibid., 423).

The Origins and Dynamics of Integration: Coming-Together and Holding-Together

To investigate the origins and dynamics of European integration, many authors invoke Stepan's distinction between holding-together and coming-together federal systems. While the former labels the federalization of (formerly unitary) states in order to literally hold the state together, the latter defines the creation of federal systems as a "largely voluntary bargain" between autonomous units that "'come together' to pool their sovereignty while retaining their individual identities" (Stepan, 1999, 23). Referring to this distinction, the EU has been put at par with the relatively small number of coming-together federations inspiring comparative research between the EU, Switzerland and the USA in particular. Accordingly, the EU is based on a voluntary coming-together of states that base their cooperation on legal contracts that preserve member state authority over key core state powers (Kelemen, 2013). In addition, the Treaty of Lisbon introduced a clause which regulates the withdrawal of single states from the Union. Article 50 of the Treaty on the Functioning of the European Union (TFEU) was invoked by the UK in 2017, triggering the treaty-based procedure to withdraw from the initial coming-together agreement. The EU hence provides for a form of secession as a legally accepted element of its polity development, which other federations rule out.

Next to these undisputed coming-together features of EU federalism, deepened integration has caused federalization processes of the holding-together type, especially inside the Union's member states. The establishment of the Committee of Regions in 1994 prompted the most encompassing ideas of federalization in the form of a *Europe of the Regions* (Loughlin, 1996). These aspirations of EU federalization by dissolving the national level and rebuilding the EU around regional sub-units did not materialize. However, the direct supranational-regional linkages—especially in terms of regional policy assigning money to regional units—laid the groundwork for conceptualizing the EU as a multilevel polity (Marks, 1996) and practically triggered holding-together federalization processes in a number of unitary and federal member states (for a recent overview, Chacha, 2020). The interconnectedness between the EU and inner-state federalization shows most strikingly in the case of Brexit (Keating, 2017a). EU membership has not only been a key driver for UK devolution, but the devolved system is so strongly embedded in the EU legal framework that Brexit creates a range of legal voids that cannot be easily resolved because allowing the devolved governments to fill the legal gaps Brexit creates would imply a drifting apart of legislation inside the UK. In addition, regional units (in particular Scotland) challenge membership in the UK's union, as they aspire direct EU membership (as similarly envisaged by Catalán nationalists in Spain). EU integration thus strengthens sub-national units and fosters inner member state federalization of the holding-together type, not least because sub-state units consider the EU as a viable framework for independent state-building.[2]

Pressures leading to holding-together type federalization are not limited to inner-state dynamics. The EU at large has developed a great range of responses to accommodate varying member state demands, which implies an increasingly differentiated system (Leuffen et al., 2013). Empirical studies on differentiation debunk earlier expectations that fall in line with Monnet's incremental functional approach according to which a multi-speed integration process means that laggards will eventually follow more integrationist avant-garde groups. Instead, it shows that initial differentiation, such as (non)membership in the Euro or the Schengen areas, gets manifested over time and thus, differentiation causes further differentiation (Schimmelfennig, 2016). In other words, the federalization of the holding-together type is mirrored on the EU level as differentiated

---

[2] Secession of state sub-units does not gain automatic EU membership but has to formally apply and negotiate membership. Northern Ireland represents an exception in this case because the Good Friday Agreement (1998) guarantees that in case Northern Ireland and the Republic of Ireland would unite, Northern Ireland would gain automatic EU membership.

member state participation in single policies that entail qualitatively differentiated degrees of membership.

Pointing to a third trend that strengthens the holding-together dimension in EU integration, Fossum and Jachtenfuchs point out that the EU's poly-crisis increased EU contestation and therefore intensified "issues of clarifying the relationship between the onus on coming-together and the onus on holding-together. These developments have brought about a strong populist pressure for renegotiating the terms of states' role and status in relation to the EU and suggest that the balance may be shifting to that of holding-together" (2017, 475–476). Beyond the question where rule should be located, the crises raised concerns about solidarity and what holds the EU together when redistributive conflicts are at stake. The responses have been issue-specific and framed in functional terms of "there is no viable alternative" in the Euro crisis. They have largely failed in the migration policy. The fact that the EU derives its solidarity from its legal principles rather than a sense of community is lucidly illustrated by Brexit. The withdrawal negotiations created an urgency to define the principles of EU cooperation in order to delineate rights and privileges of states in and outside the EU. Even though the initially explicit linkage between Brexit and further EU development weakened short of an agreement between France and Germany (Heidbreder, forthcoming), the red lines which the European Council issued for the negotiations defined which principles the EU considers as indispensable for its holding-together. The crucial linchpin that emerges is the integrity of the single market, which embraces (a) the non-negotiability of the four basic freedoms, including shared social and competitiveness standards, (b) the need to fully respect the basic freedoms by all participants in the internal market, including legal controls and sanctioning options, and (c) the clear distinction between insiders and outsiders of the single market, including a clear definition of external borders and their effective control.[3] More than the other crises, Brexit has thus shown that the mutual respect of shared rules around the single market establishes the normative core that holds together cooperation in the EU. The other crises, including COVID-19, show that the key matter of dispute is not large-scale redistribution as such but the

---

[3] Mirroring Brexit, the process of Eastern Enlargement necessitated a stock-taking and positive definition of the legal body the applicant states were acceding to. Accordingly, Eastern Enlargement caused a codification of the body of law commonly understood as acquis communautaire (Heidbreder, 2011, p. 174).

functional linkage between the EU's normative core and redistribution. Solidarity can be derived more directly when framed as a functional necessity to keep the single market running, but fails when solidarity touches upon cultural or other normative dimensions.[4]

The Institutional Balance and Functioning Logic: Divided and Integrated, Coordinated and Cooperative

Turning to the working logic of the EU's institutional structure and the underpinning functioning logic of EU policymaking, the distinction between divided (distinct competences on different levels) and integrated (shared competences across levels) federations serves as a starting point. While, in contrast to the US-divided model, some scholars classify the EU as an integrated model, such as Germany (Hueglin & Fenna, 2015, 52), most researchers paint a more blurred picture. Empirical research "depicts political processes of dividing and sharing of competences, their content and scope being determined in power struggles between national and European actors representing different public or private interests" (Benz & Zimmer, 2010, 18). In the same vein the EU is at odds with the "classic distinction between coordinate federalism, in which competences are clearly divided between the levels, and cooperative federalism, in which they are shared. In some respects, Europe challenges both varieties by undermining existing federal or quasi-federal arrangements within member states with a significant meso level" (Keating, 2017b, 622). Which working logic emerges from this?

In terms of self-rule and shared rule, the Treaty of Lisbon for the first time defines exclusive, shared or supporting competences as distinct types (TFEU, Title I, Article 2). For certain policies the EU has been conferred all policymaking authority, for example, in monetary policy for the Eurozone states. In other areas, such as public administration, it only supports authority-maintaining member states as a facilitator that offers financial or technical assistance. Next to these clear-cut cases that locate authority either on the EU or on the member state level, the bulk of EU

---

[4] Notably, the German Bundesverfassungsgericht that criticized the European Central Bank (ECB) in 2020 for having failed to sufficiently justify its crisis measures, thus putting into question the legitimacy of the legal practice of the primacy of EU law. This ruling set an example for the competition of constitutional principles between member state constitutions and EU treaties and jurisprudence—welcomed as evidence for the unlawful intervention of the EU in particular by Polish and Hungarian constitutionalists.

policies falls under the category of shared competences, itself subdivided into three types. First, in certain policies in which EU regulation has been established, member states lose their authority to regulate, for example, in most parts of the single market. Second, the EU and member states exercise authority in parallel in certain policies; thus, shared and self-rule are executed at the same time in fields such as development cooperation or research policy. Finally, member states cooperate under shared competences but preserve their authority in policies in which they decide on single measures by unanimity, most notably in foreign, security and defense policy. The EU does not only place shared and self-rule next to each other, but it also exercises intermediate modes in which the levels interact. The single policy is the functional unit within which the particular mix of self- and shared rule is defined in the treaties. Correspondingly, policymaking happens in different decision-making modes (Wallace & Reh, 2015). Decisions over policies that fall under intergovernmental decision-making clearly place the question about whether and how to share rule on the table because, by default, member states maintain self-rule except when they unanimously vote to cooperate. However, standard supranational decision-making is fundamentally different to decision-making in a state. Because the EU *is* essentially the sum of the policymaking authority conferred to it, and because the EU lacks the competence to define its own competences, each policymaking decision contains in itself basic constituent questions about the balance between shared and self-rule.[5]

To evaluate how well this system delivers, we need to consider the logic of interest aggregation and representation on which standard decision-making in the EU rests. First, the EU has no clear separation of powers. Instead, interests are aggregated and represented by different institutions with the Commission signing responsibility for a general EU common good, the Parliament for citizens directly and the Council for genuine state interests (Majone, 2002). Democratic legitimacy thus derives from the competition between these institutions (Bartolini, 2005) while partisan interest aggregation and party competition remain underdeveloped (Mair, 2008). In legislative processes the Commission as an (ideally)

---

[5] An exception to this is the exclusive competences for which decision-making authority has been delegated to agents outside the political realm, in particular the European Central Bank that can take widely independent decisions. However, member state representatives are on the governing boards of EU agencies, including the ECB, and can thus exert influence within these organizations.

a-political arbiter proposes legislation while the competition between immediate citizen concerns (EP) and member state preferences (Council) need to be matched to pass legislation. In policy execution the Commission is delegated the authority to oversee and control rightful implementation of EU regulation, but actual execution rests mostly with political administrative systems of the member states.

This system raises key questions about both output and input legitimacy (Scharpf, 1988, 2006). Regarding the actual ability to deliver working policies, Scharpf argues in his seminal comparison between EU and German federalism that decision-making is burdened by a great number of veto players that do not only impede decision-making but also, more severely, render it highly difficult to correct or even undo decisions, which he coins a joint decision-making trap. This notwithstanding, Scharpf attests the EU high levels of output legitimacy due to overall accepted policy delivery during the first decades of integration (Scharpf, 1999). However, expanding EU policies beyond the core market-creating areas and thus entering market-regulating positive integration with higher redistributive impacts renders the need for credible input legitimacy acute. Comparing the creation of legitimacy and demands for compliance by citizens in different polity types illustrates the point. Federations split these functions in different ways. Dual federalism (as seen in the USA) allocates legitimizing and compliance either on the highest (federal) or intermediate (state) level, so that compliance is demanded from the same level that citizens have legitimized to exercise specific policy authority. Unitary federalism (as seen in Germany) splits these functions. While legitimacy is produced primarily through the highest level (federal government), implementation and thereby compliance is delegated to the intermediate (Länder) level. In contrast to this the EU both creates legitimacy and demands compliance through the intermediate level (national governments). Due to the little developed direct linkage between citizens and EU policymaking, "[i]n the two-level European polity, therefore, the EU must be seen and legitimated not as a government of citizens, but as a government of governments. What matters foremost is the willingness and ability of member states to implement EU law and to assume political responsibility for doing so" (Scharpf, 2009, 181). For the functioning of the EU, this means ultimately that compliance and enforcement of EU rules depend on the voluntary cooperation of member state governments (Börzel & Heidbreder, 2017). Furthermore, policies have to be justified within the respective national context to produce legitimacy in the eyes of citizens.

In a nutshell, in the EU's daily working, single policies are the unit within which the balance between shared and self-rule is defined. The policy-dependent mix of jointly exercised authority thus follows in each case a functional logic that is negotiated in different modes. Representation in this system is channeled through institutions that enter into a competition between directly expressed citizen concerns and concerns of citizens of the 27 member states. However, as direct representation through parties and the EP remains weak, member states remain mediators to legitimize and enforce EU policies. Such strong indirect representation through the member state governments (Sbragia, 2006) hits its limits the more redistributive policies are at stake. This notwithstanding, the single market and its survival as an actual core value of the EU hints to a kind of functional-normative form of solidarity, which legitimizes economically framed redistribution. The case of the COVID-19 recovery fund *Next Generation EU* illustrates this on an unprecedented scale.

Defections and Unintended Dynamics: Democracy and Authoritarianism, Unity and Plurality

The distance between EU decision-making and citizens in the system of strong indirect representation is especially cause for claims about a fundamental democratic deficit of the EU. One response is to strengthen party-political contestation in the EP (Hix, 2008) and thereby re-direct competition from the inter-institutional to the parliamentary arena. However, not only does this strategy undermine the existing democratic architecture of the EU, it also creates severe unintended effects on the member state level. Taking up the cudgels for comparative federalism, Kelemen argues that comparative federalism literature can explain the emergence of semi-authoritarian governments in the EU (2017; Kelemen refers explicitly to work by Gibson, 2013). "This comparative federalism literature demonstrates that it is common for authoritarian enclaves (referred to variously as 'illiberal democracies', 'competitive authoritarianism', or 'electoral authoritarianism') to persist at the state level within regimes that are democratic at the federal level—a phenomenon typically referred to as 'subnational authoritarianism'" (2019, 36). Developing these insides into a "fully elaborated theory of the authoritarian equilibrium", exemplified by the "consolidation of authoritarian rule in Hungary", Kelemen identifies three explanatory factors: "partial politicisation, money and migration" (2020, 482). First, with increasing partisan competition on the EU level, Europarties that are composed of national party alliances are prone to tolerate non-conform national parties as these are needed to gain majorities; therefore, "perversely, increasing democratization at the federal level (as the EU has attempted to do in recent years by empowering the European parliament) may help to entrench authoritarian rule at the state level" (Kelemen, 2019, 36). Second, EU funding can be used to economically sustain autocratic rule because it provides autocrats additional leeway for patronage policies. Finally, economic freedoms granted by EU citizenship offer the opportunity for opponents to reside or settle anywhere in the EU and thus exit the regime, reducing necessary resistance against rising autocrats (for a more complete description, Kelemen, 2020, 482–483). "Thus, notwithstanding all the EU has done to promote democracy over the years, the union now finds itself mired in an authoritarian equilibrium, with enough partisan politics to help perpetuate local autocrats, but not enough to dislodge them" (Kelemen, 2017, 231).

Conclusion: Post-State and State-Preserving Federalism

The single defining feature of the EU as a federal system seems to be that it falls right in between all meaningful definitions of federalism. How can we make sense of this? The EU as a prototype federal model can be defined as a coming-together polity developed in repeated legitimization acts that lay down policy-specific mechanisms of shared and self-rule that are institutionalized in a legal framework depending ultimately on voluntary compliance mediated through the member states. This system has proven effective in producing legitimacy around the core principles of the single market, including redistribution to sustain the market and thereby, as Elazar envisaged, a highly efficient polity to recreate vanishing capacities of the nation-state in an increasingly interdependent global context. Yet, the EU has proven ineffective in producing solidarity in areas that are not justified by functional necessity to sustain the integrity and functioning of the single market. This said, the EU has established competences that go far beyond market creation and regulation, most prominently the European Charter of Fundamental Rights and Freedoms that gained legal force with the Treaty of Lisbon, as well as an elaborate anti-discrimination acquis. However, in these fields the EU remains mainly a regulatory but not a redistributive polity, and the reach of the EU's own democratic principles is limited to the application of EU law. The EU thus guarantees that fundamental rights are met when EU competences are being exercised, but the EU cannot promote these rights outside its policy competences. The general adherence to fundamental and social rights remains a matter of national constitutions which coexist in the EU's system of constitutional pluralism. This specific partial, policy-based functional federalization path produces unintended effects that undermine welfare and democracy on the member state level. These empirical observations recall the basic difference between the functional Monnet approach and Spinelli's radical democratic claims, according to which, only full-fledged federal constitutionalism could guarantee democratic rule. If a non-state federal system can balance the inherent tensions all federal systems encounter, it remains a matter of normative judgment and experimental polity development that continues to proceed in the EU.

References

Auer, S. (2017). Brexit, sovereignty and the end of an ever closer union. In W. Outhwaite (Ed.), *Brexit: Sociological responses* (pp. 41–54). Anthem Press.

Bartolini, S. (2005). *Restructuring Europe: Centre formation, system building, and political structuring between the nation state and the European Union*. Oxford University Press.

Bellamy, R., & Castiglione, D. (2013). Three models of democracy, political community and representation in the EU. *Journal of European Public Policy*, 20(2), 206–223.

Benz, A., & Zimmer, C. (2010). The EU's competences: The 'vertical' perspective on the multilevel system. *Living Reviews in European Governance*, 5(1).

Börzel, T., & Heidbreder, E. G. (2017). Enforcement and compliance. In C. Harlow, P. Leino-Sandberg, & della Cananea, G. (Eds.), *Research handbook on EU administrative law* (pp. 241–262). Edward Elgar.

Burgess, M. (2000). *Federalism and the European Union: The building of Europe, 1950–2000*. Routledge.

Burgess, M. (2006). *Comparative federalism: Theory and practice*. Routledge.

Burgess, M. (2009). Federalism. In A. Wiener & T. Diez (Eds.), *European integration theory* (pp. 25–44). Oxford University Press.

Calliess, C., & Schnettger, A. (2019). The protection of constitutional identity in a Europe of multilevel constitutionalism. In C. Calliess & G. Van der Schyff (Eds.), *Constitutional identity in a Europe of multilevel constitutionalism* (pp. 348–371). Cambridge University Press.

Chacha, M. (2020). European Union membership status and decentralization: A top-down approach. *Regional & Federal Studies, 30*(1), 1–23.
Council of the European Union. (2007). *Annex: ICC Mandate.* 11218/07: 26 June 2007.
De Wilde, P. (2011). No polity for old politics? A framework for analyzing the politicization of European integration. *Journal of European Integration, 33*(5), 559–575.
Elazar, D. L. (1996). From statism to federalism: A paradigm shift. *International Political Science Review, 17*(4), 417–429.
Elazar, D. (2001). The United States and the European Union: Models for their epochs. In K. Nicolaïdis & R. Howse (Eds.), *The federal vision: Legitimacy and levels of governance in the United States and the European Union* (pp. 31–53). Oxford University Press.
Epstein, R. A., & Rhodes, M. (2016). The political dynamics behind Europe's new banking union. *West European Politics, 39*(3), 415–437.
European Commission. (2017). White paper on the future of Europe and the way forward. *Reflections and scenarios for the EU27,* COM(2017)2025 (1 March).
European Parliament. (1984). Draft treaty establishing the European Union. *Official Journal of the European Communities,* (No C 77/33, adopted 14 February).
Fabbrini, S. (2005). Madison in Brussels: The EU and the US as compound democracies (Symposium: A 'United States of Europe'?). *European Political Science, 4*(2), 188–198.
Fischer, J. (2000). *From confederacy to federation – Thoughts about the finality of European integration.* Speech at the Humboldt University, Berlin, May 12. Retrieved January 17, 2018, from https://www.hu-berlin.de/de/pr/medien/aktuell/reden
Fossum, J. E., & Jachtenfuchs, M. (2017). Federal challenges and challenges to federalism. Insights from the EU and federal states. *Journal of European Public Policy, 24*(4), 467–485.
Gibson, E. L. (2013). *Boundary control: Subnational authoritarianism in federal democracies.* Cambridge University Press.
Glencross, A. (2010). Conclusion: Altiero Spinelli and the future of the European Union. In A. Glencross & A. H. Trechsel (Eds.), *EU federalism and constitutionalism: The legacy of Altiero Spinelli* (pp. 177–129). Lexington Press.
Grimm, D. (1995). Does Europe need a constitution? *European Law Journal, 1*(3), 282–302.
Habermas, J. (1995). Remarks on Dieter Grimm's "Does Europe need a constitution?". *European Law Journal, 1*(3), 303–307.
Habermas, J. (2012). *Crisis of the European Union: A response.* Polity.

Heidbreder, E. G. (2011). *The impact of expansion on EU institutions: The eastern touch on Brussels.* Palgrave Macmillan.

Heidbreder, E. G. (forthcoming). Germany. In H. Kassim (Ed.), *Negotiating Brexit: National governments, EU institutions, and the UK.* Palgrave Macmillan.

Hix, S. (2008). *What's wrong with the European Union and how to fix it.* Polity Press.

Hobolt, S. B. (2016). The Brexit vote: A divided nation, a divided continent. *Journal of European Public Policy, 23*(9), 1259–1277.

Hooghe, L., & Marks, G. (2009). A postfunctionalist theory of European integration: From permissive consensus to constraining dissensus. *British Journal of Political Science, 39*(1), 1–23.

Howarth, D., & Quaglia, L. (2014). The steep road to banking union: Constructing the single resolution mechanism. *Journal of Common Market Studies, 52*(Annual Review), 125–140.

Hueglin, T. O., & Fenna, A. (2015). *Comparative federalism: A systematic inquiry* (2nd ed.). University of Toronto Press.

Hutter, S., Grande, E., & Kriesi, H. (Eds.). (2016). *Politicising Europe.* Cambridge University Press.

Keating, M. (2017a). Brexit and devolution in the United Kingdom. *Politics and Governance, 5*(2), 1–3.

Keating, M. (2017b). Europe as a multilevel federation. *Journal of European Public Policy, 24*(4), 615–632.

Kelemen, D. R. (2013). Building the new European state? Federalism, core state powers, and European integration. In P. Genschel & M. Jachtenfuchs (Eds.), *Beyond the regulatory polity?: The European integration of core state powers* (pp. 211–229). Oxford University Press.

Kelemen, D. R. (2017). Europe's other democratic deficit: National authoritarianism in Europe's democratic union. *Government and Opposition, 52*(2), 211–238.

Kelemen, D. R. (2019). Federalism. In A. Wiener, T. A. Börzel, & T. Risse (Eds.), *European integration theory* (pp. 27–42). OUP.

Kelemen, D. R. (2020). The European Union's authoritarian equilibrium. *Journal of European Public Policy, 27*(3), 481–499.

King, P. (1982). *Federalism and federation.* Johns Hopkins University Press.

Kriesi, H., Grande, E., Lachat, R., Dolezal, M., Bornschier, S., & Frey, T. (2008). *West European politics in the age of globalization.* Cambridge University Press.

Lacey, J. (2016). Conceptually mapping the European Union: A demoi-cratic analysis. *Journal of European Integration, 38*(1), 61–77.

Leuffen, D., Rittberger, B., & Schimmelfennig, F. (2013). *Differentiated integration.* Palgrave Macmillan.

Loughlin, J. (1996). 'Europe of the Regions' and the federalization of Europe. *Publius, 26*(4), 141–162.

MacCormick, N. (1993). Beyond the sovereign state. *The Modern Law Review*, 56(1), 1–18.

Macron, E. (2017). Initiative pour l'Europe. *Discours d'Emmanuel Macron pour une Europe souveraine, unie, démocratique*, Sorbonne, Paris, September 26.

Mair, P. (2008). Popular democracy and the European Union polity. In D. Curtin & A. Will (Eds.), *Meaning and practice of accountability in the EU multi-level context* (pp. 19–62). Manheim: Connex report series no. 07.

Majone, G. (2002). Delegation of regulatory powers in a mixed polity. *European Law Journal*, 8(3), 319–339.

Marks, G. (1996). Exploring and explaining variation in EU Cohesion Policy. In L. Hooghe (Ed.), *Cohesion policy and European integration: Building multi-level governance* (pp. 388–422). Oxford University Press.

Marks, G., Hooghe, L., & Blank, S. J. (1996). European integration from the 1980s: State v. Multi-level governance. *Journal of Common Market Studies*, 34(3), 341–378.

Menon, A., & Schain, M. A. (Eds.). (2006). *Comparative federalism: The European Union and the United States in comparative perspective*. Oxford University Press.

Nicolaïdes, K., & Howse, R. (Eds.). (2001). *The federal vision: Legitimacy and levels of governance in the United States and the European Union*. Oxford University Press.

Nicolaïdis, K. (2013). European democracy and its crisis. *Journal of Common Market Studies*, 51(2), 351–369.

Sbragia, A. (2006). The United States and the European Union: Comparing two *Sui Generis* systems. In A. Menon & M. Schain (Eds.), *Comparative federalism: The European Union and the United States in comparative perspectives* (pp. 15–32). Oxford University Press.

Scharpf, F. W. (1988). The joint-decision trap: Lessons from German federalism and European integration. *Public Administration*, 66(3), 239–278.

Scharpf, F. W. (1999). *Governing in Europe. Effective and democratic?* Oxford University Press.

Scharpf, F. (2006). The joint-decision trap revisited. *Journal of Common Market Studies*, 44(4), 845–864.

Scharpf, F. W. (2009). Legitimacy in the multilevel European polity. *European Political Science Review*, 1(2), 173–204.

Schimmelfennig, F. (2016). A differentiated leap forward: Spillover, path-dependency, and graded membership in European banking regulation. *West European Politics*, 39(3), 483–502.

Stepan, A. C. (1999). Federalism and democracy: Beyond the US model. *Journal of Democracy*, 10(4), 19–34.

Tömmel, I. (2011). The European Union – A federation *Sui Generis*? In F. Laursen (Ed.), *The EU and federalism: Polities and policies compared* (pp. 41–56). Routledge.

Tortola, P. D. (2014). The limits of normalization: Taking stock of the EU-US comparative literature. *Journal of Common Market Studies, 52*(6), 1342–1357.

Wallace, H., & Reh, C. (2015). An institutional anatomy of five policy modes. In H. Wallace, M. A. Pollack, & A. R. Young (Eds.), *Policy-making in the European Union* (pp. 72–114). Oxford University Press.

Weiler, J. H. H. (2001). Federalism without constitutionalism: Europe's Sonderweg. In K. Nicolaïdis & R. Howse (Eds.), *The federal vision: Legitimacy and levels of governance in the United States and the European Union* (pp. 54–70). Oxford University Press.

Wiener, A., Börzel, T. A., & Risse, T. (Eds.). (2020). *European integration theory* (3rd ed.). OUP.

PART III

Concluding Remarks

CHAPTER 14

Conclusion: Emergence, Operation and Categorization of Federal Structures in the Post-Cold War Era

Soeren Keil and Sabine Kropp

INTRODUCTION

This book has been a long time in the making. In three of our case studies political processes substantially undermined the federalization process. In Ethiopia a new civil war erupted in November 2020 as a result of political tensions between the central government in Addis Ababa under the leadership of Prime Minister Abiy Ahmed and his former allies in the Tigray People's Liberation Front (TPLF). To date, it is unclear how many people have died, but the growing military success of the TPLF's troops has

S. Keil (✉)
Institute of Federalism, University of Fribourg, Fribourg, Switzerland
e-mail: Soeren.keil@unifr.ch

S. Kropp
Otto-Suhr-Institut für Politikwissenschaft, Freie Universität Berlin, Berlin, Germany
e-mail: sabine.kropp@fu-berlin.de

© The Author(s), under exclusive license to Springer Nature Switzerland AG 2022
S. Keil, S. Kropp (eds.), *Emerging Federal Structures in the Post-Cold War Era*, Federalism and Internal Conflicts, https://doi.org/10.1007/978-3-030-93669-3_14

meant that the war has spread to other parts of Ethiopia, causing displacement, violence and increased human suffering. Ethnic federalism did obviously not keep up to its promises. In Myanmar, a military coup in February 2021 crashed all hopes that the democratization process that began in 2010 would lead to the establishment of a federal democratic Union. Since then, the country has seen mass uprisings, which were oppressed with increased violence by the Tatmadaw (the name of Myanmar's military). The Russian invasion in Ukraine, which began in February 2022 while this book was in the final editing stage, might substantially affect the future territorial structure of Ukraine.

These drastic examples highlight a key theme of this volume—federalization processes are neither linear nor coherent or irreversible. Instead, we are dealing with highly complex situations, institutional reform processes and actors whose preferences change and adapt to internal and external developments. What is more, both cases highlight the 'incompleteness' of the federalization process. While Ethiopia claimed at least constitutionally to represent a federal democratic system (see Fessha and Dessaleghn, this volume), Myanmar was engaged in a peace process, which aimed to 'Establish a union based on the principles of democracy and federalism' (Nationwide Ceasefire Agreement, 2015, Chapter 1a; see also Breen, this volume). In Ukraine, a process of decentralization took place, but the federalism debate was damaged as a result of continued Russian interference (see Kropp and Holm-Hansen, this volume).

As the developments in Ethiopia, Ukraine and Myanmar highlight, federalization processes are complex, context-dependent and caught between different dynamics, some of which we outline later. The seven dimensions of 'emergence' outlined in the Introduction should therefore not be seen as static categories but as markers and process indicators of wider federalization dynamics. They allow us to provide a first attempt at categorization of our case studies into various forms of federalizing systems—including (1) countries in which federalization is debated, (2) cases in which decentralization is applied but further federalization is discussed, (3) cases with federal practices but without clear federal institutions, (4) systems either with some federal institutions but without full federalization, (5) cases with full federalization but with counteracting practices and (6) fully fledged federations.[1] These categories, as fleshed out further below, are a

---

[1] Dardanelli (2019, 275–280) mentions an assembly directly elected by the people of the region, primary law-making powers in at least one key area of government, considerable fiscal

first attempt at categorizing emerging federal structures, while still recognizing that the process of 'emergence' is both dynamic and non-linear. As has been highlighted across various cases in this book, the process of federalization might not lead to federation per se, and even in cases where it has resulted in proper federations, the process continues, either through demands for further decentralization and confederalization (such as in Belgium) or through regression toward more centralization and undemocratic practices (as in Russia and Ethiopia). The choice against a more static understanding of federalism and federal political system and for a dynamic, process-driven framework has been a useful one, and has reconfirmed Carl Friedrich's (1968) initial assumption that federalism as process is a much more appropriate analytical perspective than a mere discussion and analysis of specific constitutional frameworks at certain moments in time.

In light of this analytical positioning, it is then important to revisit some of the assumptions and frames developed in the Introduction. This means re-conceptualizing the origins of federalization dynamics in light of newer federal structures that have emerged in the post-Cold War era. While what authors such as William Riker (1964), Kenneth Wheare (1964) or Alfred Stepan (1999) have written is still relevant today, the picture that has emerged when looking at the case studies in this book is nevertheless much more complicated and multi-facetted. Moreover, when reconsidering the origin of federal arrangements, one also has to keep in mind that the process of emergence also affects their functioning, or what Riker labeled as 'operation' and their challenges. As will be demonstrated, we are seeing an increasing number of hybrid arrangements—not quite federal but certainly not unitary anymore.

The Emergence of Federal Political Structures

In the Introduction to this volume, we outlined seven dimensions relevant for the emergence of new federal structures. We argued that post-Cold War systems are becoming harder to classify, with fewer 'traditional' federal systems characterized by clear elements of self-rule and shared rule (Elazar, 1987; Burgess, 2006), and more hybrid regimes, which meet

---

independence as criteria for self-rule. An involvement of sub-central tiers and entities into central law-making and their participation in checks and balances are necessary to establish efficient shared rule.

some federal characteristics, but not all of them. This fuzzy classification has justified our reference to federal political arrangements or federal structures—which is less demanding than the term 'federal political system' used by Ronald Watts to categorize 'the genus of political organization that is marked by the combination of shared rule and self-rule' (Watts, 1998, 120; 2008) in a variety of ways and without or with more limited constitutional protection, which we would expect to encounter in a fully developed federation.

In the Introduction, we highlighted the following seven areas as dimensions relevant to the beginning or regressive processes of federalization: diversity and the adaptation to a federal society; the accommodation of ethno-cultural minorities; informality processes that may indicate federal practices, and encourage or discourage inclusion; federalization as part of democratization agendas; authoritarian tendencies and regressing federal structures; the use of federal instruments as tools of conflict resolution; and the imposition of federal structures by external actors. We argue that while the seven dimensions of federal emergence are visible across our cases, they are neither present in all of them nor at the same time. Instead, federalization remains a process triggered by one, or some, of the factors outlined below and can over time either be encouraged or be limited by other factors. For, while the areas we identify across our cases generally enhance federalization dynamics, we also have to point out that they, or combinations of them, may discourage the institutional manifestation of federalism. For example, the accommodation of minority rights might result in fears over territorial disintegration, and federalism becomes the infamous 'f-word'—the principle that may lead to state break-up. This can be observed in some of our cases, such as Spain, where the constitution explicitly denies the autonomous communities the right to form a federation in Article 145.1.

The patterns that emerge when analyzing the Table 1.1 in the Introduction are revealing. It is clear, for example, that federalization processes in the post-Cold War era are the result of multinationalism and the demand for minority nations for recognition and autonomy (*accommodation of ethno-cultural groups*). This is the case in all countries in our studies bar Columbia, where the conflict was much about ideological and economic issues than about ethnicity and national belonging. However, all other countries confirm Stepan's (1999) conclusion that contemporary federations (and federal arrangements) are much more the result of holding-together processes. In these systems, unlike traditional coming-together federations such as the USA or Germany, federalization processes start in order to accommodate the growing demands of minority nations for recognition and autonomy. It is therefore not surprising that the accommodation of minorities is often also linked with democratization—breaking the circle of authoritarian rule and oppression of minority rights, often connect federalization and democratization, as has been the case in Bosnia, Spain and South Africa for example. In this regard, it is also plausible that the existence of a federal society has been a key driver of federalization processes in the majority of our cases, though it has not been the driver in all of them—for they are all diverse, multinational societies, but we realize that diversity alone is not a sufficient condition for federalization. In fact, when looking at our case selection, we can see that the adoption of federal structures in order to accommodate a *federal society* takes place in democratic settings, but also at critical junctures characterized by democratization and regime change (e.g., compare the cases of Spain and Nepal). This is not to say that democratization alone will result in accommodative practices and processes (compare here the lack of these in Myanmar after 2010), but it is evident that authoritarian regimes find it hard to adapt to federal societies due to their inherent lack of responsiveness—a key finding that confirms our assumption in the Introduction.

Nevertheless, as we highlighted in the Introduction, *democratization* and federalization processes are no easy bedfellows and both are highly complex and challenging, each with their own pitfalls and difficulties (Kropp, 2019). It is therefore not surprising that democratization and federalization processes, where they can be found simultaneously, return rather mixed results. For example, in Spain democratization has hindered federalization as it has moved the country in a more majoritarian direction, as pointed out by Anderson in this volume. On the other side of the spectrum is Bosnia, where extreme decentralization within the ethnic federal system has hindered deep-rooted democratization and allowed regional elites to enhance their influence and undermine local democratization (Kapidzic, 2019).

Federalism has often been regarded as a subcomponent of democracy. Federal structures are therefore applied as integral part of democratization agendas. While the complexity in the interaction between (fully fledged) federalism and (consolidated) democracy is increasingly being studied (Benz, 2020; Benz & Sonnicksen, 2015, 2017), more evidence is needed to understand the interrelation between federalization and democratization in emerging federal arrangements. What we can corroborate from the findings in our case studies is that processes of simultaneous democratization and federalization increase the likelihood of regional authoritarianism, especially when territorial units are designed along ethnic lines. While this is not a foregone conclusion as the counter-examples of Spain, India and Nepal highlight, the presented evidence in the cases of Bosnia, Kosovo, Iraq, Russia and Ethiopia allows us to pinpoint this as a distinct danger in emerging federal structures, thereby confirming earlier research findings (Benz & Kropp, 2014; Filippov & Shvetsova, 2013). We notice that federalization can only have little or no positive impact on democratization in a number of case studies. In Myanmar, for example, there has been no substantial progress in democratization despite an intense federal debate as part of the Union Peace Agreement since 2015.

In this context it is also important to discuss not just regional authoritarianism, but the emergence of wider *authoritarian tendencies* in a number of the cases discussed in previous chapters. Authoritarianism emerges at multiple levels. Authoritarian rulers can leverage federal structures, as they allow for elite co-optation and for enhancing the number of offices that can be distributed to loyalists (as seen in Russia and Bosnia). Federal structures also enable incumbents to shift the blame to lower entities (as seen in Ethiopia and Russia) and treat subnational elites as scapegoats for policy failure.

In some cases, federalizing polities undergo flawed democratization due to the interactions between like-minded authoritarian elites at the center and in the lower territorial units. In Kosovo, for example, we see a level of non-engagement between the center and the Serb-controlled North that leads to a failure of both state-consolidation and democratization. Likewise, the demands for independence in Iraqi Kurdistan also demonstrate that the inability to implement functional federal structures is concomitant with an inability to democratize efficiently at the center and in the Kurdish region. What has become obvious across many of our case studies is the need to examine and understand further the dynamics of federalization and authoritarian governance, for it is too simplistic to deny the existence of federalization processes in non-democratic countries per se. This particularly important as political entrepreneurs might repurpose or reanimate invalidated federal structures under certain circumstances—a process described as 'conversion' in Streeck and Thelen's categorization of gradual institutional change (Streeck & Thelen, 2005, 26–27).

Another important feature of our discussion is the reliance on *informality* in the emerging federal structures discussed in this book. All cases but still war-torn Syria[2] employ some kind of informal arrangements to make the system work. However, informality—as highlighted in the Introduction—has two sides to it. In some of our cases informal political arrangements help stabilize federal arrangements in the polity, as is the case in Belgium, the European Union or in India in the past. Here, informality refers to a network of relations between the center and territorial units that are not formalized through constitutional and legal means. These networks are often essential to ensure access for ethnic minorities to political decision-making procedures. The participation of specific groups through informal arrangements might enhance participation in decision-making—a key factor of democracy—but if this takes place outside of formalized federal institutions (such as second chambers or established intergovernmental forums), it might even erode federal structures. In cases like Bosnia, Russia, Kosovo, Kenya and South Africa for example, informality tends to undermine federal structures, in some cases it fosters centralization and concomitantly subverts democratization (see also Johnston, 2014; Hale, 2015), as it is linked to corruption, to hierarchical patronal networks, to privileged access in return for political favors (for which federal structures may provide an opportunity structure, see Freille et al., 2007), or to backroom-deals that cripple democratic decision-making institutions.

Finally, in the Introduction, we highlighted the link between the use of federalization processes and *conflict resolution*. This, we argued, has become a promising tool used by international actors in a variety of contexts. However, when looking at the empirical evidence from our case studies, we have to somewhat put the connection between using federalization as a tool of conflict resolution and *the imposition of federal solutions by international actors* into question. Clear impositions are only visible in Bosnia (Keil, 2013), Iraq (Belser, 2020) and Kosovo (Skendaj, 2014). This is not to say that international actors played no role in the emergence of federal and decentralized institutional frameworks in North Macedonia, Nepal, Ukraine, South Africa or Colombia. However, here domestic elites remained in the driving seat and took the ultimate decision about the constitutional arrangements for their countries. Hence, it can be argued that we are witnessing an increase in international activity in promoting federal structures as a tool of conflict resolution, but we are not observing

---

[2] We excluded Syria because its informal practices are not linked to any federal structures or practices but to the nature of its authoritarian regime.

an increase in imposed federations and federal solutions. In some cases, there have been conscious domestic decisions against federalism and political decentralization, as Kent Eaton highlights for the most recent peace agreement in Colombia. In other cases, international actors promoted federalism or substantial decentralization openly, but domestic elites implemented limited reforms or avoided federalization, as demonstrated in the Ukraine chapter.

It has also been demonstrated that the category of 'international actors' is very diverse and context-dependent. In some cases, it refers to Western actors, as was the case in the Balkan states and Iraq; in others, it refers to regional powers, such as South Africa's role in Kenya, or kin-states, see, for example, Russia's support of the federalization of Ukraine. Kin-states often have their own agenda and are becoming increasingly influential members of the 'constitutional bargaining'. They influence discussions on key constitutional questions; in some cases they promote federalism as a constitutional tool to solve violent conflicts (as has been the case by the USA in Bosnia and Iraq); in others, kin-states interfere to prevent functional constitutional structures and use the federal idea as a lever to support separatism, as seen by Russia in the case of Ukraine. This conclusion holds true for a solution to the Syrian conflict, in which Russia, Iran and Turkey will play a major role, as well as for any future federal Union in Myanmar, in which China remains a key influencing power. The federal bargain, as described by William Riker[3] (1964, 12–15; see Volden, 2004; McKay, 2006) more than half a century ago, has become much more multi-facetted and the number of actors involved has increased. In some cases, depending on the agenda of different domestic and international actors (including kin-states), the constellation might not end in a federal bargain at all anymore, as highlighted in the cases of Ukraine and Colombia, where federal structures have been an (contested) issue in the political discourse, but not part of the constitutional negotiations. Federalization may also occur as an incremental, gradual institutional

---

[3] Riker was convinced that the formation of federal systems is to be explained by military threats. He focused on two conditions: politicians want to expand their territorial control, but do not have military capacity or refrain from conquest due to ideological concerns, while politicians who accept the bargain either desire to prevent military threat or participate in the potential aggression of the participation. Guided by rationalist logics, he set aside other possible explanations for the origin of federalism, as put forth by this book. See Volden, 2004, 91–95.

change, as the chapters on Belgium or EU reveal, and does not always end in a true federation.

What we have also learnt from the discussions in this volume is that what is classified as an 'elite' influential in the process of federalization is changing. They might not only be political elites but include military leaders (as is the case in Myanmar), ethnically based militia (as is the case in Myanmar, in Ukraine, in Nepal, in Iraq and in Ethiopia), or influential localized business and clan leaders (as discussed in the case of Colombia). Moreover, we can observe powerful and influential alliances between political elites representing minority nations and ethnic minority military groups, as seen in some of the case studies.

Federalization processes are moving away from federalism as a result of 'desire' (Wheare, 1964, 39) to federalize, or the willingness of elites to compromise and work together (Lijphart, 1969, 216), and instead we are living at a time where federal structures are clearly becoming a tool of conflict resolution and peace-building mechanism (Keil & Anderson, 2018; Keil & Alber, 2020). In all the cases discussed in this volume, with the sole exception of Belgium, there has been violent conflict between different groups. This has not always been the main driver for federalization, as highlighted in the discussions on Russia and Kenya, yet even the European Union emerged initially as a result of the Second World War. Inter-communal violence features in nearly all cases under examination, therefore substantially influencing the dynamics and the context in which the beginning of the federalization process is positioned. The idea that trust and good relations between different elites are key preconditions for successful federal structures, or the recognition of federalism as an 'end in itself' instead of just a means to achieve something else (Franck, 1968, 172) has to give way instead to negotiations (with or without international participation) on ending violent conflict and rebuilding war-torn societies. In short, what becomes a central research interest is the different dynamics of the federal bargain, the role of short-term interests (which will center around security and dealing with the results of the conflict) and long-term, sometimes unintended developments.

In a couple of cases, political solutions to ongoing questions about sovereignty, the distribution of competences and the design of institutions take place in the background of a serious threat of continued fighting and further suffering. In situations where a one-sided victory is likely, the bargaining will be severely limited as can currently be observed in Syria. On the other side, more often than not, the federal bargain only starts because neither side to the conflict is able to win and a painful stalemate has been arrived at. This is the situation in Myanmar and was the case for Nepal, while Colombia also fits this pattern. Interesting dynamics can also be observed in Ethiopia and India, where federalization was initiated by dominant political parties—as was the case in South Africa and the UK. In Iraq and post-Yugoslavia Bosnia, as well as Russia and post-apartheid South Africa, the emergence and conversion of federal structures started in the context of wider regime change.

The context, in which federalization starts and evolves over time, influences how the federal political system functions—as McCulloch and McEvoy (2020, 111) argue, a 'problematic design process means a difficult birth'. Likewise, McGarry (2017) points out that in the context in which consociational agreements are adopted not all of what is adoptable is functional, and not everything that will increase the functionality of an agreement will necessarily be adoptable or agreeable in the negotiations. There is, consequently, a clear link between the initial steps to federalization, the continuation of the federalization process and the functionality of the evolving federal structures that we shall turn our attention to now.

THE OPERATION OF NEW FEDERAL STRUCTURES

While the seven analytical dimensions discussed in the Introduction to this book helped us understand the emergence and evolution of federal structures, the discussions in the previous case study contributions also gave insight into the operation and operationalization of these polities—and the complex shifts and changes they go through. What is vital to consider are the factors that influence the federal balance—the imperfect equilibrium: between territorial units and the center, between self-rule and shared rule, between autonomy and the need for joint and unified actions (Lepine, 2015). It is therefore worth discussing in more detail what influences significant shifts in the ongoing process: the question is what enforces centralization or decentralization, how flexible adaptation can be achieved despite still existing historical legacies, and what effects external and internal shocks might have.

Centralization and Decentralization Tendencies

In his seminal study on federal systems, William Riker (1964) outlined a couple of important elements, which deserve further discussion in light of the federal structures discussed in this volume. He argued that the federal bargain that sets in motion the evolution of federal systems, lays the foundations for a political process in which political parties will over time become the main actors. He concludes that it is the design of the party system, which ultimately influences the development of a federal political system—the more decentralized the party system, and the more parties in the center are dependent on strong party structures (and powerful elites) in the constituent units, the more decentralized (peripheralized) the system will become (and remain; Riker, 1964, 129).

For Riker, the question of centralization and decentralization was a matter of party structures, but also a question of the distribution of competences, which was agreed based on a rational bargaining among actors with different preferences. He did not per se assume that countries would move between centralization and decentralization tendencies over time—he assumed this to be a much more static arrangement. By contrast, William Livingston (1952) and Carl Friedrich (1968) pointed out already more than half a century ago that federal systems are living organisms, which change over time—sometimes becoming more decentralized, sometimes facing centralization tendencies.

As the contributions in this volume have highlighted, there are numerous forces that influence the progress of the federalization process. Riker of course remains important—political parties and elites matter, and they remain the most important collective actors across the cases discussed in this book. Yet preferences of actors themselves may shift over time from centralization to decentralization (as was the case with French-speaking parties in Belgium, and the Labour Party in the UK), or vice versa (as seen in the case of the National League of Democracy in Myanmar, the African National Congress in South Africa, and the Indian Congress Party). If party structures are not consolidated, political elites can even deliberately restructure the party system, thereby enforcing the centralization of the federal structures. Here, the creation of 'Edinaya Rossia' as the party of power in Russia serves as an illustrative example. In addition to the priorities and organization of national political elites, we are also observing an increased importance of elites representing national minorities and specific territorial units—the spectrum of actors that one must consider is becoming diverse. These actors have been able to push for more decentralization in the cases of the UK and Spain, as well as in Belgium, in India and in Iraq and Bosnia and Herzegovina, where representatives of specific ethnic groups have counter-balanced centralization efforts. As Riker's focus on the US party system was limited to homogenous political parties, his analysis has certainly lost explanatory value for multinational states such as the ones represented in this volume.

External actors influence not only the emergence but also the operationalization of emerging federal structures and the decentralization-centralization process. This can have opposite effects. In Bosnia, for example, major centralization reforms such as the unification of the armed forces and the installation of a unified value-added tax and border security service all go back to international imposition through the High Representative. As Keil (2013) has argued, Bosnia's federal system was imposed and it resultantly became an internationally administered federation, because local elites had no interest or willingness to make the system work that they did not agree to. In North Macedonia and Kosovo, too, international involvement in the political process has substantially influenced federal dynamics as well as party politics between majority and minority elites (Hulsey & Keil, 2021). At times, international actors have supported centralization reforms as highlighted above in the case of Bosnia, while at other times, they have promoted decentralization and minority inclusion, as is still the case in Ukraine and in Syria.

Finding the right balance between unity and diversity, self-rule and shared rule—or the imperfect equilibrium referred to earlier—is in itself a process. In keeping with the historical institutionalist argument employed earlier in this volume, institutions evolve, they adapt and they change at key critical junctures (Steinmo, 2012) or as a result of gradual institutional change (Streeck & Thelen, 2005; Mahoney & Thelen, 2010). The case studies give numerous examples how new institutional elements are attached to existing institutions, how existing ones are defected by previously subordinate institutions, or converted, with the Russian case (after 2000) being a prime example. What was a decentralized system might become more centralized as a result of elite turn-over and concomitant institutional change as has been the case in Russia and Spain, while centralized systems might decentralize in the wake of (fragile) democratization pressures, as seen in Myanmar, India, South Africa and Kenya.

Finding the right balance is challenging for established federations and liberal democracies, in war-torn or ethnically divided countries this has been much more complex and a far-less linear and straightforward process. In other words, as holding-together federations emerge differently to coming-together federations (Stepan, 1999), it is no surprise that federal dynamics within these holding-together federal structures are different as well.

Historical Legacies and Flexible Adaptation

Above we argued that how federal structures are operationalized substantially depends on the type of actors and the given actor constellation. But analysts as well as institutional designers also need to draw attention to the wider institutional environment in which federalization takes place. While this is essential it at the same time complicates the process, because different institutions inside the same polity may embody conflicting, even incompatible 'logics' (Streeck & Thelen, 2005, 21). In the Introduction we argued that incoherent arrangements are typical for emerging federal structures, particularly if single institutions are created at different points in time—such incoherent federal structures may also misfit with other institutional dimensions.

In Belgium, Bosnia, North Macedonia, Kosovo, Iraq and the European Union, for example, self-rule and shared rule provisions are combined with different elements of consociational democracy—in some cases more rigidly than in others. In Spain, the UK, Ukraine, Myanmar, India, South Africa and Kenya, federalization takes place within majoritarian institutional provisions, which also influence the dynamics of majority and minority groups. While not all majoritarian systems necessarily exclude minorities in their governments at central level, it has been demonstrated across the chapters that a lack of minority protection and inclusion seems to increase the potential for conflict and tensions in the political system. In this regard, Spain is a good example—the more recent developments in Spain especially in the run-up and after the unilateral referendum on independence in Catalonia in 2017 have demonstrated that the initial success of Spain's model has been hampered in recent years by its majoritarian political system (Mueller, 2019). This of course does not mean that all emerging federal structures that use consociational power-sharing fare better when it comes to dealing with secessionist movements and minority inclusion.

Institutional frameworks, including the development of centralization and decentralization and the choice for or against power-sharing at the center, often build on historical legacies (Thelen, 1999). For example, while the Soviet Union and Yugoslavia were heavily flawed-federal systems, their operationalization, including the focus on ethnicity in the design of territorial units, substantially impacted upon institutional choices in Russia, Ukraine, Bosnia and Herzegovina, North Macedonia and Kosovo. This, however, is not to say that they copied the previously existing institutional frameworks one-to-one, even though legacies such as a collective Presidency in Bosnia, cooperation between Albanians and Serbs in Kosovo, and Macedonians and Albanians in North Macedonia, as well as federal asymmetries in the case of Russia can all be traced back to previously existing institutional arrangements. While 1991 remains a key critical juncture for the case studies that emerged from the Soviet Union and Socialist Yugoslavia, the dissolution of the common—formally federal—state nevertheless also laid the foundation for converting into new federal and decentralized arrangements.

While the hesitancy to adopt federal structures in most of the post-Soviet and post-Yugoslav states (except Russia and Bosnia) can be explained by the common experience of state dissolution and connected economic and political disintegration, there are nevertheless important historical continuities that can be observed in the successor states. These range from the use of federal structures as a tool of diversity management (as practiced in Russia and Bosnia) to the evolution of ethnic power-sharing mechanisms in the center (as practiced in Bosnia, Kosovo and North Macedonia). Here, federalization is an element of wider power-sharing, though only Bosnia is a federal state, while Kosovo and North Macedonia employ decentralization. Interestingly, institutional learning seems to have taken place between these cases, and among the local and international actors involved in their emergence—with discussions in North Macedonia and Kosovo both citing Bosnia as an example to avoid (Keil, 2015).

The ethnic federal design practiced in both the Soviet Union and Yugoslavia also laid the foundation for a strong focus on national identity and the creation of nation states (Grgić, 2017), which has also been pivotal in the political discourse in post-independence Ukraine. Historical legacies matter in our other cases as well, for example one reason that explains the inability of the UK to transform into a fully fledged federation can be found in the historical dominance of parliamentary democracy and the status of the Westminster Parliament as the dominant seat of democratic sovereignty. The House of Lords and the inability to find an appropriate settlement for autonomy for England are also remnants of a historically grown understanding of British statehood and democracy. In India, the long-lasting religious conflict in Kashmir is reflected in institutional choices, first through the provision of a special autonomy status and more recently through the removal of this autonomy and direct rule from Delhi, as pointed out by Wilfried Swenden in this volume.

Legacies of colonialism substantially influence discussions on federal structures (their centralization and decentralization, successes and failures, see Franck, 1968) as well as democratization processes. As highlighted in several of our case studies, the colonial heritage partially explains dysfunctional statehood, elite and inter-group tensions, authoritarianism and ongoing violence. Belser and Keil highlight the importance of these legacies for the dysfunctional federal structures in Iraq and the absence of any major federal discourse in Syria. Similar problematic residues explain the ongoing challenges to federal structures in Kenya and Myanmar. Already in 1966, Ronald Watts (1966) pointed out how new federal systems struggle with finding the right balance between unity and diversity, between centralization and decentralization. Colonial legacies may lay the ground for federal discourses and practices, but they are often undermining functioning governance, democracy and inter-group bargaining. Federal structures and discussions on federalism more generally remains a deeply contested issue in most post-colonial states.

Many cases in this book indicate that the 'formative phase' of federalization may stretch over a long time period. They also reveal that this phase does often not reflect the logics of path dependency. Processes are not necessarily self-reinforcing, and they are sometimes regressing. Institutional remnants may continue to exist, while new elements are attached to existing institutions, which may finally change their status and structure (Streeck & Thelen, 2005, 22–24). Vice versa, it is possible that institutional elements which have lost importance and function as a 'federal shell' can be activated in constitutional debates or re-activated years later or change their initial function. All this reveals that in processes of federalization, actors can employ, recombine and repurpose institutional remnants and attach new institutional elements to already existing ones in order to create something new. As a result we find a variety of incoherent, partial federal structures, which do not transform into a fully fledged federation, even when the emergence of such a federation might seem like a perfectly reasonable solution, as is the case in the UK or in Spain.

Stating this also has practical implications: a high degree of 'flexible adaptability' (Keil & McCulloch, 2021) is a prerequisite to employ these emerging federal structures. In fact, a couple of countries, such as India, South Africa and also Belgium, the UK (until 2014) and Spain (until

2010), have been remarkably flexible and innovative in their ability to adapt and further develop their federal structures and in the process calm secessionist tendencies and integrate minority nations. The corresponding chapters corroborate that stability and adaptability of multinational federal structures presuppose internalized norms and habits—as much as, if not more than, the normative commitment to federal union (McGarry & O'Leary, 2009; Walsh, 2018).

Internal and External Shocks: No Enforcement of Federal Structures?

A final factor influencing the dynamics and operationalization of emerging federal structures is strongly linked to the previous points discussed above. It refers to the importance of internal and external shocks (or so-called critical junctures in historical institutionalism, Capoccia, 2016), which shift actor perceptions or even change the leading actors within a polity.

A couple of cases have experienced drastic events. In the case of Myanmar more recently, the internal shock of a military coup has stopped the federal reform process and has ended ten years of democratization and peace-building efforts. After the terrorist attack in Beslan in 2004, Putin further re-centralized the system by disempowering the regional governors. In Ukraine, we can see how the failure to sign an agreement with the European Union in 2013 resulted in the Maidan-Revolution, followed by Russia's annexation of the Krim in 2014 and the violent conflict in Eastern Ukraine and the establishment of pro-Russian protectorates ('people's republics') around Luhansk and Donetsk. This conflict has been at the center of Ukrainian politics ever since and has played a key role in the discussions on decentralization and federalization (Kropp and Holm-Hansen in this volume). Internal shocks in the wake of shifting party dynamics have also influenced Ethiopian federalism. The coming-to-power of Prime Minister Ahmed has fundamentally altered the party system, and the relationship between the different territorial units and the center. This has, as discussed above, ended in a new violent conflict. In Spain and Iraq, party dynamics and majority-minority relations have resulted in unilateral secession attempts, which have consequently created deep-rooted constitutional crises in both countries.

During the formative phase of federal structures, external and internal shocks can basically produce different effects: they may enforce, slow down or even reverse the process. It is conspicuous that in none of the above-mentioned cases shocks enforced federalization. Instead, the central governments reacted to shocks by avoiding or stopping the devolution of powers to sub-central units, or they deliberately re-centralized power-sharing structures. Unconsolidated federal structures, on which this book focuses, are particularly prone to such moves. In times of uncertainty, when authorities see the need to take rigorous measures, concentrating power at the top of the state hierarchy seems to be an obvious approach. In ethno-culturally diverse societies, however, recentralizing strategies can easily end in a new round of (sometimes violent) conflict, as happened in some of the cases.

CATEGORIZING EMERGING FEDERAL STRUCTURES

All the cases discussed in the previous chapters have one thing in common—they all have emerging, some of them regressing federal structures—that is, countries characterized by unconsolidated federalization processes. That is not to say that we did not include any fully fledged federations, as the case of Belgium demonstrates, but we argue that even in cases where a commitment to full federalization is referenced in the constitution and exercised in political practice, the process continues. As Meier discusses in her contribution on Belgium, the full federalization of the country in 1993 has not ended debates about self-rule and shared rule, and further alterations in the relationship between regions/language communities and the center have taken place since 1993. Likewise, Russia's commitment to federalism in its 1993 constitution has nevertheless resulted in different periods of (de-)federalization, as highlighted by Klimovich and Kropp. In light of this dynamic understanding of federalization, the cases can be assigned to clear-cut categories only at a certain point of time; this also complicates attempts to integrate the cases into stable comparative groupings. Instead of providing strict classifications that could easily be outdated or challenged by political developments, or for which we lack proper data and clear measurements, we categorize the case studies according to their current state of 'emergence', as highlighted in Fig. 14.1.

Figure 14.1 reveals different clusters of cases. Note that it does neither insinuate a linear understanding of federalization processes nor do countries undergo the process stage by stage. Some cases have undergone federal regression. Also, Fig. 14.1 does not depict an ascending order of distinct phases.

Level of Federalization	Progress of Federalization Process	Cases
Low ↓ High	Centralized with Federal Debate	Syria, Myanmar
	Decentralized with Federal Debate	Ukraine, Kenya, Colombia
	Federal Practices without Federal Institutions	Kosovo, North Macedonia
	Federal Arrangements with Single Federal Institutions but without Full Federalization	Spain, United Kingdom, European Union
	Federal Arrangements with Formal Federalization but with Counteracting Practices ("Federal Shell"; Processes of Regression)	Russia, Bosnia and Herzegovina, Iraq, Ethiopia, India
	Fully-Fledged Federations	Belgium, Nepal, South Africa

Fig. 14.1 Categorization of emerging federal structures

We see a number of fully fledged federations discussed in this volume, in which federalism is directly applied within the constitutional framework (Belgium, Nepal and South Africa). These cases comply with the criteria of a federation as developed by Watts (2008) and Burgess (2006) along the axis of self-rule and shared rule (see also Kropp and Keil in the Introduction). Likewise, Russia, Bosnia and Herzegovina, Iraq, Ethiopia and most recently India are federal states, but we observe regressive tendencies in the implementation of both federal principles and democratic governance that undermine the federal arrangement, albeit to different degrees. Moreover, readers should be aware that countries featuring 'federal arrangements with single federal institutions but without full federalization' might be more 'federal' in operation than those with 'federal arrangements with formal federalization but with counteracting practices'.

In Spain, UK and the European Union we find several elements of a federal system, but the countries (union) are also lacking important features of a federation. For example, in Spain and the UK, while we can observe a high degree of self-rule, shared rule mechanisms are either very weak or non-existent. In the EU, the question of statehood and the limited autonomy of the EU as a potential federal center prevent its qualification as a federation.

In Kosovo and North Macedonia, elements of federalization are applied, despite their formal absence. Both countries feature a particular form of decentralization, which is limited in the constitution but substantial in practice. The use of consociational power-sharing in central institutions also strengthens the shared rule dimension in these countries, hence their classification as polities with federal practices without formal federal institutions. In Ukraine, Kenya and Colombia (limited) decentralization is applied in practice, but there are debates in which federalism is a contested issue. This is of course not equally substantial in the three cases—in Colombia this links to historical debates about decentralization while in the Ukrainian official discourse federalization has become a non-issue due to the ongoing conflict in the East of the country and the annexation of Crimea by Russia in 2014. Consequently, decentralization is regarded as a means to prevent debates on federalization. Finally, Myanmar (even before the coup in February 2021) and Syria are highly centralized countries, in which a federal debate has emerged as part of democratization and peace-building processes. However, the outcome of these debates and the strength of these pressures are yet to be seen. After all, in Myanmar there has been a federal debate that started before the country became independent in 1948—yet the country has never been formally federal (Siegner, 2019). In Syria, likewise, the federal debate goes back to the French mandate period after the First World War, yet the country has continued to be organized centrally and ruled directly from Damascus (Savelsberg, 2020).

Concluding Remarks

Studying emerging federal structures means studying a moving target. As highlighted in the introduction to this Conclusion chapter, the developments in Myanmar and Ethiopia demonstrate the dynamic nature of these structures. They also reveal the uncertainty that these emerging political structures face—often still unstable and unconsolidated, they are living in the shadow of a return to authoritarian rule, to renewed violent conflict, or a return to centralization and the undoing of any federalization process. All our case studies have some degree of 'incompleteness' in them, even those that fulfill the criteria of fully fledged federations (such as Belgium). It was also shown that multinational polities are fundamentally exposed to secession and potential inter-ethnic conflict (Brancati, 2008; Anderson, 2013; Keil & Anderson, 2018).

More scholarly attention needs to focus on these emerging and regressing federal structures and what they tell us about federalism and decentralization. The Introduction and the Conclusion in this book do neither provide falsifiable hypotheses about when exactly we would expect to get emerging federal structures nor reliably tell us under what conditions we will see a certain category of emergence or regression at work. The approach of this book is theory-driven, but still explorative. Considering this, future comparative research might benefit from delving into the configurative logics of federalization processes by applying more formalized methods (such as Qualitative Comparative Analysis (QCA), Schneider & Wagemann, 2012), for which this volume may serve as a starting point.

At the same time, comparing emerging federal structures allows for drawing some practical conclusions. The world in the twenty-first century has many more situations that look like Bosnia in 1993, or Syria today—just think of Libya, Somalia, Afghanistan and the renewed unrest in parts of the Arab World in recent years as examples. The findings provided by this book indicate that what is needed are not static and fixed solutions borrowed from established federations, but flexible structures able to adapt to the specific domestic context. This is easy to lay out in theory and much harder to do in practice—but the cases studied in this book highlight that it is not impossible and that there is a broad variety of evidence worth being consulted by institutional designers.

References

Anderson, L. (2013). *Federal solutions to ethnic problems: Accommodating diversity*. Routledge.

Belser, E. M. (2020). A failure of state transformation rather than a failure of federalism? The case of Iraq. *Ethnopolitics, 19*(4), 383–401.

Benz, A. (2020). *Föderale Demokratie—Regierung im Spannungsfeld von Interdependenz und Autonomie*. Nomos.

Benz, A., & Kropp, S. (2014). Föderalismus in Demokratien und Autokratien – Vereinbarkeiten, Spannungsfelder und Dynamiken. *Zeitschrift für Vergleichende Politikwissenschaft/Comparative Governance and Politics, 8*, 1–27.

Benz, A., & Sonnicksen, J. (2015). Federalism and democracy—Compatible or at odds with one another? Re-examining a tense relationship. In C. Fraenkel-Haeberle, S. Kropp, F. Palermo, & K.-P. Sommermann (Eds.), *Citizen participation in multi-level democracies* (pp. 15–30). Brill.

Benz, A., & Sonnicksen, J. (2017). Patterns of federal democracy. Tensions, friction or balance between two government dimensions. *European Political Science Review, 9*(1), 2–25.

Brancati, D. (2008). *Peace by design: Managing intrastate conflict through decentralization*. Oxford University Press.

Burgess, M. (2006). *Comparative federalism. Theory and practice*. Routledge.

Capoccia, G. (2016). Critical junctures. In O. Fioretos, T. G. Falleti, & A. Sheingate (Eds.), *The Oxford handbook of historical institutionalism* (pp. 1–20). Oxford University Press.

Dardanelli, P. (2019). Conceptualizing, measuring, and mapping state structures—With an application to Western Europe, 1950–2015. *Publius: The Journal of Federalism, 49*(2), 271–298.

Elazar, D. (1987). *Exploring federalism*. University of Alabama Press.

Filippov, M., & Shvetsova, O. (2013). Federalism, democracy, and democratization. In A. Benz & J. Broschek (Eds.), *Federal dynamics* (pp. 167–184). Oxford University Press.

Franck, T. (1968). Why federations fail. In T. Franck (Ed.), *Why federations fail: An inquiry into the requisites for successful federalism* (pp. 167–200). New York University Press.

Freille, S., Haque, M. E., & Kneller, R. (2007). Federalism, decentralisation and corruption. Retrieved November 1, 2021, from https://ssrn.com/abstract=951110 or https://doi.org/10.2139/ssrn.951110

Friedrich, C. (1968). *Trends of federalism in theory and practice*. Frederick A. Praeger Publishers.

Grgić, G. (2017). *Ethnic conflict in asymmetric federations—Comparative experience of the former Soviet and Yugoslav regions*. Routledge.

Hale, H. E. (2015). *Patronal politics: Eurasian regime dynamics in comparative perspective*. Cambridge University Press.

Hulsey, J., & Keil, S. (2021). Power-sharing and party politics in the Western Balkans. In S. Keil & A. McCulloch (Eds.), *Power-sharing in Europe—Past practice, present cases and future directions* (pp. 115–140). Palgrave Macmillan.

Johnston, M. (2014). *Corruption, contention and reform: The power of deep democratization*. Cambridge University Press.

Kapidzic, D. (2019). Subnational competitive authoritarianism and power-sharing in Bosnia and Herzegovina. *Southeast European and Black Sea Studies, 20*(1), 81–101.

Keil, S. (2013). *Multinational federalism in Bosnia and Herzegovina*. Ashgate.

Keil, S. (2015). Power-sharing success and failures in the Western Balkans. In S. Keil & V. Perry (Eds.), *State-building and democratization in Bosnia and Herzegovina* (pp. 193–212). Ashgate.

Keil, S., & Alber, E. (2020). Introduction: Federalism as a tool of conflict resolution. *Ethnopolitics, 19*(4), 329–341.

Keil, S., & Anderson, P. (2018). Decentralization as a tool of conflict resolution. In K. Detterbeck & E. Hepburn (Eds.), *Handbook of territorial politics* (pp. 89–106). Edward Elgar.

Keil, S., & McCulloch, A. (2021). Conclusion: The past, present and future of power-sharing in Europe. In S. Keil & A. McCulloch (Eds.), *Power-sharing in Europe—Past practice, present cases and future directions* (pp. 257–274). Palgrave Macmillan.

Kropp, S. (2019). The ambivalence of federalism and democracy: The challenging case of authoritarianism—With evidence from the Russian case. In N. Behnke, J. Broschek, & J. Sonnicksen (Eds.), *Multilevel governance: Configurations, dynamics, consequences* (pp. 213–229). Palgrave Macmillan.

Lepine, F. (2015). Federalism: Essence, values and ideologies. In A. Gagnon, S. Keil, & S. Mueller (Eds.), *Understanding federalism and federation* (pp. 31–50). Routledge.

Lijphart, A. (1969). Consociational democracy. *World Politics, 21*(2), 207–225.

Livingston, W. S. (1952). A note on the nature of federalism. *Political Science Quarterly, 67*, 81–95.

Mahoney, J., & Thelen, K. (2010). A theory of gradual institutional change. In J. Mahoney & K. Thelen (Eds.), *Explaining institutional change. Ambiguity, agency, and power* (pp. 1–37). Cambridge University Press.

McCulloch, A., & McEvoy, J. (2020). Understanding power-sharing performance: A lifecycle approach. *Studies in Ethnicity and Nationalism, 20*(2), 109–116.

McGarry, J. (2017). Centripetalism, consociationalism and cyprus: The "adoptability" question. In A. McCulloch & J. McGarry (Eds.), *Power-sharing: Empirical and normative challenges* (pp. 16–36). Routledge.

McGarry, J., & O'Leary, B. (2009). Must pluri-national federations fail? *Ethnopolitics, 8*(1), 5–25.

McKay, D. (2006). William Riker on federalism: Sometimes wrong but more right than anyone else? *Regional and Federal Studies, 14*(2), 167–186.

Mueller, S. (2019). Catalonia: The perils of majoritarianism. *Journal of Democracy, 30*(2), 142–156.

Nationwide Ceasefire Agreement. (2015). Retrieved July 15, 2021, from https://peacemaker.un.org/sites/peacemaker.un.org/files/MM_151510_NCAAgreement.pdf

Riker, W. H. (1964). *Federalism: Origin, operation, significance*. Little, Brown & Company.

Savelsberg, E. (2020). *Die Entstehung des Kurdischen Nationalismus in Syrien zur Zeit des französischen Mandats: Die Autonomiebewegung Hajo Aghas von den Haverkan*. Unpublished PhD Thesis, University of Erfurt.

Schneider, C. Q., & Wagemann, C. (2012). *Set-theoretic methods for the social sciences. A guide to qualitative comparative analysis*. Cambridge University Press.

Siegner, M. (2019). *In search of the panglong spirit: The role of federalism in Myanmar's peace discourse*. Yangon.

Skendaj, E. (2014). *Creating Kosovo—International oversight and the making of ethical institutions*. Woodrow Wilson Center Press.

Steinmo, S. (2012). Historical institutionalism. In D. Della Porta & M. Keating (Eds.), *Approaches and methodologies in the social sciences: A pluralist perspective* (pp. 118–138). Cambridge University Press.

Stepan, A. (1999). Federalism and democracy: Beyond the U.S. model. *Journal of Democracy, 10*(4), 19–34.

Streeck, W., & Thelen, K. (2005). Introduction: Institutional change in advanced political economies. In W. Streeck & K. Thelen (Eds.), *Beyond continuity: Institutional change in advanced political economies* (pp. 1–39). Oxford et al.: Oxford University Press.

Thelen, K. (1999). Historical institutionalism in comparative politics. *Annual Review of Political Science, 2*, 369–404.

Volden, C. (2004). Origin, operation, and significance: The federalism of William H. Riker. *Publius, 34*(4), 89–107.

Walsh, D. (2018). *Territorial self-government as a conflict management tool*. Palgrave Macmillan.

Watts, R. (1966). *New federations: Experiments in the commonwealth*. Oxford University Press.

Watts, R. (1998). Federalism, federal political system, and federation. *Annual Review of Political Science, 1*(1), 117–137.

Watts, R. (2008). *Comparing federal systems* (3rd ed.). McGill-Queen's University Press.

Wheare, K. (1964). *Federal government* (4th ed.). Oxford University Press.

Index[1]

NUMBERS AND SYMBOLS
16 Zones Most Affected by the Conflict (ZOMAC), 269
21st century Panglong Conference, 149
1947 Panglong Agreement, 151

A
Accommodation, 11–15, 24, 53, 54, 58–64, 67–69, 98, 122, 167, 179, 194, 196, 197, 205, 207, 208, 210, 239, 253, 254, 306, 307
Adaptation, 4, 10–11, 98, 99, 118, 306, 312
Adoption, 218, 219, 307
Afar, 219n4
African National Congress (ANC), 237, 239, 240, 242, 242n2, 243, 254, 313
Afrikaans, 237
Afrin, 195, 202
Agreement of Khasavyurt, 78
Ahmed, Abiy, 223, 303, 318
Ahtisaari, Martti, 132
Ahtisaari Plan, 123, 132, 133
Albanians, 121, 123, 128–131, 134, 316
Amalgamated territorial communities (OTG), 104, 105
Amhara, 219n4, 220n4, 222
Anglo-Boer War, 238
Annexation, 100, 108, 321
Apartheid, 21, 237n1, 238–240, 255
Appointment of governors, 109
Arab Spring, 192
Aragon, 49, 53
Arakan National Party, 150
al-Assad, Bashir, 193, 203, 208
al-Assad, Hafez, 193
Assad regime, 194, 201, 205, 207

[1] Note: Page numbers followed by 'n' refer to notes.

Assam, 178–180, 182, 183
Assimilation, 56, 160
Associations of Municipalities, 133
Assyrian, 203
Asymmetrical federalism, 98
Asymmetric confederation, 124
Aung San Suu Kyi, 154, 157
Authoritarian and totalitarian, 208
Authoritarianism, 16, 18, 21, 157, 158, 167, 173, 273, 293–294, 308, 317
Autonomy, 6, 8, 12–14, 19, 20, 50, 52, 54, 55, 57, 58, 60, 61, 64, 67, 74, 78, 80, 84, 88, 98–103, 105, 109, 111, 116–135, 116n1, 117n1, 150–155, 157, 159, 167, 172–174, 177, 178, 183, 193, 196, 200, 202, 204–206, 208, 209, 217, 218, 218n1, 220, 220n6, 221, 240, 241, 261, 269, 272, 306, 307, 312, 316, 317, 321

B
Baath-regime, 204
Baghdad, 196, 200, 205
Bahun, 144
Bamar, 144, 146, 152, 157
Barcelona, 53, 60, 60n2
Basic Laws, 61, 66
Basque Country, 51, 53–55, 60
Belgium, 7, 9, 20, 22, 33–46, 64, 305, 309, 311, 313, 315, 317, 319, 320, 322
Belgrade, 119, 120
Betancur, Belisario, 265
Bête noir, 54
Bharatiya Janata Party (the Indian People's Party) BJP, 169, 174–176, 178, 181–184
Bicameral, 44, 109, 110, 149, 205

Bicameralism, 202
Bihar, 178
Boer Republics, 237, 238
Bogota, 263
Border Security Force, 181
Bosnia and Herzegovina (BiH), 7, 15, 19, 116, 119, 121, 125, 134, 135, 313, 316, 320
Brexit, 62, 65, 283, 288, 289, 289n3
British Empire, 237
Brussels Capital Region, 37, 39–43, 45
Building Bridges Initiative (BBI), 251, 252
Building Bridges to Unity, 251
Building Bridges to Unity Advisory Taskforce, 251
Buthelezi, 239, 240

C
Cabinet Mission Plan, 169, 171
Cadastros, 269
Cape Colony, 238
Caste, 25, 142, 144, 145, 153, 168, 170
Castile, 49, 53
Castilianization, 53
Castro, Jaime, 265
Catalonia, 51–55, 60, 63–66, 68, 315
Catholic University of Leuven, 36
Catholic University of Louvain-La-Neuve, 36
Central Armed Police Force, 181
Central Bank, 266, 273
Centralism, 205, 225, 226, 246, 263
Centralization, 6, 53–55, 64–68, 76, 81, 88, 90, 123, 125, 168, 172, 173, 175, 176, 198, 207, 210, 217, 218, 243, 247, 248, 252, 254, 255, 261, 263, 305, 309, 312–315, 317, 322

INDEX 329

Central Ukraine, 100, 106
Chechnya, 77, 77n2, 78
Chernivtsy, 104
Chhetri, 144
Citizen Amendment Bill, 183
Clientelism, 13, 15, 24, 91, 99, 107, 111, 127, 264, 270, 271
Colombia, 25, 261–275, 309–312, 321
Colonial Office, 244, 245
Coloreds (Ethnic group in South Africa), 237
Coming-together, 151, 152, 156, 203, 237, 287–290, 294, 307, 314
Commander-in-Chief Min Aung Hlaing, 159
Commission for the Implementation of the Constitution (CIC), 249
Committee of Regions, 287
Communism, 239
Communist League of Yugoslavia, 120
Communist Party (of Ukraine), 106
Competences, 41, 42, 55, 61, 66, 67, 69, 79, 125, 132, 135, 136, 183, 199, 205, 286, 290, 291, 291n5, 294, 295, 311, 313
Confederation, 7, 46, 53, 78, 124, 125, 202, 285–287
Conference of the Presidents and Sectoral Conferences, 63
Conference on the Future of Europe, 283
Congress Pradesh (state), 174
Consociational, 19, 36, 42, 96, 111, 116, 130, 159, 169, 171, 251, 252, 312, 315, 321
Consociational confederation, 124
Constituent assembly (Nepal and Myanmar), 147, 148, 152
Constitution, 20, 37, 41, 54, 55, 59–61, 63, 74, 76, 77, 80, 83n5, 87, 98, 99, 108, 109, 124, 126, 129, 132, 133, 146–151, 153–156, 167–173, 172n1, 180, 182, 183, 195, 199, 200, 202, 203, 205, 208, 209, 216, 218–221, 223, 224, 226, 227, 239–242, 244, 246–249, 253, 261–267, 270–272, 281, 281n1, 290n4, 295, 319, 321
Constitutional Court (*Corte Constitucional* or CC), 39, 41, 42, 52, 89, 126, 203, 272–274
Constitutional Framework for Self-Governance in 2001, 123
Constitutional Treaty, 284–286
Constitution of Bosnia and Herzegovina, 122
Constitution of Kenya Review Commission (CKRC), 244, 247
Constitution of Kosovo, 123
Convention, 58n1, 61, 62, 285
Convention on South Africa, 238
Council of Legislators, 82
Council of Representatives, 199
Coup, 158–160, 193, 304, 318, 321
COVID-19, 44, 243, 283, 286, 289, 293
CPN-Maoist, 148, 155
CPN (UML), 147, 155
Crimea, 98, 100, 102, 103, 103n1, 106n3, 108, 321
Crown of Aragon, 49, 53
Cymru, Plaid, 57
Cyril Ramaphosa, 243

D

Dalits, 153
Danu Self-Administered Zone, 154
Dayton Peace Agreement (DPA), 22, 122, 124, 127

330 INDEX

Decentralization, 5–7, 11, 12, 18, 21, 24, 25, 49, 52, 55, 58, 60, 65, 68, 76, 96, 103–105, 117, 119, 123, 125, 128–130, 132–136, 148, 192–210, 226, 243, 250, 254, 263, 265–269, 271, 273, 304, 305, 307, 310, 312–318, 321, 322
De facto, 15, 18, 76, 80–81, 123, 132, 192–194, 197, 209, 219n4, 239
De-federalization, 5, 81, 91, 95–112, 266–269, 319
Dehaene, Jean-Luc (Prime Minister), 43
Democracy, 8, 11–13, 15–22, 24, 33–37, 42–45, 50, 54, 55, 58, 59, 61, 95, 98, 99, 106, 120, 122, 127, 132, 134, 135, 145, 147, 149, 156–158, 160, 167, 173–184, 192, 193, 195, 198, 200, 207, 210, 238, 244, 247, 248, 255, 261, 263–265, 271, 274, 282, 293–295, 304, 307, 309, 314–317
Democratic centralism, 225, 226
Democratization, 4, 15–18, 20, 25, 58, 68, 74, 122, 124, 134, 136, 141, 142, 147–150, 156–160, 180, 193–195, 198, 200, 201, 204, 205, 229, 273, 294, 304, 306–309, 314, 317, 318, 321
Democrats, 145
Demos, 44, 45, 60, 282
Derg, 218, 219
De-Sovietization, 102
Devolutionary federalism, 98
Dnipro, 109
Donbass, 98, 100–103, 106, 106n3, 108, 111
Donetsk, 100, 101, 103, 109, 111, 318

Dravidian South, 178
Druze, 195, 203
Dual federalism, 292
Dual subordination, 76

E
Economic Freedom Fighters, 243
Ejercitó de Liberación Nacional (ELN), 264
Elites, 8, 11, 12, 14, 17–22, 24, 25, 33, 34, 36, 37, 39, 41–43, 52, 57, 59, 65–69, 74, 76–80, 77n2, 85–87, 89–91, 98, 104, 107–109, 111, 117, 119–121, 124, 125, 128, 130, 133, 136, 145, 158, 171, 183, 195, 197, 200, 201, 206, 207, 209, 226, 242, 247, 253, 254, 280, 283, 307–311, 313, 314, 317
Entities, 6, 9, 12, 14, 17, 37–42, 56, 62, 90, 98, 101, 104, 123, 125, 127, 134, 200, 279, 284, 305n1, 308
Erbil, 196, 205
Ethiopia, 5, 12–14, 18, 19, 25, 207, 216–229, 236, 244, 254, 303–305, 308, 311, 312, 320, 321
Ethiopian People's Revolutionary Democratic Front (EPRDF), 219, 225
Ethiopian Student Movement (ESM), 217
Ethnic armed organizations (EAOs), 18, 146, 147, 149, 153, 156, 157
Ethnic cleansing, 121, 125
Ethnic federalism, 12–14, 24, 77, 119, 152, 160, 220–222, 304
Ethnic fractionalization, 142
Ethnic nationality, 144, 146, 151, 152
Ethnic separatism, 130

INDEX

Ethnocentrism, 65
Ethnofederalization, 45
Ethno-federation, 43, 45, 221
Ethno-linguistic heterogeneity, 98
Ethno-nationalist, 25, 106, 123
EU integration, 118, 135, 279, 280, 283–286, 288, 289
Euphrates, 202
Euromaidan, 100, 103, 108n4
European Central Bank (ECB), 290n4, 291n5
European Charter of Fundamental Rights and Freedoms, 294
European Commission (EC), 283
European Council, 283, 289
European Court of Human Rights, 126
Europeanization, 118
European Parliament (EP), 40, 41, 284, 286, 292–294
European Union (EU), 7, 22, 25, 42, 66–68, 105, 118, 121, 123, 128, 129, 131, 132, 135, 278–295, 309, 311, 315, 318, 321
Europe of the Regions, 288
EU's Rule of Law Mission in Kosovo, 135

F

Faisal-Constitution, 205
Fatherland, 106, 107
FDRE Constitution/FDRE constitution, 219, 221, 221n7, 227
Federal Consultation Committee, 40, 42–44
Federalism, 4–8, 12–21, 24, 25, 33–46, 52, 57, 58, 65, 66, 68, 69, 74–76, 79, 80, 89–91, 118, 120, 124, 135, 136, 141–160, 167, 170, 173–179, 181, 183, 184, 192–210, 216–229, 236, 238–240, 242, 244–246, 253–256, 262, 263, 265–267, 270, 274, 278–295, 304–307, 310, 310n3, 311, 317–322
Federalization, 4–7, 9–20, 22, 24, 34–37, 40, 43, 46, 49–69, 74, 76–80, 96, 103–105, 111, 116, 117, 141, 142, 144, 145, 147–152, 156, 157, 159, 160, 194, 202, 225n9, 262–265, 273–275, 279, 280, 282–285, 287, 288, 295, 303–313, 315–322
Federal political systems, 7, 52, 98, 116–136, 153, 195, 195n1, 305, 306, 312, 313
Federal principle, 78, 85, 195, 202, 261–264, 266, 267, 269, 273, 320
Federal Republic of Yugoslavia, 123
Federal society, 9–12, 24, 98–100, 105, 106, 110, 141–145, 156, 157, 274, 306, 307
Federal Supreme Court, 199
Federation Council, 80–83, 82n4, 86, 87, 90, 199
Federation of Bosnia and Herzegovina (FBiH), 125
Federations, 4–8, 11, 14–17, 19, 20, 34–46, 49, 52, 55, 58, 61, 66, 68, 77–80, 82, 86, 87, 102, 124, 135, 150, 152, 156, 158, 167–184, 195n1, 207, 209, 216, 217, 219–223, 220n5, 225, 228, 236–238, 240, 254, 261, 265, 278–280, 282–287, 290, 292, 304–307, 310, 311, 314, 316, 317, 319–322
FEDESARROLLO, 266
First-past-the-post electoral system, 174

First Spanish Republic, 54
Fischer, Joschka, 283
Flanders, 34, 35, 37, 38, 42
Flemish Regionalists N-VA, 46
Fragile State Index, 207
Franco (General Franco), 54
Francoist forces, 54
Freedom Front Plus, 243
Frontier Areas, 151
Fuerzas Armadas Revolucionarias de Colombia(FARC), 18, 264, 265, 268, 269
Functionality, 10, 20, 22, 118, 134, 135, 192, 195, 198, 203–208, 312

G

Galicia, 54, 60, 101, 102, 106
Gambella and Benishangul Gumuz, 220
Gandhi, Indira, 167, 172, 174, 175
Gandhi, Mahatma, 169, 175
General Royalty System (*Sistema General de Regalías*, SGR), 272
Geneva, 202, 203
Genocide, 54, 101
Ghai, Yash Pal, 144, 244, 246, 247, 252
Globalization, 283
Government of India Act, 169, 171
Grand coalition, 130, 159
Gruevski, Nikola, 131, 134, 135
Guerilla, 266
Guraferda, 224

H

Habsburgian, 101
Harar, 220n4
Havana Accord, 268, 269, 273
Hierarchy, 76, 90, 105, 151, 242, 286, 287, 319

High Representative, 122, 127, 314
Hindu, 144, 148, 153, 167–170, 173, 175, 178, 181, 183, 184
Hindu Mahasabha, 169
Hindutva, 182
Holding-together, 34, 57, 68, 111, 119, 147–153, 158, 160, 203, 287–290, 306, 314–318
Hourglass federalism, 151
House of the Federation (HoF), 223, 224
Hromady, 104, 105
Hungarian, 99, 101, 290n4
Hybrid regime, 11, 98, 99, 156, 158, 305
Hyderabad, 170

I

Ianukovych, Viktor, 102
Ideology, 18, 169, 173, 183, 204, 205, 217, 274, 279
India, 7, 12–14, 16, 25, 64, 150, 151, 167–184, 245, 308, 309, 312–317, 320
Indian Civil Service, 171
Indian National Congress, 169
Indigenous, 168, 182, 183, 219n4, 220, 222, 223
Inkatha Freedom Party (IFP), 242, 253, 254
Institute of Nationalities, 218
Integrationist, 170, 288
Inter alia, 67, 132
Interethnic violence, 117
Intergovernmental relations (IGR), 44, 62, 82, 88, 172, 200, 225, 226, 228, 249, 254
Interim Constitution 2007, 148, 240
Internal market, 54, 66, 289
Iran, 192–194, 197, 202, 208, 310

Iraq, 5, 11, 13, 15, 17–20, 25,
    192–210, 308–313, 315, 317,
    318, 320
Iraqi Constitution, 199, 203, 205
Irob and Kunama, 219n4
Islamic State in Iraq and Syria (ISIS),
    192–194, 207
Iushchenk, Viktor, 102, 107, 108n4,
    109, 110

J
Jammu, 182
Jammu and Kashmir, 167,
    169–171, 178–182
Janajati, 152
Janata Party, 177
Jatis, 168
Jazira, 202
Jewish, 76
Jinnah, Muhammad Ali, 169
Jubilee Party, 249, 251
Junagadh, 170
Juncker, Jean-Claude, 283
Junta, 218

K
Kalenjin, 243, 246, 254
Kamashi, Assosa and Metekel, 222n8
Kamba, 243
Kashmir, 167, 169–171, 175,
    178–182, 316
Kenya, 14, 15, 25, 236–256,
    309–311, 314, 315, 317, 321
Kenya African National Union
    (KANU), 246
Kenyan African Democratic Union
    (KADU), 246, 253
Kenyatta, Jomo, 246, 247
Kenyatta, Uhuru, 247, 249
Khas Arya, 144, 145, 147, 148

Kibaki, Mwai, 247
Kiev, 109
Kikuyu, 243, 246, 247, 254, 255
Kirkuk, 192
Kisii, 244
Kosovo, 117–124, 117n1, 127, 128,
    130–135, 308, 309,
    314–316, 321
Kosovo Liberation Army, 128
Kosovo Serbs, 117, 131–133
KPRF, 86
Krais, 76
Kuchma, Leonid, 102, 108n4, 110
Kurdish, 192, 193, 195, 196, 199,
    200, 202, 205–210, 308
Kurdish Autonomous Region/Kurdish
    autonomous region, 192, 197,
    199, 200, 202
Kurdish Democratic Union Party
    (PYD), 202
Kurdish National Council (KNC), 202
Kurdistan, 202, 207
Kurds, 192, 193, 195, 197, 198, 200,
    201, 203, 206
Kurti, Albin, 135
KwaZulu, 240
KwaZulu-Natal, 240, 242, 254

L
Labour Party, 57, 62, 68, 313
Ladakh, 179, 182
Lancaster Conference, 246
LDPR, 86
Leuven, 36
Leviathan, 253
Liberal Party, 57, 262, 264
Lisbon Treaty, 286
Liyu woredas, 220
Lok Sabha, 171, 177, 179
Loose multinational federation, 124
Luhansk, 100, 103, 111, 318

Luhya, 243
Luo, 243, 246, 247
Lviv, 101

M
Macron, Emmanuel, 283, 284
Madhesi, 148, 150, 155
Madras, 174
Majimboism, 244, 246, 253
Major, John, 57, 160
Majoritarianism, 157
Mandela, Nelson, 83
Manipur, 178, 182
Maoist Comprehensive Peace Agreement (2006), 146, 147
Marginalization, 102, 146, 209, 253
Martens, Wilfried, 36
Marxist-Leninist, 217
Mbeki government, 242
Mboya, Tom, 246
Meghalaya, 178, 179, 182
Mekonen, Walelign, 217
Member state, 131, 132, 282, 286–295, 290n4, 291n5
Merkel, Angela, 283
Meru, 244
Middle East, 192, 197, 198, 208–210
Minister for Home Affairs, 156
Ministries, 76, 125, 127, 152, 156, 159, 263, 269
Ministry of Finance, 88, 89, 266
Mizoram, 178–180, 182
Mobility rights, 223, 224
Modi, Narendra, 167, 174, 176, 184
Moi, Daniel Arap, 246, 247
Moldova, 102
Monarchists, 145
Montenegro, 119, 121, 123
Moscow Patriarchate, 100
Mosul, 192, 207
Movimiento 19 de Abril (M-19), 265

Mughal, 168
Multilevel governance, 171, 278, 285
Muslim, 153, 169, 170, 179, 180, 182, 183, 193, 210
Muslim League, 169
Myanmar, 7, 11, 13, 15, 18, 20, 25, 141–160, 179, 180, 304, 307, 308, 310–315, 317, 318, 321

N
Nagaland, 178–180, 182
Natal, 237, 238, 240
National Ceasefire Agreement (NCA), 149
National Conferences (Bomas), 247
National Council of Provinces, 241
National Democratic Alliance, 177, 181
National Development Council, 172
National Electoral Board of Ethiopia, 223
National Front, 264
Nationalism, 11, 53, 54, 169, 182, 196, 239, 244
National League for Democracy (Nepal and Myanmar) (NLD), 146, 147, 149, 150, 154, 157, 159
National Party, 167, 228, 237–239, 242, 294
National Planning Council (NPC), 271
National Planning Department, 266, 272, 273
"National race affairs ministries," 152–153
National Register of Citizens, 183
Nation-building, 53, 54, 99, 101, 144–146, 157, 196
"Nations, Nationality and Peoples of Ethiopia," 219

INDEX   335

Natives, 100, 110, 219n4, 220–225, 220n5, 226n10, 228
NATO, 102, 121–123
Navarre, 55
Nawab, 170
Nehru, Jawaharlal, 169, 174, 175
Neo-feudals, 104
Nepal, 13, 19, 21, 22, 25, 141–160, 307–309, 311, 312, 320
Nepal Communist Party (Centre) (NCP), 155, 160
Nepali Congress, 147, 155
Next Generation EU, 293
Nizam, 170
Non-natives, 220, 222–224
Non-racialism, 239
Northern Ireland, 51, 53, 56–58, 61, 288n2
North Macedonia, 116n1, 117, 118, 120, 121, 123, 124, 127–131, 135, 309, 314–316, 321
North of Syria, 197, 202
Nouri al-Maliki, 201
NSCN-IM, 180–182

O

Oblasts, 76–78, 85–87, 87n7, 89, 103, 104
Odinga, Raila, 247, 249–251, 255
Odinga Odinga, Jaramogi, 246, 247
Office of the High Representative (OHR), 127
Ohrid Framework Agreement (OFA), 123, 128–130
Oil stain, 35
Okrugi, 104
Okrugs, 76, 87, 87n7, 105
Oligarchy, 145
Oli, KP, 155
Orange Revolution of 2004, 108n4, 109

Orange River Colony, 237
Organic Laws, 66
Organos Colegiados de Administración y Decisión (OCADs), 272
Oromia, 219n4, 222, 222n8, 223
Oromiffa, 227
Oromo, 219n4, 220n4, 227
Our Ukraine, 106

P

Parivar, Sangh, 175
Partition, 13, 169–171, 245
Party of Regions, 106–109
Pashtan, 170
Pastrana, Andrés, 265
Path dependency, 36, 46, 101, 117, 145, 317
Patronalism, 15, 24, 99, 107, 111
Peace-building, 18–21, 24, 129, 134, 136, 192, 263, 265, 269, 311, 318, 321
People's Assembly, 251
People's President, 251
Permanency, 59
Plurinational, 50, 52, 53, 58, 59, 63–69
Polish, 101, 283, 290n4
Poroshenko, Petro, 99, 100, 102, 103, 107, 110
Power cliques, 104
Power-sharing/power sharing, 15, 17, 19, 20, 24, 42, 78, 90, 116–128, 130, 131, 134–136, 192, 194, 200, 202–204, 206, 209, 236, 238, 239, 252, 254, 255, 264, 315, 316, 319, 321
Power-vertical, 177
PP government, 66
PP government's Organic Law for the Improvement of Educational Quality, 66

Pradesh, Arunachal, 178, 182
Pradesh, Madhya, 176, 178
Pradesh, Uttar, 178
Prefects, 105, 110
President's Rule, 172, 173, 175–177, 180
Procedural democracy, 177, 178
Programas de Desarrollo Territorial (Territorially-Focused Development Programs) (PDETs), 269, 269n3
Proto-republics, 106n3, 108
PSOE-Unidas Podemos coalition, 69
Punjab, 167, 178–182
Putin, Vladimir, 74, 79–90, 318

R
Rada, Verkhovna, 106, 108n4
Radical-constitutional federalism, 282
Radical Right Populists Vlaams Blok, 41
Raion, 104
Raiony, 104
Rajasthan, 178
Rakhine State, 150, 154
Regional diversity, 99–101, 106, 110
Republic of Macedonia, 128
Republika Srpska (RS), 125, 128
Roma, 127, 129
Royalist parties, 148
Royal massacre, 145
Rule of law, 5, 11, 15, 17, 79, 120, 153, 229
Russia, 5, 7, 13–18, 25, 73–91, 98, 100–102, 108, 110, 111, 131, 132, 168, 193, 194, 202, 208, 210, 305, 308–314, 316, 320, 321
Russian Federation, 87
Russian Soviet Federative Socialist Republic (RSFSR), 74, 76
Russophile, 100

S
Saddam Hussein, 193, 200
Saint Michael Agreement, 33
San, General Aung, 146, 154, 157
Sangh, Jan, 169
Scotland, 49, 51, 53, 56–59, 61, 63–65, 68, 288
Scottish National Party (SNP), 57, 61, 65
Secession, 13, 19, 52, 57, 64, 65, 134, 145, 146, 148–151, 157, 158, 160, 175, 180, 206, 219, 237, 239, 251, 287, 288n2, 318, 322
Second Spanish Republic, 54
Second World War, 21, 34, 37, 101, 119, 145, 192, 201, 245, 253, 287, 311
Securitization, 181
Self-determination, 19, 50, 58, 59, 68, 219–221, 224
Self-government, 18, 50, 53, 54, 56, 57, 60, 62, 105, 129, 131–133, 218n1, 220, 221, 224, 246
Self-rule, 4, 6, 7, 42, 45, 46, 52, 58–64, 68, 74, 76, 80, 85, 89, 109, 117n1, 120, 168, 169, 171, 173, 179, 204, 209, 221, 224, 227, 248, 279, 285–287, 290, 291, 293, 294, 305, 305n1, 306, 312, 314, 315, 319–321
Serbia, 117, 119, 121, 123, 128, 131–133, 135, 136
Shan National League for Democracy, 150
Shan State, 150, 151, 154
Shared rule, 4, 6, 7, 14, 19, 42, 52, 58–64, 68, 69, 74, 80, 117n1, 120, 171, 179, 200, 204, 209, 239, 254, 261, 279, 285–287, 289–291, 305, 305n1, 306, 312, 314, 315, 319–321
Shia, 193, 197, 200, 201, 206, 210

Sidama, 219n4, 226
Sikkim, 178, 182
Single market, 289–291, 293, 294
Sixth Schedule, 182
Skopje, 121, 130, 131
Sluga Narodu, 104, 106
Socialist Yugoslavia, 116, 119, 136, 316
Solidarity, 41, 285, 286, 289, 290, 293, 294
Somali, Sidama and Oromo, 219n4
South Africa, 15, 18, 20, 21, 25, 236–256, 307, 309, 310, 312–315, 317, 320
South African Communist Party, 239
Southern Nations and Nationalities People (SNNP), 220, 222, 222n8, 223, 226, 227
Sovereignty, 7, 9, 57, 60, 62, 65, 66, 78, 90, 128, 182, 248, 287, 311, 316
Soviet Ukraine, 101
Soviet Union, 9, 20, 64, 73, 74, 76, 101, 315, 316
Spain, 4, 7, 12, 22, 24, 49–69, 132, 288, 306–308, 313–315, 317, 318, 321
Spanish Constitution, 66
Starmer, Keil, 68
State-building, 78
State Council, 82, 83
State dissolution, 4, 136, 199–203, 316
State Duma, 81, 82, 82n4, 85–87, 90
Statehood, 22, 50, 59, 63, 65, 96, 101, 111, 117, 199–203, 316, 317, 321
State Restructuring Commission, 153
Steering Committee, 252
Steinmeier, Frank-Walter, 103
Steinmeier Formula, 103, 111
Substantive democracy, 178
Sunni, 200, 201, 207, 210

Sunni and the Shia communities, 206
Sustainability, 207
Switzerland, 9, 64, 152, 287
Symbolic recognition, 59–60, 63, 64, 67, 68, 183
Syria, 20, 21, 25, 192–210, 309, 309n2, 311, 314, 317, 321, 322
Syrian opposition, 202, 202n3, 203

T
Tatmadaw, 147, 304
Technocracy, 266, 273, 274
Teleological, 4, 280, 284
Teleological-normative, 279–294
Terai, 151
Territorial ethnic homogenization, 121
Tharu, 153
Thatcher, Margaret, 57
Tigray, 236, 303
Tigray region, 219n4
Tikrit, 192
Transdnistria (formerly Dniestr), 102
Transvaal, 237, 238
Treaty of Lisbon, 281, 281n1, 287, 290, 294
Treaty of Maastricht, 285
Treaty on the Functioning of the European Union (TEFU), 287
Tribalism, 255
Tripura, 178, 182
Turkey, 193, 197, 201, 202, 310
Turkey and the Kurdish People's Protection Units (YPG), 201
Two nation theory, 169
Tymoshensko, 107

U
Ukraine, 11, 14, 21, 25, 95–112, 309–311, 314–316, 318, 321
Ukrainian Greek Catholics, 100

Ukrainification, 101, 102, 108
Unfinanced mandates, 88
Union Cabinet, 182
Unionism, 53, 56, 57
Union of European Federalists, 282
Unitarianism, 99, 102
Unitary state, 4, 9, 34, 49–69, 78, 98, 105, 172n1, 225, 238, 239, 287
United Kingdom (UK), 4, 5, 7, 22, 24, 49–69, 287, 288, 312, 313, 315–317, 321
United Nations (UN), 21, 128, 132
United Progressive Alliance, 181
United Russia, 81, 84–86
United Solidarity and Development Party (USDP), 146
Université Libre de Bruxelles, 36
UN Mission in Kosovo (UNMIK), 131
UN's Constitutional Framework for Provisional Self-Governance, 131
UN Security Council Resolution 2254, 207
U Nu, 146
Uribe, Alvaro, 267, 269, 272, 273
USA, 9, 16, 121, 123, 132, 193, 198, 200, 207, 286, 287, 307, 310

V
Venugopal, KK Attorney General, 182
Vertical power, 177
Vetëvendosje, 135
Veto right, 122, 130, 147, 157, 159, 169
Vikas, 184
Vishwas, 183–184
Vlaams Belang, 41, 46
Volkstaat, 240
Vrije Universiteit Brussel, 36

W
Wako draft, 247
Wales, 53, 56–58, 61
Western Balkans, 116–136
Western Cape, 242
Western Ukraine, 99, 100
Westminster, 57, 58, 58n1, 61
White Highlands, 244, 245
White monopoly capital, 243
Win, General Ne, 146
World War II (WWII), 34, 37, 101, 144, 145, 245

Y
Yemen, 192, 197, 208
Yezidi, 193
Yugoslavia, 64, 116, 119–121, 123, 136, 315, 316
Yugoslav League of Communists, 120

Z
Zakarpattia, 102
Zelenskyi, Volodymyr, 103, 104, 106
Zemli, 77
Zulu, 239
Zuma, Jacob, 20, 242, 243

Printed in the United States
by Baker & Taylor Publisher Services